Management for Professionals

More information about this series at http://www.springer.com/series/10101

Brian Dive

Mission Mastery

Revealing a 100 Year Old Leadership Secret

Springer

Brian Dive
Fairlawn
Weybridge
Surrey
United Kingdom

ISSN 2192-8096 ISSN 2192-810X (electronic)
Management for Professionals
ISBN 978-3-319-25221-6 ISBN 978-3-319-25223-0 (eBook)
DOI 10.1007/978-3-319-25223-0

Library of Congress Control Number: 2015958089

Springer Cham Heidelberg New York Dordrecht London

Printed on acid-free paper

Springer International Publishing AG Switzerland is part of Springer Science+Business Media (www.springer.com)

"This book is a must-read for all charged with developing tomorrow's leaders."

Sir Michael Perry, GBE—previously Chairman and Chief Executive Officer at Unilever, Chairman of Centrica, Chairman of the Senior Salaries Review Body, Independent Director at Singapore Technologies Telemedia Pte. Ltd, and Chairman of the Faculty Board at the Said Business School, Oxford University.

"Mission Mastery is a masterwork."

Professor Stephen J. Perkins, DPhil (Oxon) Dean Guildhall Faculty of Business & Law, London Metropolitan University, UK

"No other book on organizational leadership is as relevant today as Mission Mastery."

Gerald A. Arbuckle, Organizational Anthropologist, and author of Humanizing Healthcare Reforms

Finally, I would like to dedicate the book: To Alexander and Matthew

Contents

1 Introduction: The Secret

In evolution, nothing fails like success.
Arnold Toynbee
See Managing on the Edge by R. Pascale (1990, p. 15).

1.1 General

Why do so many organizations keep making the same leadership mistakes? This book aims to answer that question, based on the author's ~50 years' experience working around the world across a wide cross section of civilian organization in the private, public and not for profit sectors. This chapter introduces the key idea of the book, which is ***how to master an original 100 year old leadership secret in the 21st century****. It explains how the first really large learning organization was built in the nineteenth century. This leadership advantage remained hidden from "the competition" for a good 100 years, which illustrates the power and importance of good leadership. It originated in a military context. Civilian organizations tend to have a false perception of how military leadership is developed and practised, being blind to its real qualities. This revolutionary form of leadership was first practised by the "competition" 120 years after its first successful introduction. This book will illustrate there are five key components ("5 Pillars"), which underpin this success story although they have not been previously revealed. Intriguingly one Pillar is invariably overlooked and consistently neglected in civilian organizations and its absence totally undermines their practice of leadership. Surprisingly its absence is rarely commented upon in the seemingly unending outpouring of books on "leadership". The book explains what*

(continued)

B. Dive, *Mission Mastery*, Management for Professionals,
DOI 10.1007/978-3-319-25223-0_1

these 5 Pillars are and how they can be embedded in civilian organizations. In short it outlines what is required to replicate that 100 year old secret: the attainment of Mission Mastery. The key concepts of Decision Making Accountability (DMA), that are an important thread running through this book affecting civilian organizations, are outlined briefly towards the end of the chapter. DMA is treated in more depth in Chap. 8.

1.2 Tapping into the Secret

> *Where once, people accepted being 'led', as one of a large body of people, all being treated the same, all directed in the same way,* **a model based on the military** (my emphasis) *now they expect to be treated as an individual.*
> Val Gooding, A former CEO of BUPA[1]

The above quote reflects a common misconception that military organizations are all about uniform command and control whereas their civilian counterparts are bastions of individual empowerment. In reality *most civilian organizations are much closer to the military myth than they realise.* Many have developed a culture of 'no consequences' as a result and are demoralising places in which to work. This is illustrated in Chap. 9.

1.2.1 So, What Is This Book About?

No-one would deny the purpose and nature of military and civilian organizations are as different as chalk and cheese. But because of that, the common prejudice, 'I would not dream of joining the military', mutates into 'What could I possibly learn from them?'

In the field of leadership development there are fundamental things military organizations do better than civilian organizations and have done so for a long time.

I wish to highlight the things civilian leaders tend to ignore and/or are unaware of, given this resilient "command and control" prejudice. The military approach to the combination of organization design, leadership development and career planning and training is generally on another plane of excellence to that of most civilian organizations. The latter are fundamentally unhealthy and weak in the very areas where the military are strong. The military identified the route to clear

[1] See Cooper, C L (2005) ed. ***Leadership and Management in the 21st Century,*** p. 350.

accountability and a culture of trust long ago. The meandering route in civilian organizations in search of that nirvana tends to be a recurring weakness.

The core theme of the book is that effective leadership consists of five key components, which will be referred to as *The Pillars of Leadership*. Their interplay remains a 'closed book' to most civilian leaders across the private and public sectors.

As shown by the quote at the outset of this chapter there is a well worn belief that the military is all about "command and control" and civilian organizations are all about empowerment. As far as I can determine the unhelpful term "command and control" came from Peter Drucker. At a seminar in London during 1984 he described how the German Banks, such as Dresdner, were very impressed by the success of the Prussian army in its war with France in 1870–1871, deciding to copy, what he termed its "command and control" approach in managing a generally illiterate front line. Drucker missed the critical factors contributing to that success and the legacy of his misunderstanding continues to feed an enduring myth.

My observations over the last ~50 years suggest actual reality is precisely the other way round. The military have empowered their leaders whereas civilian organizations generally have not. The latter have favoured a philosophy of micro management. This was first espoused as scientific management at the beginning of the twentieth century, which took an inhuman, engineering approach based on the division of work, which was reinforced by the approach of process re-engineering at the end of the century. Both initiatives are based on a "man is a machine" approach to work, which is broken down into countless processes and sub processes notwithstanding the occasional exception to this trend such as some of the work of Socio-Technical Systems Analysis. Even though more people have become more educated in the twenty-first century, many civilian organizations are still prone to divide work up into tiny tasks most of which are meaningless in isolation, as if their employees were still illiterate.

It is deeply ironical that many civilian organizations' negative view of military organizations is in fact invariably a mirror image of themselves.

When in the field, NATO generals today have been trained to communicate *what & why* but not *how*. As will be shown in Chap. 2, those details are left to *leaders and their teams who have been trained in mastery of the relevant tasks and skills who are then left to decide, what is appropriate in a given situation given the overarching brief.* They are not given minute, detailed instructions, of the type that have ripped the soul out of much office work in the twenty-first century.[2] The military test their officers and men via realistic "experiential training" (such as war games), whereas civilian organizations "test" their leaders by having them talk in a

[2] An interesting book on this theme is: *The Case for Working with Your Hands: Or Why Office Work is Bad for Us and Fixing Things Feels Good* by Matthew Crawford (2009).

classroom about how they would theoretically lead in a case study being discussed. Civilian training focuses on the individual but is typically weak in demonstrating purpose, context, skills and the practical accountability leaders require to succeed. Worse than that, it seems quite a few are not aware of this gap.

The secret of this book is not of the conspiracy variety. It grew out of a set of principles that evolved into a military organization's new operating model in the latter half of the nineteenth century. It was a leadership initiative that was not detected by either its allies or the enemy. They both assumed success was based on a secret weapon: but did not detect what it was. In the late 1980s, after a period of peace and information exchange, the former enemies finally recognised and adopted this operating model themselves—the ultimate compliment. Today the gap in leadership knowledge and practice persists in civilian organizations, despite the patronising quote at the top of this chapter. Good leadership is hard to devise, build and recognise and harder still to replicate. That is the essence of this secret.

This book aims to help close that knowledge gap in civilian Organizations

1.3 The Inspiration for This Book: A Study of the First Large Learning Organization

The more I read and thought about this conundrum the more it started to dawn on me that there has been one example of an organization that produced high quality leaders in its field for at least 100 years. But it was ignored and its secret remained undetected.

It was the first learning organization, which was very large and had built an organic, self-adapting approach to leadership.

But what is even more astounding is the realisation that this successful development has been missed (or ignored) by business school academics/researchers that have actually sent the study of leadership down a rabbit hole obsessing about the differences between "leadership" and "management." The source of this distracting development seems to have been an article by A Zaleznik in the *Harvard Business Review* of May–June 1977, entitled: "Managers and Leaders: Are they different?" It seems this academic side show contributed to the fact that the great leadership secret of this book was not latched onto by the competitors for over 100 years.

1.3.1 An Emerging Idea

In 2000 I read, what at that point seemed to be the definitive account of the Battle of Britain, namely Stephen Bungay's *The Most Dangerous Enemy.* This interest had been stimulated by the fact that my first boss, Colin Gray, a most impressive but modest man, was the 7th ranked ace in the Battle of Britain. While Bungay identified key individuals who clearly contributed directly to the victory—such as

Churchill, Dowding, Mitchell and especially Parks—he seemed to be moving away from the standard approach to military history of simply writing a "boys' own heroes" approach to the conflict. As an ex business consultant, who could speak German he managed to get access to both countries' war records. He seemed to approach the Battle as a conflict between two organizations: the Luftwaffe and the RAF. He dug into the different approaches to strategy, tactics, technology (such as the issue of radar: spurned by the Luftwaffe but not the German navy as HMS Exeter, Achilles and Ajax discovered when confronting the Graf Spee), communications and leadership. This enabled him to conclude, contrary to public opinion up to that time, that the Battle of Britain was "not a close run thing".

A couple of years later I read his next book, *Alamein*. This was a really revealing study.

By now Bungay had tapped into a theme of leadership in the professional German army that stemmed from a root and branch re-organization of the Prussian army at the beginning of the nineteenth century.

He showed that the British image of German officers as Prussian, heel clicking "yes men" intent only on following orders was totally incorrect. Worse, he revealed that the misplaced perception was actually, heel clicking apart, a mirror self image of the British army and its leadership philosophy.

It emerged there were two schools of thought on how to tackle the predictable uncertainly of war. One was to have a clear master plan: the British/American approach. The other, which the Germans called *Auftragstaktiker (*from Auftrag meaning "mission"), was to have a very clear mission (the "what" and "why") but to leave the "how" to the initiative of *highly trained* officers and men, since one cannot fully predict the reaction of the enemy once battle commences. Thus a detailed plan is likely to be quickly and increasingly irrelevant. The biggest sin a trained German officer could commit, once battle started, was *not to use his initiative* in the face of unfolding events. The opposite was the case for his British counterpart, for whom it was a sin to act without orders. M. van Creveld (1982) pointed out that in 1939 the US Army had a similar philosophy to the British. They also put great faith in planning and control, which were treated as paramount. In reality this leads to decision paralysis and inaction in the field. Rommel for example knew this, which is why he liked to move quickly and take the initiative away from an enemy likely to be waiting for the next order.

I could now understand why commanders such as Freyberg a New Zealander and O'Connor an Irishman got frustrated with some British commanders. The former did not need to be told to take advantage of a changing situation and achieve their "mission" faster than was expected. This led to the danger of being isolated (O'Connor was captured at the front) if they achieved their objective, as they invariably did, more quickly than the ponderous armoured brigade expected in their rigid planning. Rommel, by comparison, was trained to flex his infantry, artillery and armour according to the fluid demands of a given situation. The stove-piped 8th Army organized into separate silos was not as fleet of foot in the heat of the battle.

*This insight sent me on a journey to identify the vital secret components of what NATO now calls **mission command** – their translation of the original "Auftragstaktik".*

1.3.2 Outstanding Leadership Is Difficult to Replicate

Firstly this book will demonstrate a path to outstanding leadership that is achievable but is not easy to attain and is even more difficult to replicate. Recently leadership development and career planning have clearly failed in many organizations, despite the unending hype to the contrary. These failures have been dramatically evident in the years leading up to and post the GFC. Chapter 5 on leadership development will demonstrate how and why career path planning has been flawed in many cases. Some even argue it is a waste of time in today's 'fluid, digital world'. So why, if managers hate coming second, don't they embrace a wining leadership formula?

Part of the problem is there are no shortcuts: it takes time to develop leaders. On 1 August 2014 James Henderson, just appointed CEO of William Hill after 29 years in that business, said: "If there is a bit of advice I'd give anybody about their career, it is not a sprint. It's a long haul and opportunities do come if you work hard and deliver results." That applies whether the "long haul" is in one or more organizations. Too many civilian organizations seek the quick fix, which is not available. The successful components will be explored thoroughly in Chaps. 5 and 6. Leadership is not instant gratification despite the alleged aspirations of generation Y.[3]

1.3.3 Outstanding Leadership Is Not Mono-dimensional

Secondly, leadership is not mono-dimensional. This book will aim to unravel this mystery by providing a multi-dimensional analysis and solution that is practical and which has worked for a long time. The principles that underpin Mission Mastery are universal and my contention is they can be applied in the public, private and voluntary sectors of civilian organizations and in different cultures around the world. If the mission is clear people can be held to account to deliver it while simultaneously being developed through a series of well orchestrated leadership learning experiences to learn, grow and become better in the process.

[3] "Leading a team is not a long-term ambition for Gen Y" *People Management* 31 January 2015.

1.3.4 Why Has This Insight into Outstanding Leadership Been Ignored?

Thirdly why has this obvious success story been ignored by academia? In November 2014 A. N. Wilson bemoaned the fact that a conference set up by the British Museum on the topic: *Germany—Memories of a Nation,* with an excellent array of German speakers, was sidetracked into a discussion of the Nazi horror story, led by an historian, M. Fulbrook, "*who should have known better and schooled the audience on the positive legacy of the Holy Roman Empire*." I suspect the history of the wars since 1870 distracts academics from studying German lessons of worth from that era. (Yet, as Norman Davies reveals, they continually and conveniently ignore the devious politics, grandstanding and appalling atrocities of the Russians.[4]) It is all still too close for comfort. If people were really aware of the ruthless mayhem caused by Edward III in France during the fourteenth century they would be horrified at the slaughter of non combatant villagers, which was a feature of his campaigns. But Edward is an historical hero to the English, the victor of Crecy and Poitiers, the founder of the chivalrous Order of the Garter, who first raised the English flag of St. George going into battle alongside the Royal Standard: a "Perfect English King".[5] Distance and time lend enchantment to the view. I suspect our current 'proximity' and what that entails for many people, is one reason why these leadership insights of a Prussian general have been overlooked. The negative experience of his fatherland is still, for many, too close and too raw for living memory. One of my grandfather's lies buried in the Etaples Military Cemetery twelve thousand miles from home and my father also volunteered to fight, ending up in the desert theatre—against Rommel. That is what prompted me to read Bungay's *Alamein* in the first place, which in turn took me deeper into the unfolding mystery of *Auftragstaktik.*

Finally it is instructive to consider the contrasting approaches to the 'teaching' of leadership in military and civilian organizations. Military staff colleges have a heavy input from those who have succeeded in the field. By way of contrast, the key criterion enabling someone to *lecture* on the practice of managerial leadership in universities is usually the possession of a PhD in "management". Many have never actually led anything: either inside or outside academia. Sadly events since 2008 have made it insultingly clear that successful leadership is not just about having an MBA or having a case study written about your organization.[6]

Talking about leadership is not leadership.

[4] Davies N, (2012) *Vanished Kingdoms,* see Chap. 7.

[5] See Mortimer I, (2008).

[6] See Mintzberg, H (2003) *Managers not MBAs: a hard look at the soft practice of managing and management development.*

1.3.5 The Focus Is on Transformation

Some readers might be thinking: "Wait a minute: this is all very well and good but who won the last two World Wars? Not the Germans. So what can we learn about leadership from them?" It was no doubt fortuitous that a constitutional monarch, who insisted two of his sons should serve as Corps commanders, was of indifferent military ability in WWI. Vincent (2003) has pointed out that (fortunately for us!) auftragstaktik was abandoned by Hitler in his disastrous personal direction of the German armies in WWII. Like Napoleon he 'knew better than his generals'. So, yes, that is a fair question: but my focus is on the Prussian/German army as an organic learning system and as I will touch on below it was not *its* performance that led to defeat.

After a great disaster in 1806, when defeated by Napoleon, the Prussian army went through a period of deep self analysis and introspection, which then led to massive organizational transformation and cultural change culminating in a totally new approach to leadership. It was the latter which was significant but intriguingly the 'competition' did not recognise what was going on. The fact that Germany had totally flawed political leadership for 50 years in the twentieth century, whose mistakes led to two major wars and their ensuing defeats, should not distract us from the quality of the military's performance twice asked unwisely to fight on two fronts. Fortunately political incompetence explains why Germany did not win WWI or WWII, a fact that has probably distracted us for far too long from the leadership revolution that had occurred before the political mist descended. It is worth noting that notwithstanding those two outcomes, the famous American officer and war historian, Trevor Dupuy, commented on the relative performance of the Germans and the patchwork quilt of Allies, in 1977 as follows:

> *"On a man for man basis the German ground soldier inflicted casualties at a 50 % higher rate than they incurred from the opposing British and American troops under all circumstances."*[7]

Beevor painted a similar picture during the fall of Berlin in 1945. It would seem Germany's defeat has coloured some people's view of that field reality.

1.4 The Five Pillars of Mission Command

I have identified five key pillars that underpin mission command. But they are not explicitly spelled out, which helps explain why they remained undiscovered for so long. You might be saying to yourself: "Here we go again, another consultant '7S' type solution to the world's problems." But this is not an approach dreamed up on a

[7] T. Dupuy (1977) *A Genius for War* p. 234.

consultant away day. (The background to the 7S model was shared in detail by Richard Pascale at a seminar in London organised by the Economist in March 1992. He explained how he and a colleague crafted a set of headings to provide some discipline for an offsite brainstorming meeting with a third colleague who, although creative, was apt to "go all over the place at once." After a few moments silence that third colleague said: "If we label all your headings with "S" we could sell it as "The 7S model.")

My thoughts resulted from searching for workable solutions to real problems in real organizations in many countries over many decades.

I have distilled these insights by studying the success of a change process that started just over 200 years ago in one organization. I realised that behind this transformation there were key components I have been stumbling towards and endeavouring to apply with increasing understanding for almost 50 years. Not only that but there are features of these components that most civilian organizations still get wrong and/or are not even aware of.

These pillars do not seem to have been clearly identified elsewhere. The Royal Navy's (RN) description of mission command identifies "8 Principles", (set out in Chap. 2), which are underpinned in turn by these five Pillars.[8] Interestingly the RN describes Lord Nelson as a natural implementer of mission command.

But the key point here is that neither the RN nor the Eighth Army institutionalised mission command in the way the Germans did.

Not even Rommel, who led 45,000 trained Germans in the Deutsches Afrika Korps (DAK), could turn the 55,000 Italians under his command into an equally proficient fighting force. One of the reasons was the Italian army had not been trained in the principles of Auftragstaktik. It also explains why the DAK could keep fighting effectively when Rommel was absent. The mission was clear. His *trained men knew what they had to do and how to do it*. They were part of an organic, self directed learning organization.

The purpose of this book is to describe these five pillars in some detail and explain how they can be migrated to any civilian organization, although it is not a simple journey. The goal then for such an organization is to achieve ***Mission Mastery.***

[8] See Band, J Admiral, Commander in Chief Fleet *Mission Command: a view from the Fleet Battlestaff:* the Royal Navy.

1.5 The Theme of the Book

Competitors can copy relatively easily everything an organization does, except the way its people are led and the way they respond.

Managerial leaders know that possession of a genuine secret is the first step along the path to success. It should lead to breakthrough change and first mover advantage that will deliver best in class performance. Companies spend hundreds of millions on research and development in search of that competitive breakthrough that can ring-fence market advantage. Screeds have been written about the theory of effective leadership but its practice remains elusive. This book helps demonstrate why.

1.5.1 What This Book Is Not About

While the inspiration for this book stems from a military leadership transformation this book is not suggesting civilian organizations should become pale military clones.

It is clear that a career in the military is fundamentally different to anything in the civilian world. The military mission is to win a battle during warfare. Survival is paramount. Skills' mastery is a more critical given the objective is to be achieved in a life or death environment. A military career is akin to a vocation. A subordinate must be prepared to step up immediately when a superior is killed. The protocols are crystal clear. Even for civilian organizations in the competitive private sector the odds are not in that league. Hence the military has very clear authorities and behaviours, which reinforce its purpose, such as saluting disciplines and uniforms that make rank obvious. These "absurdities" contribute mightily to the persistent idea that the military is all about command, control and mindless obedience. Although civilian organizations do not deal in "life or death" realities they do need delegated and clear accountabilities in order to be effective but they too often seem to confuse form (e.g. saluting) with substance, such as clear accountability, value adding hierarchy and effective leadership development, which are the bed-rock of effectiveness in action. As will be shown in Chaps. 5 and 6 the military have a better grasp on these three realities than many civilian organizations.

1.5.2 The Book Outline

Turning to the structure of this book: it will consist of ten chapters.

The second chapter, after this, will describe the background to the revitalisation of the previously successful Prussian Army following its traumatic defeat at Jena-Auerstedt at the beginning of the nineteenth century. The work and influence of the

Generals August von Gneisenau[9] and Gerhard von Scharnhorst will be touched on. The third player in this trinity was Carl von Clauswitz, who wrote the classic, "*On War*"*:* Later in the nineteenth century came the in most significant General of them all—Helmuth von Moltke—who extended their earlier thinking building an unsurpassed system of distributive leadership first practiced during the rout of the French in 1870.[10] He wrote the first important (short!) treatise on strategy, well before business school professors and consultants commandeered the topic, which is set out in the appendix. He set up in effect the first management training school (his War Academy) for the training of his officers. Selection of the best and most intelligent was conducted with great rigour. Much of the training was based on experiential learning in the field. Contrary to popular belief he trained his officers to be prepared to disobey an inappropriate order. (The Nuremberg trials have helped perpetuate a myth that Prussian/German officers were obsessed only with following orders. It seems fair to say that applied to the SS not the general professional officer corps). Other countries did not have then a comparable, professional approach to the selection and training of their officers.

Chapter 2 will describe the basis of auftragstaktik, now known as mission command in NATO, highlighting the new insights.

Chapters 3 to 7 will outline the five Pillars of Mission Mastery in some depth, with a chapter on each of the Pillars.

The five Pillars are as follows:

- A clear direction (mission) effectively communicated to all layers of leadership
- An organization structure of minimal layers aligned to levels of accountability to facilitate the cascade of the mission
- Effective leadership development aligned to those levels
- Experiential learning tailored to those levels
- A culture of positive values, which is an outcome built upon the first 4 pillars.

A holistic approach to leadership and leadership development is not new. Jay Galbraith's "5 star" model, Harold Bridger's "Pentagram" and Bill Tate's "Systemic Leadership" are just three examples of a holistic approach to leadership. Indeed Ignatius of Loyola espoused something akin to these five Pillars when founding the Jesuits in the sixteenth century. He set out the mission for his Institute. He wrote a clear constitution that reinforced that mission. He set up a clear accountable structure of government appropriate to the mission. He set up extensive training to prepare his followers for their mission including the now famous Spiritual Exercises as the means to embed transformative behaviour in his candidates. Part of their education prior to ordination included experiential

[9] I will follow the stylistic convention where after the first mention of an individual whose full name is "von" as in von Gneisenau, the honorific will be omitted.

[10] Von Moltke the elder to distinguish him from his nephew, German Chief of Staff in WWI, who was not nearly as distinguished.

assignments in various demanding social situations, usually among the poor and underprivileged. He ensured in his lifetime that a firm culture of identity was established that would guarantee the authenticity of the mission he founded. He of course did not refer to a learning organization but it would seem this is in fact what he built. Was it a coincidence I wonder that he had been a soldier earlier in his life? Much of the civilian work to date on leadership has been rather theoretical, as will be shown in Chap. 5. The findings in this book are based on an analysis of what has worked, studying why it has worked.

Chapter 8 will explain the background and basic tenets of the Decision Making Accountability Solution Set (DMASS).

Chapter 9 will outline what happens in an organization, when the 5 Pillars are not fully robust. The case study will focus on extensive work my team and I have done in the British Civil Service. It will be shown that when the 5 Pillars are defective the outcome is a culture of "no consequences". This is the opposite of Mission Mastery and the result can be a soul destroying work environment for talented people.

Chapter 10 will return to the three questions posed at the end of this chapter. It will hopefully provide some markers along the road for those aspiring to move in this direction in the future.

Finally, Moltke's paper on Strategy, written in 1871, is set out in an appendix.

1.6 A Word About Decision Making Accountability (DMA)

Clear accountability and the concomitant authority are a pre-requisite of the high performing organization.

At this stage it is important to flag that a key theme running through the book is *accountability, which is calibrated in value adding decision levels* in employment organizations that exist for a purpose. It will be treated more extensively in Chap. 8. Its complementary seam is hierarchy, or *layers of leadership*. In a healthy organization there should be a one to one alignment: a single layer of leadership to each level of accountability.

In the military context the 'residents' of levels of accountability are *battle echelons*: e.g. a battalion at the third level, a brigade at the fourth and so on. The front line (most junior role) is the first level of accountability. The organization design and nomenclature is established, clear and universally understood. Notwithstanding the different terminology across the three Services, the degrees of accountability are constant. For example, it is axiomatic that a Lieutenant Colonel accountable for a battalion reports to a Brigadier accountable for the brigade, NOT another Lieutenant Colonel. (The military reference here is to the field organization in battle formation, not various peacetime permutations.)

In the civilian world the picture is more blurred and confused, as it is often not obvious in practice where the different levels of accountability reside in a specific organisation and therefore whether the existing *layers of leadership* are aligned to different levels of accountability. This is further complicated by the fact that whilst there is a tried and tested way to identify levels of accountability in civilian organizations (see below), this method is not known to most managers.

Many civilian organizations do not know how to identify levels of accountability let alone how they should dovetail with hierarchy. They in effect have "Lt. Colonels" reporting to "Lt Colonels" and "Brigadiers" reporting to "Brigadiers" (in the same spine of accountability), and so on, because in accountability terms they do not know the equivalent accountability of a "battalion" or a "brigade". This muddle undermines good leadership development.

The fundamental problem in civilian organizations is the lack of a consistent, widely accepted nomenclature or understanding that provides a blueprint for how layers of management need to align to levels of accountability. This is the civilian OD disease, which also undermines the development of effective leaders.[11]

1.6.1 The DMA Solution Set (DMASS)

DMASS maps accountability and aims to address this OD disease by identifying the discrete and individual decisions which any individual makes in their job within an employment organization that exists for a purpose. (Thus it usually does not encompass a partnership, a cooperative or voluntary association such as a kibbutz, even though they all have a leader.) Once accountability is clear it serves as the basis for organization design, leadership development (including the assessment of potential) and reward. DMASS is a 'Solution Set' because it is a flexible approach: it does not offer a one-size-fits-all answer on every occasion. It is based on a set of universal principles that can be flexed to meet and fit any individual organization's design and people needs, providing a tailored, appropriate solution unique to that situation.

An individual's decisions should be different from those of the people who report to him or her and from those to whom they in turn report. Similarly the person in the layer above should be taking decisions that are adding value to the larger team and so on. This is the key to effective decision making in an accountability hierarchy. Each layer has discrete, non overlapping decision rights.

The DMA Solution Set is based on one simple idea.

[11] OD in this book refers to organization design.

Does your work add value to the customer, (the patient, the consumer, the constituent) and that of your colleagues?

The Solution Set is a conceptually integrated mental framework, based on that simple idea. *Two key concepts in this context are* ***layers and levels***.

1.6.2 Layers and Levels

The distinction between layers and levels is fundamental and lies at the heart of the thinking underlying this book.

The Levels of accountability have to be identified before the layers of hierarchy can be clearly established.

- **A Level of accountability** is a decision making zone with discrete and different decision rights, which differ from those of the levels above and below. The level is constant across an organization, in that the quality of decisions to be made, are essentially the same in terms of accountability, whatever the function, or type of job. The total number of levels varies between organizations of different sizes, complexity and geographical reach, which results in greater uncertainty to be resolved and managed.
- **A Layer** is a job in the structure of an organization on the vertical spine of line management accountability (line of command, in the military). It is the hardware of the organization. A spine of accountability is commonly referred to as a reporting chain. A layer resides within a level of accountability. If there are no discrete, different decision rights in a role there is no 'space' for that layer. Layers also reside on the same horizontal axis across the structure when in the same Level.

The Golden Rule of DMASS: ***Only one layer of leadership is needed per level***

- **Compression** occurs when there are two or more layers of leadership within one level of accountability. It means two or more people are working in the same decision space and therefore are not each adding value to their direct reports. (There are occasional situations above Level 1, where the compressed lower role might not be a leader.)
  Compression is the opposite of empowerment

Layers are counted down from the top line of the organization. The role of CEO, for example would be layer 1—reference will be made to the "CEO" throughout for the top full time executive role in an employment organization, even though this term is not always used in some countries, which may refer to a "President," "Director General", "Permanent Secretary" and so on, when describing the top executive role.

Levels on the other hand are counted up from the most junior role at the customer/patient front line, invariably, but not always, at the first Level of accountability.

Personal accountability occurs when an individual is answerable to a higher authority for work, resources (people, money, systems and/or specialist knowhow), outcomes, service and/or results that can be measured in terms of quantity, quality, cost and time.

This accountability is not shared—teamwork is—and it necessarily involves rewards or sanctions. *Accountability entails consequences.*[12] Unclear accountability degenerates into a culture of no consequences which leads to organizational inertia: an example is provided in Chap. 9.

Personal accountability is assessed via the Seven DMA Elements which are spelled out in more detail in Chap. 8.

1.6.3 Empowerment: A Blend of Moltke and DMA

The Fig. 1.1 below, aims to illustrate how in column (a) most leaders tend to believe they should control the "what", the "why" and the "how" of the work of the team for which they are accountable. By intervening in the "how" they are actually intervening unnecessarily in the work of their staff in the lower reaches of the organization and disempowering them. They are working in their subordinates' decision space, micromanaging and de-motivating them. Column (a) illustrates this by indicating the box of autonomy in each lower level is getting narrower and narrower as one moves down the reporting chain. The front line work is eviscerated by those above not delegating the authority commensurate with what they claim to be holding their team members to account for. This becomes even more marked if there are unnecessary layers in that spine of accountability. The further down the hierarchy one progresses the more empowerment is ebbing away, often as a result if inadequate training, over layering in many cases.

Column (b) on the other hand is the basis of *Space to Lead:* training staff in the "how" of their work set in the context of "what" needs to be done and "why". In this instance each layer on the spine of accountability is more empowered than the corresponding layer in column (a). This picture (b) reflects the reality of back-

[12] Klatt B et al. (1999) *Accountability: Practical tools for focusing on clarity, commitment and results.*

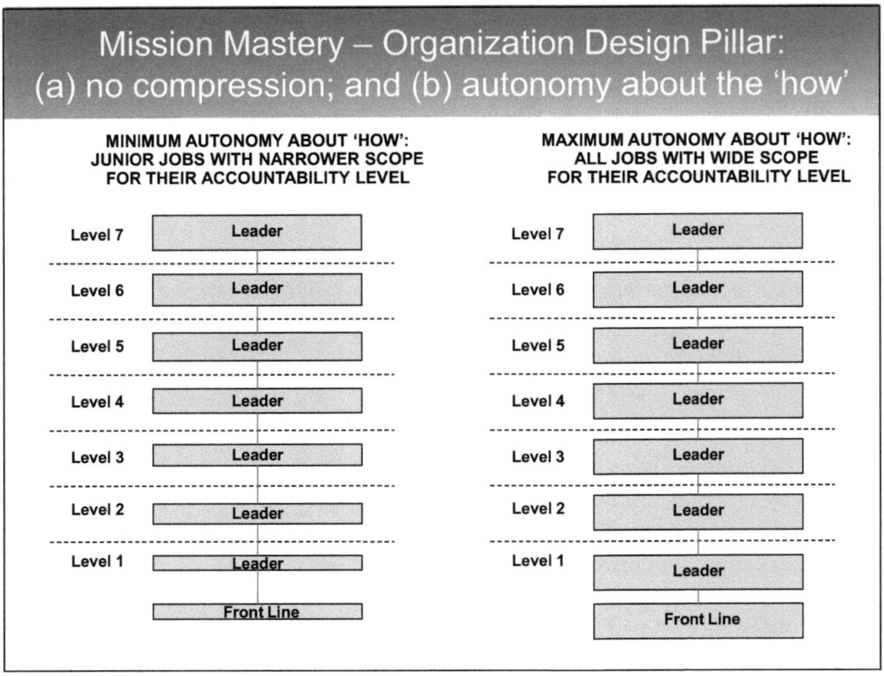

Fig. 1.1 Mission mastery and empowerment

briefing (see Chap. 2) in which each layer in the organization enjoys its full autonomy appropriate to their level of accountability in the chain of command. They are all 'fully in the picture' appropriate to their position. They are clear on what needs to be done and why and have been equipped to do it. They do not need to be continually told "how to do it".

Civilian organizations still have much to learn from best practice in the military in the critical sphere of leadership and the development of good leaders. That is the message of this book: we will examine the *five Pillars* in turn to learn both their contribution what they each reveal about the 100 year old leadership secret.

1.7 The Experience Underpinning This Book

Seven years ago I wrote *The Accountable Leader*. It was aimed at a gap I had detected in the studies and literature on leadership, which ignored the issue of accountability and good organization design. As I have worked for more organizations in both the private and public sectors in different countries since, it has become clearer that this gap is endemic in civilian organizations, whether in the private or public domains. It is a recurring problem. Good leadership is not expensive and yet it is rarer than gold. After almost 50 years working in the field

I continue to be amazed at the millions of dollars misspent on leadership development and training not aligned to accountable work or context.

It seems most leadership training initiatives take wing like swifts in late summer, make a crazy sweep in line with the fad or fashion of the day, skimming back in the end to their starting point, having achieved little. Many organizations continue to squander their money by putting individuals into situations where their ability to lead is constrained by bad organization design. This is often coupled with faulty assessment of the capability of their leaders and a lack of appropriate career planning.

Leadership is a multi-faceted subject and the pursuit of mono-faceted solutions based on style, personality, fad or fashion of the day, will continue to fail.

As my last book was published in 2008, the world lurched into a series of leadership crises. They have spanned politics, banking and financial services, the media, and public services such as the police and health. The West has been bedevilled by mediocre political leadership during this period. Corruption amongst politicians has been shown to be widespread and it continues.[13] But this book is not about politicians. They are not elected on the basis of competence or proven ability to do a job. But CEOs of banks, newspapers, broadcasting corporations, police forces, and hospitals are appointed on that assumption. Competence to lead is expected of the head of one of these organizations. So why have there been so many catastrophic failures?

Some might argue that this is a result of rising secularism, politics/ideology materialism and a concomitant erosion of ethical standards and an obsession with celebrity so commonplace today in many countries. Two narratives have emerged to explain the Global Financial Crisis (GFC): one focuses on *moral failure*, which fostered the obscene reward practices fed by the greed of some leaders in banks and a number of public entities such as world sporting bodies, which seem to spawn corruption. The moral failure theory sees a misalignment between personal aggrandizement at the expense of the best interests of the organization as the compelling cause. The second narrative is that of *cognitive failure,* whereby key individuals believed propositions that turned out to be untrue. Policy makers were caught up in the same flawed cognitive environment so market mistakes went unchecked because regulators shared the same illusions and false assumptions as the financial executives.

It seems various socio/legal initiatives have muddied the waters of selection on merit, which have blunted the development of leaders. That also might be so, but favouritism is not new and is not the focus of this book. I wish to highlight the recurring systemic mistakes civilian organizations continue to make in their

[13] E.g. the EU is yet to have all its accounts ratified in an objective annual audit.

approaches to leadership development and suggest how they might be overcome. The fundamental issue that remains unresolved is the question of effective governance. Post the GFC it seems the pendulum is swinging too far in the direction of control, which is increasingly being put into the hands of people who increasingly have little experience or insight into what they are 'controlling'. The mere passing of a law does not install competence.

At the beginning of 2105 an article on "Decoding Leadership: What really matters" in the *McKinsey Quarterly* (January 8) maintained four types of behaviour apparently made the difference between strong and weak organizations "in terms of leadership effectiveness." The insights offered were: "Be supportive, operate with a strong results orientation, seek different perspectives and solve problems effectively." This article dramatically illustrates that many civilian organizations and their advisors are still only in the foothills of understanding leadership. It is depressing that even in 2015 some still think the key to good leadership is simply 'to focus on behaviour'. Provincial 'solutions of the day' such as "Neuroscience is the answer" will continue to blossom. But even today most civilian approaches to leadership development are flawed and/or inadequate. It is these shortcomings I wish to highlight to a degree but more importantly suggest how they can be overcome. Certain key military insights will be flagged as we proceed along this road, which I believe have great relevance to civilian organizations.

1.7.1 Held to Account

The focus of this book is civilian employment organizations that exist for a purpose and have a clear mission. Someone has to be held to account for the proper delivery of that mission. That in turn presupposes that there are leaders at every level who are competent and can contribute effectively to that overall purpose. I wish to show how leaders can be developed at every level in civilian organizations. This is *distributed leadership* and it is the subject of this book. It means having competent leaders at *every* level of accountability not just the top of the organization. Good distributive leadership is a critical piece of the high performance puzzle, yet its delivery remains an unfinished jigsaw for many organizations around the world.

The challenge of distributive leadership is finding a way to build an organic, learning organization that is well led throughout and continuously adapts to the challenge of a changing environment.

As I have consulted to more and more organizations I have been struck by how often the same shortcomings variously reoccur across the private, public and not for profit sectors. Clearly an unhealthy organization is not a good seed bed for the growth of the effective leaders it needs. But what makes an organization unhealthy and how can it be recognised?

By the end of this book you will know the answer.

During the book I will address three vital questions and revert to them explicitly in Chap. 10:

Firstly, what was the essence of mission command, which remained secret for so long?

Secondly, is that leadership secret, which first emerged over 100 years later, still relevant today?

Thirdly can it be replicated in twenty-first century civilian organizations and if so, how?

Some questions to consider

At the end of each chapter I will pose some questions for you to consider. In the case of Chap. 1, they are:

1. How is the Mission Mastery journey relevant to your organization?
2. Where do you see it will have the most benefit?
3. What are the advantages/risks of embarking on this journey?

What Is Mission Mastery?

2

Mission command is the difference between those military strategists who wanted to ***manage chaos*** *by controlling* ***how*** *and those who wanted to* ***exploit chaos*** *by commanding* ***what and why.***
Stephen Bungay
(2011) The Art of Action p. 70

2.1 General

This chapter identifies the essence of Mission Mastery. It tracks back and explains what led to the transformation of the Prussian Army during the nineteenth century, why and how it happened. It touches on its famous heritage of success that was shattered in the defeats of 1806. Ironically the value of that defeat for twenty-first century management is the response orchestrated by four key individuals, whose work led to the gestation of the first large learning organization. The two who over time have had the most influence are Clauswitz—of "On War" fame—and Moltke, the scourge of the French in 1870. The great learning here is the leadership secret he unfurled, which remained undetected for another 100 years. In the military context the German description of "Auftragstaktiker" was recast in English by NATO countries as 'mission command'. We then briefly examine how mission command has played out in the Royal Navy. The goal of this chapter is to capture the essence of mission command and open up the discussion of what it might look like in a civilian setting. I am suggesting that when the essential components are successfully migrated from their military setting, the approach becomes Mission Mastery in the civilian world.

B. Dive, *Mission Mastery*, Management for Professionals,
DOI 10.1007/978-3-319-25223-0_2

2.2 What Is Mission Command?

If working in large organizations can be a bad experience, trying to improve things can make life even worse. Machiavelli presciently identified the challenge:

> *Those who stand to gain from change will be lukewarm in support while those who perceive they will lose out will be strident in their opposition.*

The inspiration for this book is the story of how a large organization, once a byword for success, suffered a traumatic failure and then successfully reinvented itself. Key individuals led a major, sustained change process leading to its total revitalisation. It took many years to complete. It is something most ailing organizations aspire to but rarely achieve.[1] The really fascinating part of this story is the fact that even when the façade of this new edifice was noticed the underlying leadership foundation stone was not detected. During this process it invented what has become known as *mission command, a new form of leadership, still virtually unheard of by twenty-first century civilian managerial leaders.*

Mission Mastery is the successful migration of the key, relevant tenets of mission command from a military to a civilian context. It is the optimisation of the pillars of Purpose, Organization Design, Leadership, Experiential Learning and Culture in a non military organization.

2.2.1 1806: The Seeds of Failure Are Often Sown at the Height of Greatness

This story begins in 1806. That is the year Napoleon defeated the powerful Prussian Army at Jena and Auerstedt. It has been argued that Hegel saw 1806 as a seminal moment—the end of history, "because he felt Napoleon brought into being the principles of liberty and equality underlying the modern state."[2] Defeat is always traumatic, especially when it is totally unexpected. Prior to 1806 the Prussian Army had a proud military record of success, reaching its apogee under Frederick the Great.

Frederick the Great was probably the most talented person to ascend a royal throne in Europe in the last 1000 years. He was a gifted musician who played the transverse flute and composed 100 sonatas for the flute as well as four symphonies. His court musicians included C. P. E. Bach, Johann Joachim Quantz and others. He challenged J. S. Bach with a musical conundrum in 1747 at Potsdam "Setting him an awkward chromatic theme on which to extemporise first in three, then in six

[1] For example, on 5 July 2013 in *Knowledge Wharton*, Jeff Klein and Gregory Shea claimed that 70 % of change programmes fail. While the evidence for that percentage was not totally convincing most would agree that failure occurs far too frequently.

[2] Fukuyama *The End of History & the Last Man*, p 64.

parts" that led to Bach's composing *The Musical Offering*.[3] It seems their musical views clashed as Bach had to resubmit it. Frederick was a man of letters with a genuine interest in the art and philosophy. He was interested in the Enlightenment movement, corresponding with some of its key figures, such as Voltaire, for many years. In 1739, Frederick wrote his *Anti-Machiavel*, an idealistic refutation of Machiavelli. He was an accomplished linguist. In addition to his native language, German, he spoke French, English, Spanish, Portuguese, and Italian; he also understood Latin, ancient and modern Greek, and Hebrew.

But Frederick the Great is best known for his brilliance in military campaigning and the organization of the Prussian army.

He and his father before him, had effectively build Prussia into "an army with a country" by the time he died (1786). A key element of that tradition involved the famous Junkers—Prussian officers drawn exclusively from the ranks of the aristocracy. Strict rules and a culture of loyalty to the Prince had been established by Frederick William I (1713–1740), the "Soldier-King" obsessed with both the army and achieving self-sufficiency for his country. This tradition is the origin of the outdated image of the disciplined, mindless heel clicking, Prussian officer automaton that is the delight of the film producers and comedy writers.

Given this history and context the Prussian army was over confident and complacent in 1806. Following the debacle three men recognized that and set out to change things in a way that had far reaching effects into the C20th.

2.2.2 The Immediate Aftermath

The need for radical change is often stimulated by a burning platform. The Prussians recognised their platform was a tinder box! But more important, successful change can take hold when new leaders who are not contaminated by the old regime have the foresight, courage and ability to see a way forward. In this the Prussians were better served than most organizations. Following their traumatic twin defeat they wisely undertook a review to ascertain what had happened and why.

Three personalities were significant in this process: General von *Schaarnhorst*, who was chief of staff of the Prussian Army in 1806, Field Marshall von *Gneisenau*, who although of humble origins served as one of Prince Hohenlohe's staff-officers and fought as a company commander at Jena, and *Karl von Clausewitz* who was acting as adjutant to Prince August at Auerstadt. Schaarnhorst was later his mentor and by Waterloo Gneisenau was Blucher's Chief of Staff. Over time, Clauswitz has become the most famous as a result of his magnum opus, "*On War*", edited and published after his death in 1831 by his wife. These three were part of the organizing committee which set to work on reconstructing the Prussian army.

[3] Gardiner, J E (2014) *Music in the Garden of Heaven* p. 227.

It is worth noting that this trio were not Junkers. Therefore they were not beholden to the previous legacy.

Firstly they observed that far too many Prussian Generals were around 80 years old and there were too many generals even for an army of ~190,000 men. Clearly there were plenty of sinecures in force. Furthermore these officer posts were filled only by aristocrats who bought their commissions—as the inexperienced, untrained Wellington had done in the British army.[4] By way of contrast they noted that Napoleon's younger marshals had achieved their posts on merit.

Secondly they also noted the French army worked at a faster tempo in the field. Schaarnhorst observed: "We fought bravely but not cleverly enough." The French officers seemed to operate with certain clearly understood principles and then were expected to exercise initiative as the battle unfolded. And it seemed they had the authority to take decisions without referring back in the heat of the battle. This led to a fundamental conclusion: *the Prussians needed to develop a more professional officer corps* (bear in mind most front line soldiers were illiterate at this time) with the authority and know how to take effective decisions in real time.

2.2.3 Three Critical Steps Then Followed

In 1808 the Prussian army introduced general conscription, something again Napoleon had introduced in France. In the past the wealthy could buy their way out of conscription.[5] This was no longer possible in the new regime. Officer ranks were now open to all strata of society. This also meant a better leavening of talent was coming into leadership roles within the army.

Secondly promotion was now to be on merit not length of service. The earlier custom of paying sinecures well into "retirement", when the officers in question were barely able to climb onto a horse, was phased out.

Thirdly they realised that leadership training of officers had to be introduced and practiced more effectively to ensure the army was led by a professional cadres with the ability, authority and preparedness to take key decisions in the field.

In 1810 a "General War School" was established to enhance officer education and training. *The blueprint of the ideal candidate and the key qualities being sought also changed.* It was no longer de rigueur to be obsessed with bowing to authority.

[4] Holmes, R (2003) *Wellington The Iron Duke*, p.29 "Purchasing of Commissions persisted in the British Army until 1871" Keegan J, (1994) *A History of Warfare*, p14.

[5] This was still a problem for the Russian army as late as WWI, according to Hastings, (2013) p.15.

Instead intelligence, a strong will, independence of mind and determination in the face of obstacles were being sought. The training was general and technical to ensure a common understanding and approach across the officer group of the Army. There was also thought being given to training in the practice of what we today would call "values". A key value for a Prussian officer was "honour", which seemed to mean something like "being true to yourself."

There was even teaching in due course as to when it might be appropriate to disobey an order if it conflicted with the demands of honour.

Sun Tzu had already sanctioned the possibility of disobeying an order 2300 years earlier (See Griffith's translation p. 172). Sun Tzu's work had been translated by a French Jesuit—J. J. L. Amiot—in 1782, who introduced his work to Europe. It was quite well known by the end of the eighteenth century and was probably read by Napoleon. It was Moltke who introduced it in the Prussian context. This was an important first step in the acculturation of a new officer class but as will be shown further important changes were brought in later in the nineteenth century. This early analysis laid the ground work for what I have called "Experiential Training", which will be covered in more depth in Chap. 6.

2.3 Learning in the Military

The military is one form of organization that has learned consistently from its mistakes. The cynic would argue they make plenty so there is plenty of scope. There is also clearly a major incentive as the performance stakes are higher than in other forms of organization. Learning leads to less loss of life. While it is true that there have been countless examples of military disasters and "managerial cock-ups" there has also been a clear tradition of learning from what went wrong even though some such as Barbara Tuchman (1985) have questioned that. Civilian organizations don't generally let on about their cock-ups and therefore rarely learn from them.

This ability to learn and adapt is most clear in the military approach to organization. There have been reorganisations throughout history to accommodate new uses of 'technology' including new approaches to weaponry, logistics and training, to gain competitive advantage. One Lt. Colonel told me recently, "Today I suspect our generals would struggle with the intensity of firepower and digital information available to the front line commander compared to their day only 20 years ago." These have mostly affected the deployment on horizontal axis of organization design, such as the introduction of cavalry and so on, but the vertical axis—the line of command or layers of leadership—has been largely unchanged for many centuries.

2.3.1 The Line and Staff Distinction

The military were the first to figure out the critical difference between "line" and "staff" to ensure the line of command in the field was not overly cluttered with non value adding layers 'in support'. Only line jobs—the line of command—are on the spine of accountability. Staff jobs support the spine of accountability. They are not placed between the accountable leader and the team, nor more importantly the accountable leader and his boss.

Most civilian organizations still have not reliably figured out this key distinction and its impact on hierarchy, which tends to be heavy as a result. *The influence of job evaluation and grading systems and their wrongful migration into the domain of organization design is the main cause of this distortion in civilian organisations.* These systems have wrongly migrated into the space of organization design and leadership development with quite devastating negative consequences. In civilian organizations the disease of "every grade a layer" tends to be widespread. Specialists in civilian organizations, such as engineers, are placed on the spine of accountability in order to get the 'right' grade (because the job evaluation system offers more points for bigger budgets and more staff and the shortcut to these is to insert another layer into the structure) to pay the 'right' money. Civilian grading systems frequently bedevil organization design (and leadership development) as a result.

The military, unlike civilian organizations, value the staff roles. General Omar Bradley is alleged to have said: "Amateurs talk about strategy, professionals about logistics." It is the supporting logistics that ensure success in the field: strategy in action. The orchestrated leadership development paths of generals veer across line and staff roles throughout their career, as was already evident in the career paths of our three Prussian reformers. Civilian organizations don't tend to see this as important, which is not surprising since they invariably don't know how to distinguish and calibrate the value of these jobs.

The ability to adapt and really learn from experience has a long history in military circles. Keegan has pointed out the use of technology (e.g. the introduction of horses and chariots) delivered clear advantage at first until copied by opponents.[6] He has also shown that lack of adaptability and learning, even of a cultural, social nature, has led ultimately to failure. Among the classic examples he cites being the demise of the Marmelukes in Egypt and the Samurai in Japan, as effective fighting forces. Landes gives a dramatic description of the "*Celestial Empire's (*China*) stasis and retreat*" based on lack of adaptability and institutional learning following the heights achieved in the early medieval period when it boasted the largest, most impressive navy in the world.[7] This also occurred in the Chinese civil service which by the late nineteenth century was becoming corrupt and unable to adapt the industrial and technological needs of the era, with fatal consequences, even though

[6] Keegan (1994) *A History of Warfare* p.34.

[7] Landes (1998) *The Wealth and Poverty of Nations* p335ff.

it was unmatched for well over 1000 years as it selected top bureaucrats on merit. When the value of selection on merit is lost in a blinkered, cultural time warp it is the first step to leadership failure.

2.4 Learning in Civilian Organizations

Over the years I have noticed many major, sometimes global, projects fail in civilian organizations. Yet it is virtually unheard of for companies to study the lessons of failure to ensure they are not replicated, let alone appoint two or three "generals" to review the 'failed' situation.

2.4.1 A Global Finance Project

I recall a global project in a large company aimed at the seamless gathering of finance information from around the world to be collected in real time straight into the corporate office. Although this was a high profile project, which involved some of the top finance executives in the company and involved about forty managers from one of the world's leading technology companies working with them, with a budget running into millions, the project failed. There was a mild investigation into why this had happened, but the process was politicised and the true reasons for failure did not emerge. Real learning did not occur: it was lip service at best.

2.4.2 A Pan European Marking Project

In another situation an international company had a major, very public, marketing failure with a new product introduction. It was established that the failure was essentially a technical shortcoming. The company maintained lessons had been learned and that this would not happen again. I happened to be interviewing a number of the technical managers in this company at the time and it was clear *the lesson had not been learned.* None of the managers gave the same reason for the failure. There were no examples of co-ordinated new steps being taken as a result of this episode. The so-called learning was cosmetic designed for the benefit of analysts and other external observers.

2.4.3 The Lessons and Price of Project Failure?

The only company I have encountered that claims to formally study project failure is Motorola. In that company apparently anyone given a major project to manage is first asked to study previous projects of similar complexity that have not been the total success that was envisaged. They then examine the reasons for failure in order not to make the same mistakes.

It is of course difficult for ambitious junior managers in an organization with a heritage of promotion from within, to unmask the incompetence of those in the very positions to which they aspire. Some companies such as Enron, Andersen Consulting and Lehman Brothers, for example, never recover from a major setback. Shell Oil is one that did. It rectified governance, organizational and leadership mistakes over its cavalier estimation of oil reserves in 2004. As a result the then chairman, Sir Philip Watts, and his heir apparent, Walter van de Vijver, were sacked. In further moves Shell overhauled and improved its previously archaic and flawed governance structure. Arie de Geus argued in 1979, that Shell was a learning company and it would appear he was right. BP wobbled badly over its oil spill in the Gulf of Mexico, which led to the departure of the CEO. At the time of writing it is not that clear yet whether fully effective remedial action followed or indeed whether the company has fully recovered.

If, as it seems, civilian organizations are generally not too good at learning from their own mistakes it is not too surprising they rarely bother to learn from other organizations. Tesco and Matsushita are two exceptions who have been known in the past to be 'rapid followers'. Sun Tzu said: "Know your enemy (competition) and know yourself: then in 100 battles you will never be in peril." Lip service is often paid to the practices of competitors but it is a brave manager who would suggest the company might learn something from the military. These cultural silos seem to be reinforced by academics even if only by omission.

The closest civilian practice aimed at learning from others is called *benchmarking*. But on closer examination the basis of comparison is often flawed, as apples are matched with pears. The other disadvantage of benchmarking is its backward looking character. Benchmarking cold statistics would not have helped our three Prussians' project as their enemy *behaved in a different manner* and no amount of benchmarking and studying sheaves of metrics would have provided the insights they uncovered. They had to recognise that different behaviour and understand what drove it. Part of their great strength was the fact that they had been in the field and could dredge their memories of that experience to draw out the differences that were critical to the end result. Their analysis was not simply from behind the desk.

It is not easy to survive a major setback and very few organizations have the proven intelligence, insight, courage, resilience and integrity to revitalise themselves from within. Most fail, disappear and/or are taken over. Thus the steps set in train *after* Jena by the Prussian army are, impressive, significant and worthy of study.

2.5 Clausewitz's Contribution

Clausewitz had experience of both line and staff roles *in the field*. He was not a backroom boy. He was in a staff role during the defeat of 1806. So he knew how to plan and how to act directly in the field. He was said to be the intellectual one of the three reformers. He apparently had been writing down his thoughts as early as 1803.

When appointed to the War College in Berlin in 1813 he was able to dedicate more time to his magnum opus, *On War*, which in fact he never finished. He is famous for the phrase "War is the continuation of policy by other means." It is debatable whether this epic and often quoted statement is quite that clear. He used the German word "politik", which is potentially ambiguous in that could be translated as either 'policy' or 'politics' in English. Hence it is also claimed he said "War is the continuation of politics by other means." While Thomas Hobbes argued in *Leviathan* that the roots of war were found in the nature of man, Clausewitz *seemed* to believe they stemmed from the nature of politics.

On war is indeed a magnum opus in the best German tradition and there are probably few readers who have stayed the course: I have not. It is in places highly abstract and philosophical. The Germans have a word for the effort needed to produce (and read!) a work of this length, depth and complexity—'gruntlich'. There is no exact English translation—officially "thorough"—but the word conveys nose-grinding hard work, requiring determined and single minded persistence and perseverance to complete something over a long period of time. It was his Sisyphean life task, which he too never quite completed.

Clausewitz's great and unique insight was to focus on the gap between planning and execution. Planning is straightforward but implementation is not because of what he called "friktion".

2.5.1 "Friktion"

'Friction' in English but the German word has wider connotations. It is the resistance that occurs when one tries to put a simple plan into action. It has probably been best described by Paret (1976):

> *Friction refers to the uncertainties, errors, accidents, technical difficulties, the unforeseen and their effect on decisions, morale, and actions.*

Friction seems to have been "*derived from physics, a concept which is invoked to explain the discrepancy between real and idealised mechanical processes*".[8] Clausewitz developed the analogy further: "*This enormous friction, which is not concentrated, as in mechanics, at a few points, is therefore everywhere brought into contact with chance.*"[9] He divided friction into two parts: numerous chance events and numerous difficulties which work against the execution of precise plans. Much of that friction stems from the action of the enemy (or competitor, in civilian life), which cannot easily be anticipated.

My experience suggests few organizations give real or deep thought to the competitors' likely reaction to their new initiatives. Clausewitz's insight has

[8] A. Rappoport's 69 page (!) Introduction to Penguin's 1982 edition of *On War* p.14.

[9] On War (1982) p165.

major implications for the crafting and implementing of strategy, which we will pick over in more detail in the next chapter. He argued war was an art not a science, as some of his more senior Prussian commanders believed at the time. It is never easy to argue against the grain of superiors. He believed friction was inevitable, could not be avoided or eliminated but it could be mitigated and managed. He further distinguished between external and internal sources. Bungay has pointed out that "The existence of friction is why armies need officers and businesses needs managers".[10] Clausewitz was also interested in and explored the question: "What makes a person succeed in the art of command?" He identified several essential qualities that a commander must possess, although he noted differences. He believed two were of primary importance: courage and intelligence. We will explore his views on leadership and those of others, both military and civilian in more detail in Chap. 5, on Leadership Development.

He also places great emphasis on training, which will be the subject of Chap. 6. The major difference between the military and civilian organizations is the importance the former place on *experiential* or *rehearsal training*. This is rare outside the military where academic/class room discussion tends to hold sway. But its effectiveness is increasingly challenged, for example by Henry Mintzberg.

Clausewitz highlighted this training pitfall early:

> "*Activity in war is movement in a resistant medium, just as a man in water is unable to perform with ease*. . .*This is the reason that the theorist is like a swimming master who teaches on dry land the movements required in water, which must appear grotesque and ludicrous to those who forget about the water*. . ..*This is also why theorists who have never plunged in themselves or who cannot deduce any generalities from their experience, are impractical and even absurd, because they only teach what everyone knows – how to walk.*"[11]

There are a number of insights in *On War* that will play out in all five pillars in this book. Interestingly Clausewitz does not seem to say much about the structure of an army. This is not surprising since that issue had been hammered out well before his time, as indicated above and mission command was able to treat structure largely as a given. *It is also most probably why the critical influence of organization design is so often overlooked* by civilian managers and academics, who might have dipped into *On War*.

> ***It is important to note that it was not the structure of the Prussian army that was the cause of failure at Jena. Nor was Napoleon's inherently superior.***

[10] Bungay, S (2011) Op cit p32.

[11] On War (1982) pp165–166.

This is very different to civilian organizations where faulty organization design is too often the root cause of failings in strategy implementation and leadership development. Northern Rock, which experienced the first run on a British bank in over 100 years, is a case in point. Although it could justify up to 6 layers of leadership it had up to 11.

2.6 Moltke's Contribution

If Frederick the Great was Europe's pre-eminently talented prince, then Field Marshall Helmuth von Molke could lay claim to being its preeminent soldier. This Helmuth Von Molke, The Great, is not to be confused with his "much less gifted nephew", of the same name who was a favourite of the Kaiser and who rose to the rank of Chief of Staff in WW1 because of it. It was ironic that after 1890 the elder Moltke argued that Europe's fate should thenceforth be decided diplomatically rather than on the battlefield: he thought the usefulness of war to Germany was exhausted."[12] The difference between him and say Wellington was the fact he left an unparalleled blueprint for running a successful organization, which lived on beyond his victories in the field. He is the man who took the ideas of the three reformers and accelerated their implementation. He re-built an Army and created a General Staff that was without peer in Europe in his time. This was recognised by the Allies at Versailles, ~50 years later, who demanded it be dismantled.

He was that very rare combination: a leader who had a flair for both operations and strategic thinking. He understood how things worked but wanted to make them work even better. He possessed key personal gifts: he was a clear and decisive communicator, an innovator and an implementer. Many of his ideas were written down in succinct essays and memoranda. His three pages 'On strategy' is a masterpiece: it is set out in the Appendix. He was a true, rounded leader of men. He was honest, generous and modest not given to flamboyance or posturing.

2.6.1 "Auftragstaktiker"

He developed what today would be called the German army's operating model. He was the father of Auftragstaktiker. (Auftrag normally means "task" or "assignment" but "mission" is the favoured military translation. A mission is a "task with a purpose".[13]) Today the Bundeswehr—German military—refer not to Auftragstaktik but "Fuhren mit Auftrag" (leading by mission).

[12] See Hastings (2013) *Catastrophe Europe goes to War* p27.

[13] Bungay op cit: note 32 P.257.

Today NATO refers to this operating model as mission command although others such as Bungay & McKinney[14] as 'mission leadership'.

Unusually, following a victory over the Austrians at Koniggratz in 1866, Molke produced a *post mortem report*, in which he highlighted two problems. He felt the instructions from above were not getting through accurately to the lower reaches of the army who as a result worked independently of each other, which could have undermined the overall strategy and the result of the battle. On this occasion they got away with it, but he saw it as a major organizational flaw affecting the behaviour of the army in the field that had to be overcome. He recognised it was vital to connect these two extremes as it was not possible in a large army for the Field marshal to have line of sight of all the men in the field. This was a powerful, common sense but unique insight.

In this he was grappling with a challenge that is even more demanding in a large global company. The person at the top cannot manage events and people directly at the front line across 100 countries. Yet it is vital for success that communications from the top to the front line are clear and not corrupted by traversing multiple layers of hollow hierarchy. Peter Drucker (1969) maintained that each layer of management diluted the message emanating from either end of a company's hierarchy by 50 %. Drucker was a management philosopher who rarely provided hard evidence for his views but there is no doubt that too many layers is a problem in far too many civilian organizations. The problem layers are those that are not needed because they are not adding value and so needlessly distort and delay communications.

But the even greater problem in most civilian organizations is they do not know how to identify the hollow layers that might exist.

Although I have worked in at least 70 organizations across 70 countries I have come across very few organizations that have put formal, sustained effort into training their managers how to communicate in clear, simple language down to and including the front line. ASDA—part of Wal-mart—is one that excels in this respect. In 1869 Molke he put his thoughts on paper in a document called "*Guidance for large unit commanders.*" It is probably the first written document providing advice and guidance on leadership for senior officers (and executives) and it was unchanged up to 1939 and today its content is apparently recognisable *in some documents of NATO and US forces,* according to Hughes, D. J. editor (1993) in *Molke on the Art of War*. It is worth recalling that large private sector businesses did not really come into being until the around the 1870s and public sector bureaucracies were only emerging in any force at that time. Formal guidance and education of top managers was nonexistent and therefore unheard of at the time, hence the great significance of Moltke's guidance for his 'top leaders'.

[14] Bungay, S and McKinney, D (2003) Mission Leadership, *Ashridge Journal,* Spring.

His next great insight was to split the concept of 'command' (leadership) from that of 'control'—contrary to the myths about the military model being only about "command and control".

He envisaged a process that entailed officers giving far fewer minute instructions the further down the chain of command they travelled. This is exactly the opposite to twentieth century civilian management practices built originally on the tenets of "scientific management" and more recently, "process reengineering", both of which beatify attention to detail. Action in civilian organizations is too often constipated by an obsession with building 'operating models' invariably dividing work into meaningless (on their own) components of processes and sub processes. They have removed the soul from much white collar work; at a time in history when there have never been so many educated people available to do meaningful work at the customer interface.

When Moltke was confronting the challenge of how to cascade information effectively down, across and up through a large organization he was dealing with a front line then that was largely illiterate and yet he treated them with more trust than today's process engineers. In designing what is now recognised as mission command, he enshrined a set of behaviours in the military which went in the opposite direction to that favoured by twenty-first century civilian organizations.

Moltke's great insight was clarifying "the mission"—the "what" and the "why"—which could be described clearly and succinctly. Provided officers were well trained in the practice of leadership and soldiers in military tasks, the "how" did not need to be spelt out in detail.

And of course it (the "how") could not be, especially once battle began. Molke's solution was to define *the mission*—the *what* & the *why*—at the top of the organization. *Effective* training for both officers and soldiers would mean they would know the relevant *tasks* at the front line—the *how*—needed to achieve the mission. The next challenge was he had to define a way of connecting these two strands of mission and task, the *what* and the *how*.

The answer became Auftragstaktiker or mission command, which is the *exploitation of chaos* by commanding *what and why*.

The British Field Marshall Sir Nigel Bagnall is credited with bringing mission command into his army and subsequently into NATO in the 1980s.[15] It was first used formally by NATO in the Gulf War of 1991.

[15] Bungay (2011) Op cit, p.78.

2.6.1.1 The Invisible Thread: Back-Briefing

The invisible thread of Moltke's approach was training, especially ***leadership training, coupled with back-briefing****, which tied together three layers in a communication cascade.*

Back briefing, in essence a feedback loop, entailed sharing the brief from above and then asking the subordinate to summarise that brief back before passing it down to his team. In this way back-briefing automatically locked in three layers of leadership to the mission. Back-briefing is a cascade process from the top of the organization but *what was new was the emphasis on two way communication.* The front line had line of sight of the strategy and the top leadership had line of sight to operations and tactics but without trying to formulate them.

In order to take action people need to know the overall intent—*What and why.* A clear, accountable structure enables the message to be passed on quickly: 'this is what you are going to have to do and why, to fit in to the overall mission.' The leader one layer down has to then crystallise how this task will be broken down into further tasks for the direct reports. That leader in the lower layer is then asked to repeat the original message back up to the leader above (in the next higher layer) summarising what he/she will do together with a summary outline of those to be carried out by the team—direct reports. This is the closing of the communication loop.

A key question for any organization is, what does anyone need to know to make a decision and take action? Moltke's answer was to introduce *back-briefing* aiming to lock-in three layers at a time into a clear understanding of what has to be done and why. In a large organization with more than three layers in total this results in an overlapping cascade of locked in layers plugged into the *same relevant message.* It becomes the basis of orchestrated action with everyone on the same page coupling together the needs for information and action. Figure 2.1 gives a pictorial example of how the "3 layer loops" would work in an organization, where the CEO's role is Work Level 5, chosen because it illustrates the critical integrating link of a WL 3 manager who happens to be common to each of the three loops.

In back-briefing the first thing the subordinate needs to know is *what* and *why*—the overall aim or intent of the work to be done. This comes from the layer above—e.g. level 5 in Fig. 2.1. So the level 5 leader in this example starts by giving the brief. Given this information the person in level 4 is asked to figure out *how* this might be achieved. Having quickly figured that out that the subordinate is expected to close the communication loop by repeating back up, both their understanding of the boss's message while adding in the tasks *(how)* they now need to carry out. The boss is checking the understanding of the brief while gaining verification and insight into how his or her directions can be carried out. In this way subordinate leaders are able to check on the understanding of the intent and its implications before passing it further down the line to their subordinates.

Briefing and back-briefing are then repeated at each layer. So the level 4 leader, having checked his or her understanding of the direction that has been given, briefs the leader at level 3. This is the brief the Level 4 has agreed with the Level 5, based on the original brief the former was given. The Level 3 in turn is asked to back-brief

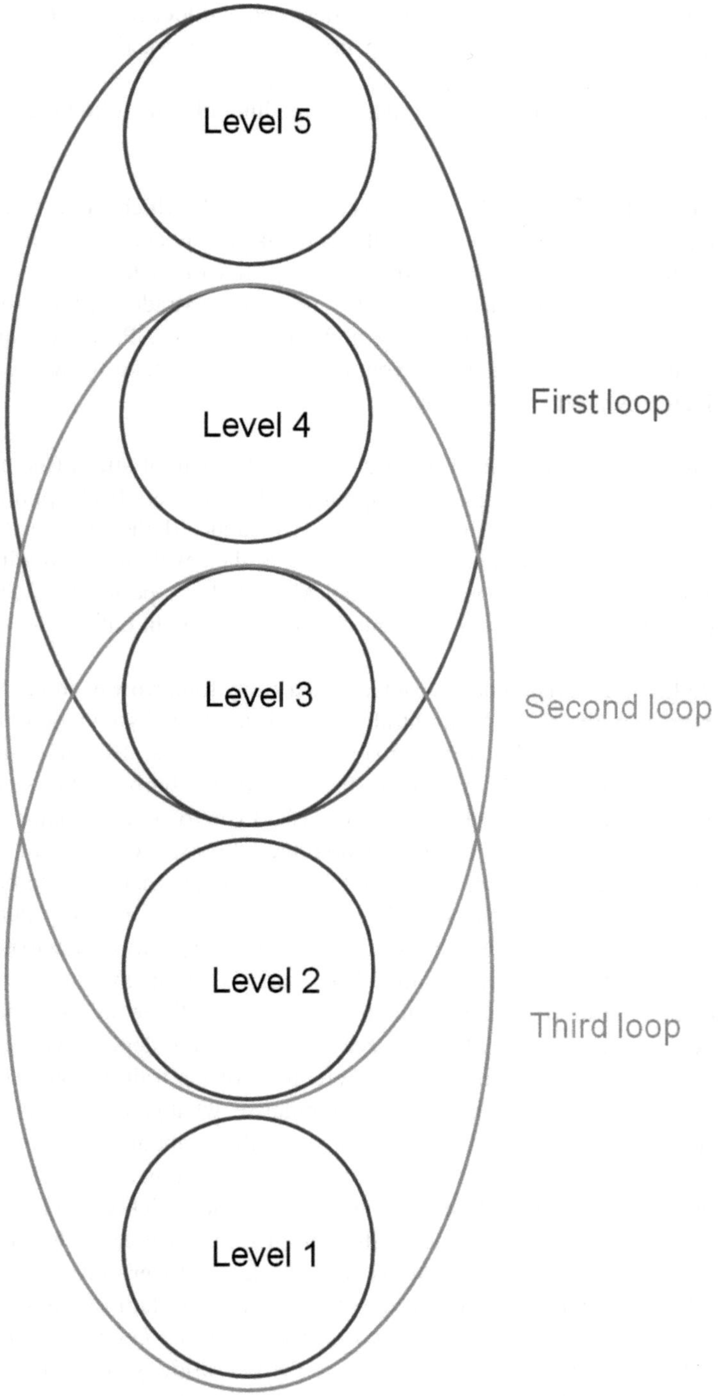

Fig. 2.1 An example of back-briefing

the level 4 boss to ensure the mission is understood and locked in. (The back-brief could lead to some revision of the top brief given the practicalities of a given context.)

An example, in military terms, could be something like the following simplified version.

Level 5 to L4: "I have been told we are to capture town A, which has a river running through it. This is part of the Corps' thrust to take the adjacent shipbuilding port, ABC, which is key to achieving Army V's objective of controlling the east coast river mouths. There are three key suburbs to the West straddling the river, which I want your brigade to capture by nightfall tomorrow. Please confirm your understanding of which suburbs you are to attack and take by when. Do you anticipate any problems with that?"

The subordinate would then brief back, outline his plan of attack (the how) and highlight issues where he might need support, such as artillery back up, timing and method of communication with his artillery colleague. If they feel in *this brief discussion* there are insurmountable or obstacles the levels above might not be aware of the L5 may need to re-enagage quickly with his superior. But ideally that would not be necessary if the overall mission is well thought out.

Level 4 to L3: Our division has to capture town A, by tomorrow evening. We have to capture suburbs X,Y,Z by nightfall to set this up. I need your battalion to take suburb X, defended by armed road and rail bridges: two in total. Your colleagues, Bill and John will take the other two suburbs at the same time. Confirm you are clear on what I have just asked you to do. Any major obstacles to that plan you are aware of? They would then discuss the outline of "how" in some more detail until both a clear and satisfied about what needs to be done.

Level 3 to L2: The division plans to take town A by tomorrow evening. Our brigade has to take out suburbs X,Y,Z before then to make it happen. We are to neutralise suburb X in the same timeframe. Your task is to secure the two bridges immediately in front of us to ensure that can happen. There are two key bridges but the road one is the key to our success. I want you to deploy two platoons to capture the road bridge and one to take control of the train bridge. The attack must start in precisely one hour so let's summarise. what you understand you and your teams have to do and briefly how you will go about it and whether you anticipate any significant problems we need to discuss now. The superior officer will probably have more experience and can critique (quickly) the L2's method of attack and build in reassurance to their discussion. Once the L3 is comfortable the "how" is do-able and understood he will ask his officer to brief his men.

The Level 2 officer will then brief his direct reports in a similar fashion on what and why, *choosing which squads of men to set about which key tasks*—the how in which they have been trained—to capture the two bridges in the first instance. Once again he will seek understanding, feasibility and commitment. He is now into the real practicalities and may stress the advantages of surprise and *how* to maximise this advantage: so the final comment might be: "Right let's synchronise watches".

If his team have not been adequately trained for their specific tasks the chances of success could be remote, depending on the deployment and competence of the enemy.

In this rather simplistic description the brief is becoming narrower under the umbrella of the general mission but increasingly specific to match what is needed at each lower level of accountability. Emphasis in the briefings is on *brevity*. Hence the tasks become ever more specific and detailed, tailored to the context of the relevant mission, until the front line has been included. In short each leader is saying, "This is what *we* have to do and why, how are *you* going to do it?" Since the process directly locks in three layers at a time it can be seen that in the example of Fig. 1.1, it so happens that the level 3 leader is the lynchpin in this hypothetical example, participating in three back briefs: those of 5-4-3, 4-3-2 and 3-2-1 making it the critical leadership pivot in that instance. For each leader the starting point is the intent of the leader above.

The military call this process "mission analysis". Bungay favours "strategy briefing",[16] but since levels 1–3 (99 %+of a typical work force) do not have strategic accountability I prefer "back-briefing". Back-briefing provides a clear line of sight downwards toward operations and tactics while at the same time affording a line up to strategy while also aligning support functions to the action (s) agreed upon.

The "what", "why" and "how" of back-briefing are not absolute terms. They are relative terms given meaning by the job context: their battle echelon or Work Level. As so often is the case, the key success depends on matching work and capability to context.

This is course is the ideal but things don't always work as smoothly as that in the real world. This is where culture and values, based on realistically flat structures and clear accountability as the basis of good leadership development and training, come into their own. The implied thought for the empowered subordinate is:

"What would my boss order me to do if that person he was in my position and knew what I know now?"

The purpose of back-briefing is to enable people to act successfully both independently but in unison as a collective. It unifies effort up, down and across the organisation.

[16] Bungay op cit p. 148.

2.6.1.2 Potential Sources of Friction

Moltke's insight recognised that invariably *friction* tended to stem from a lack of one or all of the following:

- Knowledge
- Alignment
- Effects.

These gaps tend to lead to three predicable outcomes:

- More information and data is called for to close the knowledge gap.
- More detailed instructions are given to improve alignment with the plan
- More detailed controls and measures are imposed to help ensure the right effect is achieved.

The combined outcome is delay and frustration, which makes the overall situation worse. Bungay has analysed this aspect of Moltke's thinking in some detail so I do not intend or need to replicate his excellent analysis. However I think these gaps are so serious and potentially debilitating I have called them ***thee strategic traps*** and discuss their impact in more detail in Chap. 2.

2.7 So, What Is Mission Command?

The essence of mission command is ensuring trained leaders understand their mission—a task within a purpose—but are left free to decide for themselves how best to accomplish it.

Today we would say mission command is about *empowerment and trust*. Most civilian organizations today claim to espouse this philosophy but *few know how to deliver it. Mission Mastery would close that gap.*

This is because trust is built first on clear accountability combined with commensurate authority. Accountability and authority are two sides of the same coin.

Mission command was not developed as a theory in some academic dark room. It was developed as a *set of practices* devised to overcome sub optimal performance that had been observed in the field. They were refined to ensure they worked and were further improved in the light of experience. Mission command is also *scaleable* and *transferable,* which means it can be enhanced and migrated to civilian organizations.

For Moltke the mission would be set out in clear, simple terms by the most relevant senior commander but the 'how' was not specified in detail. Once they understood the purpose behind their immediate task the officers reporting to the relevant commander were both able and expected to make subsequent decisions based on the situation as it unfolded but still in line with the overall brief. This of course enabled them to react to changing circumstances as the chaos of a given battle unfolded. In this way they could exploit unexpected opportunities. They were obliged to take initiative and junior officers were trained to take over a unit up to the size of a battalion, so that these units would not be paralysed in the field if a commanding officer was immobilised. They were acutely aware that *inaction was the cardinal sin for a leader.*

Training focussed around field exercises so that the tactics were well understood by all and *rehearsed* throughout the army. This enabled the army officers to react quickly in unison so that they could improvise effectively in real crises. After the Battle of Tannenberg in WWI, where the Germans despatched the Russian divisions with surprising ease, the Austrian staff officer, (with the Italian name!), Pallavacini noted of the Germans: "They must have a secret weapon."[17]

They did: it was mission command which later emerged as Blitzkrieg in WWII. A young Charles de Gaulle argued that France's hopes depended on a career based army with powerful and mobile forces. His views were set out in two books in the early 1930s. "Prime Minister Daladier and most of the top brass dismissed his views. Young German commanders read de Gaulle's books from cover to cover and swiftly incorporated his offensive-oriented strategy into their own army".[18]

2.7.1 The Contrasting Approach of the "Competition"

Bungay points out that the British doctrine to avoid battlefield chaos was to control it centrally through a 'Master Plan'—an attempt to control the *how.*[19] Junior officers were only allowed to change their actions if circumstances changed, and needed authority to do so, which led to delay. *Initiative was effectively banned.* After months of detailed planning the Battle of the Somme in 1916 was a debacle as officers were hamstrung by lack of orders. In fact Haig and Rawlinson could not even agree on the overall objective. Their minutely detailed plan for the Battle of the Somme (sketched out by those sitting ~100 miles from the Front in Montreuil), is a graphic example of failure by the planning and control school. Alan Clark (1961) *Donkeys,* or Max Hastings' *Catastrophe* (2013) are among the many who remain unimpressed by the "leadership" of these generals.

They were examples of generals trying to *manage chaos* by trying to control the *how* by spelling it out in minute, fixed detail. If, like Alexander, Julius Caesar, Wellington or Rommel they had actually bothered to visit the front they would have surely realised the shortcomings of their detailed academic plans and the shocking unsuitability of the terrain they had chosen for the battle.

[17] Hastings op cit p 398.

[18] Kladstrup D and P (2002) *Wine and War*, p.32.

[19] Bungay, S (2002) *Alamein,* Aurum Press, London, p.34.

Incredibly this folly was repeated 2 years later at Passchendaele when apparently those at HQ had no idea men were drowning in a sea of mud in October 1917.[20] The future Major General Inglis noted on 4th October: "*The tragedy of the attack [at Broodseinde] is that we were tied down to strictly limited objectives for we could have walked to Passchendaele almost unopposed that morning. . .at the time we cursed the British tactical methods.*"[21] No doubt the largely needless 270,000 British and Dominion subsequent casualties were also unimpressed by Haig's decision making. Shortly after Inglis' observation he apparently over-ruled three layers of generals, with knowledge of the terrain and insisted their men attack in knee deep mud and pouring rain on 12th October. When that failed in predictable slaughter another immediate attack was ordered, with half their comrades lying in no-man's land, according to Vennell (2014). It further highlights the severe limitations of the planning and control school that believed it could control chaos—the "how".

The debacle at Suvla Bay in the Gallipoli campaign occurred, according to Alan Moorehead, when the British troops decided to go for a swim on coming ashore *because they were awaiting further orders.* Meantime Mustafa Kemal sprinted round behind the hills to secure the high ground that the British could have taken earlier, largely if not completely unopposed.

Andrew Gordon[22] noted the Royal Navy was not much better in WWI. He thought the gravest weakness of the Royal Navy was its officers' rigidity of thought and subservience to higher authority: captains waited upon the orders of their admiral and if these were confused or absent subordinates never dared to think or act for themselves. He provided examples to make his case.

As French[23] (not the WWI general!) noted, the British, ignoring battlefield evidence, continued to believe *they* had a talent for improvisation and the Germans were unimaginative and methodical. Ironically it was the "rigid Prussians" who were the fast, imaginative, improvisers.

Most companies are apt to believe their competitors are not as good as them, irrespective of evidence to the contrary.

Bungay again: "*Although the British deluded themselves with fantasies about Germans rigidly obeying orders and planning everything down to the last detail (because of Teutonic thoroughness) the Germans knew their enemy. The Afrika Korps noted that the enemy's 'higher level commanders would show reluctance to make swift decisions' while junior officers 'show a lack of independence and inflexible methods'. As late as the Gazala battle the intelligence branch of the*

[20] On November 7th after the slaughter, General Kiggell, Haig's no. 2 paid his ***first*** visit to Passchendaele **4 months** after the battle began and said: "***Good God: did we really send men to fight in that?***" J. Vennell (2014) *The Forgotten General,* p.177.

[21] Lindsay Inglis. Diary, vol 2.p61.

[22] Gordon, A (1996) *The Rule of the Game: Jutland and British Naval Command.*

[23] French, D (2000) *Raising Churchill's Army*, Oxford University Press. (Not to be confused with WWI general Sir John French.)

*Panzerarmee noted with the bemusement of men to whom mission command was a way of life: 'Their orders were schematic and went into the smallest detail. The middle and lower command were consequently allowed little freedom of movement. . .**a certain shyness of action existed.** (My emphasis) Of all the factors which can be cited to explain how the Germans beat the odds for so long, both in the desert and elsewhere, their use of a mission-based command system, and their opponents lack of it, is the most important*".

In other words they did have a secret weapon. It was the quality of their leadership and training.

2.7.2 The Royal Navy's Approach to Mission Command[24]

The Royal Navy (RN) is an example of how mission command has migrated from one disparate organization to another and is therefore an example of how mission command could cross the military/civilian divide. *Mission Command was formally introduced into the British Armed Forces in ~1987—more than 100 years after Moltke introduced it in Germany*. The RN has now instituted mission command on its own terms to fit its ethos. It approach is defined as follows:

"*Mission Command is the assignment of a mission or a task to a subordinate, having provided that person with a framework of understanding or context and the support/resources needed to succeed. It is a robust system of command design (i.e. leadership, in civilian organizations—author) to promote and to achieve a sense of unity of effort at all levels.*

For those bold enough to apply it, this approach *has proved to be* the most appropriate way to contend with the demands, uncertainties, and frictions of command in war. It requires:

- Development of trust and mutual understanding between leader and lead
- Timely and effective decision making
- *Initiative at all levels*

The manner of its application cannot be stereotyped: the leader's style of command must also reflect the overarching situation, including the capability and understanding of his subordinates. It needs acceptance that the leader on the spot is probably right and that the subordinate will call for assistance if needed. In which case, the logic is:

[24] This material is based on "Mission Command A View from the Fleet Battlestaff" (undated). I was given a copy when visiting Portsmouth HQ in 2004.

If there is silence, then all is well.

In other words it calls for trust that the subordinate will call for help or advice if needed. This calls for relationships that are creative and constructive not dictatorial and therefore de-motivating.

"The Nelson Touch"

This is the first heading in the RN's current bible, British Maritime Doctrine. It extols Nelson's simple instructions, his belief in delegation and the time and effort he spent in getting his captains to understand his intentions. Nelson may well have been a mission commander, first showing signs of this at the battle of Cape St. Vincent in 1797 but the real point here is this:

The RN did not endeavour to institutionalise this approach to leadership for nearly another 200 years.

2.7.2.1 The Royal Navy Sets Out Eight Principles of Mission Command

Unity of Effort

"*This is the most important principle.* Mission command calls for a form of leadership that devolves decision-making. This has to be done in a way that does not dilute unity of effort or undermine effective teamwork. This can only be done if the sense of purpose is clear and the team members are appropriately trained."

"Unity of effort" is further enhanced if the subordinates understand the intentions not only of their commander but the two layers of management above. ***In this way three layers of management understand the consistency of the aim.*** *This ensures the strategic and operational levels of activity are 'on the same page'.*

Most civilian organizations struggle to have two layers of leadership acting smoothly in unison, let alone three or even four. One of the pervading reasons for this of course is that too often there is no 'blue water' or clear accountability between the many layers of civilian management that should be making different decisions.

Decentralisation

This seems to be the Navy's word for 'empowerment'. The idea is to set decision levels as low as possible. This enables people to "use their initiative within their delegated freedom of action and provides them with a greater sense of involvement and commitment." The aim is to ensure that the person with the most up to date information is empowered, within the clear and agreed parameters of the mission, to take a decision without information being needlessly passed up and down the spine of accountability.

Trust

Everyone agrees this is critical but as already indicated most civilian organizations find this incredibly difficult to achieve. But as the RN makes clear, "Trust is one of the cornerstones of leadership. Like respect it must be earned. There are few short cuts: it is based on professional competence, personal example and integrity. Trust so slowly gained, can be lost quickly especially in extreme conditions." Once again there is no mention of the command structure, which is based on clear accountability and it is *a given* in the RN.

Lack of clear accountability and the necessary authority undermines trust in an organization.

It is pointed out that for trust to work it must be reciprocal. The leader must have trust in and the trust of the followers.

The critical insight of mission command is the recognition that the basis of reciprocal trust is a clear, mutual understanding of what each is seeking to achieve. Accountability and authority is clear and understood.

Delegation Not Abdication

The challenge here is to keep "a firm grip on events with a sensible minimum of control measures." Allowing too much unfocused application of initiative makes co-ordination difficult if not impossible. It is stressed that the key to success is to get the right balance "between control by superiors and subordinate freedom. Never underestimate the difficulties of achieving this balance: it is a fundamentally important skill to develop which will require a good deal of serious thought, including *an accurate assessment of subordinates' capabilities.*"

Mutual Understanding

"A good leader (the RN word is "commander") ensures he understands his subordinates and they understand him. Only then can they conduct operations in a cohesive and effective manner."

"Do not fall into the trap of detailing how they are to achieve their goals. *That is their business.* But ensure your subordinates are aware and understand the higher level constraints and limitations you are all working under."

There is a clear expectation that a subordinate must ensure the leader's intentions are understood and then aim to carry out that intention. In the context of mission command, it is likely the subordinate will have to work out personally how to meet that intention. It is incumbent on the subordinate to seek clarification but not get into the detail of means—the how. This has been covered by training and earlier skill acquisition.

Timely and Effective Decision Making

Mission command calls for timely and effective decision-making at all levels. It is a blueprint for distributed managerial leadership. The Royal Navy puts a lot of emphasis on the ability to make the appropriate judgement and to act as "required at your level of decision making". Once again there is a paradox: how to avoid being precipitate acting on too little information and when to take advantage of "fleeting opportunities". This nicely encapsulates the fact that each and every leadership decision involves and element of inherent risk.

The Navy accepts "that many tactical decisions will have to be made on the basis of incomplete information—but if the mission is well understood this maximises the chance of the right decision being taken by leader or lead."

Responsibility for Decision-Making

(There is a tendency for the words 'accountability' and 'responsibility' to be used interchangeably by English speaking people. I am told that in other European and Asian languages there is only one word for accountability. So when the Royal Navy refers to "Responsibility" I treat that as "Accountability".)

The Navy is adamant that a strong leader takes difficult decisions. And while a "wise leader will heed sound advice, the final responsibility rests at your level and your level alone." Once again the pressure to use initiative is implicitly being stressed. Equally important is the exhortation, "You must expect and demand that your subordinates unflinchingly take the *decisions for which they are responsible*." This is very much in line with Gerry Kraines' (2001) view of responsibility: "What an individual demands of him or herself, has to do with one's conscience, aspirations and internal standards." Accountability for decision-making is not simply top-down and passive: it entails a proactive commitment.

Given the life and death nature of much of their work, the military also tend to stress and expect a more intense commitment to 'teamwork' and colleagues, which is more demanding and far-reaching than what is called for in non-military organizations. While it is clear the stakes can be much higher in military as opposed to non-military scenarios, nevertheless the *principles* underlying successful mission command are common to both military and civilian situations. Although many civilian organizations talk a lot about culture and their efforts to build the equivalent of a successful esprit de corps in reality the outcome is little more than cold tea. This is because they see culture as an input not an output.

Communications

Finally, the Royal Navy emphasises the importance of communications. This is no surprise given that history shows that virtually every great commander, whether on land, sea or air, has been noted for their ability to communicate and inspire their followers. Conversely most defeats reflect communication cock-ups. Bungay (2001), when analysing the Battle of Britain saw a critical advantage accrued from Dowding's communications system—see p. 65. He summed up Rommel's ability to beat the odds against him for so long as: "better equipment, tactics, training, *the acquisition and use of information* and generalship"—p. 25 (2003). In theory this was obvious but the British underestimated the training, leadership and communication advantage of their desert enemy. In short, his mastery and practice of mission command.

The importance of communications is underestimated in most change programmes, which is why they tend to fail so often. When Unilever successfully implemented Work Levels in 1997–1998 across at least 100 countries the company spent over £1 m on communications and training materials. And that did not include the time of those involved in leading and designing the communications efforts. The RN has noted, "There is a widespread perception that the intrusiveness and pervasiveness of modern communications can act against the principles of mission command. Well, of course it can. But it need not and should not." The antidote in mission command terms is very clear, and stems once again form the "clarity of command", i.e. leadership based on clarity of accountability. Today great pressure can emanate from the sheer volume of information available from modern communication systems, such as the Internet, face-book etc. It is simply a newer form of friction. This need to communicate quickly in real time is taken for granted in the twenty-first century. If the clarity of intent from the leader is lacking and the associated context for freedom of action is ambiguous for the follower(s) then confusion and/or inaction simply occurs even more quickly.

The Navy recognises "The volume of modern communications and the associated increase in expectation can actually result in key pieces of information or instructions 'not getting through'. Or it may get through in a technical sense but not be recognised for its importance. Mission command ensures modern communications can act as an enabler not an inhibitor." This is because the inherent distributed leadership, the clarity of purpose and the consistency of intent across three levels of accountability helps ensure the relevant communications 'hit the right spot'. (We will return to this issue of layers of leadership and levels of accountability throughout the book. The military have cracked this relationship with only one layer of leadership per level of accountability. Civilian organizations have not as a rule, and therein lies their problem.)

2.8 The Link Between the RN's Mission Command and Mission Mastery

The RN's '8 principles' are in fact underpinned by the five pillars of Mission Mastery, which to recall are:

- Purpose
- Organization design
- Leadership development
- Experiential learning
- Culture

Unity of Effort consists of devolved decision making which can work effectively only when there are clear levels of accountability with discrete decision rights. This is reflected in the DMA Solution Set where one layer of leadership is required per level of accountability.

The military do not refer to levels of accountability, but "battle echelons."

The battle echelons represent the spine of accountability or chain of command. However there is built-in organizational redundancy between Level 1 and Level 2 to take account of the expected likelihood of casualties in battle. For example of the 458 British casualties in Afghanistan ~4 % were officers, but only one was above Captain (level 2). Even the term "lieutenant" means "holding in place of" or being ready to step into the breach when the person above is killed. Thus there seems to be institutional over-layering in the lower reaches of the officer cadres that is not justified in a civilian management organization. The chain of command for an army in the field is clear: through platoon, company, battalion, brigade, division, corps and ultimately army. (The Royal Air Force and the Royal Navy also have ranks aligned to seven levels of accountability, at present.) Furthermore the ranks are also clear for each of the key levels of accountability. Thus a lieutenant colonel commands a battalion, a brigadier a brigade and so on up to the four-star general in command of an army. The military have geared their training and career path planning to these established benchmarks—covered in more detail in Chap. 5. Moltke trained his officers to be both ready and able to "step up" one level or possibly two levels) in an emergency: i.e. on a temporary basis. This was part of the strength of his cascade system of involving knowledge of the mission for the two layers above.

Civilian organizations do not tend to have this clarity. For example, the common phrase "business unit" could mean anything from the equivalent of a Battalion to a Corps—see *The Accountable Leader* pp. 139–140 for a more detailed description of business units in civilian organizations straddling Levels 3–6. Worse than that civilian organizations do not as rule have a clear understanding of what kind of leader or manager should run each of these undefined business units. They are generally not aware of where the critically important divide between operational accountability at Level 3 and the onset of strategic accountability at Level 4. Nor the fact that crossing that Rubicon is fundamentally different to a move from Level 2 to Level 3 for example.

This confusion is often manifested in faulty organization design resulting in haphazard leadership development. The military are quite clear what the difference between their key levels entails and there is evidence of their understanding that good Level 4 (one star) generals—a Commodore in the RN—might not make it to the next level of Rear Admiral *owing to the different leadership demands involved in the role and therefore required of the individual as he (still invariably he) progresses further away from line of sight management.*

2.9 How Does the RN's Version of Mission Command Mesh with Mission Mastery?

The eight RN principles of mission command are firmly underpinned by the five pillars of Mission Mastery.

Table 2.1 The dovetailing of the RN's mission command and the five pillars

Mission command	Five pillars of Mission Mastery
Unity of effort	Purpose Organization design
Decentralisation	Organization design Experiential learning
Trust	Culture
Delegation	Leadership development
Mutual understanding	Experiential learning
Timely and effective decision-making	Organization design Experiential learning
Responsible decision-making	Organization design Leadership development
Communications	Culture

Unity of Effort presupposes a hierarchy of clear, unambiguous accountability—the Pillar of structure.

'*Decentralisation*' really equates to empowerment in the Mission Command context. This depends on a sound Pillar of organization and that of Rehearsal Training.

'*Trust*' links to the pillar of Culture and also presupposes clear accountability. If an organization is not clear about its levels of accountability then leadership development and career planning will be jeopardised which in turn is a drag factor on establishing a positive culture of trust. "Trust does not reside in integrated circuits or fibre optic cables. It is not reducible to information."[25]

'*Delegation*' links to the Pillar of Leadership, which in turn presupposes a robust and accountable structure.

'*Mutual Understanding*' is also a subset of an accountable structure and the training needed within the relevant context.

'*Timely and effective decision making*' and '*Responsible decision making*' are directly linked to a structure of truly accountable roles and the Pillar of experiential learning.

'*Mission Command and Communications*' are a subset of the Pillar on Culture.

There is also no explicit reference to the importance of organization structure and its critical contribution to mission command but as the Table 2.1 shows it explicitly underpins four of the eight RN principles. As with the three wise Prussians, structure tends to be 'a given' which can be taken for granted. But civilian organizations are generally much younger and the evidence suggests they cannot take this pillar for granted. The principles of mission command cannot be implemented successfully without being firmly grounded on all five Pillars.

[25] Fukuyama F. (1995) p.25.

2.9.1 "The Park Touch"

Although pilots in principle have more scope for individualism and initiative blinkered leadership (and ambition?) can blunt their effectiveness. Keith Park was the great air war commander who, according to his boss Hugh Dowding, Air Chief Marshall Fighter Command and Arthur Tedder, Chief of the Air Staff, won the Battle of Britain. He intuitively practised mission command despite intense opposition from dyed in the wool elements in the RAF hierarchy who mirrored the planning school shortcomings of WW1 generals. Led by the unimpressive Leigh-Mallory, they engineered to have him and Dowding fired "at a high level conference on 17 October 1940 in a monument to stupidity" while the blitz of London continued.[26] This would be about the worst blot, by "the dingiest clots", on the history of decision making in RAF. Bungay has proven in *Most Dangerous Enemy* that the Battle of Britain was not a close run thing in the end as popularly imagined, but it would have been, at best, had this insane act been perpetrated earlier that year.

> *A crucial component of Park's thinking was that the basic tactical unit had to be the squadron not the big wing (the opposing view), that the tactics needed to be flexible....and that fighter squadrons had to be allowed freedom and flexibility to move fast, climb high and strike with single-minded determination to shoot down German planes.*[27]

Big wings of fighter planes could not achieve this because "*the speed of the air battle was the critical consideration. Both strategic and tactical movement were too rapid to allow precious time to be wasted on assembly, formation and manoeuvre. All the evidence—at the time and since—is the big wings did not work. They were visible from great distance and command and control was difficult*"[28] It is revealing that average top brass don't easily take to mission command thinking and the loss of control, yet interestingly Park, (like Nelson in the RN), was the most respected of the RAF commanders being the only one who regularly visited "the front". His hurricane was the last plane to fly over Dunkirk on the 4 June 1940 and he regularly took to the air during the Battle to see things for himself and flew to inspect men and airports following sorties. He (and Dowding) mastered the "what" and "why" leaving the "how" to well briefed, variously trained and highly committed pilot officers and their support on the ground. Unlike his officer colleagues Park knew what worked in aerial battle (he was an ace from WWI) and fortunately his unwavering approach won the Battle of Britain with the support of Dowding. (After being fired from the critical 11 Group defending London and a large sweep of Eastern and Southern England, he was sent to Malta where his 'new' tactics reversed fortunes and led to victory in that battle routing Kesselring and later he was equally successful in Asia enabling Slim to expel the Japanese from Burma. Bungay likens him to Wellington but notes, "Waterloo was only 5 hours: the Battle

---

[26] Faulkner, N 2015 Park the man who won the Battle of Britain, in *Military History*, July Issue 58.

[27] Ibid p.21.

[28] Ibid p 23 and 24.

of Britain was a concentrated 5 months. His record makes him the greatest fighter commander in the short history of air warfare."[29] Park is the only air general in history that never lost a battle—*in the air!*)

2.10 Civilian Organizational Transformation Is Rare

Few civilian organizations have led or undergone a major transformation as successfully and on such a scale as the Prussian Army. It is unheard of in the civilian world. The morphing of Nokia from an old world industrial company founded in 1865 into a leading electronics company at the beginning of the twenty-first century is probably Europe's greatest internal company transformation. When I completed an assignment with Orange in 2005, Nokia's mobile phone was no. 1 in the world, for a short period. Only a few years latter part absorption by Microsoft and a new vision in 2013 has signalled another turn in the road.

It seems Shell and Unilever are the only global companies to have survived long term on the FTSE 100 along with a handful of others in the US and Switzerland. Who could say whether the new kids on the block, such as Apple, Microsoft, Face book, and Google will be around in 15, or let alone 25 years' time? This amounts to a few minutes in the time-sands of military history. The spectre is those who live by technology, die (quickly) by technology. Transformation of civilian organizations is not becoming easer. Philips invented television, the CD and co-invented the DVD yet sold its business in television and audio-video in 2011. Its prime focus today is the innovation of new health technology, where its main competitors are General Electric and Siemens. These companies, with heritages in very different industries, recognise that the universal and permanent need of the twenty-first century and the opportunity therefore, is providing new health solutions so that people reach new standards of health and well being as they generally continue to live longer.

Mission Command in a military setting is the assignment of a mission or a task to a subordinate, having provided that person with a framework of understanding and context together with the support/resources (including training) needed to succeed. When it migrates to a civilian organization it becomes Mission Mastery.

Questions to consider

1. How does your organization measure up against the five Pillars of Mission Mastery: Mission, Organization Design, Leadership Development, Experiential Learning and Culture?
2. What are your organization's strengths and weaknesses in these five areas?

[29] Bungay S (2001) *The most dangerous enemy*, p.383.

3. Is your organization better at adapting to changing circumstances and learning from them than your competition?
4. What practices and beliefs is your organization holding on to, which are holding you back?

Mission Mastery: Pillar 1—Mission

3

No plan of operations can extend with any degree of certainty beyond the first encounter with reality. Only a layman could imagine he is watching the logical unfolding of an initial idea, thought out in every detail, and pursued to its conclusion.

On strategy
H. Von Moltke, 1871.

3.1 General

As described in Chap. 1, Mission Mastery is the successful migration of mission command to civilian organizations. It is the optimisation of the Pillars of Mission, Organization Design, Leadership Development, Experiential Learning and Culture in a non military organisation. This chapter is about the first of these five Pillars: purpose. So the first key step is the defining of the relevant purpose, which Moltke called 'mission', the prime Pillar. He moved quickly from the abstract concept of 'mission' to its concrete delivery, by describing how the process amounted to the mastering of its elements of what, why and how. He then separated the delivery of what and why from that of how. Top leadership was accountable for "what" and "why". Delivery of "how" was the role of less senior leaders down to and including the front line. This led inexorably to a focus on the quality of leadership training and general execution in lower echelons since Moltke realised that training was the glue that held together the demands of what-why-how in the field, where friction was to be both expected and had to be overcome.

B. Dive, *Mission Mastery*, Management for Professionals,
DOI 10.1007/978-3-319-25223-0_3

3.2 The Core of Mission Mastery

The focus is now on purpose or 'mission' which is at the heart of mission command. The best treatment of this Pillar of Mission or Purpose is Stephen Bungay's book *The Art of Action (2011).* I will skim the surface here and refer briefly to his core ideas. But he did not cover the other four Pillars in the way I will in the remainder of this book.

This is generally elaborated into strategy in civilian organizations, although the difference between vision, mission and strategy is often blurred. This is a large and somewhat vexed topic, which is not central to my argument. I found Campbell's et al. (1994) treatment in *Corporate-level Strategy,* a good synthesis of the key ideas.

For Moltke, 'mission' equals purpose and mastering its elements of what, why and how.

It is rare to find a bold statement of a truly compelling mission in a civilian organization based on a clear purpose. An exception occurred in November 2010, when Paul Polman, the CEO of Unilever, set out his mission to double the size of the company by 2020. That overall goal was not that unique or surprising in statistical terms but the path mapped out to achieve it, was original. It consisted of eight uniquely ambitious pledges:

- Help more than a billion people improve their hygiene
- Bring safe drinking water to 500 million people
- Double the proportion of the company's portfolio that meets the highest nutritional standards
- Halve the greenhouse gas impact of its products across their lifecycle
- Halve the water associated with the consumer use of its products
- Halve the waste associated with the disposal of its products
- Source 100 % of its agricultural raw materials sustainably
- Link 500,000 smallholder farmers and small-scale distributors into its supply chains.

Early progress has been impressive but the proof of the pudding will be in the 2020 eating. Each year since, in the Annual Report and Accounts progress on the *Sustainable Living Plan* is reported against each of the three 'big ambitious goals' and monitored against nine specified targets. *Many high sounding strategies remain just that, because they are not implemented.* Failure to implement strategy can stem from weaknesses in content and/or process. The latter tends to be the more commonplace as the crafters of strategic intent are often unhorsed by the hurdles within their organization. Four critical ones that have been identified are[1]:

[1] Chan Kim W, and Mauborgne (2006) *Blue Ocean Strategy* p150.

- The cognitive hurdle—the organization is wedded to the status quo
- The resource hurdle—limited resources, in quality and quantity
- The motivational hurdle—unmotivated and resistant staff
- The political hurdle—internal opposition especially from powerful vested interests

This insight helps explain why 'a good plan is easily miscarried in the breech'. In August 2014 McKinsey & Company[2] reviewed what ~2000 "global executives" *thought* made for good implementation. They highlighted three things:

- Ownership and commitment
- Prioritization and planning
- Accountability

Nothing new or surprising there you might say, until you look at what is meant by "accountability":

> Line managers eliminate performance variability through tight monitoring and quick responses. This includes effectively using key performance indicators (KPIs) that the organization tracks at the right frequency, conducting regular performance discussions with team and regularly assessing employees against individual goals and targets.

That is not a robust description of accountability. It is merely the description of a performance management process. There is more to accountability than simply monitoring performance. This focus on metrics and KPIs will be highlighted below as the basis of a strategic alignment gap noted by Moltke: the *effects gap*—the gap between actions and the desired effects. A gap in effects or outcomes invariably encourages more controls, which can work against achieving the desired outcomes. The favourite control mechanism is the use of metrics, which these days is often the balanced score card. When it becomes too detailed the danger here is the emphasis switches from output to input.

I have seen an international company's score cards in Asia become far too detailed, which served more as a rod to beat up national managers than enhance the performance of the business. A control mentality adds to overheads and can lead to disempowerment of the business units and key managers because it is tracking too much detail. This leads to the danger of working in the wrong Level: (a boss working in the team member's Level, occupying their decision space). Historically business schools have tended to breed over reliance on metrics and mathematical models. The trouble is metrics come after the event and too much emphasis on these metrics can lead to micro management. It is not accountability. It can be a step towards a bullying culture of pseudo leadership.

[2] "Why Implementation Matters" (08.08.14), R. Pustkowski, J. Scott and J. Tesvic.

Accountability means being answerable to a higher authority for the delivery of work, (involving resources: people, money, systems and specialist know how), outcomes, service and results that can be measured in terms of quality, quantity, time and cost.

Accountability consists of seven decision zones of discrete decision rights, which vary by level as is summarised in Chap. 8 as part of the DMA SS. It provides an example of how the quality of decisions changes across the Work Levels. Measurement is the thermometer, the means, not the goal.

3.3 Moltke's Four Great Insights

Moltke's insight went deeper than the four hurdles already highlighted. *His uniqueness was he focussed on content and process simultaneously.* He was interested in making things happen.

3.3.1 The First Great Insight: There Is No Such Thing as a Perfect Plan

Building on Clausewitz's concept of "friction" he concluded, somewhat controversially at the time, that the plan was simply a goal, the strategic intent, the start of a journey in a certain direction—*the mission.* But he knew the direction needed to have a purpose. Aristotle was probably the first to point out that the human being is goal oriented. We are motivated by purpose. We strive to achieve that chosen purpose, to do something worthwhile, to make a difference. This is reflected in the behavioural work of the 1960s—McClelland, Likert and Herzberg for example. The reason why so much white collar work in civilian organizations in the twenty-first century is being criticised is because people feel they are not making a meaningful contribution at work and therefore to their lives. This case is well argued in *Meaning Inc* by Gurnek Bains et al. (2007).

For too many people, office work is a boring, rather mindless activity lacking direction, meaning or purpose. This is because it invariably lacks clear accountability, which is the basis for building trust and satisfaction in an organization. In reality too many people become disconnected from the organization's purpose or mission. Many don't see any point to their job or how it fits into the overarching mission of their unit, let alone the organization. It is a sad fact that much white collar work in the twenty-first century has become as mindless as twentieth century blue collar work. The learning from the delayered blue collar work structures has not always migrated to the white collar domain. Alleviation often came from automation. Level one work with a prescribed destination, whether white collar or blue collar, can usually be automated and the job removed but often with social implications for the unskilled. It is the cost of that automation compared to the labour cost that becomes the decisive factor. In the twenty-first century more people are more educated so the potential for alienation is potentially greater especially when hierarchy heavy structure remains. It is not uncommon to see front line jobs removed but too much superstructure retained: Northern Rock, after the GFC, being one example where that occurred initially.

3.3.1.1 Moltke on Mission and Strategy

Much has been written in recent years on strategy. There is no need to add to that. The most commonly recognised problem today is not so much the quality of the formulation of strategy as *the failure of implementation*. Good strategy is ultimately about execution. The aim of this chapter is to briefly summarise the unique and original insights of Moltke in this area and point to some key lessons that have great relevance also for civilian organizations.

The 1950s and 1960s were a time of rebuilding after the Second World War. Half of the world was closed (communist) and American companies especially, prospered during a time of little to no international competition. This period witnessed the growth of strategy departments, strategy consultants and strategy professors all singing the glories of long term planning. Then the upheaval of the 1970s (the two oil shocks and the advent of effective Japanese international competition) shook the old certainties. Central planning departments started to be dismantled, with people like Jack Welsh at GE leading the way. By the faster moving even more competitive 1990s the value of centralised long term planning/strategy departments was seriously questioned. "The world is moving too fast to be thinking more than a year or so ahead" became received wisdom. The advent of the Internet and social media accentuated this thinking with its focus on the short term and real time. It is equally clear today that ignoring the long term is not the solution but neither is a large central strategy office combined with a network of strategy departments in business units. The problem of the right long term planning horizon remains today even though Moltke expressed some misgivings about over dependence on its reliability.

Purpose for Moltke was enshrined in "Mission". He avoided the current confusion in many civilian organizations over "vision, purpose and strategy."

Mourkogiannis (2006) tried to tackle this confusion in his book on Purpose, arguing there are only four basic purposes for civilian organizations. One for example, is altruism, but his argument that Wal-mart is an example of altruism was not totally convincing.

> *The mission of a civilian employment organization is to meet a permanent and universal need, which enshrines its social and moral purpose.*

From the late 1980s I chaired the Conference Board's Council on International Organization, which consisted of about 20 of the world's leading companies. We used to meet on a regular basis to discuss common issues affecting Organization Development, particularly following the collapse of the Berlin Wall. One outcome was a shared realisation that the money being spent on expensive strategy consultants rarely led to anything being implemented. We noted that business school professors' focus was on the '*what*' of strategy not the '*how*' as most of them had never run a division or a function let alone a business or international organization. They had rarely *successfully* implemented their theories. The '*what*' and the '*why*' are clearly important: get that wrong and the organization will struggle. But it is not enough on its own to ensure a successful outcome. Moltke recognised this. His unique contribution was to think through how a large organization can execute the '*what*' '*why*' and '*how*' simultaneously. He realised the challenge was consistently getting the *right things done*. Today it is called 'strategy in action'.

Sometimes a so-called strategy is little more than mental acrobatics bouncing upon hubris. A recent example was the then CEO of RBS, Fred Goodwin's rationale to purchase of Amro bank. The strategy was (only) to be the biggest, which is not a strategy. His thinking was flawed, which ultimately led to failure on a dramatic scale. This was predictable as I wrote in the Kogan Page house journal in July 2007, before the takeover unravelled. The motivation was suspect as it was seemingly driven by a desire to block Barclay's CEO, John Varley, from buying Amro. Varley had put Amro in play. Goodwin's reaction was a non strategy, which subsequently doomed RBS. And Varley—also pursuing a suspect strategy "to become one of the top 5 banks in the world"—was possibly the luckiest banker in history as a consequence. By May 2014 the then CEO of Barclays, Peter Jenkins, sold many of these newly acquired operations in Europe including the Investment bank—~16,000 jobs—as "they were not strategic business for the bank". It is quite incredible to read that in 2007, when the RBS planned to take over ABN Amro the only question considered by the Board was: "Can we do this?" not "should we do this?", according Ian Martin in his book (2013) on this sorry tale. And it never apparently considered "What Barclays might do in response." Moltke would have fired the lot, to sustained ripples of tax payer applause no doubt!

Goodwin and Varley ignored that premise. One ruined his bank: the other would have had he not been "trumped" in his desire to acquire ABN Amro. They both ignored what is required to craft a relevant mission and orchestrate successful organizational change. A takeover of a huge organization calls for a well thought through holistic, systemic approach. The glint of more money and power is a tempting but poisonous cocktail. The links between strategy, organization structure, the quality of the leadership and training needed to deliver constructive *integrated* change together as part of a positive and appropriate culture are all needed to ensure success ideally reflected in increased customer satisfaction, improved employee engagement and enhanced financial returns. *It seems many top civilian leaders still tend to believe in their perfect plan.*

3.3.2 Moltke's Second Great Insight: The 'What' & 'Why' of Strategy Must Be Separated From the 'How' and Mastered at Different Levels. This Is Now Known as Mission Command

He realised that to exploit uncertainty, strategic leaders should focus on crafting *what* and *why*. But he also recognised leadership throughout a large organization needed to ensure the simultaneous mastery of *what, why & how* at different but appropriate levels.

The strength of mission command is its clarifies and couples mission (why) and strategy (what) together with a proven means of putting that strategy into action (how). It is unique as a system in seamlessly fusing quality of thought with sound execution throughout a large organization. It is doubtful whether anyone has written a better, short—just three pages- paper on strategy than Moltke—see the Appendix. His invention and elaboration of the power of the process of mission cascade *and its feedback loop across different command levels* (or levels of accountability) was revolutionary. Civilian organizations still appear to be struggling to master this critical process. As far as I can see many academics and strategy consultants have still not solved the conundrum of how to deliver and embed strategy in very large organizations. Their tendency is still to focus on the *what* (the content) without mastering the *how* (execution). Great military leaders such as Alexander the Great,[3] Julius Caesar[4] and Frederick the Great practised naturally the key ingredients of mission command. The Royal Navy makes that claim of Nelson. Certainly the first three leaders were strong on mission, strategy (use of intelligence) organization, training, and leadership development with promotion based on merit. But none of the above *institutionalised their approach to leadership* in a way that it lived on after them. Perhaps, prior to Moltke, Ghengis Khan was to the closest to that ideal.

Moltke's uniqueness lay in the fact that ***he institutionalised this approach*** *to leadership in first the Prussian and then the German armies.*

The fact that so many civilian leaders, consultants and academics have still not understood the connection between strategy in action, effective organization design and successful leadership development in the twenty-first century rather accentuates the man's genius.

3.3.2.1 What Purpose?

Ideally a civilian organization should exist to meet a permanent and universal need in society. The expression of the need may change over time given developments in social mores and changes in technology. For example I have been working with a European not for profit organization that was initially founded to meet the scourge

[3] **Bose, P** (2003) ***Lessons from the great empire builder: Alexander the Great's art of strategy.***

[4] Meier, C (1998) Julius *Caesar* p.299.

of polio in the 1940s and 1950s. Now that polio has been defeated it focuses on helping those with severe mental and physical disabilities. Today, its committed people are meeting a different need but one that is equally critical to the well being of that society. But as the country has been going through a financial crisis, the environment has required yet another root and branch appraisal of its strategy. Given that, the next requirement is the clear identification and relevance of its current mission (or purpose) and the activities needed to carry it out. In a number of civilian organizations, this is not always crystal clear but is usually referred to as the 'strategy'. The 'purpose school' does not seem to have gained much traction in civilian organizations, which talk more of their strategy or mission, although not always with clarity.

Chandler seems to have been the first to point out in his seminal work that organization structure follows strategy, in 1962. The key to the organizational architecture is context: in the military this is reflected in the system of battle echelons. In the Prussian mission command system senior officers were encouraged to give broad direction (*what and why*) rather than issue detailed orders about *how*. The latter was an outcome of training. Middle ranking and junior officers were encouraged to use their initiative both to exploit emerging and unexpected opportunities and to go to each other's aid (teamwork). Over time the desired behaviours were systematised and became part of the ongoing training of officers. (Moltke's innovations in training and development will be explored in Chaps. 5 and 6). The focus of strategic leaders was on what to achieve and why but not how to do it. The latter was implicitly linked to three of the other Pillars, *organization, leadership development* and *rehearsal training—see the next three chapters.* The quality of training was such that it is a 'given' for these officers.

By way of contrast it is not generally a 'given' in civilian organizations, which are prone to have very detailed plans and instructions, coupled with lengthy job descriptions covering processes and sub process but light on accountability. This was still largely the approach of American and British generals during WWII leading more to decision paralysis than prompt action. Harper (2005, p. 252) writes of General Mark Clark's command system "giving orders planned in great detail more like the British Generals of 1915 and 1916" as late as the battle at Monte Cassino. Beevor writes of the cultural inertia of the British during the D Day invasion when the recurring desire to stop for a cup of tea shocked their American and Canadian allies. "The other British failing came from a demarcation mentality, of not doing anything that was not strictly your job", which he put down to a trade-union mindset. He also noted ominously that "The Germans were far more professional, mainly as a result of their training system of *Auftragstaktik*, which was a commander's obligation to achieve an objective on his own initiative. This gave them much greater flexibility of response."[5]

[5] Beevor A (2012) *D-Day: The Battle for Normandy* in *A new foreword,* pp xviii and xx. Later in the book (p.32) he describes how Hitler over ruled his generals such that "his policy was contrary to every traditional tenet of the German general staff, which insisted on flexibility."

Moltke's new approach replaced the previous system of top down, one way, autocratic orders. It was now a matter of 'missions', which simultaneously took in the needs of two to three battle echelons in his back briefing cascade system. *Each mission consisted of "a task and a purpose".*

Once briefed, the lower level had to restate the mission ***("back-brief")*** *to the layer above before briefing the next level down and so on to the front line.* This helped overcome noise ("friction") in the communications process.

The level of accountability of the leader, accounted for the complexity and extent of the task and its purpose. Clearly this Pillar of Purpose on its own is not enough to ensure success. It is vital that the five Pillars are put into practice together. This is both the great challenge and power of Mission Mastery for civilian organizations. It is a complete package, a systemic approach, not just a technique or, dare I say it, another fad.

Implementation is a plan encountering the "friction" of reality.

In mission command the defined task was set in the context of a higher purpose (the reason for the action) and organization (the battle echelon). The simplicity/complexity spectrum of the task was set by the context of the battle echelon—the level of accountability. This process is fundamentally about providing clear, short communications within a context of unambiguous accountability. This seems obvious but poor communications or lack of timely communications is probably the most common failing on the battlefield—and probably even more so in those civilian organizations which lack these disciplines. For example, most civilian 'Cascade' processes are typically top down only (as the word implies), e.g. usually communicating last year's results and this year's targets.

Each of the individuals and units in the military would have been trained to discharge their respective tasks. The foreseeable "unexpected" event such as an ambush would have been well rehearsed in advance. This may not be in the detail of time and place, but with certainly as to type and likelihood. The officer only has to shout "ambush" and every individual knows what to do. Management are apt to overlook the fact that most "unexpected" events can be predicted and anticipated in type and form.

Civilian planning typically ignores the possibility of friction.

3.3.2.2 Formulation of Purpose

Civilian organizations are often surprisingly hazy about their fundamental raison d'etre or purpose. They tend to become enmeshed in a confusing plethora of mission, vision, purpose, strategy, objectives, goals, tactics and values. They rarely break down purpose into relevant missions and tasks for *all* the levels in the organization. The fact that they might have too few or too many leadership layers does not help. Management by Objectives in the 1960s was an excellent civilian initiative to move in this direction but unclear hierarchical accountabilities meant it degenerated into unhelpful bureaucracy.

This concept has re-emerged latterly in ideas such as "the golden thread" and "line of sight". The type of comment that enabled a forklift driver at NASA to explains his job as "Putting a man on the Moon." Missions are then dovetailed to deliver the grand Mission. A clear context of accountability Levels helps make this purpose live.

The mission or purpose of an organization is really the touchstone for its existence (the identification and meeting of a permanent and universal need) but that purpose is not always easy to define. I was once addressing a group of managers from non profit organizations and said somewhat naively: "Well I don't intend spending any time on 'Mission' as you will be clear on that." At which point, to my surprise, most of the audience burst out laughing. "Mission depends on where the money comes from" I was told. Family firms invariably seem to run aground at the third generation. Family aggrandizement is not a worthy or sustaining mission for the members of the whole organization. When the mission is fuzzy and confused then "task" implementation tends to be erratic and ineffective. The other four Pillars work best when the mission is clear.

In Chap. 9 we will see the example of the British Civil Service where the mission of many departments is not really clear and how accountability is undermined as a result. In the same chapter we will see an example of a company that has crafted a clear "2020 strategy" and how that flows through to the organization architecture and ultimately leadership development. But mission is not enough.

Health organizations have an obvious mission, but their organization, performance and culture of "care" leaves (increasingly) much to be desired. T. L. Lee, a professor of medicine at Harvard, pointed out in 2010: "Taming the chaos of healthcare requires a new breed of leader at every level." (*Harvard Business Review, April 2010.*) But as doctors know, diagnosis is relatively easy but appropriate delivery is often a challenge in a different league.

3.3.3 The Third Great Insight: The Three Strategic Traps

Moltke accepted that as soon as strategy is put into action there would be "Friction". The enemy ("competition") would react, often in an unexpected way and thereby generate resistance. This reaction can sometimes be predicted and anticipated but often not. The quote at the beginning of this chapter makes that clear. Implementation must be dynamic. Strategy "*is the art of taking action under the pressure of the most difficult conditions*" identifying gaps and constraints on performance, which need to be overcome.

It is also worth remembering that around the 1860s the German approach to education and thought leadership was probably unparalleled in Europe. German thinking was greatly influencing Americans founding their new universities such as Illinois in 1867 and those of California and MIT in 1869. "*It was about now that the attractions of the German system began to be appreciated, with several professors and university administrators travelling to Prussia, in particular, to study the way things were done there.*"[6]

Watson has pointed out that German thinking was highly influential in more fields than just the military. "*The fact that they led the way in history increasingly implied that theology was itself an historical development and this encouraged the emergence of biblical criticism*". He also maintained that it was the Germans who were responsible for the idea that education should be the responsibility of the state "*and it was a German idea that the university should be the home of scholars (researchers, writers) and not just teachers.*" This intellectual ferment demonstrates that Moltke was not living in a thought backwater and it is not surprising therefore that the most radical thinking in the organization of military matters in the world was also emanating from Prussia/Germany at that time.

Surprisingly (today) Moltke's paper on strategy in 1871 is short. He would not understand the need for strategy consultants' unending sessions of death by Power Point or the academics' voluminous textbooks, aiming to school us in the delights of their thoughts on strategy. Strategy is complex and requires deep thought but civilian organizations, consultants and academics have made a complex subject unnecessarily complicated. The gift of a truly intelligent leader is an ability to simplify the complex and communicate in a way that is understood by all, right down to and including the front line. This is the need that Moltke recognised in 1866 when he realised the major challenge in a large organization is orchestrating a method of rapid, accurate communication from the top to the bottom, which is not distorted by the process, so that it is clearly understood at the front line. Hastings—op cit—argues this was largely the undoing of the huge German military machine in WWI, ironically led in 1914 by Moltke's nephew.

3.3.3.1 Three Sources of "Friction"

In his most recent book Bungay focussed heavily on what I am calling Pillar 1 and I am aiming to build on his excellent analysis here.[7] In his study of Moltke, he highlighted the "Discipline of Execution" noting that planning is not difficult in a predictable environment, as was the case in the Western world in the 1960s, which witnessed the mushrooming of bureaucratic planning departments. "*We can make plans, take actions, and achieve outcomes in a linear sequence with some reliability...In an unpredictable environment, this approach quickly falters.*"

Although Clausewitz had listed 12 sources of friction in 1812: Moltke distilled the causes of failure into three categories:

- Not enough information (or imperfect knowledge)
- Lack of alignment between a plan and actions taken
- The wrong outcomes or results. (Since civilian organizations in the public sector don't refer to 'results' as a rule I will refer to "effects" and "outcomes".)

---

[6] Watson, P (2005) *Ideas A History of Thought and Invention from Fire to Freud*, p. 700.

[7] Bungay S (2011) op cit p45ff.

Today's unpredictable environment creates gaps between plans, actions and results. These are what he saw as the three strategic gaps. I feel they are more devastating than that and will refer to his insight as: *the three strategic traps.*

3.3.3.2 The Knowledge Trap

The first trap to be wary of is the gap is between knowledge and plans.

This is the difference between what we would like to know compared to what we actually know.

This depends initially on the quality of knowledge and information available. It is what we *need to know* compared to what we actually know. The implication is we cannot create a reliable plan since we don't have sufficient knowledge of the future. A lack of knowledge generates the inevitable tendency to collect more data and 'information'. This is apt to cause delay and indecision. Tom Peters called this 'analysis paralysis' and it is a frequent tendency of highly intelligent people who are often aware that they have not covered all the knowledge bases. This means they are forced to hypothesise or guess. Being bright they can logically explain and rationalise why they cannot take a decision as yet, since they need more data. It is the first comfort stop of the expert. It is no comfort to the person who is facing a sick patient or an angry customer and has to take a decision now. This process inevitably consumes valuable time and still may not resolve the basic lack of sufficient knowledge or information. It inevitably slows down the decision process.

In his paper *On strategy,* Moltke wrote:

> *The successive acts of competition (Moltke's word was "war") do not follow a premeditated design but are acts of spontaneity guided by judgement. Every case is unique. It is a matter of seeing through the fog of uncertainty in which every situation is shrouded, making an accurate assessment of what you do know, guessing what you do not know, reaching a conclusion rapidly and then vigorously and unwaveringly following it through.*

3.3.3.3 The Alignment Trap

The second trap is lack of fit between plans and actions.

This is the difference between what we want or expect people to do and what they actually do.

Misalignment is often reflected in top-level frustration at the outcome of events and lower-level confusion and de-motivation. If, as can occur, the initial briefing is not clear and then people are encouraged to use their initiative chaos is likely to ensure. *The trap then is to impose more controls as a sticking plaster to compensate for an inadequate plan.* This is what Molke observed in 1866 at the Battle of Koniggratz, which he summarised in his post mortem "Memoire" report to the king in 1868. The *constant imposition of more controls and instructions leads to constipation of effort and greater chaos.* This causes an organizational whiplash effect at the front line as a result of a never-ending stream of new instructions from 'on high'. In Chap. 9 we will witness the damaging effect on policy formulation in Whitehall caused by politicians' unending initiatives in an attempt to "produce" positive daily headlines. Awareness of this trap led Moltke to introduce his revolutionary doctrine of "briefing and back-briefing."

The aim of back-briefing is to create and maintain alignment at all levels in the organization.

For something to be clear it must first be simple. Successful briefing is not just about the process. It is a skill, which needs to be taught.

3.3.3.4 The Effects Trap

The third trap occurs when efforts or actions do not produce the desired effects and outcomes.

This is the difference between what we expect our actions, and/or those of our team, to achieve and what they actually achieve.

The 'wrong' effect or outcome also encourages more controls. The favourite control mechanism, as already mentioned, is the use of more metrics, which these days is often the balanced score card. *The danger here is the emphasis switches from output to input.* Excessive numbers of controls with a focus on past events do not meet the needs of a patient or customer today. Checking past performance does not necessarily help current performance. The approach needs to be more client-centred focusing on what is happening rather than what might have happened in the past, *if correctly measured.* This approach can lead to disempowerment of the relevant "business units."

This malaise has hit social work in the UK. For example there have been a number of disasters involving the deaths of children in the "care" of social workers, with two of the worst being the London Borough of Haringey. This resulted in a classic falling into the effects trap: more controls to stop more children's deaths. More layers of hierarchy have been put into children's departments in Local Authorities. Professor Munro's report in 2012 into this matter recommended part of the solution was social workers needed to have more accountability. The same recommendation that came from Lord Laming's report in 2003 as a result of the inquiry into the death of Victoria Climbie in 2000 in the same London borough! Neither Laming nor Munro defined or set out what they meant by accountability.

In actual fact our field work in a number of Local Authorities since then revealed their children's departments had added in more layers of control. This of course actually ***diluted accountability*** *and made the situation worse. It results in* ***more risk*** *not less!!*

As I write, scandals indicating paedophile activities have been rampant in places such as Islington, Rochester, Oxford and Westminster, not to mention the BBC. And yet some people who were lead politicians in these sink pits have gone on to Westminster to prosper as ministers/high profile chairs of parliamentary committees. Enquires and committees are proliferating but the record suggests they will tumble into the three strategic traps, since in these cases there is widespread evidence of cover up and blackening of witnesses who were abused. When accountability is opaque justice is obtuse.

Historically business schools have tended to breed over reliance on metrics and mathematical models. The trouble is metrics come after the event and only serve to re-spin the cylinder of the three shortcomings. There is also a danger they became the master (the end) not the servant (the means).

When top leaders delegate authority for decision making they are giving away some power but not their accountability. They need to delegate but must not abdicate. They also have to bear in mind that metrics provide only information. The interpretation of the relevant metrics and the will to take the right action is the task of the wise leader.

These three traps accentuate friction. We cannot control all the variables in a given situation. *But what is really important is learning how to avoid these three traps:*

Unless these traps are avoided the ensuring complication, confusion and delay, adds to the ensuing friction. It is the classic manifestation of top down control, which in a hierarchy heavy organization degenerates into inertia—see the case study in Chap. 9. Moltke realised from experience that falling into these three traps went directly counter to his aim of building an empowered, learning organization. Officers had to be trained to both recognise and avoid them.

3.3.3.5 The Solution

Any potential solution must address all three traps. Moltke's advice was as follows:

Decide What Really Counts

On the *knowledge trap* his advice is to plan only what can be meaningfully planned based on sound judgement stemming from the information available and the likely consequences of inaction. Acceptance of some uncertainty is inevitable. Rather than gather more data Moltke advocated, acknowledge the imperfection in data, adjust the plan and focus on the essentials that can and need to be achieved.

As it is not possible to construct perfect plans work on the outcomes your organization can achieve, which you really want. In other words formulate the strategy as intent, not a detailed plan. This must be *tailored to the level of accountability of the direct reports,* whether they are (at different levels of accountability) in Cape Town (national), London (regional) or New York (global).

Get the Message Across

On the *alignment trap* he recommends an information cascade process (his famous back-briefing loop) with each layer adding something to the one above but all united by an understanding of the intention of the top layer(s). The lower the level the more detailed the plans may be. Thus each layer will know less than the one above about the larger context but know more about the local situation. Alignment is around intent (what to achieve and *why*) while autonomy is about actions (*what to do and how*). The cascade of information was orchestrated on a clear need to know basis. No more, no less.

Having worked out what matters most, now pass the message to others and give them responsibility to carry out their part of the plan. Keep it simple but be clear about your intention telling them *what & why.* Don't tell them *how* to do it (if you know they have the skills and experience). Then ask them to tell you what they are going to do—back-briefing.

But note *it presupposes subordinates have jobs with clear accountability and effective training to carry out those tasks.*

Give People Space and Support

On the *effects trap* he is keen to foster individual initiative but within clearly delineated boundaries (the intent). There should be implied freedom to depart from the letter of the original brief it the local situation demands it to meet the overall intent. *He was not in favour of tightening control.* This was because the fundamental principle he felt needed to be inculcated was a belief in independent action and initiative by subordinates once they know the mission. He tended to see the organization not so much in terms of strategy and implementation but more in terms of what Bungay calls a "thinking-doing cycle" of learning and adapting. What I call "a dynamic learning organization".

Do not try to predict in detail what effects your actions will have. It is not possible. Give your team clear boundaries—defined by their level of accountability—within which they can take decisions as appropriate. Encourage them to adapt their actions within those guidelines to realise the overall intent of your instruction. In other words encourage initiative appropriate to the situation. Don't try to work in their level and do their job.

Many readers will recognise these traps. When things go wrong the call goes out for more information, more control and more metrics. Inertia is then likely. The business school emphasis in recent years on strategy (*what & why*) and general management has tended to paint an overly simplistic picture of what it takes to be an effective leader in a learning organization. This probably helps to explain why over

30 % of CEOs that moved prior to the completion of their contract in the decade 1995–2006, were removed from office.[8]

This in a nutshell is the culmination of the four great Prussian reformers work, which transformed Frederick the Great's army of robots into a self adjusting organism—**a learning organization.**

*This was because **they viewed their army as a living, adaptive organism, not a machine**.*

3.3.4 The Fourth Great Insight: The Definition of Operations as the Link Between Strategy and Tactics

One of the most common sources of confusion in civilian organizations today is the lack of clarity between strategic and operational accountability. I would be a wealthy man if I received a dollar, every time I heard a self assured young brand manager say: "I am responsible for the strategy of product x or product y". 'Strategy' is probably the most over-used and inexact term in most organizations' management lexicons. If this difference between strategy and tactics, between mission and task, is not clear and understood throughout all levels in an organization, then Mission Mastery will remain only an aspiration. We will examine more thoroughly the importance of this Rubicon between operational and strategic accountability in the next chapter and then study the implications for leadership development in Chap. 5. These are critical components in the development of distributed leadership. For Moltke:

> *Strategy is about fighting the right battles. 'Operations' is about winning them.*

He saw three types of activities that were critical to success in the field:

- Tactics
- Operations
- Strategy

Tactics and operations were principally about efficiency (doing things right): strategy about effectiveness (doing the right things). Moltke's insight was realising his armies needed to be simultaneously efficient and effective. *Fight and win the right battles.* Prior to that, the German high command tended to worship at the altar of scientific efficiency. Moltke was adamant that war was not science since obviously you can't control enough of the key variables, least of all the enemy. In this

[8] S. Wheeler et al, 29.05.07, The Era of the Inclusive Leader, *Strategy & Business*.

context there is a certain irony in the fact that the very word "strategy" comes from the Greek word—strategos—a military commander.

Given his conundrum about how to communicate quickly and effectively from Commander in Chief to private, in a huge army, Moltke took his insight a step further.

He aligned *tactics to the frontline soldier*—in the terms of the DMA Solution Set, Work Level 1.[9]

He then aligned *operations to "junior and middle ranking officers"*—effectively Works Level 2 and 3.

Strategy was the business of the top echelons—Work Levels 4–7: the 1–4 star generals. (The rank of Field Marshall is usually a 5* role but does not exist in peace time as a fighting rank. Strategic roles are likely to be up to half of 1 % in a large organization. As will be shown later about 0.4 % is closer to the norm in the private sector compared to 0.7 % in the public sector, but these figures also vary by industry.)

He recognised the organizational communications challenge was greatest in "junior and middle management." This is where things seemed to go wrong even in the successful battle of 1866 against the Austrians. Although the Prussians won, Moltke detected communications got gummed up, delayed and distorted in middle and junior management ranks, which had an adverse impact on front line effectiveness. This is consistently the same problem that emerges time and again in civilian organizations, usually because there are too many junior and middle ranking management jobs. Moltke's case was different in that he realised that the structure was sound but the behaviour of his troops was not. He therefore had to revitalise the training and leadership of junior and middle management to ensure that did not happen in future.

This was a brilliant and original insight together with his plans to address this weakness.

Ironically, given the lesson of Jena, it was the French who first felt the brunt of his leadership innovations in their comprehensive defeat in 1870. Based on my experience across 70 countries, supplemented by our data base of over half a million jobs that we have analysed, we now know that the number of leadership jobs in a large organization breaks down *approximately as follows*[10]:

---

[9] See Chap. 8 for more detail on Levels.

[10] These are only indicative ratios since in reality the % of leaders in any organization varies depending on the nature of the activities: the number of leaders required varies according to whether activities are labour intensive (lower %s), capital intensive (higher %s) and/or knowledge intensive (higher %).

- *Up to* 0.5 % of jobs are typically in Work Levels 4+. For example in large private sector organizations the roles in L4+ have been in a range from 0.1 % (labour intensive) to 0.4 %. The comparable number in the military seems to be 2.5 %.
- ~7 % of jobs are typically in WLs 2+. The distribution of leader roles is influenced by the nature of work at the front line and could be higher for knowledge intensive work.
- Thus generally speaking ~90 % of jobs tend to be in Work Level 1 where often up to 10 % of those could be leaders—NCOs in the military, supervisors/team leaders in civilian organizations. Some roles with NCO rank or of supervisory grade may be specialists with no subordinates and therefore would not be leaders.

This means ~15 % of employees could be leaders—as some job holders in WL 2+ are not leaders. This correlates with leaders having an average span of control of 6.6 %. It also suggests that the number of leaders needed in a well structured organization tends to be less than most people imagine.

The military have one distinct advantage over most civilian organizations since they know how to identify the right number of battle echelons and therefore the number of layers of leaders they need in a given situation. Although they have up to 7 battle echelons and 19 ranks the former drive organization design and the later pay. Once again it is important to stress that not every rank equates to a battle echelon given their understanding of line and support. The ranks, which serve as the basis for pay, drive key protocols, which come into play in an emergency. They are prime indicators for example, of who should step up in an emergency if a leader is taken out. The ranks do not muddy the water of organisation design as happens with grading systems in the civilian world. The military seem to carry excess "buffer stock" in leadership roles between WLs 1 & 2, given the wasteful nature of warfare. They have institutional compression of officers in WL 2 but not from WL 3. The rank indicates who has precedence in an emergency even though they might be in the same echelon. For example, if there are two lieutenants one of whom should 'step up' if their captain is killed then the officer promoted first to that rank has the right/obligation to step up, and everyone in the company knows that. The average life expectancy of a junior officer in Moltke's time until the end of WWI was calibrated in hours during battle. A system of cover—governed by ranks—which everyone understood, was essential.

Moltke unerringly put his finger on the problem of communicating strategy from top to bottom in a large organization. The problem is alive and well in twenty-first century civilian organizations where bloated middle management hierarchies are not uncommon. Without the discipline and logic of levels of accountability virtually every organization I have consulted to around the world has been over managed. This can be pronounced in junior and middle management—the so called middle management bulge—but compression is not uncommon at the top of the organization where big egos wrestle for decision space.

Describing operations as a link between strategy and tactics does not seem shatteringly brilliant until civilian managers tumble to the insight that he is taking for granted an organization structure of clear accountability. They are often a step further back as it is rare for them to reliably identify value adding layers of "junior and middle management". Moltke saw the problem clearly and thought through how to solve it.

> *The scary thing is the same problem is widespread in civilian organizations today, but even IF the leadership acknowledge it, they usually do not have the means/know-how to solve it. Their response is akin to giving a machete to a blind man and telling him to trim the overgrown grass.*

Readers will have noticed that I am admirer of Stephen Bungay's writings. But a quote from *The Art of Action* illustrates I believe, just how far civilian managers and academics are, as yet, from understanding the power of Moltke's insight about operations as the link between tactics and strategy *and its relevance to their own organizations.*

Bungay states: "*We might say (very broadly) that strategy involves business units, operations involve departments and functions and tactics involves subunits whether in support roles or with direct customer contact.*"[11]

As I have shown in *The Accountable Leader* a business unit can be anything in a civilian organization from WL 3 to WL 6—a battalion commander to a Corps commander in military terms. That provides a huge margin for error, which most are not even aware of. Similarly "departments" can be at various levels of accountability, depending on the size and complexity of the organization. For example is "the department" in the national office in Cape Town, the regional office in London or the Corporate Office in New York? In an effective structure they would all be at different levels of accountability adding value to the jobs below. Some "departments" head Functions, which are the classic support roles heading Finance, HR, Legal, IT etc. Even in a WL 5 organization (where the top role is WL 5) a number of functions could be at Level 4, whereas in a large global organization they could be 2 or 3 WLs higher. Now even allowing for the shrewd "very broadly" caveat above is of little real help to a civilian organization if it does not know where its levels of accountability reside.

> *The difference between military and civilian organizations is the military know which ranks equate to which Levels of accountability, whereas civilian organizations rarely know how their grades play out in terms of accountability levels.*

---

[11] Bungay Op cit p219.

3.4 Strategy in Civilian Organizations

If a civilian organization's strategy is meeting a permanent and universal need it should continue to exist for a long time. Unlike military organizations, private sector companies tend to have a short life span. The original FTSE top 30 was set up in 1935, but today only two companies, Shell and Unilever, are still in existence as fundamentally the same businesses. R. Foster of Yale University has been quoted as saying that today companies on the S&P 500 index "typically exist for only 15 years.[12] It is now common knowledge that the model companies listed in books like *In Search of Excellence* and *Built to Last* have not lasted. In *Managing on the Edge,* Pascale noted in 1990 that already two thirds of the cases in Peters and Waterman's best seller had slipped off the "excellent" list within a decade from publication. Similar contentions have been made about the sample in *Built to Last* by Foster and Kaplan in 2001. Unlike the public sector, businesses invariably build their strategy around the desire to grow. But the record of successful innovative growth driven by the strategy of an existing company is not great. For example Chan Kim and Mauborgne found that 86 % of attempts to grow were merely incremental improvements such as line extensions. They contended this adversely impacted revenue, profit and viability in the longer run.[13] Does anyone really believe a recently appointed CEO of Apple, exiting the fashion industry (!), is worth a $72 million "hello" payment? That largesse is more reminiscent of the greed and loss of moral purpose that led to the downfall of some banks.

3.4.1 A Strategy Case Study[14]: An Achievement Gap

Does a clear strategy guarantee successful achievement? Consider the following case study.

A few years ago we were working with an international services company. We were involved in a close study of key operating divisions in one country. The MD of one proudly told us his agreed strategy was to increase 'his' business by 50 % in the next 3 years. He presented that as the "what" and that he was more than confident of achieving this in a highly competitive, developed industry where overall growth was not significant. An "ambitious and motivating strategy" we were told.

The first doubts arose when we looked at the division's recent track record in attracting new business. It was not impressive to put it mildly. We undertook a series of interviews in the organization. What emerged was alarming. The division

[12] Williams D.K. "Staying in business forever: how to create a 100 year old company", *Forbes* 10.4.13.

[13] Chan Kim W, and Mauborgne R, (2006) *Blue Ocean Strategy* p7.

[14] All case studies quoted in the book are real cases that I have worked on over the years. There will be a number of times when I refer to a case study that has negative lessons to offer. Those, such as this one, will be kept anonymous. But where there are positive lessons to share, which an organization is prepared to share, which is rare, then the organization will be referred to.

was massively over managed with three layers of management in one level of accountability: that equivalent to a battalion. Now there is no way an army in the field would have three lieutenant colonels running a single battalion in a hierarchical relationship. They know that a battalion commander reports to a brigade commander in the next higher battle echelon. We found that the spine of accountability went through supervisor, to site manager, to a district manager, to a regional director to an operations director. The three managers above the site manager all called on the client over a weekly, 2 weekly or monthly period. The agenda being discussed was not clear. When we asked an individual why they were visiting and what they discussed the answer was typically: "My (subordinate) manager discusses the day to day stuff, I focus on strategic issues" No one defined clearly or succinctly what they meant by "strategic issues."

Micro management—working in the wrong level of accountability—was widespread and helped explain the performance of the units. The most senior role-holder under the MD talked of spending 70 % of his time "in the field" of an over-layered field force. The MD also described himself as "the salesman for the division winning new bids and dealing with the strategic issues", even though he had a general management brief on paper. (I was by now getting a little suspicious that this MD seemingly had been promoted above his level of competence and that was also part of the problem—as it often is.)

When we shared our findings with the MD he got very aggressive. It is noticeable that those out of their depth often attack (bully) as the first form of defence.

- "You have not understood my business
- Relationships are the bedrock of our success
- My managers do more than make decisions
- We have to match the seniority of our clients
- We don't need to focus on cost as the client pays that in the contract."

The compression (too many managers in one level of accountability) meant the best managers were very frustrated as others were in their decision space. The danger in this situation is the best managers, who are marketable, move on and the average performers remain in the organization. That then creates a bubble in the talent succession pipeline which restricts growth. And yet this company's stated strategy was to grow by 50 % in 3 years! Leaving aside all other problems it was becoming patently obvious this division did not really have an *appropriate strategy*, its organization design was sub optimal and the quality of management to achieve this stated ambition was a question mark since they were neither trained nor empowered for the task in hand.

This MD had not realised that you do not need a layer of sales management to interface with every layer in a client organization. In fact some of his clients were in the military and he seemed to have assumed that each rank needed another layer of management to deal with the rank interface. He appeared to have no idea of their line/staff demarcation and that for example the rank of colonel was not a layer in the operational chain of command.

While these discussions were going on the division lost out on two new bids the MD had been "sure of getting." The reason was his pricing offer was higher than his competition. (I am not making this up!!) And this was one of the largest companies in the world.

Exam question: Would he have survived under Moltke?

3.4.2 The Lesson

A clear strategy (at the International Group in this case) is not enough. A major problem in this case was a growing realisation that the MD was seemingly not up to the strategic demands of *his* job. He came across as authoritarian. Adorno, T et al. (1950) and Dixon, N. (1976) have studied authoritarian leaders and autocrats. Autocrats seek responsibility and are able to trust others when there are grounds to do so. They are intelligent, able to grasp the essentials of a situation while remaining self confident and comfortable with uncertainty. Authoritarians do not have those qualities hiding instead behind the trappings of their 'office'. Authoritarians are people who are conventional and uncritical of and submissive towards those in higher echelons, inclined to think in rigid categories and tend to follow rules and procedures. They thrive in a stable situation. They like to appear tough and can be unpleasant for peers and subordinates to deal with. They are dysfunctional in a team and if they reach the top can be destructive since they have insufficient intelligence as a rule and lack the people skills and ability to assess and judge subordinates. Trust is not a tool in their leadership kit bag. Authoritarians do not develop and grow people. They micro manage in most circumstances and tend to bully rather than lead, especially when things go wrong. Blaming others is their default position. An authoritarian manager who has been promoted beyond Work Level 3 is an unguided missile in any organization.

Although this MD was in a strategic role akin to that of a one star general he was displaying authoritarian behaviour. His task *was not* to simply pass on the "what" of the Group's global strategy. He was expected to flesh out the "what" for his division in one of many countries. The 50 % strategic growth target was the overall international goal. A good MD would then go to work to ascertain whether his part of the business could achieve only 18 % growth or 60 % for example. The former would mean challenging those above: not a predilection of authoritarians. He had to work out what was right for his operation, not simply mindlessly hand down an inappropriate target for his managers, who could only fail no matter how well versed they might be in the "how".

Even more worrying was the fact that there was a further major shortcoming in his structure at the critical third level of accountability. We have plenty of evidence to show that the increase in the number of jobs in Level 3 (not reporting to each other!) is the key driver of growth in an organization's structure. But as this division was severely compressed in level 3—as bad as I have seen—this was a major drag on potential for growth even if the divisional mission had been appropriate. Friction was multiplying exponentially in this case across the three pillars of mission, organization design and leadership development and training. The culture was also impaired.

So to return to the question as the outset of this section, the answer clearly is: "No, a clear strategy does not guarantee growth." The health of the other four pillars is equally important and any shortcomings in those will jeopardise the delivery of strategy. In this case they had become hurdles to implementation. Inept leaders are unlikely to *deliver* a clear strategy let alone train and develop good leaders. They are apt to resort to bullying tactics when things don't go "according to plan."

If we consider this "general's" performance against the criteria set out in this chapter needed to connect strategy and tactics the conclusion is clear.

This manager fell at each of the four hurdles in Sect. 2:

- The Cognitive hurdle—he was wedded to the status quo
- Resource hurdle—he stymied critical resources in Level 3
- Motivational hurdle—he bullied and did not motivate staff
- Political hurdle—he failed to challenge his superiors and win them over to the strategy his division could deliver. He did not win cooperation from his peers to help win new business.

He also fell headlong into the three strategic traps in Sect. 3.3.:

- His divisional strategy was undermined by a lack of knowledge of his own market. He suffered not from a surfeit of unnecessary knowledge but a dearth of necessary information. He did not tap into the group *knowledge* available to him.
- His sales force organization was *not aligned* to the needs of the customers. His solution was to apply more layers of control to the field force.
- *Results were slipping* given the above two inadequacies.

And therefore:

- He could not decide what really counted
- Consequently he could not get the key message(s) across to his team
- He did not give people space and support.

These shortcomings all stemmed from the MD's inability to devise the right mission; hence tactics remained dislocated from strategy.

You might be thinking: "But what was top management doing and why did it tolerate this shambles?" That is a very fair question. The division was profitable at the time (although slipping) and the arrogance of profit is a powerful source of disguising reality, the more so when other divisions are less profitable, even unprofitable. The logic tends to be: "We are profitable so we are clearly good". I once consulted to the national telecoms company in the Maldives, which at the time although small, was one of the most profitable companies I had encountered. But there was no competition then, so making a profit was not difficult. The company was not healthy. But some managers in the private sector make the mistake of thinking they must be very good because their company is profitable. It does not necessarily follow.

The point of this case study is that while strategy based on a sound mission (of Group in this case) is important it is only the starting point of Mission Mastery. If the MD cannot devise and agree the right "what" then there is little chance his staff will be able to move into "how" mode. Poor organization design and lack of appropriate training will greatly undermine any change of successful delivery of the requisite "how".

3.4.3 A Distinctive 'Footprint': Research on How It Should Be Done

A consultant, with whom I have worked, Alaric Mostyn of Stonecourt, has conducted research on how to build faster, more responsive organizations that have a successful record of growth. The large sample consisted of 214 companies. He detected that high growth; high profit companies do different things when compared to other business. He divided them into "Growth champions", who were the more successful and "Others".

He identified six main drivers and four enablers. Not surprisingly they straddle the five pillars of Mission Mastery, hence I will return to them as appropriate in the succeeding chapters.

Three that relate directly to mission and strategy in action are:

- Clarity on the sources of growth—Growth champions 93 % v Others 74 %
- Focus on a few initiatives—Champions 70 % v Others 44 %
- Disciplined execution *at all levels* (my italics) and promoting excellence in execution—Champions 78 % v Others 44 %

In addition 91 % of Champions had clearly articulated and well understood business models. Only 56 % of Others met this requirement. This meant 70 % of Champions were more effective in deciding trade-off decisions, whereas Others reached only 45 %. Finally 70 % of Champions used strong metrics and feedback loops compared to only 38 % for Others. In order to reach these standards of performance the Champions "streamlined their organization design", which I will explore in the next chapter. Better leadership development also contributed to their "better, faster decision making", which resulted in a measurably different "change ready cultures" and "climates of trust". These two factors will be returned to in Chaps. 5 and 7 respectively.

When strategy is defective it is very hard for the other four pillars to function. It is likely to lead to all five wobbling, at which point the task of constructing the edifice of Mission Mastery is bordering on the impossible.

Some questions to ponder.

1. Is your organization's mission clear and if so how well do those whom you lead understand the what and why of the strategy and are they well trained to perform as a consequence?
2. How confident are you that the two layers below you understand your objectives?
3. Do you recognise any of Moltke's three traps in your organization: if so what needs to be done to overcome them?
4. Do your leaders spend more time on controlling and generating friction in the organization rather than giving space to lead: if so what action is needed by you?

4 Mission Mastery: Pillar 2—Organization Design

Organization design is an opportunity to grow leaders. Don't organize around people but define roles that will stretch and grow talent. Design is a leadership responsibility—not a consensus activity. Design decision making should not be delegated.

Kesler and Kates

Kessler, G. and Kates, A. (2010) *Leading Organization Design*, p. 7.

4.1 General

This is the fulcrum chapter of this book. Firstly, because mission command does not highlight the need for good organization architecture: that had been established centuries ago in a military setting and was therefore taken for granted. Secondly, faulty design is consistently the abiding weakness in the civilian organizations I have encountered around the world in the last 50 years or so. It is the missing link, which undermines their leadership development regimes. Organization design consists of two axes: one horizontal (its reach) the second vertical (its height.) In the 1970s I did a lot of research into effective design of the horizontal axis under the leadership of Roger Roes. We focused on issues of shape, such as geographical, functional, divisional and matrices delving into the right balance between centralisation/decentralisation, spans of control, over specialisation and unnecessary duplication. In the 1980s I realised the driver of effectiveness is the vertical axis. Layers drive spans not the other way round thus it was necessary to have a mental framework to identify the correct height of an organization to ensure

(continued)

B. Dive, *Mission Mastery*, Management for Professionals,
DOI 10.1007/978-3-319-25223-0_4

the two axes are in equilibrium. My findings revealed many civilian organisations do not have such a framework; hence the focus of this book is on the vertical dimension of the organization not the horizontal linkages, as there is generally no shortage of material on the latter.

4.2 The Fulcrum Pillar

Organization design is a leadership competence. Clear decision making underpins good organization design. Over 50 years ago Peter Drucker wrote:

> *An analysis of decisions is required to find out what structure is needed. A decision should always be made at the lowest possible level and as close to the scene of action as possible.*[1]

Kesler and Kates on the same theme wrote: "*A primary purpose of an organization is to make decisions.*"[2]

Art Kleiner agrees: "*The basic building block of organizational action is not the job, the team, the project, the process, the share or even the dollar. It is the decision.*"[3]

Jay Galbraith is equally adamant about the importance of organization design for a leader: "*The successful execution of leadership today requires an ability to design and change the organization. There is no more challenging and important task.*"[4]

In my experience THE major failing in organization design stems from leaders who lack of a robust conceptual framework of proven principles that can be flexed reliably and consistently to ensure an effective fit in any given situation.

The work of academics tends to lack practical rigour but that of consultants, conceptual rigour. Consequently unhealthy organization structures remain the norm rather than the exception. "Organization" is a wide ranging term that can be linked to 'operating models', processes and the whole strategic agenda of mission, structure, people and systems. In this context the focus is on structure and organization design.

---

[1] Drucker P. (1964) *The Practice of Management*, p17.

[2] Kesler G, and Kates A (2011) p.7.

[3] Kleiner, A (2003) *Who Really Matters*, p14.

[4] Galbraith J. (2010) Foreword, *Learning Organization Design*.

4.2.1 The Hidden Cornerstone

Optimal organization design is the cornerstone on which the edifice of leadership and therefore Mission Mastery rests but it is the hidden element.

It therefore can be easily overlooked and invariably is. This is because the issue of effective vertical structure in the military world has been static for centuries. It is not something which needs constant re-analysis or fundamental change. When change, e.g. because of technology, is called for it affects the horizontal alignments. There is no need to tinker with the vertical command or leadership structure. It is already established as the critical platform for both successful operations and the critical concomitant, leadership development.

The founders of mission command could take their organization shape and structure for granted because historically it was known to be effective. This is the trap that awaits the unwary civilian observer who might wrongly assume there is no need to worry about their structure because Moltke was silent on this issue.

This can mean the criticality of organization design remains a blind spot in too many civilian organizations although their leaders could be forgiven for thinking mission command has nothing to say on the subject. *It doesn't because it did not need to.* But that is not the same as saying 'structure is not part of the mix and therefore does not matter.' The early classical theorists in the twentieth century—Fayol, Barnard and Taylor—focused on efficiency not effectiveness. The human relations school (Mayo, Maslow) again ignored the shape of the organization to focus on behaviour in the organization largely in reaction to the earlier 'man is a machine' school of scientific management. . Other academics that turned to their attention to structure concentrated on improving Weber's 'bureaucratic' and 'authoritarian' model. The alternatives suggested included 'non hierarchical' (McGregor 1961), 'organic' (Burns and Stalker 1961) 'democratic' (Emery and Trist 1965). Others pursuing this theme included Bennis, Blake and Mouton, Lawrence and Lorsch. Galbraith, Reddin and the BIOSS School, Jaques and particularly Rowbottom, Knight, Kinston and Billis in the 1970s and 1980s started to wrestle more directly with the issue of effective organization design.

The great Prussian reformers did not have to change their army's depth of the structure since they already knew that it worked. Their challenge was to make it work better by overlaying it with better leadership capability. The structure of the Prussian army did not need fundamental redesign. It needed better, more capable leaders who could lead the transformation and emerge victorious in the field. *Thus a close study of mission command does not immediately offer new insights into organization design.*

One too few or one too many layers of leadership and the decision making process in the organization is undermined. See Figs. 4.3 and 4.5 below for examples of both situations. *A great many civilian managers do not know whether they have an appropriate hierarchy.*

An effective structure is the fulcrum pillar of the Mission Mastery edifice.

There are two important considerations here. Firstly, while all five Pillars are critical, a faulty structure can severely undermine strategy in action, leadership development, training and the development of a positive culture, as we saw in the previous chapter. They stand or fall on the strength or weakness of this Pillar. A mission will not be delivered effectively over the longer term in an organization of opaque accountability. This in turn hampers career planning and the development of leaders because it is difficult to impossible to consistently produce good leaders in a badly organized entity of non jobs. These are jobs without discrete decision rights. While one can't fail in a non job it is impossible to display one's talent, which is therefore wasted.

An ineffective structure is the pervading source of friction in civilian organizations.

The Chinese were aware of this a long time ago. "When expectations are clear and organization structure is appropriate for their tasks, people will follow their leaders and follow them even under difficult circumstances"[5]

If civilian organizations are not effectively organized, their leadership development schemes will be little more than lotteries buffeted by social fashion, legislative quotas, internal politics and/or the latest management fad.

4.2.2 Accountability and Subsidiarity

In the nineteenth century Pope Leo XIII introduced an idea known as ***the principle of subsidiarity***—see Rerum Novarum 15 May 1891. It is no longer a new idea but management academics thrive on putting old wine into new skins, so today it is called 'empowerment', but it is truly astounding how few people know how to *implement* this philosophy. It means that whatever people are able to do for themselves ought not be removed from their competence and taken over by other people. Decisions should not be made at higher levels if they can be competently made at lower levels. Subsidiarity means leaders must acknowledge these boundaries and hold people to account in their roles.

[5] Krause, D.G (1996) *Sun Tze The Art of war for Executives*, p115.

Time and again I have come across CEOs who have crassly removed a layer, any layer, 'since that will empower my staff' (and remove cost!). Removing the wrong layer in an over layered structure merely makes a bad situation worse. Subsidiarity was arguably what Drucker had in mind when he said organizations must be strong at the centre and strong at the periphery. Ironically it is an idea that is now corrupted in Europe, 124 years after it was introduced. Top down EU initiatives are prone to strip local communities of their decision rights. This has given rise to a proliferation of self serving central bureaucracies whose top down value-add is at best questioned and at worst resented.

It is of course all very well accepting the principle but how do you put it into practice? That in essence was the challenge I was confronted with in 1986. "Empowerment" was fashionable talk but was not a noticeable reality on the ground. There was no recognised practice that met the ideal notwithstanding initiatives such as Volvo's work with 'leaderless' groups in the 1960s. The search for an answer to that gap led in due course led to my crafting the DMA Solution Set, which presupposes the principle of subsidiarity—see Chap. 8. What I have learned since is subsidiarity (or empowerment if you like) is more honoured in the breach than observance.

4.3 Sources of Organization Design Friction

The principal stresses undermining structures tend to be one, some or all of the following.

4.3.1 The Issue of Size

Size is often a particular source of friction for those wishing to change an organization's design. It seems the larger an organization the more likely it is to have a sub optimal structure. It is invariably manifested in the silting up of middle management. The other two areas that can be problematical are supervisory layers and the top of the house where COO jobs can exist based on faulty logic. COOs and CEOs have been found in the same level of accountability: "one looking out and one running the business". The main justification for a temporary COO is when the incumbent is the dauphin. An example occurred when John Varley was COO of Barclays some months prior to succeeding CEO Matt Barrett.

Adam Pearce's data base of over 50,000 leader jobs has revealed that average spans of control decrease from Level 5 down to Level 2 and then increase for supervisors in level 1. The widest spans are often those of the chief executive and supervisors at the front line. Nevertheless frequent unnecessary over layering of supervisory roles (two or even three layers in Level 1) explains why their averages are not a wide as they could and should be. One reason is confusion over 24 × 7 shift work patterns. See Table 3.1 for an example of middle management bloat (over-layering). The red line indicates the total number of layers needed given the

7 levels of accountability justifying therefore up to eight layers. The decreasing spans of control in the right hand column point to where most of the real problems lie: layers 4–8. In order to pinpoint precisely where the overlayering resides it is necessary to undertake a Probe of the relevant spine(s) of accountability.

4.3.2 Job Evaluation

Job evaluation is another factor, which frequently undermines organization architecture. The various job evaluation systems are driven by size factors despite claims to the contrary. These systems are mostly bespoke consultant offerings but some are the result of internal policy and/or national union negotiations in some countries. For example the true accountability of significant Local Authority roles with a cost budget of "only" a billion $ are seriously down played in comparison to bank roles which are assessed against many nebulous "billions of $". We have found jobs 'assessed' by points based job evaluation systems given the same points when in fact they are two Levels apart. It is this erroneous logic that frequently distorts organization design in civilian organizations, because it encourages the adding of unnecessary layers, which then undermine the basis of their leadership development. Grade driven HR policies tend to undermine organization design and leadership development.

The table below shows an organization that field work revealed justified up to eight layers of employees, since it had seven levels of accountability. As can be seen it has up to 12 layers in places. The red line indicates the acceptable maximum *number* of layers. It does not mean the jobs below the red line should be removed since these are people doing real work in most cases. The problem is mostly in middle management—note layers 4–8 where average spans of control illustrated on the right hand column become progressively smaller. This shows where the worst over layering is evident: A classic case of middle management bloat (Fig. 4.1).

Middle management bloat seems to be widespread in civilian organizations.

4.3.3 Globalisation

Globalisation has at times triggered some ineffective structures. A recurring issue is confusion between centralization and decentralization. This often occurs if the accountability of value added decisions between the national, the regional and corporate offices is not clearly delineated. Major changes in legislation (e.g. 1992 in Europe removing customs barriers) enabled the introduction of pan European structures. Some organizations moved too quickly before they had embedded pan European systems, which created undue 'internal' friction. The rapid advance in technology coupled with outsourcing (e.g. in the supply chain) has led to a questioning of the need for the traditional P&L accountable country manager

Filled Positions By Filled Hierarchical Tier

	Unit 1	Unit 2	Unit 3	Unit 4	Unit 5	Unit 6	Unit 7	Unit 8	Unit 9	Unit 10	Total	Average Span
Layer 1											1	**10.0**
Layer 2											10	**5.6**
Layer 3	7	5	12	11	4	6	3	2	3	3	56	**5.6**
Layer 4	27	14	95	50	11	43	22	2	9	3	276	**4.6**
Layer 5	51	37	459	202	18	175	101	6	38	3	1,090	**3.6**
Layer 6	41	93	1,229	611	27	400	343	6	26		2,776	**3.0**
Layer 7	23	52	2,488	1,185	14	745	707	1	4		5,219	**2.2**
Layer 8	10	49	2,357	1,387	7	662	1,251		2		5,725	2.3
Layer 9	4	19	1,170	789	1	341	1,181				3,505	4.0
Layer 10			353	403		13	1,406				2,175	6.4
Layer 11			28	97			815				940	4.7
Tier 12				1			27				28	-
TOTAL	164	270	8,192	4,737	83	2,386	5,857	18	83	10	21,800	2.9
Average Span	2.1	2.7	2.3	2.7	1.9	3.5	4.2	1.4	2.6	1.8	2.9	

6,648 filled positions (30% of the total of 21,800) are in layer 9 to 12, if vacant leader roles are not counted as a tier

brian.dive@dmac1.com adam@sbudesign.com

Fig. 4.1 An example of bloat in middle management

role. Today a significant number of multinationals have moved to multi country organizations (MCO) structures around the world. External trading groupings such as EU, NAFTA and Mercosur help facilitate the relevance of these structures, some of which are still experimental revealing new organization design challenges. These new structures create new leadership development problems as the traditional P&L country manager role, typically WL 5, were great for general management development as they were usually accountable for a fully fledged business including key support functions. In Chap. 11 of *The Accountable Leader* I describe an example of the importance and impact of three different types of country management roles at Level 5 in the development of a manger and how it helped him reach Level 8.

4.3.4 Impact of the Global Financial Crisis (GFC)

The most recent GFC in 2008 has led to undue focus on cost cutting. "Undue" in that it has been usually neither guided nor based on sound organization design principles.

Any fool can cut costs in a large organization. The trick is to know when to stop and why, to avoid cutting corporate muscle.

When surgery is needed it is best done with the OD manager's laser of sound principles, not the accountant's knife. Ham-fisted cost cutting has been too prevalent since 2008. Although numbers have noticeably reduced in the banking industry, they needed to, but have the right layers been removed? I have worked in about ten financial services organizations: they were all, bar one (a start up), hierarchy heavy. Prior to the GFC banks were known in some countries as 'the civil service of the private sector'. The lack of accountability and knowledge of their own industry and its products was frighteningly exposed in 2008. One could not imagine leaders in the oil, consumer goods, retail, automobile, pharmaceutical or mining sectors being so ignorant of the makeup of their own products, services and technology. Although cost reduction was necessary in the banks, it was not always done based on a sound knowledge of organization design.

The knife is still the OD method of choice in many civilian organisations.

4.3.5 The Asset Trap

Failure to recognise when a competitive advantage has run its course and/or needs to be reconfigured can lead to an asset trap impacting effective organization design. The obverse can also apply: such as when to acquire assets to gain competitive advantage. Tesco powered to no. 1 in the UK grocery market racing past Sainsbury (which had been number one) based initially on its property expansion of hypermarkets. It quietly secured the prime sites from under the noses of its competitors. Today with the growth of on-line shopping and more price competition in the wake of the GFC some of those assets appear to be a potential liability. From 1999 Tesco has also been building its on-line business, which is now the second largest in Europe. It could be best placed to adapt to the latest preferences of shoppers in the longer haul. Its total of stores is becoming an asset drag and already it (and other retailers) is starting to close stores, which has considerable organization design (and other), implications.

4.3.6 Changing Technology

Closely linked to the above is the issue of changing technology. Managing the cannibalisation of one part of the business by another is a major challenge when faced with technological change. Consider the newspapers trying to battle with the advent of on-line services. Does your brand die or can it be morphed into another format. If it is meeting a permanent and universal need (for news) then another way must found or corporate death beckons. The *Guardian* is bankrupt but it is trying to compensate the halving of its print circulation by expanding its on-line business. The jury is out as yet since it is currently living off its investments. The organization design implications have to be managed quickly and adroitly.

The previously nationalised telephone company BT is a good example of how competition has (slowly) enhanced that company's performance and product offering as it leads the way in up-rating its digital services building on its investment in fibre. Changing a previously lumbering public sector monopoly has been an enormous challenge. It has taken over 20 years to turn the ship around. As I write BT has targeted the company EE as its way back into the mobile market and at the same time has moved into televising sport. This has necessitated significant changes in the company's operating model and structure calling for a change in number of support roles compared to those that are customer facing. It has also sharpened accountabilities as a result of implementing Work Levels.

Technological changes can outflank previous strengths as IBM found in the 1990s and Nokia more recently. During the 2015 Davos Conference the head of Microsoft pointed to the end of the Internet. If he is right this is likely to be another seismic shift with organization design implications for companies in the technology sector.

4.3.7 Spurious OD Principles

Relying on spurious "principles" of organization design is another pitfall. For example some consultants sell projects measuring an organization's 'spans of control' based on fixed formulas about the ideal numbers. One international company continues to sell "8 x 8" as "the answer". The fact that clients still "buy it" illustrates the shallowness of some CEOs' organization design knowledge. This then enables the sale of cost cutting projects on the basis of this "principle" and set dangerously invalid targets for spans and layers. In 2012 the CEO of one of the world's largest banks proudly announced that with this consultancy's help he had moved his company to 8 layers and that "everyone now had 8 direct reports." An interesting description of an average span!

In another example in the US we saw a global financial services company was helped by another consultancy to lift its average span of control by two decimal points to save millions of dollars. Our subsequent analysis established it had two unnecessary layers, which if removed would actually empower its management.

Spans and layers are key components of organization design and are closely linked. Tall structures are prone to narrow spans, depending on the nature of work at the front line. For example we have worked with organizations with relatively large average spans that were still over layered because the work at the front line was straightforward, with prescribed outputs suitable for large spans. This is counterintuitive and can mislead "de-layering" initiatives. Generally flatter structures tend to be reflected in wider spans. Thus the shorthand for some is to simply drive for broader spans since that will trigger removal of layers. Whether they are the right layers to remove tends to receive less consideration. So while spans are the inverse partners to layers it is important to realise that:

Levels validate or drive layers which in turn drive spans. Spans do not reliably drive layers.

Beware of the advisor who talks about 'spans and layers' as that linvariably betrays an obsession with spans and an inability to reliably assess value adding layers. If so it will not resolve the problem of suspect organization design. Hence our LSA software, designed by Adam Pearce, focuses on *an analysis of levels, layers and spans*: the order is important.

Studies of "spans and layers" not aligned to levels of accountability are potentially very dangerous when invoked as 'the' reason for a change in organization design.

The challenge is then to identify the pinch points in the structure: those layers which are in the same decision space or level of accountability, eroding space to lead. They are the areas of compression and disempowerment. If the corrective laser of accountability levels is missing, guesswork prevails, which is a formula for traumatising employees.

In Chap. 9 more insight is provided via a major case study to show why spans need to vary and on what basis.

4.3.8 The Contribution of Process Re-engineering

The impact of process engineering has had some negative impacts on organization architecture. It was originally introduced to 'get rid of the silos in functional structures'. It has too often built in horizontal silos reinvigorating the worst aspects of Taylor's scientific management. As with the recent GFC, the 1980s were a difficult decade with many businesses reviewing their core strategies and using re-engineering as a cost cutting device. This initiative did not solve the widespread problem of hierarchy heavy structures.

4.3.9 The Contribution of Fads and Fashions

Fads and fashion seem to unduly influence patterns of organization structure. Managers can be seduced by the search for "the new". Following the much vaunted introduction of the matrix structure in the NASA moon project of the late 1960s a number of multinationals, such as Hoechst, Shell and Unilever toyed with formal matrix options in the 1970s only to move away from them in the 1980s and 1990s. A true matrix structure entails two hard line bosses. Philips "tilted its matrix" around this time and in doing so moved into to loss for a short period, which cost the first non-family CEO his job. It seemed they did not foresee the internal friction entailed in radically changing the structure in a global organization. The influence of the previous profit accountable country "barons" was underestimated, which led to undue confusion leading to slower reaction times and declining market shares with innovation becoming bogged down.

All international companies have a matrix of interests (function, product, geography, customer, technology for example) that need to be successfully managed but that is not the same as having two hard line bosses. This has not been helped by some writers talking about managing a matrix of interests as "a matrix structure."[6] Accountability is a zero sum game and the presence of two hard line bosses necessarily dilutes accountability. The matrix organization is best suited to the management of large projects, hence its introduction into NASA. Apart from that it tends to be suboptimal for two reasons. Firstly the authority of two hard line bosses tends to lead to a decision making impasse in the case of disagreement. Secondly the only true point of conflict resolution is the top left hand corner of the matrix: the CEO. But people try to avoid that, which means politics proliferate. The outcome is slow decision making at a time when technology and the customer demands faster and faster responses.

Another initiative was the "process organization" which was largely old wine in new skins. It was fashionable for a while but it was not really a fundamentally new concept. At the top of the organization "Processes" appeared to be more akin to the re-naming of 'old fashioned functions' such as sales and personnel, which become customer management (although it is a brave sales manager who claims to 'manage' a customer such as Wal-Mart or Carrefour.), human resources 'process owners' and so on. Some writers even more confusingly wrote of "process functions".[7]

The 'network organization' favoured by Miles, was another brief meteor, which appeared to explain the success of Benetton and publishing companies that were among the first to outsource much of their work to places like Taiwan, retaining key sources of competiveness such as design and development skills in-house. Subsequently outsourcing and off-shoring have become important cost driven initiatives aimed at improving financial results (although not customer service it seems), which have changed the location of some key roles but have not their fundamental accountability. It is not uncommon in the twenty-first century to find members of a top executive team in an international organization based in different countries.

4.3.10 Organization for Growth

Structuring for growth is a major challenge. One can move too quickly or too slowly. Too quickly and the new initiative is killed by the cost burden. Too slowly

[6] For example, see Kesler and Kates (2011).

[7] Fisch, G. G. in *Organization Structuring* (1971) edited by H.E. Frank.

and the opportunity is missed. In the1990s Ford moved to a global functional structure to help manufacture the global car. The structure was clearly aligned to the new strategy. It was a huge change and may have been premature as it was not considered a success at the time. Indeed the CEO bit the dust. The amount of time in meetings and travel it created for top executives was underestimated. Today with the internet and video conferencing it might have had a better chance of working.

Often the major constraint on growth aspirations is not money but the quality and depth of leaders with potential for a bigger job. The potential of managers assessed against Levels can facilitate growth. When Unilever was about to re-enter Vietnam it assessed the country could sustain a Work Level 5 national organization given the population and the average per capita income. At that time the resources in the country required leadership at only Level 3 but in order to ensure the operation grew quickly it appointed a "List 5 manager"—i.e. a manager in WL 4 with confirmed potential to move to WL 5. The move was successful and the growth materialised as planned.

4.3.11 Organization for Privatisation

A very challenging form of organizational change is required when government or public sector organizations migrate to the private sector as part of a privatisation or corporatisation programme, as they are variously called around the world. This can be a huge culture challenge for both the former employees and the new top management.

As will be shown in Chap. 6 on culture, the outcome and its quality depends critically on the successful implementation of the other four Pillars. Top private sector managers do not realise that performance/ people management and financial accountability are invariably weak to nonexistent (see Chap. 7) below WL 4 across large public service organizations in central government. The HR department's focus is often on employee relations without a great deal of OD knowledge and experience in managing large organizational change projects.

Since junior and middle managers invariably do not own the levers of change their ability to drive innovation initiatives is often untried. Yet this is precisely what the new top management expect and they wrongly assume their managerial leaders have this capability. Invariably they do not, which is often the major source of friction in the newly privatised organization. If the privatised entity retains most of its current top management this is potentially a major ball and chain limiting progress. *The 'secret weapon' is working in reverse.* I have seen evidence of that public service ethos lasting over 20 years in the "new" organization. It poses specific challenges, which are not usually anticipated in the delivery of glossy new brochures.

4.3.12 Managing M & A Re-Organizations

M & A activity in the private sector is another source of friction in the area of organization design. Those acquiring are prone to the arrogance of size and an attitude of 'we know best otherwise we would not be able to acquire (little) you'. In 2002/03 I was working with the Amersham pharmaceutical company which was actively planning to launch Work Levels across their international organization in April 2004 as part of their reward strategy. But in October 2003 they were unexpectedly taken over by General Electric and folded into its medical division. A GE reward manager (maybe WL 3) was dispatched to listen to what Amersham was doing in the reward space. At the very short meeting it was made clear that "GE HR systems are second to none." It is possible GE could have learned something if they had had an open mind to what was good in Amersham. People issues (assets and liabilities) are the aspect of M&A work that are invariably not considered and often underestimated. It is not straightforward because the way people behave and perform can be, as we are seeing in this book, a secret weapon beyond the insight of the 'numbers boys and girls'. History tends to be written by the victors not the losers—mission command not withstanding!

The trickiest "merger" is when a smaller company takes over a larger one. I was working for a sizeable international telecoms company that was acquired by a smaller national operator. The CEO from the smaller company now had to run an operation that was in a higher level of complexity. The CEO was full of confidence and placed many of his people in the key new roles on greatly enhanced reward packages, with the CEO's the most controversial. The organization design was the result of 'provincial' thinking and it did not take long to see that a capability problem was manifest across the top of the new structure. The best people in the larger company voted with their feet once the state of play was obvious to all. Not that long afterwards the company was broken up and sold in parts to other competitors.

Mergers as a result of industry rationalisation can be another source of ineffective structures. The UK ship building industry has been decimated in recent years largely as a result of government policy. This has forced mergers for survival. Having worked with one of the key survivors it was clear they had a legacy of unnecessary structures, job grades and systems, which were the result of the industry's recent history. They had not been rationalised and were generating make-work and confusion added to which the company was struggling to identify talent with potential for further growth.

In 2009 I interviewed a leading IT Director who had just left one of the country's major banks. He explained the large number of Legacy IT systems there, which were the vestigial footprint of the banks it had acquired over time. The systems had never been fully integrated. In his view these systems were then held together by "bubble gum and sticking plaster." Sure enough, in 2013 they crashed and customers could not access their money for days. This happened not once but twice that year and customers in Northern Ireland were affected for weeks.

I have also found similar problems in the public sector when different health bodies were merged without thinking through the new organization design needed. In one case our field work revealed Directors of regions in Level 4 reporting to a Level 4 COO. One of the directors, who had spent less than a year in Level 3 in the previous structure, was struggling. The architecture in these two directorates was sub optimal, but with different problems. One had severe compression in Level 2 (people in the health world seem to get a new grade and 'promotion' every time they pass another exam *irrespective of their accountabilities or decisions they take/ don't take*, which is apt to generate compression) while the other had unmanageable spans (over 20), which were too broad *given the intensive nature of the work being done by professionals at the front line.* Instead of giving the struggling director coaching and help, the COO planned to merge the two suboptimal directorates. Probably the only thing he could do to make a bad situation worse. The interviews we conducted revealed enormous frustration, as junior and middle managers could see more or less what was wrong but it remained unresolved. Key players voted with their feet, as often happens with the best talent, which by definition is mobile.

Perhaps the saddest case of failed acquisitions involves the UK Cooperative Group. This proud 150 year old company once had 40 % of the UK grocery retail market. Today it would be lucky to register a sixth of its former glory. It blew its proud heritage in a series of unwise acquisitions, which included the failing retailer Somerfield and the similarly problematical bank, Britannia. The board and top management sadly became infamous in 2014 for its unwieldy structure coupled with weaknesses across all five pillars of Mission Mastery.

4.3.13 The Key Steps to Achieve Successful Change of Structure

As with the first pillar, strategy, the key to success is "structure in action". This is never clearer than when there is a change of structure. New CEOs seem to be pathologically driven to changing structure, especially at the top, when they are appointed. Many of the 12 shortcomings above are quite common occurrences where the motivation of these CEOs seems to be aimed at 'having an immediate impact on the (sometimes also new) direct reports.' A common outcome in an era of cost cutting is the consolidation of the top team into fewer jobs. This has occurred in more than one UK Local authority. It looks a good cost saving move to the uninitiated but small spans at the top tend to correlate with over-layering.

Poor execution is just as lethal in the domain of organization design as it is in the case of setting strategy. In my experience the process needs to be guided by ten critical work streams, often working in parallel, once the top structure is agreed by the governance body.

3.13.1. Choice of structure (functional, geographic etc) aligned to the strategy. This is a major OD topic but one that has been written about quite extensively by others so I do not intend to major here on this content issue of organization design.

3.13.2. Completion of that total target organization design based on the right number of minimal layers aligned to strategy and the requisite levels of accountability.
3.13.3. The target structure to be built top down (but only the first two layers) ***and*** bottom up from the customer/patient as appropriate.
3.13.4. Time lines and agreed milestones for implementation with programme management including a clear governance process to discuss and agree changes and monitor progress against the agreed roadmap.
3.13.5. Organization design training—for example in the DMA Solution Set so that the process can be owned by line management not the OD consultants
3.13.6. Design the detail of the key accountabilities of the new roles, ideally on one page, maximum two.
3.13.7. Leadership assessment of potential incumbents for the key new jobs
3.13.8. Appropriate appointments as required. This can then move to individual training needs analysis and development plans once the roles have been filled, as required.
3.13.9. Training in how to work successfully in the new structure, including clarification of any new horizontal linkages stemming directly from the new structure. This is often done via workshops starting with the new top team.
3.13.10. Communications and engagement of *all* stakeholders inside and outside the organization.

The one element of this ten point plan which is likely to be short-changed in my experience is that relating to communications and engagement.[8] *It is probably the most common reason why the friction of organizational change is underestimated jeopardising the total change enterprise. It may also help to explain Klein and Shea's claim in chapter 1 that 70 % of change programmes fail.*

4.4 History of Military Organization Design

Dawson[9] has demonstrated that early military development consisted of three stages. These may be described in capsule form as the warfare of the siege, of chariot and of infantry. Around 1000 BC came the breakthrough involving the rise of mass infantry formations supported by cavalry, dramatically increasing the scale and frequency of warfare and *giving rise to centralized, bureaucratic multi-states that could command hitherto unprecedented resources.* Large infantry based armies

[8] See Chap. 9 of *The Healthy Organization* on Mobilising Change based on the five phases of change e.

[9] Dawson, D (2001) *The First Armies* p.210.

needed supporting structures and organization to support them to get to the field of battle with all its consequences.

For example the organising 'principle of 10', referred to in Exodus[10] was probably first used even more rigorously by the Persians, in the sixth century BC.[11] In the fifth century BC the Chinese army organised ten sections of ten into a company.[12] The Persians organization was arguably a refinement of the Assyrians, the first empire to build a logistics bureaucracy to support its army in the field that was later broadly applied by the Greeks and the Romans.[13] One of the greatest organizational innovations during this era was the introduction of the phalanx formation by Philip of Macedon. Philip seems to have been the first to have a professional army that was very well trained and served by choice not conscription. Bose maintains that Philips's army hierarchy "*Was only 7 levels deep to keep him in touch with the troops at the lowest levels and that the armies of the Roman Empire carefully studied Philip's pedagogical approaches.*"[14] It seems significant that all these armies, whether in the East or the West, all arrived at virtually identical, workable, flat command structures. The Roman standing army probably had the flattest structure of all these armies consisting of maniple (a squad of 10) reporting to a centurion (usually 80 soldiers) to a cohort (6 centurions), to a legion (10 cohorts): being one of ~25 legions that reported directly to the Emperor.[15] This flat structure of the Roman army aided decision making, accountability and empowerment, which would seem to be a key factor in its long tenure of success. Keegan noted that Ghengis Khan divided his army into "tens, hundreds and thousands – which anticipated the modern Western system of sections, subordinate to squadrons and squadrons subordinate to regiments" the terminology used for cavalry formations, which of course was Ghengis Khan's forte.[16] My colleague, Adam Pearce, has analysed our data base of clients covering more than half a million jobs based on 32 organizations and found their average span of control was 6.6. All but three had too much hierarchy, which indicated there was plenty of scope for improvement.

Military organizations have been around longer than large civilian employment organizations. The hierarchy of military organizations has been largely settled for ~2500 years. There have been great advances in the complexity in warfare technology that have affected the horizontal dimension of structures in the main but not the vertical, which has remained largely if not completely, unaffected. Thus depth or

---

[10] Exodus 18, 25.

[11] Cook, J M (1998) *The Persians,* p.149, where he records Herodotus referring to Xerxes army being built up in powers of 10. See also *Herodotus Histories,* translated by G. Rawlinson (1996) Book Seven *Polymina* chapter 81, p542.

[12] Sun Tzu, op cit. p. 135.

[13] Dawson, D op cit.

[14] Bose, P (2003) *Alexander the Great's art of strategy* p.14.

[15] Fields, N (2009), *The Roman Army of the Principate 27BC—AD 117,* p.15.

[16] Keegan, J (1994) *op cit* p 204.

height of structure is not something that the military tend to think about today since it is now largely taken for granted although they struggle with effective peacetime structures as the numbers under command become less. To repeat the earlier message:

Military structure did not need revision by the Prussian reformers. It was not a contributing cause to their earlier defeat and that of Napoleon was not better. They could take it for granted, unlike their civilian counterparts.

Although Philip of Macedon ran a standing army on professional lines the Romans were probably the first to solve the problem of maintaining a permanent professional army on a long term basis that was well led, well organized, well paid, well trained and well motivated as they could be offered citizenship and a pension at the end of their service. Many retired to farms in Iberia for example. They rarely mutinied despite the fact that the Roman Army was often a rather cosmopolitan mixture of different nationalities. Ghengis Khan was also noted for choosing his officers on the basis of talent, who were well trained with strong discipline over behaviour including central control over booty.

4.4.1 The Key Element of Military Structure

So structure—the depth of layers—in the military has been generally agreed and largely unchanged for a long time. The layers of command are clear as is the quality of leader needed at each layer. There is a common language and common understanding on both counts: number of layers and quality of leader needed at each layer.

This is not the case with civilian organizations based on my fieldwork around the world.

It seems the organization for a four star general in the field would be in Level 7 and could therefore justify up to eight layers of hierarchy. (Layers are counted down to and including the front line—the most junior role. Levels of accountability are counted from that front line upwards including the top role. Thus an organization with seven levels of accountability could have up to eight layers of hierarchy: the front line plus a layer of leadership for each Level.) In fact the military tend to have one more based on compression in WL 2. I have worked in civilian organizations in both the public and private sector with 12–14 Layers of hierarchy when mostly no more than 7 or 8 are justified.

How can this be? Navigating a way towards an answer to that question is the focus for the rest of this chapter.

As hinted above the services are not perfect. The Army, Navy and Air Force all have their Christmas trees of Generals, especially in peace time. They are prone to building symmetrical structures given inter-service rivalry. Given the massive downsizing of the Royal Navy since World War I for example, it is debatable whether it still has seven levels of accountability. At the end of WWI the Royal Navy had strength of 437,000 officers and men. Today it is less than 40,000 but maintains the same array of ranks. So although better in many respects than their civilian counterparts the military are known to resist change. I was recently asked to look at the headquarters of one of the services and was somewhat surprised to see such rigidly symmetrical structures across the services, which appeared to be driven by the desire to match ranks if called to a joint services meeting. "If *their* one-stars (1-stars) are attending we had better send a 1-star too." I queried a 2 star post compressing the role below but was told "We need that rank because he interfaces with the Americans and their general is a 2 star" And of course the giveaway was 4 star generals reporting to 4 star generals within more than one of the services.

At one point I was asked to submit five different pricing options for a possible project to satisfy Services politics. At that stage I lost interest as the project did not really seem to want an objective answer, which may have been the problem with the Betts Review. This was a royal commission set up to review of the UK military in 1993 but perhaps the brief was too wide. One of Betts' recommendations was to remove one rank (of 19). The review team, being made up of civilians, seemed to confuse rank, grades and organization design. The military duly implemented the recommendation and removed the rank of Field Marshall, which in peace time is vacant other than for honorific incumbents such as the Dukes of Edinburgh and Westminster!

4.5 Organization Design in Civilian Organizations

4.5.1 The Danger of Top-Down Organization Design

The major organization design problem today in many *civilian organizations is, irrespective of their shapes (functional, geographic etc) they still do not know how many layers of management they need nor how to identify the correct number.* No amount of process reengineering or new operating models can repair organizational spinal curvature. Fiddling with the ribs is no way to cure a damaged central nervous system. A common mistake I observe in civilian organizations is organizing the total structure top-down. It is the starting point of the link to strategy, but only the starting point. Experience shows, *if this approach progresses beyond the top two layers it invariably leads to the insertion of span breakers into the structure.*

A span breaker is a job that adds comfort to the boss but does not add value to the key reports and hence the customer or the other members of the team. It is not justified on the spine of accountability.

The best way to test the value adding decision rights in a spine of accountability is to interview job holders from the front line to identify what decisions they take and what decision support they need from the layer above them and so on. In that way the value adding decision rights can be plotted along a spine of accountability or be shown to be unnecessary duplication.

In other words good organization design is simultaneously a top down and bottom up process.

4.5.2 Is Hierarchy Still Valid for Civilian Organizations in the Twenty-First Century?

Consideration of the vertical axis leads inevitably to the issue of hierarchy. Today "hierarchy" is a somewhat pejorative term loaded with emotion. It is easy to see why. Most people work in civilian organizations that are badly organized with far too many layers of hierarchy some of which are therefore full of sound and fury adding nothing. They work in defective bureaucracies

A bureaucracy disconnected from its mission, its customer and performance is a denial of what Weber had in mind. Unfortunately today that is "the bureaucracy" most people experience.

An over-layered bureaucracy is a totally demoralising experience. It invariably means someone else is working "in my decision space, duplicating my work". Then work has no clear purpose, is of little consequence, since "I cannot make a difference." People need to feel their work is worthwhile. They rightly bemoan the cluttered hierarchy above them and can clearly identify layers "where nothing really happens" despite the trappings of titles, large offices fancy salaries and mouth watering bonuses. They are disempowered and rightly angry. (In August 2014 the CIPD reported that the ratio of average CEO pay of the FTSE 100 to the respective average employee was 143:1. In 1975 the Diamond Commission argued that 5:1 was the "right" differential. The Sudreau report in France took a similar stance at the time. How times have changed.)

People have described these situations of frustrating helplessness to me as "working in a blancmange", "hamster management" and "running in treacle". Other manifestations are, "seniority trumps talent", "avoidance of redundancy is more important here than assessment of performance", "filling the latest minority quota is the name of the game." These comments tend to be the more strident in relation to 'white collar' work, which in the twenty-first century too often splinters into rather soulless processes and sub processes the purpose of which is not clear to the people "doing the work." In every case itemised above, the structure in question was very hierarchy heavy. Today fashionable CEO platitudes claim to have "done away with hierarchy", "removed a command and control culture", "and flattened the structure to get close to the customer, speed up communications and release our staff's talent". These are noble aspirations to right-size an organization, which invariably seem to capsize when lacking a conceptual framework that can identify too much or too little hierarchy. "Hierarchy" is often associated today with authoritarian management and top down control, which is confusing style with substance.

4.5.2.1 Hierarchy Is the (Necessary) Response to Increasing Complexity

Hierarchy is needed to cope with increasing complexity. It is a term known in mathematics, biology and information theory that reflects qualitative increases in complexity. It is the link with complexity that is important here. Organizational accountability is associated with making more complex decisions reflecting a more extensive environment calling for a more comprehensive response, taking more time to achieve order and mastery. Most people I speak to in large organizations are aware of the fact that they have too many layers of hierarchy but at the same time do not know what the answer should be, or how to find out. I was running a webcast once in the US, which revealed the following.

> 72 % of participating companies (about 40, mostly large North American) indicated they felt they had too many layers of management *but did not know what the right number should be.*

Organizations also tend to be confused by status issues. I remember being in a country visited by a delegation of top Chinese politicians. They all wore the same navy boiler suits but you only had to look at the cut and type of cloth to know who the top shots were. Those in denim arose early in the hotel to clean the shoes of their "comrades" in gabardine.

Organizations cannot function without appropriate accountability or in other words appropriate hierarchy.

4.5.3 Strategy and Structure: Know Your "Business"

In his famous work, *Strategy and Structure Chapters in the History of the Industrial Enterprise* written in 1962, Alfred Chandler established that 'structure follows strategy'. This is important in the case of decoding the top structure, which could be functional, divisional, geographic, product, customer based or matrix in shape depending on an organization's strategy. In fact most structures are a hybrid of these factors. For example the underlying structure in most organizations is functional but even there sales will be organized by geography, finance by function/specialism and the supply chain by technology depending on the industry. Some, such as Roger Roes saw matrix as the interim stage from a functional structure growing towards becoming another large division or company. Thus it could be argued there is really no pure organizational format. Strategy (or mission) is (or should be) the principal influence on the design of the top horizontal axis. The problem is that while a clear strategy is a prerequisite for high performance it is not enough on its own. It does not necessarily follow that an organization has an effective structure simply because the strategy is "clear". The two are related but quite distinct. An example of a simple statement of strategy being undermined by an ineffective structure was given in the previous chapter. This means leadership development and career planning (the subject of the next chapter) are also undermined when the structure is flawed as we also saw in that earlier case study. Strategy and structure are both totally undermined by weak implementation. Moltke recognised this but unlike many 21st managers he knew it was unacceptable for a leader to simply put this in the 'too hard' basket. That was unacceptable since there must be a logical solution—*the back briefing cascade of mission command was his answer.*

But if strategy is not attuned to the environment there is a clear likelihood that organization structures tend to become ineffective. The recent recession and stagflation in Europe and Japan has seen the resurgence of cost reduction programmes. Too few seem to have relied on sound organization design principles to revitalise their sclerotic organizations. Some initiatives have been noticeably unimpressive. I summarised one in a paper: *Can Councils be run effectively without a CEO?* In recent years Europe has been the underperforming problem child for virtually every multinational I work with. Given the protectionism, corruption and inefficiency of the EU that is hardly surprising. Take just one example. In 2014 the European wine industry received another 1.6 billion euro subsidy while their competitors in other countries did not receive government subsidies and yet it is the latter's market shares that are growing. Europe is clearly starting to reap the whirlwind of its unaccountable bureaucracy and its unemployed young people under 30 are paying a grievous, predictable price.

Toyota is an example of a company whose strategy and performance has recently been impacted by a suboptimal structure. It dominated management awards for excellence for years but in 2010 it had to recall thousands of cars in the US to rectify faults. Part of the problem was its faulty organization design and a lack of single point accountability in the US, one of its largest markets. Sales in San Francisco and manufacturing in Kentucky both reported independently to Japan. This is the risk for some global companies that are dividing the world into functions reporting directly into corporate.

4.6 Structures for Growth

A recurring OD challenge is one already referred to above in Sect. 3.9: "How do we organize for growth?" Growth in the US and Europe was commonplace until he 1970s. Two major oil shocks and the arrival of Japanese competition then led to the difficult 1980s. We were then subjected to an avalanche of books on "Japanese management" examining the secret of their success. These analyses were time bound and surprisingly naïve explanations, as I learned when visiting Japan in the 1980s.

During 2012/13 I ran a number of OD workshops in Asia. Given the challenge of high growth in that part of the world this was a major concern/challenge for them The growth in GDP for Malaysia (where I was running some of the workshops) for example during 2012 was 6.4 % in national GDP: 17 % for the construction industry. Many of these organizations worried about 'how to structure for growth' and how to attract and retain talent 'which is in short supply'. Yet the great majority of these companies already had around 8–11 layers of leaders and nearly all of them could actually justify only between 5 and 7 layers at most. *They already lacked effective organisation structures but all were planning to add to them* ***because they were growing!*** They are simply repeating the mistakes which American and European companies made in the 1960s during their times of easy growth. This is actually quite depressing and it shows how little has really been learned in the field of organization design during the last 50 years. The back-of-the-envelope "degree" is still prevalent.

My colleagues and I have found the key to building effective structures for growth is to *focus on the number of Work Level 3 roles required*. These jobs are the backbone of a successful organization. They are the operational general managers who run hypermarkets, large factories, oil refineries, distribution centres, call centres and major corporate office departments. In every organization it is important to identify what drives the Level 3 units in a given situation: such as moving into a new country or orchestrating a takeover. For example working with one retailer planning to expand internationally we established the number of level three stores required to move a country management role over time from Level 4 to Level 5 to Level 6. This could be extrapolated from the roll out plans for mega stores over a clear 5 years strategy/plan. This had critical people implications given their current capabilities.

It is very rare for a large organization to grow a level of accountability. For example an organization where the top job is in Level 6 would need to have at least 500 jobs in Level 3 to warrant a move to Level 7 and then ~4000 for Level 8. Where this does occur *there are huge implications for organization design and whether the current employees have the potential capability to also grow a level. Finding the right amount of money is rarely a problem, compared to finding the right number and quality of people*. I recall visiting Tesco in Korea in 2001, when it had less than five hypermarkets. The plan was to move to ~50 in 5 years. The building and financing was clearly a logistical challenge but finding the requisite number of experienced Korean Level 3 managers was a daunting challenge. How can you build managers with sufficient experience and expertise as fast as building the stores? Part of the solution was buying Wal-mart's footprint in the country. Finding/developing competent distributive leaders at Level 3 and above is the most common source of friction in a growing organization.

4.6.1 The Distinctive Footprint[17]

We established in Chap. 2 that high growth; high profit companies do different things when compared with other businesses. They have a "distinctive footprint". One of the four enablers of that footprint's features, in addition to those affecting strategy, discussed in the previous chapter, is "*simpler structures*": 61 % for "growth champions" versus 49 % for "others". The second enabler based on those simpler structures with clear accountability was "*Fast cross company innovation*"*:* 91 % for growth champions and only 56 % for others.

Mostyn's research showed there are three smart ways to build pace, delivery and growth.

1. Streamline the organization design
2. Create better, faster decision making
3. Build more effective executive teams

On streamlining the organization design they reported that more than ever organizations (Stonecourt said "businesses", but clearly these findings apply to any civilian organization in the twenty-first century that aspires to the delivery of first class customer (patient/pupil) service) need to be managed for speed and flexibility. They noted that too many models are built on out of date beliefs undermining organizational performance.

He concluded that given a strong, relevant and clear strategy it is vital to:

- "Identify where the centre should add value"
- "Relentlessly reduce management levels (For "levels" in this context read "Layers")
- "Reduce clutter from job design and sharpen performance management."
- "Define decision rights and simplify accountabilities"
- "Embed the few key organization behaviours that will unleash the success of the design."

This research emphasised that clear accountability results in simpler, transparent structures which foster creativity and innovation. I have witnessed marketing and advertising departments where lack of discipline and accountability "to foster creativity" has resulted in chaos and de-motivation. Indeed in one bank we studied, the risk function was both too deep and had twice the number of horizontal interfaces it needed—and reported in its annual accounts! After the GFC in 2008 the importance of risk departments became very high profile for obvious reasons but legislation does not specify the addition of "mandatory layers" of leadership. But new laws are sometimes used to justify rich structures. This happened after the Enron debacle, which resulted in the Sarbanes-Oxley Act. Finance and

[17] Material continued from Chap. 2.

Underwriting departments tended to use it to justify extra, unnecessary layers. New legal work might lead to new jobs but is invariably a spurious reason for adding layers of hierarchy.

4.7 The Civilian Approach to Hierarchy: How Tall Is too Tall?

This was the question I wrestled with almost 30 years ago when I was global Head of Organization at Unilever. No-one could tell me how tall Unilever should be and why and as I explained in the Introduction, finding the answer to that conundrum gave rise to the DMA Solution Set with its core concept of Work Levels.

I now realise Unilever was an excellent test bed since at the time it was a conglomerate of 300,000 employees selling in 200 countries with a substantial presence in 100. Furthermore it consisted of capital intensive businesses (such as chemicals), labour intensive businesses (such as tea estates and plantations), knowledge intensive operations (such as research laboratories) plus countless consumer goods operations, trading businesses, restaurants, shipping lines and not to forget a complex head office based in London and Rotterdam reflecting its historical share holding. Across all of these entities was a common interest group of 20,000 managers, 6 % of whom would, at any one time, be working outside their own country.

4.7.1 The Key to Unlocking Hierarchy

As part of the field work it became clear that once the total number of Levels of Accountability (or Work Levels) was known it was possible to indicate the maximum number of hierarchical layers that can be justified in any employment organization that exists for a purpose. This is because:

One and only one layer of leadership is needed in each level of accountability.

This was an insight first suggested by the Brunel school but dramatically reinforced by my early field work in India during the late 1980s and on numerous occasions subsequently. The Levels of accountability reflect the increasing decision making complexity in an organization, which is the key to how much hierarchy is justified. The key question about the height of a given hierarchy in organization design is to determine the total number of Work Levels. Thus if the top job in an organization is WL 5, we know there can be *up to 6 layers of hierarchy*. The most junior role at the customer front line is a layer, with scope for a leader in each of the 5 Work Levels above it. Hence *up to* 6 layers in an organization where the top role is in WL 5. If, as can occur, the front line is in Work Level 2 then there would be scope for only 3 further layers up to the top role. This is the skeleton to which the organization edifice of hierarchical layers can be aligned and against which horizontal linkages can be matched.

> *It can now be seen that if an organization does not know how many levels of discrete decision rights exist within its spine of accountability then the task of deciding the right number of layers is guesswork. That in turn disrupts the process flow across the organization and undermines leadership development.*

For example, from work done in the British Civil Service we have determined that the post of Permanent Secretary, the top executive job in a government department, can be at Level 5, 6 or 7. Some are possibly WL 4, although we have not interviewed in the smallest departments. Some departments also have a permanent secretary grade below that of the CEO Permanent Secretary. One office in Whitehall had **three** layers of permanent secretary.

But as they were not aware of their total number of levels, each of the departments we have worked in, turned out to be over layered. Similarly the top jobs (CEOs) of companies on the FTSE 100, or the Dow Jones 500 are not all at the same level of accountability. The same applied to Local Authority CEOs, the top 250 of which seem to be Levels 4–6 (in a handful of cases).

During the last 10 years my colleagues and I have consulted to a significant number of international banks. They had CEOs at various Levels of accountability. They were not aware of this prior to our work and were also (except one case, which was a start up) consistently over layered. There have been major job reductions across the industry since 2008 as a result of the financial crash, which have been estimated at 180,000.[18] Those that have not used the DMA accountability laser probably were not as aware of the difference between those roles adding value and those not. For example, depending on the levels of accountability we have recommended tailored solutions of 5 × 7 (up to five layers with a span on average of 7), 6 × 6, 7 × 7 and 8 × 8 for example. The answer has to be adapted to the facts. Be wary of consultants who offer "8x8" as THE solution. See Chap. 8 for more comment on Spans.

In one example Adam Pearce helped a bank devise an effectiveness ratio of "8x8" (*up to* eight layers including the CEO with an average span of 8 or more) after detailed analysis of the bank in question. Then a new CEO came in and decided, with no obvious OD logic, to make the ratios more demanding and delivered a new diktat of "7 x 10" (*up to* seven layers with an average span of 10). There was no organization design logic for the change other than perhaps to signal "things are getting tougher under the new regime." Following this guideline the new CEO removed some key direct reports creating an accountability gap in the Level below

[18] The Evening Standard 14 October 2013.

his. This resulted in an unrealistic span of direct reports, which in turn led to a breakdown in the CEO's health. Sadly this was a predictable possibility.

The height of hierarchy calibrated in value adding layers with discrete decision rights gives a unique insight into the optimal average span of control. This varies according to the number of layers needed. Generally, depending on the nature of the work at the front line, the average span of control should not be less than the number of layers required.

Establishing the correct number of leadership layers and the corresponding appropriate spans of control continues to be a matter of guesswork and meaningless metrics for too many organizations and consultants. "Guidelines" are rarely based on discernible logic.

4.7.2 Organize from the Customer (i.e. "Bottom Up")

Top managers are trained to think 'strategy to structure'. The structure should follow once the strategy is clear. This is important for the top two layers of an organization—the horizontal shape of the organization—which should be designed first. But CEOs and many consultants are apt to design the rest of their structure top down. The great danger in this approach is it tends to build in expensive jobs (span breakers) that do not add value (make qualitatively different decisions) to those of people further down in the organization. .

Good organization design has to be top down, linked to strategy and bottom up from the customer.

Once the top two layers are designed it is best to build back the vertical structure from the customer front line. We recently worked in an organization of ~100,000 people following a firm of accounting consultants who had just designed in the top three layers "to fit a new operating model." The problem we then demonstrated was the presence of compression (two layers in one level of accountability), which directly involved the third layer down from the top. Having plotted decision rights in this organization from the customer front line we had established there were seven levels of accountability available with severe compression at the new layer 3. This was immediately a major roadblock to a significant organizational change programme. The top management's first reaction was to tell the rest of this huge organization that their subordinate leaders must fit their team structures into the four leadership layers remaining. This was both unprofessional and impossible but it protected the "brothers in law" at the top of the organization. This organization already had one of the worst engagement scores we had ever seen. That was not a surprise to us given our insight but the consultant solution was a potential disaster. When my colleague pointed out to one director that her structure was the worst he had ever seen she took umbrage, complained to her boss who summoned my colleague to explain himself. Which he did with a vengeance pointing out it would be more professional if the manager in question took her accountability more seriously.

Effective organization design is like building the Sydney harbour bridge, where the work started on each side of the harbour, meeting in the middle. Similarly good organization design "meets in the middle." The top two layers are aligned to strategy and then the edifice is built up from the customer interface. As can be seen, the design blueprint is tailored according to the total levels of accountability known to be available. Once that is known it is relatively straight forward to resolve the horizontal design issues.

4.7.3 Orchestrating the Horizontal Linkages

As I have pointed out, the horizontal element of any structure needs to be in balanced and in sync with its vertical needs. Clearly if an organization is over layered, that disrupts its lateral information linkages. Networks are dislocated as people are invariably dealing with colleagues at differing levels of accountability who therefore do not have *equally relevant authorities,* when it would be easier and smoother if they were all in the same plane. A common manifestation of this is multi-layered decision meetings, which should have only one layer higher than the regular attendants: the decision maker. When people are not clear who can decide what, meetings get over layered as a form of insurance. The outcome is typically inertia or confusion or a combination of both. More information is needed, more time is requested, deadlines slip, and discipline and efficiency tend to suffer which in turn feeds more meetings'.

There is a whole industry around trying to clarify these ambiguities. The focus is on identifying who needs to be involved and who can decide what. One popular method used is, RACI (responsible, accountable, consult, inform). RACI is generally associated with Galbraith, but his "A" was "approve". Galbraith says he was working at Boeing during the late 1960s in Seattle in their commercial airline division, which was struggling to make a programme-function matrix work, when a local consulting firm introduced him to the idea of RACI charts.[19] I am told most other languages do not have two words (responsibility and accountability) for the same concept in an organizational setting. Thus they find it distinctly unhelpful and confusing as they don't see a real conceptual distinction. I favour DICE (identify who decides, needs to be informed, consulted and who executes.) The main value is to get all the concerned participants who work in a lateral linkage across a section, department, function or total organization in a room and work the issues with all the key players and thrash out a working agreement. In the top layers of a multinational

---

[19] *Designing Matrix Organizations that Actually Work* (2008) pp236–38.

this process could take a good 3 days with the key players in the same room, to achieve both clarity and agreement.

The fact that I have not written a lot on the horizontal dimension of organization architecture is not to suggest it is unimportant. There are two reasons for this "neglect". Firstly because there is no shortage of material on processes and operating models that are key lateral elements helping to explain how organizations work. Secondly, they are usually treated in isolation as if they provide "the answer" to effective organization design. This is a heresy I am aiming to redress. The horizontal and vertical axes of organization structure need to be balanced, otherwise one can be overly emphasised to the detriment of the other. Equally, it is important to note that it is the vertical axis that drives organizational effectiveness not the horizontal one. Conducting countless "DICE" exercises will not deliver traction in an organization with a broken spine of accountability. This is the reason why my focus is relentlessly on the vertical requirements of sound organization design. This is also the shortcoming of focusing only on the span of control.

In order to achieve organizational equilibrium both the horizontal and vertical axes need to be balanced against each other. It is therefore important to have a mental reference frame against which the chosen architecture can be analysed and critiqued: such as levels of accountability for the vertical and DICE for the horizontal. This will help ensure the structure is both tightly aligned to the strategy and motivating for those working in the organization.

4.7.3.1 Horizontal Overload in a Large Local Authority

Not so long ago we were working with a very large Local Authority. The Head of Social Services was under pressure to save money. He decided to halve the number of District Managers across his large geography and asked us to help show how this could work. We studied the districts, from the front line focusing on the case load burden of the respective social workers and determined the key ratio was the number of cases that a front line social worker could meaningfully cope with. That in turn dictated the number of cases that could be safely managed by a District Manager linked to specific geography and the staff needed in a single district and therefore the number of direct reports that a WL 2 District Manager could manage. For example if a social worker could handle up to 25 cases, the tipping point for a district manager turned out to be around 1000 cases, with appropriate direct report supervisors. That then guided to total number of staff, including support roles, for a given district. We illustrated that a move from 12 District Managers to 6 would have a potentially disastrous impact upon the organization's provision of social care and were therefore able to provide better alternatives.

This was a good case of the needs of the horizontal axis needing to be balanced with those of the vertical axis. It was also further evidence of the danger of top management working back from the desired budget outcome as a criterion for effective organization design.

4.8 What Distorts the Structures of Civilian Organizations?

Military organizations have ensured there are no redundant roles in the design of the officer command structure from the layer of company commander. It is fair to assume this has grown from the practical demands of battle when each officer needed physical line of sight to his troops and his superior officer. Although von Moltke (also known for his powerful telescope) recognised this was a particular challenge to be overcome the larger the army became, he saw the answer in terms of better behaviour and communication orchestrated via better training.

4.8.1 The Problem of Grade-Driven Structures in Civilian Organizations

Most civilian organizations have a system of grades needed to help establish fair and equitable pay. They are typically underpinned by job evaluation schemes. Thomas Paterson pointed out over 40 years ago: "Job evaluation is mainly concerned with reward and, in particular, with differential reward."[20] He explained that the grades are usually underpinned by a factor rating methodology expressed in points and that there are six different generic approaches to grading jobs:(p. 41ff), plus of course, a seventh: the Paterson method. So job evaluation systems invariably calibrate jobs in points. These points are derived on a quantitative basis driven by factors such as size of revenue, budgets and assets, and the number of subordinate staff. The bigger these are the higher the points. They do not focus on or calibrate the quality of decisions needed but rather the quantity of resources proximate to the job. I have seen a case where a company decided to have its store managers run three stores not one. It was a clear cost saving and the job evaluation points were increased by the new factors covering more sales, people etc, so the remaining store managers were happy as their grades were increased. But adding a WL 2 job to a WL 2 job does not guarantee WL 3, because the quality of the decisions has not changed. (This fact can also highlight unwise organization design plans, as in this case, where the initiative failed and the company returned to having one manager per store. It is always risky to break the key OD principle of single point accountability.) Hence they have great difficulty "adding up" and "sizing" the worth of specialist jobs, such as a research scientist with few or no subordinates and a tiny budget. They then resort to averaging the factors! See Chap. 5 for an example of assessing three jobs the same echelon across the services, with different financial ratios.

[20] Paterson T. T. (1972) *Job Evaluation*, p.126.

Grading systems have moved into and undermined organization design and leadership development in civilian organizations, for which they were neither designed nor intended.

Grading systems undermine organization design as follows. The quickest way to get more points in a grading system is to *insert another layer in the hierarchy*. This way you will inevitably have more staff and therefore a bigger budget. These factors drive up the job evaluation points, which results in the higher grade with new fringe benefits, for example. In reality this means the job evaluation/grading system ends up driving organization design. Grading systems are fundamentally blind to the demands of organization design. Job evaluation enthusiasts challenge this but have never been able to explain why every large organization I have consulted to or worked in, which had a grading system based on a points rating approach, has always been markedly over-layered.

Grading systems are notoriously prone to cost and grade drift—I give a detailed example in Chap. 9. They are not genuinely objective or scientifically reliable, despite the cosmetic points rating systems and are too often prey to internal politics. For example the top manager who insists grade x must be upgraded to y and has the power to make it happen. Often examples of faulty grading occurs when organizations decide what pay they wish to offer an individual (especially one recruited from ‘outside’) and then look for the grade that provides the right money answer, since grades usually have a corresponding money range. This is often the case with unclear distinctions between line and staff jobs, even though Taylor noted that difference in civilian organizations as early as 1911 in his book, *Shop Management*. Thus the disease of grade to grade reporting creeps into the organization, spawning more layers. In theory it should not happen but I run into it all the time. This over layering silts up the structure with hollow or pseudo jobs, wasting both talent and money. Too often 12 grades result in 12 layers as invariably the philosophy is: “every grade = a layer.”

Work Levels applied appropriately are not prone to vertical inflation like grades. If my boss is in Level 3 I cannot also move into that level and report to that person as that would be compression. The only option would be to create another Level 3 job in parallel to the boss’ job. This could lead to cost inflation but it is much easier to detect and challenge as a ruse to get round the discipline of Levels. But if there are 15 grades what logic stops me moving from “grade 10 to grade 11” if my boss has enough clout? The evidence repeatedly suggests “nothing inherent to the job evaluation system” stops this upward drift.

Grading systems also eviscerate true leadership development because people start to plot their personal development in terms of the grades into which they are moved. These are usually only *administrative promotions* or changes in a label. They do not reliably map changes in accountability, which would signal a real promotion. But these “grade promotions” invariably include an increase in pay and sometimes new fringe benefits or larger bonuses as well; hence they are keenly sought after. They also suggest "progress up the career ladder" is being made so they are doubly popular. Now if people are being promoted into hollow jobs without distinct and discrete decision rights they are inevitably working in someone else's decision space. This is de-motivating and dissatisfying especially for those who are talented.

Put simply, civilian organizations are not clear about the distinction between their layers and different purposes of organization design and reward hence their systems have become muddled. In the military officers of a given rank are generally paid the same. A 4 star general is usually paid about 5 times that of a 2nd lieutenant. In civilian organizations that ratio could be 500 to 1. I don't know of any justification for such pay ratios—certainly not the spurious one of "the market". It can be seen immediately that if grades are unreliable they are not helpful in assessing a true market value. (Most market surveys are not worth the paper they are written on, but that is another story.) Unlike the military, civilian organizations have tended to use grading and pay systems as the currency for leadership development and organization design. On that basis the military would have 19 layers of leadership and the three services would be structurally constipated and unlikely to fire a bullet in anger. The implications for leadership development and career planning are dire.

So when grades add unnecessary layers to the management hierarchy they are undermining both the effectiveness of the organization design plus the leadership development and career planning within the organization.

4.8.2 The Identification of Clear Accountability Is the Key

In order to overcome the problem outlined in 8.1, the following steps are suggested.

Step 1 Given the current strategy, identify how many levels of accountability should exist in a particular organization.

Step 2 Calibrate the exact number of layers of leadership that are then required. This is based on **the golden rule**: "*There is decision space for only one layer of leadership within each level of accountability.*"

Step 3 Rectify the muddled structure (either over-layered or under-layered – see examples in Figs. 4.2 and 4.4) to ensure it is healthy.

I have now worked in about 70 different organizations:

- At the outset not one of them knew how many levels of accountability existed in their organization
- Therefore, not one of them had a totally correct alignment between accountability and hierarchical layers across the entire organization.

Unclear accountability is the great scandal of twenty-first century civilian organizations: i.e. not just banks!

4.8.3 The Probe Process

A Probe is a process whereby a series of interviews is conducted along a spine of accountability, starting at the front line (the most junior role). Usually a number of Probes have to be conducted, depending on the size and complexity of the organization, to establish the top Work Level in the respective departments and therefore those of the CEO's direct reports, which in turn establishes the WL of the CEO.

The typical output of an individual Probe covers a great number of issues, one of which is s diagram along the lines of that set out in Fig. 4.2. A Probe is a series of interviews conducted along a reporting chain or spine of accountability from the most junior role holder to the most senior. The jobs are assessed against the seven DMA Elements (see Chap. 8) in order to identify their level of accountability or Work Level.

In this example below it identifies a severely compressed department with duplication of accountabilities in Levels 1, 2, 3 and 4. A significant number of these jobs are not adding value in this department. Unravelling this confusion and overlapping decision rights is not a task for an inexperienced OD interviewer.

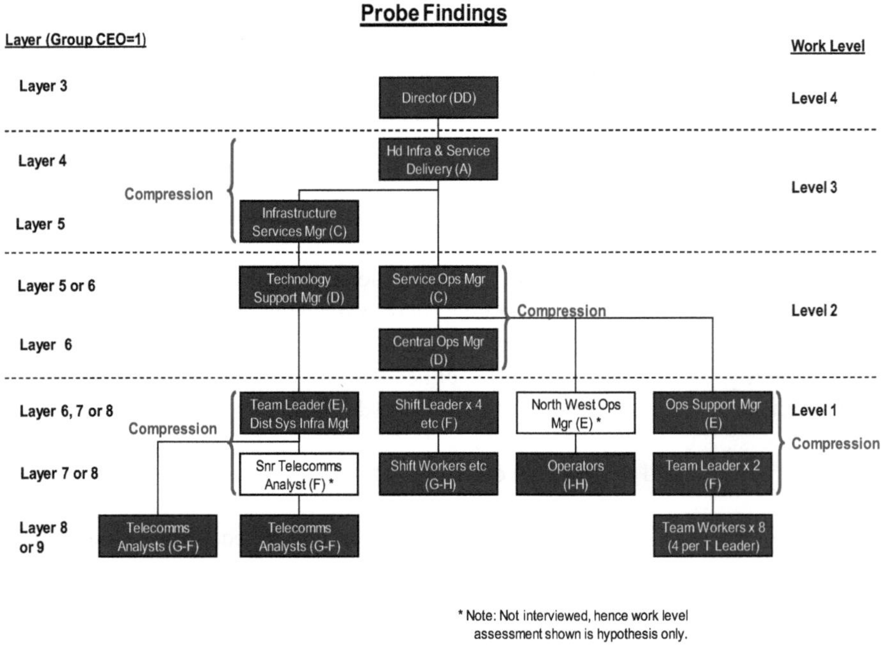

Fig. 4.2 Probe of a department in a bank

Implementing the appropriate change is not straightforward as the roles needed in the new structure need to be re-defined to reflect the different levels of accountability and the respective DMA Elements.

Given this fieldwork, recommendations would be made as to how the department should be re-structured to align jobs with the identified levels of accountability. Not surprisingly regulators struggle to get on top of these issues and seem to be still over reliant on grading systems. This does not help identify best organization design practice added to which they don't have statistically valid and reliable methods of establishing fair pay for bank executives. Some bank CEOs continue to witter on about the need to pay "the market rate for talent". What market rate? How measured? What talent? What has happened to the need for performance? This is an insidious development, where "performance" has been placed on the back burner.

As can be seen Fig. 4.2 is a heavy structure with four cases of compression across Levels 1, 2 and 3. In Level 1 a layer of supervisory leadership could be removed as there was no difference in the accountability and therefore the decision rights of the two layers even though given different titles such as Team Leader and Operations Support Manager, for example even though they have different grades: G to E. Similarly the two compressed roles in Level 2 (grades D and C) are not both required in the line, since neither was a job based solely on expertise. The same logic applied in Level 3 where layers 4 and 5 overlapped in the same line decision space. And note grade C is in both Level 2 and Level 3! Now how could that be? And what happened to grade B in Level 3 as we jump to grade A for some reason. Clearly these jobs did not both have discrete decision rights, despite having different grades, hence both were not required.

When there is a pronounced lack of decision rights in a given area or function I have found it useful to set that out pictorially in a Decision Matrix. To ensure anonymity the job titles have been omitted and the grades changed. Logically every management decision box should have a black √ with no red Xs. See Fig. 4.3 below. (This is a different organization to that shown in Fig. 4.2.)

Sometimes a department is lacking a layer of hierarchy. This is not so common and is more difficult to identify. Figure 4.4 provides an example.

In this case the bank had been under pressure at the onset of the financial crisis in 2008. It had to cut costs so it slashed the number of jobs in the IT department. This illustrates the danger of the accountant's cost drive moving into the OD manager's space. The reductions went too far and cut into the muscle of the department. To make matters even worse in this case the bank's strategic aim was to attract more customers to its on-line services. A sound strategy totally undermined, by unguided cost cutting resulting in bad organization design. The Head of IT was constantly dragged down a level of accountability to sort out operational problems. The strategic work suffered. And worse, the post of COO, filled by a previous marketing generalist, was not adding value to this department, based on our findings.

Grade	Resources				Budget		To Make Change to		
	People Accountability	Direct Reports	Appraisals & Ratings of Reports	Selection of Reports	People	Finance	Process	Structure	People
A	0	0	n/a	n/a	X	X	X	X	X
B	10	10	√	X	X	X	X	X	X
C	c100	10	√	X	X	X	X	X	X
D	c170	8	√	X	X	X	X	X	X
E	c500[4]	4	√	√	X	£38k	X	X	√
F	c2,200	9	√	√	X	£350k	X	X	√
G	c8,000	6	√	√	£195m	£5m	√	X	√
H	c11,500	7	√	√	£232m	£8m	√	√	√
I	c10,500	6	√	√	£244m	£6m	√	√	√

Fig. 4.3 Decision rights in a customer centre and above

Two things needed to happen in this organization: the MD IT needed to report to the CEO and the gap in Level 3 needed to be filled. Thus one job needed to be added and the reporting line to the CEO refined. There were also cases of one over one reporting on the spine of accountability, which in my experience is rarely if ever effective. One over one at the end of a spine can be effective *if there is work for both incumbents.*

The next task would be to design a target organization based on the department's mission and essential business 'givens' calibrated against the three levels of accountability available, refined by a rigorous assessment to establish more realistic spans of control. Each of the new jobs would need a one page definition of its key accountabilities. This would be a major undertaking in a department, which is now crucial to helping to deliver the new customer strategy but whose present structure is not fit for purpose. Unless such a review of the structure was undertaken, the strategy would be holed below the water line before it was announced.

4.8.4 Ten Typical Shortcomings

This case study outlined in Figs. 4.2 and 4.4 identified ten major shortcomings stemming directly from the unhealthy structure that was in part both over layered and under layered in different parts of the bank.

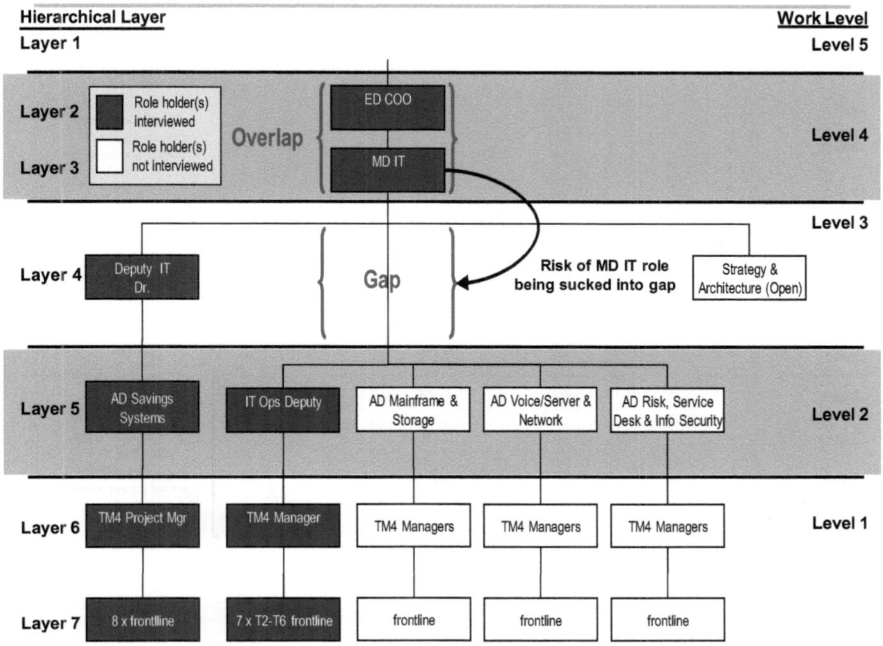

Fig. 4.4 A Gap in IT

- There were 11 layers of employees where only 6 are justified
- There were two management layers too many across the organisation.
- There were too many layers of supervision in most departments
- Average spans of control were too low (4.9 overall)
- There was a plethora of job titles in management, aligned to similar layers, which fed the over-layering
- The job evaluation system was suboptimal (with ~20 grades), which in turn drove the over-layering
- The 'competencies system' was also suboptimal and did not distinguish reliably between performance and potential
- Management budget accountability was lacking in too many management jobs and therefore financial disciplines were weak
- Management accountability for people and performance was not clear
- Middle management needed to have sharper focus on continuous improvement, change and productivity. At the time unclear accountabilities meant they did not always own the levers of change.

When identifying the number of accountability Levels the next task is to extrapolate the findings from this field work to the total organization. The field

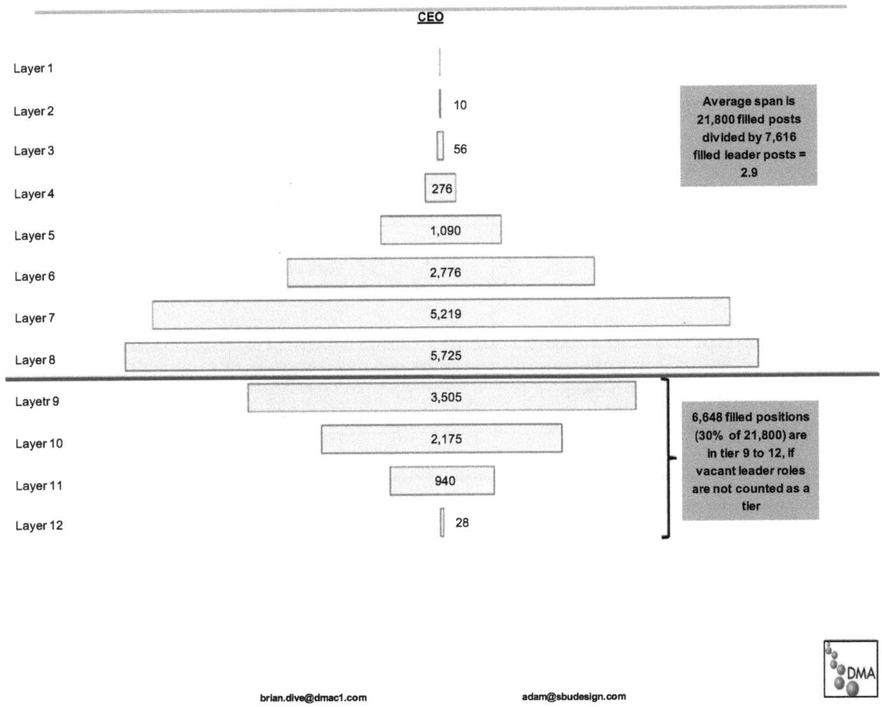

Fig. 4.5 An example of 12 layers from a Leader in layer 1 with an average span of only 2.9! across ~22,000 employees

work enables us to get a fix on the top role in the organization, i.e. its level of accountability. Once the level of the CEO is established we are in a position to show, in macro terms, whether the total organization is over layered and if so, to what degree. This is done by the application of specially designed software programme.

This approach can then flesh out the implications of the *golden rule that there is scope for only one layer of leadership per level of accountability.*

The result of the initial Probes in another organization summarised in Fig. 4.5, show it had seven levels of accountability but far too many layers of "management." There were many areas where there were more than eight layers, as the red line highlighted. Thus the red line is indicating where the Rubicon of healthiness resides. Jobs below the red line suggest too much hierarchy is involved. *It does NOT mean that jobs below the red line are at risk. These are usually the jobs doing the real work, which means the problem is above them.*

It is self evident there are significant problems between layers 6 and 9 of the management structure but the analysis thus far does not reveal precisely which jobs are hollow and lacking distinct decision rights. The most encouraging reaction we find is line management take to this process and content very quickly. They find it "easy" to understand. So, once the structure platform is robust we can address how to develop the leaders who can perform in the challenging roles, which will be the focus of the next chapter.

Clear accountability with appropriate authority is the pre-requisite for effective organization design. It is also the basis of building trust in an organization and the platform for leadership development.

Some questions to ponder.

1. How many levels of accountability exist in your organization?
2. Does it therefore have too few or too many layers: where are the pinch- points?
3. Are the number of layers and average spans in balance: if not, where is the problem and how can it be solved?
4. If good people have underperformed in a new job how much was due to the person, the accountability of the job and/or the structure?

Mission Mastery: Pillar 3—Leadership 5

Instead of assuming that leaders are mostly born not made – an assumption Ron Heifetz claims 'fosters both self-delusion and irresponsibility' – I start with the assertion that executive leaders are both born and made, but mostly made, based on a significant amount of research showing that executives do learn, grow and change over time.
Morgan McCall
McCall M W Jnr (1998). *High Fliers: Developing the next generation of leaders*. P4

5.1 General

Leadership development needs to align two tectonic plates that are inherently prone to shift out of kilter. The two plates in question are the job and the person: accountability and capability. When they are aligned and in sync personal growth can occur. The problem is, if this relationship is not understood, they are apt to rub up against each other leading to disruptive outcomes for both the person and the organization. The accountability plate can be stabilised. But capability is inherently unstable because it is the more likely to grow and change over time. *The fundamental challenge of leadership development is matching the moving capability of an individual to the appropriate accountability plate at a point in time*. It is vital therefore to have a valid and reliable way of assessing both plates simultaneously. But if *both are in flux* individual development is akin to a game of roulette, reduced to guesswork. This chapter will show that the military seem to have the better grip on this challenge. Their battle echelons are stable and their approach to matching

(continued)

B. Dive, *Mission Mastery*, Management for Professionals,
DOI 10.1007/978-3-319-25223-0_5

personal capacity and accountability is road tested and reliable. In many civilian organizations *both plates continue to move and are rarely dynamically synchronised.* Generally a lot of effort (and money) goes into building capability but not into building an appropriate organization design. The bonzai oak tree does not grow to its full height because its roots are restricted by the tiny box in which it is placed. Similarly, hierarchy heavy organizations produce stunted bonzai managers. "*A bonsai manager is one whose growth has not run its course, as he has not been able to draw sustenance from his natural environment. As a result bonsai managers are not able to work at the top of their potential*"[1] Elsewhere in his excellent book Gopalakrishnan defines the stunted manager as one who is "*Operating and working at a level which is well below his potential.*"[2]

5.2 Leadership Is More than the Person at the Top

Now we are into the heartland of this book: leadership development. It is surprisingly a problem for many civilian organizations but less so in military organizations as will be shown in this chapter. The challenge continues to be underestimated. Consider just one example. In 2004 a struggling Marks & Spencer's appointed a new CEO. Much was made of how he would reverse the share slide, revitalise the company's leadership and develop his successor from within while improving overall performance. When he stepped down in 2010 his successor was the third external CEO appointment in a row: i.e. no internal successor had been developed and during his tenure, the company's share price had moved from 315 pence in 10.06.04 to 314 pence in 10.06.10. M&S was once the no. 1 retail company in the UK. Why couldn't it produce the top leaders it needed?

Strategy on its own, even if appropriate, does not produce leaders. Faulty organization design hampers the development of people.

I had noted on an assignment in the company during 2003 that the key ingredients for successful leadership development were not aligned. The strategy was being questioned. The company had suboptimal structures in key areas of the business and had broad banded pay not accountability. As a result it predictably lost control of some critical costs. The approach to the assessment of capability and potential was unreliable, not helped by the presence of hollow jobs. HR leadership did not seem to have overcome the legacy of a bullying culture, which was an

[1] Gopalakrishnan R (2007) *The case of the Bonzai manager: Lessons from Nature on growing* p.xi.
[2] Ibid: p.53.

overhang from the 1990s, described in *The Rise and Fall of Marks and Spencer* (2002) by J. Bevan. As events proved, this challenge needed much more than a short term fix notwithstanding the claims of a flamboyant CEO whose time at the helm was accompanied by a revolving door of top talent. Both tectonic plates were constantly in motion. There is more to leadership development than smoke and mirrors.

McCall and Hollenbeck's work on the development of international executives concluded:

> *Challenging experiences force people to learn new things: bland experiences don't.*[3]

Hierarchy heavy organizations spawn hollow jobs. A hollow job lacks clear accountability and is therefore "a bland experience". It is the inherent danger in the current fashion for "agile organizations" where everything is "fluid" and tends to foster a chaotic approach to growth and learning. You cannot fail in a hollow job but you cannot succeed either. As Kessler and Kates pointed out,

> *Organization design is an opportunity to grow leaders. Don't organize around people but define roles that will stretch and grow talent. Design is a leadership responsibility – not a consensus activity. Design decision making should not be delegated.*[4]

In short, good leadership development calls for a series of taxing experiences that enable individuals to learn and grow and, in some cases, demonstrate potential for *effective future leadership* at an even higher level of accountability.

5.2.1 Leadership Development Models Have Changed, Haven't They?

There is today a belief that the need for and the methods of, leadership development have fundamentally changed in the twenty-first century. This is because it is felt people no longer have a job for life and therefore thoughts about 'growing up' in one organization are no longer relevant or even possible. Thus why bother studying the military whose leadership model is out of date since it presupposes a life time career mostly in one organization. Added to which there is plenty of evidence of large civilian organizations that lack vitality, feeding the image of the 'bureaucratic monster'. In 2014 The Economist noted "Too many civil servants, especially in Continental Europe, swirl around a bureaucratic Gormenghast but rarely leave it. Nearly four fifths of German senior public servants have been in public administration for more than two decades. The French state, under Hollande, is governed by a caste of unsackable functionaries, resistant to change."[5]

---

[3] *The Lessons of International Experience: Developing Global Executives* (2002), p.10.

[4] *Leading Organization Design,* (2010) p.7.

[5] Mandarin Lessons, *The Economist*: 09.08.14.

Since ~2000 and the onset of the Internet there has been a veritable explosion of small, fast moving, innovative, entrepreneurial companies in a number of countries. They tend to be knowledge rich enterprises that have a high front line that require flatter hierarchies. Their vibrancy and competitiveness is one reason why the aftermath of the GFC did not reach the depths of the Great Depression's unemployment. But even so, Bill Gates started with one work station and Sam Walton with one shop. A quick glance at the Fortune 500 over the last 5 years reveals even those new organizations are not getting smaller. The five largest companies I have worked with since 2000 have a combined total of around 3 million employees. The need for good distributive leadership persists.

Today people generally change jobs more frequently than their parents (who did not necessarily have jobs for life) as companies disappear and/or are gobbled up by competitors or capitalist predators. But those who reach top leadership positions of large organizations, whether in the private or public sector, invariably spend substantial periods with one or two organizations or federation of organizations along the way. This has been noted for leaders in international companies as McCall and Hollenbeck's research (2002) illustrates. Some, such as GE, Procter & Gamble, have a reputation for building leaders that move on to other companies, depending on how their own prospects play out in the mother ship. The best organizations accept this is a by-product of good leadership development programmes. Good military officers similarly relocate into the civilian world with consistent ease. While some people are less mobile than in the past, with more married spouses running their own business or a in a national profession such as legal militating against international transfer, it is also noticeable today that more and more people are like a young Thai woman whom I met recently, who travelled to study at UCLA and then took her first job in Brazil. Models and assumptions about expatriation (even the word's meaning) are constantly being re-invented.

Today the person wishing to develop over the lifetime of their career faces two potential imposters: working in the same organization for life or working for many different organizations. The option of staying in the one organization makes it easier in principle to recognise those jobs that genuinely offer a positive new challenge and personal development. The risk is loyalty and progress may be over ruled by the 'political' prejudice of the day as the 'newly beatified' are advanced in one's stead. Thus one's progress may be unfairly disrupted, indicating it might be time to leave the meaningless Gormenghast. The advantage of moving to more than one organization means these tactical blockages can be avoided. But assessing the real accountability of a new role in a different organization is more difficult. It may not be the step up one thinks and with few reliable benchmarks the possibility of making a wrong choice is potentially more likely. In short the development risks of both career patterns are not insignificant. Given the widespread absence of sound accountable roles and reliable assessment of individual performance *and potential* in many civilian organizations this decision is fraught with error.

But the principles of leadership development are, I would argue, constant. If you accept that leaders are born and made, but mostly made, then it seems to me you cannot escape the inevitability that they need an orchestrated set of experiences, (what I refer to below as boundary moves) which enable them to *learn, grow and develop* ***as leaders***. The fundamentals of this development process are a job with clear purpose, real accountability and learning support, which provide the stretch that continues to take a talented person outside their comfort zone but not outside their learning zone *at the appropriate time*. And of course, personal choice and circumstances will govern when, where and whether someone will choose to seek that experience.

It is a subjective call for an individual to decide when and how often to change companies in pursuit of that personal growth development equation. In practice many personal questions come into play: what job, which organization, what sort of colleagues, how can I learn, when is the right time for the next challenge and where? The organizational dimension is no less complex. Is the organization's mission one I admire, is the job under review one with clear accountability in which I can make a difference both to the customer and my own growth, are the promotion stakes really based on merit, what is the organization' s record on learning and personal development, do those who leave prosper more than those who stay? Would the new job be a real promotion?

I have reasoned earlier that if an organization does not have a sound approach to organization design, building in real jobs fostering personal growth, then leadership development is probably a misnomer. In this chapter and the next I will highlight the importance of differentiating leadership competencies aligned to levels of accountability to facilitate that process. When these are lacking it is very difficult to impossible for a talented individual to learn, grow and develop other than in a haphazard manner.

If, as I am suggesting, it is already difficult enough to find a leading organization to work in that has these positive attributes, then dancing from employer to employer does not make the process easier: rather the converse. The argument in this book so far is, many civilian organizations fall short and/or lack some of the Pillars that underpin genuine leadership development and personal growth opportunities. Experience also suggests these opportunities for personal growth do not correlate with the best salary/bonus offerings, despite the siren calls from head-hunters or coaches with vested interests.

It is fine to be an advocate for a musical chairs career but the corollary is it does not make orchestrating growth as a leader in the twenty-first century any easier and in fact probably lengthens the odds against. This is because the underlying principles that govern how one learns, grows and develops as a leader, which is what these next two chapters are about, are not widely in evidence today. To quote an old sporting adage: form is temporary class is permanent. Leadership is a matter of class. Substance, not form is the issue. Once you understand the principles underlying the process it is easier to guide the desired outcome.

5.2.2 Followership

Mary Parker Follett was the first writer to emphasise the importance of the 'followers' for a good leader. If people do not want to be led they will not be led. Distributive leadership highlights this phenomenon. Leaders *in the organization* have to both lead and be led. This is manifest in the readiness to be led; the willingness to accept other leaders' decisions, understanding that one's role is to help implement these decisions, whether or not one totally agrees with them, provided they are not immoral, unethical or illegal instructions. This entails the ability to offer advice and opinion without perceiving this to be control of the decision or transfer of the authority: the ability to understand the leader's intent and then act accordingly, to conduct ones actions within it. It also means having the courage to speak truth to power: recall Moltke's ultimate test, to disobey an inappropriate order. In mission command terms this amounts to the ability of lower levels of leaders simultaneously leading and providing direction to their own team while at the same time performing as a member of their line manager's team. In essence this is the mission command process that aims to enshrine back-briefing.

Distributive leadership involves the recognition that, by definition, most leadership careers will plateau before reaching the top. Some individuals may then find themselves in too small a pond with too many big pike in it to reach their natural level but in the more fluid commercial world a move to a different firm should resolve this. In discussion with a high flying Air Force officer, he explained that he resigned at 42 since he could see the ratio of high potential officers to Air Vice Marshall roles available meant further progress was not guaranteed and that it was better to change careers sooner rather than later. In this case he had subsequently a very successful career in civil aviation.

Clearly the vast majority of leaders inevitably reach a natural ceiling that is likely to be due to intellectual capacity, level of technical knowhow, quality of interpersonal skills, personal ambition or any number of other factors. This in no way makes them lesser leaders and indeed they can often be better lower level leaders than those with more stratospheric potential moving up too quickly. The way the military have established the Warrant Officer role in the experiential training of young officers in their first posting is a good example. An experienced Sergeant will invariably be paid more than the young Lieutenant: something a civilian grading system would not institutionally allow. In fact Fukuyama maintains: "*NCOs in Germany have been entrusted with broader authority than their counterparts in France, Britain or the United States.*"[6]

Effective distributed leadership depends on having soundly designed appraisals of performance and potential. Mission command has it, Mission Mastery needs it.

[6] Fukuyama, F (1995) *Trust: the social virtues and the creation of prosperity* p.221.

Implementation is the key challenge, as it is with the Pillars of Mission and Organization Design, or in this case, *leadership development in action*. It seems the friction between policy and delivery in growing leaders is a pervasive problem in civilian organizations.

The evidence demonstrates there is no shortcut to good leadership development. This seems to be underestimated by ambitious CEOs at the helm of 'agile' civilian organizations. Learning leadership is a maturation process that takes time to nurture. The effects trap is a cadre of bonsai managers: those whose growth is stunted by a cluttered structure that does not afford sufficient space for them to grow to their full potential.

5.2.3 Two Lens of Leadership

There are two perspectives of the word *leadership*. On the one hand it refers to *a position* in an organization—a leadership position. On the other hand leadership refers to *a kind of performance*—behaving in a leader-like way. The two concepts are different and independent but should be totally integrated in a given situation. One can be in a leadership position but not behave as a leader and there can be people with leadership capability who are not in a leader role. Worst of all is the situation where the position does not really have clear leadership accountability despite a fancy title, which means the incumbent can't truly lead, irrespective of capability.

In this chapter I plan to summarise the different approaches to leadership development espoused by military and civilian organizations. The military focus on the individual in the context of a role with clear accountability. *They address both ends of the leadership equation: the matching of the position and the person.* By way of contrast civilian leadership theory tends to focus only on the individual. This may be because the academics that invariably are the sources of civilian leadership theory have not always experienced leadership in action. The context of the job and the clarity of its accountabilities tend to be overlooked consequently half the leadership equation is neglected. They are prone to fall into the strategic traps of too much irrelevant knowledge, combined with faulty alignment resulting in the wrong outcomes or effects.

5.2.4 Two Dimensions of Personality

Leadership development, like recruitment, is not a foolproof process. It is difficult and fraught with potential error. In short it is a sophisticated guestimate of future performance (as is potential assessment). Hogan (2007) has pointed out that personality consists of two qualities. One, known only to the self: (identity) and the other observable by others (reputation). Reputation concerns what you do:

identity why you do it.[7] Identity is the more important but remains inscrutable to the observer—and psychological tests. "*We can talk with knowledge about reputation, but our observations about another person's identity are speculative at best.*" This explains why leadership development is so difficult.

The military observe the unknowable *identity* in a job context where behaviour (*reputation*) can be assessed and via their experiential training (see next chapter) individuals are checked for character flaws/impairments that might surface in battle. In assessing reputation only, based on theories and personality tests, the civilian approach is less comprehensive and is therefore more prone to error. The psychopath shines in an interview situation. In order to overcome this shortcoming Hogan designed his test, The Hogan Development Survey (HDS) in 1997, which aims to detect whether any of 11 potential personality disorders might be present.

We saw in Chap. 2 how a CEO's ill conceived strategy bankrupted his bank. But the failure of CEOs is not simply a matter of the wrong strategy; it is invariably the outcome of a company's flawed assessment and leadership development process when the CEO is promoted from within. In theory the internal selection is easier and more reliable than the external one. Effective selection, leadership development and career planning play a critical role in the preparation of a successful CEO. Iain Martin's shredding of Fred Goodwin raises questions in this respect.[8] The evidence he presents strongly suggests Goodwin was over promoted. So how on earth did Goodwin get to become head of RBS? His was a promotion from within. His foibles should have been evident and well known.

It suggests RBS' HR leadership development and selection criteria (and the HR leadership?) were inadequate and did not recognise that their tectonic plates were misaligned.

When the bank was castigated on all fronts, especially for its culture of greed over bonuses, the HRD at the time tried to argue in *People Management* that it was not the fault of the HR department!

The spectacular crash of another bank CEO around the same time seemed to stem (perhaps unknowingly) from a flawed career path. He was a darling of his Alma Mater business school. He rose rapidly through the ranks in an international retail business. I had insight into that business and it would seem he reached Work Level 5 there, at best, but not the role of CEO. (I have shown elsewhere that overly rapid progress through WLs 3 and 5 correlates with lack of success in the top levels of accountability. See Chap. 6 for more detail on boundary moves.) He then was headhunted to become CEO of a WL 7 bank. So:

He moved to another industry and in addition skipped a level of accountability, which is known to be highly risky. He undertook three strategic boundary moves simultaneously, which is not recommended even for the most talented leaders.

---

[7] Hogan, R (2007) *Personality and the Fate of Organizations*, p.8.

[8] *Making it Happen Fred Goodwin, RBS and the men who blew up the British economy.(2013).*

When an organization does not know its levels of accountability this sort of "leadership development" mistake is easily made. I later interviewed someone who had been in this CEO's top team. It was clearly felt the leader in question did not fully understand the workings of the bank let alone the industry. His focus, having been a retailer, was on selling more and more mortgages, which just happened to be the basis for bonus payments! The rest is now sad history. It is hard to imagine IBM, Matsushita, Nestle, or Shell taking such a cavalier approach to the grooming and selection of one of their CEOs.

The key question here is: "What makes someone a successful leader and is it possible to develop those qualities in leaders at every layer in an organization?" The Corporal with a squad of 8 soldiers, the night shift supervisor with a team of 20, the production manager with a department of 150, the call centre manager with a staff of 1000, the Brigadier with a brigade of 3000, the country manager with 20,000, the Major General with 40,000, the European MD with 160,000 or the global CEO with 400,000, are all leaders across 8 levels of accountability. They are all held to account in roles that are fundamentally different. But Corporals do not typically become Generals or Heads of State, notwithstanding one notable exception: Hitler. (Napoleon was referred to at times as "The little corporal" but in reality he was commissioned as a second lieutenant in the La Fere regiment at the age of 16.)

5.2.5 Two Approaches to Leadership Development

We will now briefly examine and contrast the approaches to leadership development in military and civilian organizations. The first thing to note is that military wisdom comes very much from people who "have been there, done that." That is, from people who have been leaders in the field. Civilian leadership wisdom tends to be imparted mostly as academics' theories, rarely practised in the field by the propagators.

Yet both military and civilian writers share the same shortcoming. They both focus almost exclusively on leadership at the top of the organization. They rarely describe or even allude to distributive leadership. They tend to obsess with the leader *of* not the leader *in*. Yet self evidently most leaders are the latter not the former. And usually one needs to master the latter to succeed at the former. Learning how to do that is the recurring conundrum for leaders that are made.

5.3 The Military Perspective

> ***There is no such thing as a born leader. It is something you have to learn.***
> Recruiting slogan, Royal Military College Duntroon

The critical military question is: what makes a person successful in the art of command? Harper points out that a "*survey of military literature reveals considerable agreement on the essential qualities a commander must possess although there are differences of emphasis.*" [9] Clausewitz felt a 'great commander' needed to have a number of essential qualities.[10] This focus on "great" suggests Clausewitz and a number of the military sources quoted in this chapter are concerned primarily with THE commander—the 4 star general or field marshal. He singled out two qualities that he felt were of primary importance: courage and intelligence. Clausewitz cites two kinds of courage: physical courage or indifference to danger and moral courage. He saw intelligence as a prerequisite as one needed a "fine and penetrating mind" to think through the fog of war. He identified four factors present in war—danger, physical effort, uncertainty and chance. The latter three apply also in civilian situations, especially for a business in a competitive market. Competition is the civilian form of "friction". He believed "*a great force of mind and understanding is required to progress with safety and success against these opposing elements.*"

Moran saw courage in terms of "will-power", which tends to have its limits and can be burnt out.[11] He also described courage as a moral quality: "*It is not just a gift of nature like an aptitude for games. It is a cold choice between two alternatives.*" Wavell felt "robustness" was the first essential of leadership allied to courage. While physical courage is rarely needed in the civilian world there is a requirement for moral courage in leaders, a fibre which is too often lacking today. Take the example of Steve Jobs. A man, who cheated on his first business partner, initially denied paternity of his first child, closed the company's budget for charitable donations when as a billionaire he became CEO of Apple and who invariably parked his Mercedes in the disabled car park space close to the entrance of his office.[12]

One form of moral courage needed by leaders *in* an organization, as against the leader *of* the organization, is the ability to question and even challenge commands when they are felt to be tactically inappropriate or ethically wrong. Speaking up in a corrupt and wasteful organization like the European Union's bureaucracy takes courage. Bruno Wakefield reported in Brussels (06.11.12) "The EU's auditor failed to give a clean bill of health to £89 billion of spending "affected by material error." The EU Court of Auditors reported that controls over 86 % of the EU budget "last year were only partially effective." 2014 was similarly unimpressive. It is also disconcerting that in the lead up to the banking crisis so few risk managers had the moral fibre to speak up. One exception was Paul Moore, at HBOS who warned of reckless borrowing. Shortly after warning senior directors that the bank was lending a dangerous amount, he was dismissed by the CEO, James Crosby: the latter was later stripped of his knighthood but not before the bank had to be rescued by the taxpayer.

---

[9] Harper, G (2005) *Kippenberger*, p.15.

[10] Clausewitz, Carl von (1982) *On War* (1832), p 140.

[11] Moran, Lord (1945) *The Anatomy of Courage,* Constable, London.

[12] See The Daily Telegraph obituary Friday 7th October 2011.

A third factor mentioned by Fuller and others is good health. Arguably this is what Wavell had in mind when he talked of "robustness." Robustness seems to me to be closely related to the very topical quality of resilience, which allows individuals and organizations to perform consistently in times of unexpected or high demand. The ability to bounce back ensures continuity, gives a critical strategic advantage to the organization and helps protect the individuals it employs. Three key factors that contribute to resilience have been identified by John Bruce Jones of Stanton Marris: Resourcefulness, Connectedness and Cheerfulness. The last of these echoes the way that a positive mindset manifests itself in military contexts—a realistic optimism that fights negativity with every weapon including black humour.

Wavell and Dixon identify a fourth element—fighting spirit or the will to win.[13] Being proactive rather than just waiting for things to happen. Great leaders face their true test during a crisis such as defeat, where their true robustness can be assessed. Rommel was impressive under pressure unlike Montgomery who could be guilty of "puerile pride".[14] His behaviour was described by Hogan as one of the sources of likely mental derailment.[15] (More recently Beevor suggested Montgomery suffered from Asperger's syndrome, a form of autism which makes it difficult to enjoy normal social relationships and interactions.)[16]

Dixon felt that incompetence stemmed mostly from fear of failure which leads to paralysis in decision making and an overcautious approach—recall the knowledge trap in Chap. 2. Hopefully the person prone to freezing under pressure will be identified in rehearsal training. I provide an example in the next chapter of a bank manager who froze during an experiential learning case study when confronted with a totally unexpected change of events.

John Mulgan summarised a subordinate's view as well as anyone:

> *By this time I had seen enough of war to know that the first essential of command is competence. Personal charm, or savage discipline, or individual bravery are good things in their place at the right time, but men, I know now, would forgive any vices in a commander so long as he is capable.*[17]

Molke knew there would always be some element of risk in a leader's decisions. "*A commander who in each case offers directions, which are at least sensible, even if not optimal stands a good case of success*". His officers came to understand that an omission or failure to act was a graver charge than making a mistake in the choice of means based on the best information available. In his 1871 paper On Strategy he wrote:

[13] Dixon, N.F. (1994) *On the psychology of Military Incompetence.*

[14] Beevor A, (2014), *D Day The Battle for Normandy.* P.184.

[15] Op cit, p.125.

[16] The Times 23.05.15.

[17] Mulgan J, *Report on Experience* (1967) Blackwood and Janet Paul, Auckland.

> "*Whatever the vicissitudes of events, a commander will need to keep his mind fixed unwaveringly on his main objectives, but he can never be certain beforehand which paths offer the best hopes of realising them. Successive actions*[18] *do not follow a premeditated design but are acts of spontaneity guided by judgement…Making an accurate assessment of what you know, guessing what you do not know, reaching a conclusion* ***rapidly*** *(my emphasis), and then vigorously and unwaveringly following it through.*"

Dixon highlighted yet a fifth element of leadership. "*An ideal military leader is one who manages to combine task excellence with an equal flair for the social or heroic aspects of leadership. Such leaders combine extreme professionalism in the realising of military goals with a warm humanity, which earns them the lasting affection and loyalty of their men*".[19] This is a description of resilience or cheerfulness under pressure: maintaining a positive outlook and humour. This also reflects the ancient Chinese belief spelt out 1000 years ago that "*The essence of leadership is in winning people. The essence of winning people is in perceiving their feelings.*"[20] So, ability to win respect, affection and loyalty while maintaining a sense of humour is the fifth and final quality expected of a good leader.

That is the ideal: even so it is self evident that not all military commanders tick all the boxes, which is also the case with civilian leaders.

5.3.1 Summary of Military Leadership Qualities

The military consensus suggests five essential qualities are needed for a successful commander (leader):

- Courage, physical and moral
- Intelligence
- Good health, physical and mental
- Will to win
- Ability to instil genuine affection and loyalty.

A read-across to civilian organizations seems relevant. Physical courage is not often a key requirement in civilian organizations. Above average intelligence is needed from Level 4+ where an ability to think from first principles is most definitely a requirement of strategic accountability. A will to win may not be so critical in a public sector or not for profit organization. In those organizations it

[18] Molke said "acts of war" and "military judgement".

[19] Harper op cit.

[20] Cleary, T (1995) translator of *The Tao of Organization*, p.224.

would hopefully manifest itself as a "Will to provide winning, best in class, service." Finally the best civilian leaders are noted for instilling genuine affection and loyalty—e.g. Konosuke Matsushita.

5.4 Military Leadership Development

The military approach to leadership development is meticulous in content, process and job context. While the nature of activity, information and availability of weaponry at the front has dramatically changed the delivery of information and firepower in the digital age, the command structure is fundamentally the same. Training has radically altered the field officer's skill to manage new weaponry but accountability has remained constant. A captain still commands a platoon, a major a company and so on.

5.4.1 Officer Selection and Career Development

The basis of military leadership is founded on the training of officers who are prepared to enter the field at the cusp of what I refer to as Work Level 2.

Those thought to be potential officer material are put through a rigorous selection process followed by 'basic training' particularly in tactics and leadership. This can be a university graduate but not necessarily. And it is possible, although not common for someone to be selected from Other Ranks. This is a prolonged assessment in fact, which for the Army lasts 48 weeks and broadly similar times for the other services. It includes theoretical and practical assignments. The candidate enters the programme as a 2nd Lieutenant and if successful, passes out with the rank of Lieutenant and is assigned to a platoon. He (still usually he) is given accountability for leadership of the platoon but is in training and is expected to learn leadership from an experienced sergeant. Only a fool would ignore his mentor and would be seen to fail then and there. After 2 years from inception the officer should have become a captain. Progress to captain is effectively automatic subject to meeting the training requirements, themselves part of a prolonged selection process. Progress to major and above is not automatic.

Assignments (tours) tend to be 2 years duration and it would typically take at least three, more likely four, successful postings to be confirmed as a major. One at least of these tours would be "at the desk", i.e. in a support or "staff" role. This blending of line and staff accountabilities starts early and continues throughout an officer's career. The first explicit assessment based on performance in-role comes in the move from captain to major. It depends on an appraisal of performance in the field and assessment of potential ("merit") against clear guidelines. The services have a rigorous system for assessing potential via selection boards of more senior ranks, usually from outside the relevant unit. They rely on the performance appraisals by the relevant superior as *one* key input into the assessment. A high flier would typically reach major around age 32 and would be in charge of a company. (I have talked to those in the other services and found they follow a virtually identical pattern. E.g. a high flier in the Air Force said: "I progressed through these positions because I was assessed to be competent at each stage and if my potential assessment was positive the next step was always a "boundary" move. I was a Squadron Leader (Major) at age 32 and a Wing Commander (Lieutenant Colonel) at age 39.") They are likely to attend a junior staff college programme as part of their leadership development.

The military is much more thorough in the testing of its leaders than civilian organizations where they tend to rattle through Level 2 in a couple of years clamouring for "promotion", which helps explain why leadership tends to be brittle near the top of functions such as finance, IT, marketing and HR in the civilian world and recently in general management as mentioned in the Introduction. The leadership embedding process in the military is slower but arguably more thorough and comprehensive, developing greater resilience than in civilian counterparts. This is arguably because the consequences of poor leadership of the front line are more critical in the military. Ironically civilians can rocket through to the top echelons of their organizations, with inadequate preparation, where the consequences of inept leadership can also ruin many lives.

It would seem there is a bulge in WL 2 in the military while the new captains bed down on the cusp of WL 2, under the full Level 2 leader, the major. Strictly speaking this is over layering. The history seems to be that the military have to expect 'wastage' in battle and historically the 'life' of a junior officer in the field is prone to be very short as they are at the front with their men. For example of the 16 British officers killed in Afghanistan since 2001: 15 were captains. That may also explain the name, *lieutenant*, "holding in place of" or "standing ready". The step up guidelines are very clear in an emergency, which is what the lieutenants and captain are effectively learning: how to be a good Level 2 leader.

The next key job in the line of command (next WL up) is leadership of a battalion, the role of lieutenant colonel. After 4 years as an effective major, one then enters the formal promotion zone. This is an even more searching rigorous selection process of boards of senior officers who both focus *on the potential* of the candidates and know the likely future job requirements. They also have a detailed insight into relevant pipelines, many of which call increasingly for specialist knowhow and experience. Once again the major will have done at least 4 years in substantive rank before being eligible for promotion. At this rank and colonel, there are defined retirement ages (in the early 50s) to help facilitate promotions. This process is open and understood by officers who can also request career interviews, especially if they miss a selection board or a promotion they were chasing. (It also easy to see how clumsy cost cutting by politicians can shred these pipelines.) The potential Lieutenant Colonel is likely to attend a senior staff college course run on a tri-service basis (with international military and a few UK MoD Civil Servants among the student body) as part of the preparation for intended promotion.

It is interesting to consider the differences of various field/line/operational/command postings at the equivalent of Lt. Colonel that could occur across the services:

- Commander of a battalion or regiment (in the UK Army, these are partially interchangeable terms—e.g. battalion for infantry, regiment for cavalry) leading some 6–700 men with a discretionary budget of ~ £1.5 m. The staff cost would amount to ~ £16.5 m
- Commander of an Apache helicopter regiment with personnel strength of about 400, but with 18 helicopters at a capital cost of ~ £0.7 billion.
- Commander of an advanced Type 45 class of guided missile destroyer with a complement of 191 and a value of £1.05 billion for the platform alone.
- Commander of a Vanguard class nuclear submarine, with a crew of 135, with capacity to carry up to 16 missiles, each with 8 warheads so a total of 128 warheads. The value of the vessel/platform alone is in excess of £1.5 billion.

A civilian job evaluation scheme would internally haemorrhage trying to plot the relative importance of these four WL 3 roles because they do not evaluate accountabilities but place disproportionate weightings on financial values that then drive the "answer" and distort the spine of accountability.

The next level of command is one star (1*) General. The selection process is essentially the same. To recap: a Sub-Unit Command Board sits to select Majors for Company Command positions, a Major Unit Command Board sits to select Lieutenant Colonels for Battalion command and the selection process of individuals for 1* command is somewhat less rigid and formal—but it will ultimately be a decision for the 4* Chief of the General Staff (for Army 1* command positions) or his RN and RAF equivalents. In addition there is recommended attendance at the Higher Command Staff College, also run on a tri-service basis. The process becomes increasingly political at the top to the point where appointment to 4* needs approval by the prime minister. Some see that as "checks and balances," others as a slippery slope since PMs are not noted for their military leadership competence, Churchill's enthusiasm notwithstanding. So the key point is this: whatever the level sought, the leadership testing in the field and the selection assessment process for potential is stringent, clearly established and well proven. Few civilian organizations bear comparison.

It should be noted that the selection process does not allow for the skipping of a rank (in peacetime) even though given the line-staff demarcation there are sometimes more than one rank within a level of accountability – e.g. Lt Colonel and Colonel in the equivalent of WL 3 but not reporting one to the other.

This is a very short summary of a rigorous and consistently thorough process of leadership development aligned to accountability. I have interviewed a number of military "Whitehall warriors flying desks" in London who have all been rather impressive. That could not be said of all their civilian counterparts. The military approach to training, leadership assessment and career planning is robust, based on years of trial and error.

My field work with civilian organizations consistently suggests that even high potential leaders need two, ideally three, different postings—different learning experiences—in WL 3 and similarly in WL 5 for those who go on to succeed at WL 6+. This seems to be the proven basis of successful leadership development in the military.

5.5 The Civilian Perspective

Civilian writers and academics have also not written much about the "10,000 leading the 90,000"—*distributed leadership*, or the leadership required at every layer.

5.5.1 The False Leadership Dichotomy

There is a widespread tendency for 'leadership' to be separated from 'management' in the work of civilian writers, which is a false dichotomy. However the work of Jaques and Clements (1991) on "Executive leadership" is a notable exception to this trend although their work was primarily focussed on the military. This "distinction" was first aired in an article by Zaleznik in 1971 it seems and was later endorsed by Bennis and Nanus (1985),[21] Bennis (1989),[22] and Covey (1989),[23] arguing that 'Managers do things right: leaders do the right things'. This is really a misleading spin on Peter Drucker's original insight into the difference between effectiveness and efficiency spelled in *The Effective Executive,* 1967. Bennis describes the manager as one who 'administers, maintains, focuses on systems and control, has a short-term view, who asks how and when and focuses on the bottom line.' He sees a leader as someone who 'innovates, develops, focuses on people, inspires trust, asks why, and has a long-term view and an eye for the horizon.' This is described as the difference between "perspiration" and "inspiration" and so on. Both categories are leaders, perhaps operational versus strategic in WL terms. Charlton is another who lists pages of differences between "leaders & managers".[24] The assertion that 'leadership' and 'management' are oppositional concepts is misleading and

[21] Bennis W and Nanus B (1985) *Leaders the strategies for taking charge* with the strap line: "Managers do things right leaders do the right things."

[22] Bennis, W (1989), *On Becoming a Leader* p45.

[23] Covey, S (1989), *The Seven Habits of Highly Effective People* p101.

[24] Charlton, G (1993) *Leadership*, pp23–27.

unhelpful. The activities described now as 'management', now as 'leadership', are all, in fact, often carried out, at different times, by the same individual.

It seems to me that leadership and management are actually on the same conceptual continuum. They are simply towards different ends of that spectrum.

What some writers describe as 'management' seems to be poor leadership; and what they describe as 'leadership' is good management. Some leaders are good and some are not. To call the latter "managers" seems to be an intellectual cop out. I have found that in civilian organizations the distinctions between "manager", "leader" and "director" are too often confused, muddled and unhelpful. Sometimes their activities are not fundamentally different; notwithstanding different titles, but on other occasions they are and would therefore align to different levels of accountability. There is no consistency, unlike the military.

Bungay adds an additional nuance.[25] He seems to buy the Zaleznik thesis that managers and leaders are a different species. He states:

The director (one who commands) is detached, calculating and flexible
The manager is engaged, realistic and pragmatic
The leader is committed, passionate and determined

Depending on the leader's level of accountability he or she can (and should) be all of these things. It is not an either/or situation. Or putting that another way: the qualities of an effective leader are the same for an effective manager.

I am not convinced that Bungay's three descriptions are real distinctions. I certainly would be very wary of a leader who is only "committed, passionate and determined." Heaven knows where he or she might take me. He further suggests "*Directing is intellectual; managing is physical and leading is moral.*" [26] I think the distinctions he is driving at can be more firmly grounded by considering a leader's role in its context—its level of accountability.

It is the role that demands different types of leadership because the work required is different, calls for different types of decisions and, therefore, calls for differing capabilities and flexibility of style.

[25] Bungay S op cit. p216.

[26] Bungay S op cit. p228.

The military are generally better at recognising what is required, for example, of a 2* role and therefore whether an individual 1* general is ready for promotion. In most civilian organizations this is rarely as clear because the leadership roles are not well demarcated. An example of grade alignment confusion exists in the UK Civil Service, which some years ago aligned its grades to military ranks. The trouble is they seem to have moved over time such that the CS believes a Senior CS Grade 1 is the same as a one star general. Having interviewed over 50 SCS1s it is clear they are not in the same level of accountability despite the official "alignment". The nature of work or leadership required in operational levels of accountability (up to Level 3, e.g. a battalion commander in the field) are different in strategic Levels (Level 4 and above, e.g. 1* general +). The latter would fit into Bungay's "developing strategy, giving direction and building the organization", whereas the former (operational accountability at Levels 2 and 3) would align to his "resourcing, organizing and controlling" or what he refers to as "management".

At the outset of this chapter I listed a number of leaders' roles that were a likely spread from Level 1 to Level 8 (corporal to CEO of an organization with 300,000+ employees). Referring back to that list it is clear that the leadership brief for the corporal was likely to focus on the task and the team, whereas the battalion commander would be more into "resourcing, organizing and controlling" and the 4* general into "strategy development, building the organization and providing overall direction". If the person currently in the role of corporal moved up through the organization the more his accountabilities would be evolving in scope and complexity. But he would be expected to lead just as effectively in each of those situations.

5.5.2 Three Things Are Now Clear

- Firstly the foundation of effective leadership is an organization structure of clear accountability.
- Secondly leadership requires selecting a person with the requisite capability to match the relevant accountability
- Thirdly it takes time for an individual to learn, grow and demonstrate successful leadership across all the different levels of accountability, assuming they have potential to do so.

The civilian world lacks the consistency which is a feature of the military. This also explains why in civilian business units, "directors" seem to pop up in different levels of accountability, depending often on the national culture, custom and usage of language. These days, on Linked In for example, one can take an advertisement with a title, such as 'Managing Director' and, by studying the text, identify jobs that could be three Levels apart. In one global company I am familiar with, a WL 3 leader in the US is called a "director" but a "manager" in Europe. At WL 4 the US leader is a vice president but in Europe a director. Now if this company had not understood and determined that accountability was the driver of leadership development it could have got into a horrible mess as it moved its executives around the world as part of their leadership development. It would most likely have wasted both talent and money. Even more serious is the fact that the most prevalent leader in civilian organizations—the supervisor/team leader/front line manager—does not seem to even register on academic leadership radars. In the military the supervisor equivalent is the NCO sergeant/warrant officer, part of the rank system in Work Level 1.

5.6 Civilian Theories of Leadership

Zaleznik, Bennis and Bungay have over-complicated the complex issue of leadership in civilian organizations and are in danger of taking us down an Alice in Wonderland rabbit's burrow. The search is invariably for outstanding examples of leadership, leaders at the top of an organization who have stood out in their time above peers and competitors. The Harvard Business Review (2001) on *Breakthrough Leadership* is a classic case in point. Its review of ten leading books on leadership focuses only on the top jobs and various individuals who are either in or have occupied such jobs. The assumption seems to be that if you analyse the lives of top leaders in various walks of life somehow the formula for success inevitably emerges and it will be relevant to all of us.

This is all rather reminiscent of the now discredited trait theory of leadership that was in vogue shortly after the Second World War.

5.6.1 Charismatic Leadership

The original seed bed of charismatic leadership seems to be Thomas Carlyle's "great man" theory.[27] The most influential of these approaches was the charismatic leadership in the perfect bureaucracy mooted by Max Weber (1922). His ideas were later adapted to feed the transformational leadership school. The studies dealing with leaders of the community lead to a series of what Kakabadse and Kakabadse (1999) called "dichotomous leadership models". One of the first of these was the transactional/transformational model of leadership: Burns (1978), Nibly (1984), Bennis and Nanus (1985), Tichy and Devanna (1986), and Kaplan and Kaiser (2003).

Another approach is the 'leader as hero, the leader as tyrant, the leader as liberator, the leader as father figure' and so on—seemingly another mutation of Carlyle. Owain Franks noted over 10 years ago that the focus on the 'top dog' as charismatic leader now "*appears to be coming to an end*".[28] The approach lauding the 'super hero' has been holed below the waterline by the recent rogues' gallery of people from politics, the media, social services, business, banks, newspapers, the

[27] Carlyle, T (1840) "The Hero as Divinity" in: *Heroes and Hero-Worship.*

[28] Franks, O (2003) Introduction to, *Mastering Leadership,* FT/PWC, London.

police, and health. It seems no civilian field is immune. Sadly it illustrates the dangerous double edged sword of the so-called charismatic leader with a "strong" personality. If anything today the search is for the anti-hero.[29]

Jim Collins talks in *From Good to Great* of 'level 5 leadership' being "quiet, humble and modest." But Collins is writing only about the *style* of leadership at the top of the tree not accountability. Other "leaders of" theories included expectancy theory (Vroom), path-goal theory (House and Mitchell), and re-enforcement theory (Scott and Podsahoff). Robert Kogan (2007) believes that personality is the key to how leaders behave.[30] But even well equipped, balanced personalities struggle to make an impact when placed in an organizational vacuum. Bob Garratt is unequivocal: "*Overblown optimism and greed have led to the present dismal situation of the 'celebrity CEO"*. For him the answer is clear. It lies in better

- Accountability
- Probity (honesty)
- Transparency.

And he was writing *before* the global financial crisis![31]

One of the problems of focusing on companies led by charismatic leaders, as Peters and Waterman *In Search of Excellence* (1982) found, is explaining a little later why such leaders and their companies have a habit of subsequently losing their way. Finally it seems that charismatic leaders are notorious for not developing or choosing outstanding successors. I leave the last word on this aspect of leadership to Alistair Mant who realised that the more complex the job and its level of accountability the more "brainpower" was required to master it and lead others.

> *The hot issue in 'leadership studies' ought not to be personality or charisma or even vision – it ought to be the brainpower or the ability to handle complexity under pressure. This is so obvious to me, as a student of worldwide cock-up's and blunders, that I have difficulty in seeing how anybody could see things differently.*[32]

5.6.2 The Importance of the Situation, Contingency Theory and the Task

A refinement of earlier work, contingency theory, argues effective leadership varies according to 'the situation': but the situation is not precisely defined. Much of the leadership material we are reviewing here is concerned with the Anglo-Saxon world—especially America. This might in itself be taken as an objection to the

[29] Financial Times: 15/16 June 2013, p.17.

[30] Hogan, R (2007) *Personality and the Fate of Organizations.*

[31] Garratt, R (2003) *Thin on Top* p.3.

[32] Mant, A (1997) *Intelligent Leadership,* p282.

possibility of applying its findings elsewhere—would not the 'situations' examined be too specific to a particular culture? In my experience cultural differences can be unduly exaggerated. The need for accountable leadership is universal as various ancient Eastern writers, such as Tzu (on military, 500 BC) and Cheng Yi (civilian eleventh century AD) noted long ago—for more detail on Cheny Yi also known as Ch'eng I, see Chap. 8. The Chinese maintained a civil service selected on merit (academic achievement) for almost 1500 years. It was set up by the Sui emperors (581–618) and effectively dismantled when the Qing dynasty was overthrown in 1911. This idea of selection on merit finally started to seep into parts of the Western European psyche in the mid nineteenth century. An early example in that context is Northcote and Trevelyan's report on the British Civil Service instigated by Gladstone in 1853, which advocated selection on merit.

Blake and Mouton introduced a leadership model ("the grid") that was bi-polar in that they stressed the importance of balancing task and people.[33] The various leadership styles were expressed numerically. Thus someone who was task obsessed would be categorized as a "9/1" leader and someone who was highly people sensitive was "1/9". Fielder seemed to like this approach.

Reddin[34] felt this was inadequate since it ignored the situation, the third dimension, which he saw as the key to effectiveness. He accordingly designated his approach "3-D theory", which did attempt to take account of the situation. The 3 dimensions were: task, people and the situation, which when managed in balance was then seen as "effective". Thus, in Blake terms, Reddin argued sometimes it was 'right' to be 9/1 (an officer under fire, for example) and therefore 9/9 was not always the ideal leadership style. Hershey and Blanchard took this a stage further, adding an aspect of 'relational behaviour' that took the team more into account.

John Adair[35] focused on the variables of task, the individual and the group. His approach is called "Action Centred Leadership", which consisted of three key simultaneous challenges: achieving the assigned task, managing the team or group and managing the individual. Adair was working mostly with the military so effective structure was a given and therefore not commented upon.

More recently, Professor Andrew Furnham, the eminent business psychologist, has co-authored a book on leadership.[36] This surveys the sea of leadership, its currents and developments and proposes a helpfully simple model for leadership capabilities: Setting strategic direction, Building and sustaining relationships, Delivering Results. The intersections of these domains define other capabilities such as Planning and Organizing, Creating Alignment and Team working. These insights closely overlap with the ideas in the DMA Differentiating Competencies,

[33] Blake and Mouton (1964) *The Managerial Grid: The Key to Leadership Excellence.*

[34] Reddin, W (1970) *Managerial Effectiveness.*

[35] Adair, J (1979). *Action Centred Leadership.*

[36] Furnham A and Pendleton D (2012) *Leadership: All You Need To Know.*

touched on below, Sect. 8.4: as they see the key variables in leadership as strategy, operations and the interplay of personal ability. DMA sharpens these ideas by setting them in an accountable context.

All of which leads me to suggest that leadership theory is progressing to a point where what is important is the ability to lead in an assigned level of accountability that Moltke would see as one calling for a tactical, operational or strategic response, attuned to the relevant context or battle echelon.

5.6.3 Style Must Be Relevant to the Substance Required

These approaches all conceive of *the behaviour* that is appropriate in a given situation with a focus therefore on leadership *style*. It is an advance on earlier work but the contingency school is still incomplete. Even in 2015, as I wrote this book, McKinsey consultants were still advising that the key to "Decoding Leadership" was only a matter of the right behaviours, such as "being supportive, operating with a strong results orientation, seeking different perspectives and solving problems effectively." This is devalued currency.

If *"a primary purpose of an organization is to make decisions," it is important to identify the behaviour (decision making) and abilities that might be required at different levels of accountability.*[37]

In other words the level of accountability is the ultimate leadership contingency.

In reality, the behaviour and performance of a supervisory leader at the front line of an organisation would be quite different *in substance*, not just style, to that of a middle or top manager. Their basic accountabilities are fundamentally different and this calls for different types of decision-making and correspondingly different behaviour. It is theoretically conceivable that they could have the same leadership style given the culture and history of a given organization and their different positions (in different countries) but it is much more likely their styles and ways of working would need to be different. Managing applied research scientists in New York for example calls for a different approach to managing tea pluckers at Kericho in the Kenyan Highlands even though they were once in the same company, Unilever. This is because these managerial leaders are at different levels of accountability, based on the work being done at the front line.

I have found nothing in the extensive work of the various civilian writers on leadership which differentiates between the quality of work and the corresponding leadership required at different layers of accountability in an organization—other than Jaques and Clement.

[37] Kesler and Kates p.7.

This is the core weakness of civilian leadership theorists.

Their initial preoccupation was with looking for the "right way" to lead. Earlier theorists tended to be rather rigid and later researchers more flexible, as they recognized the importance of matching different leadership styles to different situations; and though it was an important refinement, it was not the complete answer.

They did not analyse the substance and type of leadership needed in different types of **accountable situations**, where more than the right style is needed.

The most widespread leadership challenge occurs as people take the helm at different levels of accountability throughout their career. Their personal growth needs to match this journey.

5.6.4 Summary of Civilian Leadership Qualities

The civilian approach also centred upon five different leadership qualities but not the same as those of military theorists:

- The traits of the leader
- The importance of the "task" (incompletely defined)
- The importance of the individual to be led
- The importance of the group
- The importance of the "situation" (incompletely defined)

But the basic conundrum remains.

These civilian theories do not explain how a leader in an over layered hierarchy of unclear accountability can be effective, let alone learn and grow as a leader. Indeed, the real worry is, the problem is invariably not recognised, giving rise to a jungle of bonsai managers.

5.7 Civilian Leadership Development

It would seem the Romans were the first to appreciate that the development of leadership was a qualitative, time consuming process. They recognised that the time dimension of leadership development depends on the clarity and accountability of the job. Hence, their guidelines about when the different levels of leadership (quaestorship etc) could be achieved." No one under the age of thirty could seek election to even the most junior magistracy." The related moves upwards were also time delineated.[38] An intriguing question is: "Had the Roman civilian government learned this from their military leaders?"

5.7.1 The Fundamental Challenge

Matching accountability and capability is the fundamental challenge in the growth and development of leaders because on the one hand, levels of accountability are stable while on the other, human capability is not. People can learn and grow. Large organizations might move up or down from say Level 7 over time depending on their circumstances and history. I have seen only one or two examples of this. But the consistency of accountabilities in Levels from 1 to 5 would not change fundamentally even in those situations.

Aligning and synchronising capability with accountability is the fundamental challenge of successful leadership development.

This alignment or matching challenge is the friction that undermines leadership development in civilian organizations. The focus has been invariably on the person to the detriment of the critical link with the accountability of the role. Not enough attention has been paid to the alignment of the two. Indeed more often than not civilian organizations are not able to make this match. This inevitably undermines Individual learning, growth and leadership development. When career planning is fundamentally erratic and haphazard it quickly becomes politicised—see Chap. 9.

The need to achieve alignment between an accountability level and the personal capability of an individual is the great challenge for civilian leadership development schemes in the twenty-first century.

When capability of the person and accountability of the role are misaligned, it causes personal stress. According to Csikszentmihalyi, when the two are matched, the person is 'in flow' or in a state of optimal psychological balance. But if the job is outside a person's level of competence—either too low or too high—this will generate stress.

It takes time to learn how to lead. It is also vital to identify the right learning steps, making the right moves at the right time. An example is the time it takes for women to reach the top of civilian organizations. In 2015, 5 % of the FTSE 100 CEOs were women, while 23.5 % of board members were women. These facts reflects the fact that the path to CEO is time dependent and is not a quality

[38] Holland, T (2003) *Rubicon: The triumph and tragedy of the Roman Empire*, p.103.

change that can be driven by quotas.[39] Fieldwork I have conducted over almost 50 years in more than 70 countries suggests many different jobs or boundary moves are needed to maximise personal growth of the most capable individuals. The best field work on this topic has been done by Morgan McCall and his colleagues.

There is no substitute for experience in roles with clear accountability, as the source of leaders' personal growth throughout ***a well designed organization****, especially for those who have the capability to reach the top echelons.*

5.7.2 Accelerated Development: Does It Really Work?

The so-called 'war for talent' is an idea that surfaced in 1997 but for which I have not seen any convincing field work. It remains high profile for three main reasons.

- Firstly too many civilian organizations do not have a robust organizational architecture.
- Secondly jobs with clear accountabilities are not present in sufficient numbers.
- Thirdly, crashing inexperienced people through a series of hollow jobs, devoid of discrete decision rights, is setting people up for at least frustration and at worst, failure.

This creates the impression that there is an everlasting shortage of talent. It is a myth borne on the back of poorly designed organizations. Accelerated development is considered today to be the answer. It will 'ensure' various minorities get more top jobs, 'making up for the sins of the past.' But in reality it results in a waste of talent more often than not. There are no shortcuts in this game. Leaders have to walk before they can run. Building programmes based on the exception is wasteful, stressful and highly risky for those involved. The military understand that. The nature of leadership has changed in the military as new technologies have come into play over the centuries and mission command is mastered but the underlying accountabilities of battle echelons have remained constant.

It is the same in civilian organizations albeit their existence is much shorter and prone to be transitory, at least in the private sector. It is also a fact that 'civilian echelons' are rarely stable. The job with fixed boundaries has been dead for some time, as I have discussed in *The Healthy Organization*, Chap. 10. McGrath in *The End of Competitive Advantage* (2013) downplays the importance of roles and structures. When she says "*so leaders must change jobs regularly*" she is in danger of throwing out the baby with the bath water. As I have tried to show, it is the level of accountability and the number and pattern of learning and growth opportunities that are more significant than the job in isolation. There is an inherent danger in what she calls "continuous reconfiguration". It is similar to the thought that 'there is no one way to organize', therefore 'any structure will do'. Good leadership

[39] Daily Telegraph 20.05.15.

development is more subtle than that. It is not simply a game of musical chairs. The military understand this.

I have witnessed young Brazilians moved too quickly though levels of accountability by a naïve CEO hoping to produce leaders at WL 5+. But they did not make it because their time in Level 3 was too short. Afrikaner companies in South Africa did not have a conspicuous record of promoting Afrikans into significant jobs between 1947 and 1992. But the moment Mandela was released from Robben Island it suddenly became de rigueur for young Afrikans to be slotted into significant roles before they were ready and for which they had not been appropriately prepared. The lack of development over two generations meant there was not a meaningful pipeline of talent ready and available. It also meant that too many would struggle in these new roles. The desire to progress minorities, although well intentioned, is not always constructive. The overwhelming evidence suggests many of those from minorities are skipping a level (or levels) and/or key boundary moves in this process and therefore will struggle to succeed in the higher reaches of accountability.

Ironically there is a real danger this approach may resurface or reinforce old prejudices that kept people down in the first place.

In 2014 the CEO of an international company, influenced by the new "wiki-leadership" fad, briefed his talent manager to devise a system that would enable young graduates to reach the equivalent of WL 4 at age 26. *The evidence suggests he will end up with a field of broken reeds.* (In Chap. 8 of *The Healthy Organization* I refer to research where I plotted the international career development of successful and slightly less successful senior managers across ten variables that might influence their career progress. One variable was 'age at WL reached'. In an initial sample of 26 international leaders who reached WL 7+, the average age at which they reached WL 4 was 37. And these were high fliers! In a second sample of 286 high potentials, the average age of those successful in reaching WL 4 was 40. Interestingly, this is not dissimilar to the pattern in the military, where the age distribution would seem to be a bit higher still.) The evidence of history suggests that technology changes do not change the fundamental realities of leadership development, whatever the fad or fashion currently in vogue.

Political agendas may change but the number and nature of accountability levels do not. 'Accelerated development' only works when it is based on sound knowledge of both the level of accountability and the capability of the person in that level coupled with training/coaching and the requisite period of gestation to achieve mastery in the relevant number of different roles (learning experiences). All are vital for future success in the promotion stakes.

5.7.3 The Distinctive Civilian Leadership Footprint

One of the four key "Enablers" of the Alaric Mostyn's research into high growth, high profit companies was *Leadership built from within*. (The others were simpler structures, Fast cross-boundary innovation and Change ready cultures.)

I am a firm advocate of leadership from within since, as Moltke demonstrated; it is not easy to copy and therefore is potentially a huge source of competitive advantage. But of course leadership development, based on promotion from within, is not enough in isolation (as will be demonstrated in Chap. 9) since it needs to be based on all five Pillars of Mission Mastery to be successful. Stonecourt's research revealed that in order to work well, this internal leadership development is facilitated by:

- Fast and good quality decision making
- Decision making linked to good metrics *and* execution
- The following ingrained patterns of behaviour
  - A climate of trust, encouraging and recognising need for change
  - Constructive conflict management
  - Shared commitment
  - Personal accountability
  - Bias for action.

Teamwork and leadership is not always ideal at the top: Mostyn also noted that:

- Excellent senior managers can be disappointing when together
- The more senior the team the more difficult it is to be a real team
- There are low levels of discipline and effectiveness in top team meetings.
  - Only 5 % have a rigorous and disciplined process
  - 65 % focus on 'information sharing' not decision making
  - 48 % of all these meetings get sidetracked and run out of time.

5.8 The Importance of Aligning Capability and Accountability

The fundamental challenge of leadership development is the alignment of the right calibre person to the appropriate level of accountability.

Progress in civilian organizations tends to be based on grade promotion. There are usually more grades on offer than the number of levels of accountability available. In one bank the top management were all in *one senior executive* grade. The bank had seven levels of accountability but we found up to eight layers in the one senior exec grade. There were another six grades to conjure with as well!

This undermines the quality of promotion and dilutes learning. The question is: "How do people traverse these levels in their careers?" This in turn opens up four vital issues about:

- The way potential is assessed,
- The type of training required
- The career planning options available to move *across and up* through the levels of accountability
- Awareness that some levels more important than others

The major concern for most organizations is finding (and retaining) the appropriate number and quality of leaders to ensure the organization succeeds, or at least does not fail. It is about orchestrating the training and development of leaders 'in' the organization. This in turn means the organization's structure must be designed with meaningful jobs that are aligned to the purpose of the organization, add value to the customer and the work of others, while enabling individual leaders the opportunity to learn and grow at the same time. *This is the basis of a healthy organization.*

There are five key stages in this process for any organization:

- Identify the total number of levels of accountability
- Work out the number of value adding layers and therefore the jobs with clear, discrete and distinct decision rights
- Construct a set of differentiating competencies aligned to levels of accountability to help identify talent with potential to progress
- Train top management in how to use the differentiating competencies (Differentiating competencies help earmark the type of behaviours needed at the next level of accountability. Thus they can differentiate what is required between two levels of accountability.)
- Assess accurately individuals' potential to traverse the different layers

Many organizations continue to spend millions on "leadership development" programmes that ignore these five stages. These programmes tend to be motivational "full of sound and fury, signifying nothing" in terms of reliable personal development in a real job. Their training and education is cosmetic not medicinal.

5.8.1 Bankrupt Ideas on Leadership and Hierarchy Are Alive and Well

It is distressing to note that as recently as May 2014 the UK's professional body for HR held an L&D show which concluded: "Poorly targeted training and 'outdated' structures create barriers to talent improvement" It went on to say that "rigid organizational hierarchies are one of the main barriers to improving management and leadership skills at work." This "research" seemed to be based simply on asking

HR managers what they thought. No wonder leadership development has stalled if HR managers still really believe hierarchy per se is the problem.

5.8.2 Assessing Leadership Potential

Since a large number of organizations don't have effective structures it is not surprising to learn that many so called "leadership competencies models" are hardly worth the paper they are written on. The critical importance of the context—the level of accountability at which leadership is exercised—is invariably neglected. The development of leaders is not simple but it does not need to be complicated. It seems some CEOs and their HRDs, are prone to fall into the three "Traps" described in Chap. 2.

Faced with the ***Knowledge Trap*** they set out to build a detailed approach to their brave new world, bordering on overload. We encountered an example of this in the previous chapter: Northern Rock had ~20 job grades for "pay and promotion" but linked to them were a corresponding number of competencies "to identify potential leaders" that actually focussed on performance not potential. This would have been a nightmare of bureaucratic endeavour for a line manager trying to assess a subordinate using this approach because it was not fit for purpose.

Then faced with erratic results top management would typically slide into an ***Alignment Trap***, expressed as "It seems not everyone understands the new system yet. We need to help embed it among our managers." This would have the HRD drafting *more detailed instructions and guidance* leading to another round of seminars and workshops, first for the HR community and then key line managers, so they can better understand the system. The flawed underlying content remains untouched as the effort goes into more process.

But still the outcome is not good. "We seem to have some good potential top managers in the pipeline, but is it the right number?" We checked the list and when subjected to the rigour of applying differentiating competencies aligned to levels of accountability, for the first time, only one person survived the cut. The Exec team went from smugness to shock overnight. This is the predictable ***Effects Trap***.

So what we are now likely to have proposed is a set of new mechanisms designed to provide better results. More effort *and control* is called for to ensure the right result is achieved, such as "a more robust set of metrics." So we witness an emphasis on timeframes for completion, discussions about the appropriate time needed to fill in the forms, detailed analysis of distribution curves of performance and potential categories—by product group, by region, by function. The danger is the actual quality and accuracy of *content* and fit with reality of the appraisals is lost in the obsessive drive to create metrics to justify decisions.

In Northern Rock for example, the conceptual content of the programme was not reliably measuring what top management thought. The bank typically had two to five layers of leadership jobs more than it needed across the bank. The job evaluation system was far too diffuse and was also feeding the over layering. The competency model was linked in detail to the faulty job evaluation scheme and therefore did not measure an individual's potential to move upwards and/or across the organization. *The leadership development programme was for the most part an elaborate, well meaning exercise in futility.* Sadly this is not unique in civilian organizations.

I was recently working in a public sector organization where I was told "We have a good leadership development system" When I probed a little further what was being said was: "Everybody believes in it and 93 % of the forms are completed on time. There is scope for some improvement but overall the performance commitment is very satisfying". A little later I interviewed the CEO who said:

> Now don't write this down, but my biggest problem is quality of people.
>
> "You surprise me", I said. "I have seen your performance appraisal records and I noticed *all of your managers* were rated '1 or 2 (Where 1 is excellent and 5 is unsatisfactory.)
>
> Yes, and to be honest I have an HRD who is a liability, but as you know it is virtually impossible to get rid of someone in the Civil Service on grounds of incompetent performance. It is worse than the teaching profession. The unions will argue I am the problem not the HRD as this individual has always had good ratings form other managers and directors across Whitehall. As you will have noticed the HRD is from a minority and I have no wish to open Pandora's Box.

5.8.3 The Vexed Issue of 'Competencies'

Most companies today use "competencies" systems to help identify leaders, but they tend to be very unreliable as McCall (1998) has pointed out:

> *"Even though it has been known for decades that no single set of traits defines all successful executives in all situations, the belief that it does has been resurrected in one-size-fits-all competencies. Ironically leadership development began with 'Great Man' theories that were debunked by contingency theorists, only to re-emerge as "competencies". Entirely new personnel bureaucracies have emerged to translate these competencies into human resource programmes."*

Boyatzis (1982) would appear to have been the first to argue for the development of competencies as a basis for leadership development, but it has since degenerated into a quagmire of definitional confusion, as he admitted at the Third Italian Competencies conference in Rome during 1998. George Klemp (1998) is a cogent critic of this mess. In 1990 Prahalad and Hamel coined the term "core competence", which seems to be the origin of 'core competencies', which have proliferated since.[40] They are usually 'capabilities' or in reality simply another word for skills.

---

[40] Prahalad C.K and Hamel G (1990) "The Core Competence of the Corporation", *Harvard Business Review, v.68 no.3.*

They do not identify potential. The term itself does not help as "competence" suggests capability to do something but "competency" was not previously a word in common English usage. Some 50 years ago its primary meaning was "Sufficiency of means for living."[41] Today 'Competency' implies first "an ability to do something well and secondly, sufficient income to live."[42] To carry out a specific job is generally a task requiring skill. But skills reinforce the quality of performance ***in a level***, not potential for the next job at a higher level of accountability. Yet today most HRDs see their 'competencies' as indicators of potential, which is why so many leadership development approaches are floundering. Herwig Kressler pointed out in 2003, that "*Potential is among those terms that have lost their clarity, having been trampled and hackneyed through extensive use...While there is no simple technique of personal development there is however knowledge of* ***contexts*** *(my emphasis) and principles, which can facilitate understanding and be of practical use.*"[43]

The reason so many competency models fail is because they mix values, skills and leadership behaviours and do not therefore measure potential reliably linked to an accountable context.

The resulting conceptual mishmash means "competencies" invariably do not reliably measure promotability to the next level of accountability and future effectiveness. Firstly, because the tectonic plate of accountability is suspect or does not exist and secondly because the capability plate is flawed and unreliable. This means an individual cannot be reliably assessed. The result is too many HR potential assessment systems are neither valid nor reliable. Measuring personality in a vacuum is not the answer either as it does not identify who has potential for promotion.

5.8.3.1 Values

Values are important. They help shape culture in an organization—of which more in Chap. 7. But they do not identify who should or can be promoted. They are ***badges of belonging***: "To be a member of this family you must practice these values." So if, for example, a value is "integrity", you don't get promoted for being honest, you get fired for being dishonest. So, from the perspective of leadership development the quality of the values practised should be the same at every level in the organization. Values are behaviours, but as they apply equally at each level of accountability *they do not differentiate* and indicate who has potential for a move to the next Level.

[41] The Concise Oxford Dictionary (1960).

[42] Collins Dictionary of the English language (2010).

[43] Kressler H W (2003) *Motivate and Reward: performance appraisal and incentive systems for business success*.p.79.

5.8.3.2 Skills

Skills or 'core competencies' relate to task-mastery. They can be specific (engineering, nursing, legal etc) or general (project management, people management etc.). They are the key ingredient influencing the quality of ***performance in a specific level of accountability***. Thus in the family of financial skills we find the technical accounting requirements of a Level 2 management accountant are different to those of a national treasurer who may be at Level 3 or a head of audit at Level 4 in an international company. Technical skills drive performance in a Level: they do not reliably indicate a more demanding performance requirement can be met in a higher level. Part of the reason being that from Level 3 and up general management skills tend to become increasingly more important in the majority of situations. *Yet it is common practice in civilian organizations to promote on the basis of proven performance in the lower Level.* It is assuming the best maths teacher can run the school. Clearly something over and above expertise in the teaching of maths is required to be able to run a large secondary or high school. In a well run organization the manager at the next higher level—"the accountable parent"—would be responsible for assessing performance and making a recommendation to the accountable grandparent about potential. The grandparent(s) would make the decision to ratify the potential proposal or not. This is well orchestrated in the military approach to assessing potential as described above in Sect. 4.1. It is patchier in civilian organizations.

5.8.4 DMA Leadership Model of Differentiating Competencies

Most competency models do not *differentiate* between the requirements of different levels of accountability, which is why they are not reliable indicators of potential for higher leadership positions. The DMA Leadership model is the alignment of an individual's leadership behaviour and performance to a given level of accountability. The underlying logic is as follows: 'If these are the decisions you have to make in this role, then these are the behaviours we need to see at this Level.' The individual is assessed in and against the requirements of a meaningful, accountable context based on their behaviour as they take keys decision aligned to the Level. A DMA leadership competency does not presume a 'Great Man' solution because it is context not personality driven. It is defined as:

A *set of behaviours, which ensure an individual's performance is effective when calibrated against the demands of a given level of accountability.*

> ***The DMA Competencies are "Differentiating" because they also help to identify who has potential to move to the next higher Level by studying what is required at that new level and comparing current behaviour against that yardstick.***

Table 5.1 DMA competencies aligned to the Work Level Elements

Seven DMA elements	Six DMA differentiating competencies
• Nature of work (& Timeframe)	• Setting direction
• Resource complexity	• Leading resources
• Problem solving	• Analysing and decision making
• Change	• Driving change
• Natural work team	• Influencing colleagues
• External interaction	• Managing the external Environment
• Timeframe	• *Values based non differentiating competencies e.g. passion, energy, commitment*[a]

[a]Non differentiating competencies are the same for every level: i.e. they do not change (or differentiate) form one Level to the next. The optimal number of differentiating competencies is about 6: 8 or more is far too many for busy line managers added to which reliability suffers

The seven Work Level Elements identify the decisions that need to be taken at each level. The *Competencies indicate how one should behave (think and lead) when making those decisions.* They summarise the standards of effective performance at each level of accountability and can identify who to promote to the next level (Table 5.1).

Successful behaviours are cumulative; meaning that at higher levels managers should already be demonstrating the required behaviours from lower levels. To recall Kressler's dictum, the model is a set of principles linked to a context that will enable an organization to:

- Communicate clearly to jobholders those behaviours, which are required for top performance at their respective Work Levels.
- Identify priority competency development needs for individual managers in their current or likely future roles.
- *Identify individuals who, at their current level, are demonstrating behaviours, which indicate they have potential to move to the next higher Work Level.*

These managers represent the bench strength of high potential leaders.

5.8.4.1 Filling the Promotion Pipeline

Differentiating competencies are the key to facilitating the identification of potential of future leaders, who make up a given promotion pipeline. But the length of these pipelines varies depending on the total number of Work Levels in a given organization. The pipeline is sometimes referred to as *cover*: i.e. how many Individuals in say Level 2 have confirmed potential (assessed against DMA Competencies) for Level 3, expressed as a percentage of the total number of Level 3 jobs in this instance. All managers are expected to practice the corporate values and perform well technically in their current Level. These are givens. They may not be an outstanding performer but must meet the standard requirements of the current job. Often high potential leaders move up quite quickly and don't stay long enough in role to demonstrate outstanding performance. But for these relatively small cadres we are now looking for more than performance. They must be able to provide *evidence* that can differentiate between what is required at this Level and the next higher Level. We are searching for ***differentiating behaviours***. We also know that time and number of learning experiences spent in some levels is a better predictor of success at higher levels than others. Conversely too little time spent in say Level 3, is a high risk promotion to Level 4.

In one international company I was asked to verify how many of the top executive jobs had a successor in the pipeline. It had just been identified as a Level 6 company and therefore we were looking for managers in Level 4 who could move into Level 5. "No problem," said the HRD, "we have identified 11 individuals with potential to reach the top executive team." But they had not been thinking in terms of progression from Level 4 to Level 5 in their previous assessments. The earlier assessments were heavily reliant on performance in current jobs not the requirements of the next job. We then assessed those individuals against the yardstick of the DMA Differentiating Competencies looking for *evidence* checked off against the newly introduced definitions for Level 5. In this process it is vitally important there is a consensus view of the whole top team on the relevance and accuracy of the evidence provided before an individual is confirmed as having potential for the next level of accountability. The grandparent CEO of the individual in question would then ratify that view. Those successfully assessed would be placed on *List 5*, in this instance, confirming the belief they had potential to proceed to Level 5. Then an appropriate training/career plan should then be put in place to ensure this plan unfolds, all other things being equal. Interestingly and somewhat predictably in this instance the number of successors based on the new criteria fell from eleven on the list to just two, a dose of reality which rather unnerved the CEO. But at least he now had a more reliable reading on the strength or otherwise of the key promotion pipelines.

5.8.4.2 The Military Competencies' Hook

All the military officers I approached talked about the importance of being assessed for potential and while they discussed the process, and their own experience of it, they did not feel they could share 'the secrets' of how the assessments were made. But it is very clear that the concept of potential is well understood in the military, being part of what they refer to as "merit", which is a different usage to that of civilian organizations that tend to see "merit" in terms of fairness and reward payments for performance. A lot of effort goes into establishing competent Level 2 and especially Level 3 leaders across the military, who are the natural feedstock for the ranks of generals. The system is open and those who cannot move up to Level 4 are retired in their early 50s, which gives them an opportunity to build another career in "CivvyStreet", which is invariably the case.

5.8.5 The "Promotion Obsession" in Civilian Organizations

Promotion in civilian organizations is a move upwards, usually reflected in *a change of grad*e and an increase in the reward package. The latter is the driver of the first more often than not. The first question I always get when introducing the idea of say 6 Work Levels to replace say, 16 grades is: "How will we promote people?" But the more fundamental questions are:

- What exactly is a promotion?
- Why is it sought?
- How should it be delivered?

It is necessary then to change the nature of the "promotion debate" away from external drivers such as grade and status to the work to be done and its consequences for the learning and development of a talented person.

Promotion is about learning, growing and developing while enjoying enhanced rewards. The administrative grade change (understandably) muddies the water of personal development because it signals more status and increases one's pay packet. Thus the idea of a true promotion is diluted in the same way performance is now becoming irrelevant in banks' as CEOs chase talent via the mythical mantra of "paying the market rate." The assertion that the financial services market is cooked by captive consultants and their pliant remuneration committees is another part of the story. The performance anchor is becoming irrelevant it seems. If companies introduce Levels it makes sense to modify their reward practices. For example if someone moves three times "sideways" in Level 3 as part of their learning and development, they should have a pay increase each time they move, just as if they had a new grade. Fringe benefits can be aligned to a level as dictated by market analysis, and so on.

Morgan McCall et al highlight the following blend of experiences as being among those that are keys to the growth of an individual leader.

- Foundation assignments
- First management job
- Business turnaround
- Business start-ups
- Joint ventures, alliances, mergers or acquisitions
- Managing a project
- A stint in headquarters.

These promotion possibilities amount to what I call 'Boundary Moves' to enhance personal learning and development. I will touch on these in the next chapter as they are vital sources of experiential learning.

A Boundary Move takes an individual out of their comfort zone but not beyond their learning zone. They facilitate personal growth.

For example, a manager running a department within a large store at say WL 2 was newly promoted to run a WL 3 Hypermarket. Let's assume it was already very successful with outstanding staff meeting all its annual KPIs (increased sales, improved customer service, reduced overtime cost, less wastage, lower staff turnovers, and improved engagement scores). In reality this store would almost run itself in the first year. If at that point this person was promoted to Level 4 to run 15+ hypermarkets it is highly likely he or she would struggle and possibly fail as a Stores Director. But if after say 2 years this manager was sent to complete a turnaround of a failing store in another city, which was successfully completed after about 3 or 4 years following which the next assignment was to open a new store in yet another city, the pattern is clear. This high flying manager will have had three key boundary moves or *learning experiences*—within the same Level—prior to a boundary move to the next higher Level to become responsible for 15 hypermarkets likely to be in one of the three situations encountered in the last 7 years or so. The chances of success at Level 4 are now much more likely. Each boundary move could, I would say, should, lead to a pay increase, as the further evidence confirms the potential to move up to the next level of accountability.

In other words it is not just time in Work Level that guarantees leadership development but the quality of the ***different learning experiences*** *offered within that Work Level.*

5.8.6 The Importance of Tracking High-Potential Leaders

"Tracking" implies the ability to plot career paths up to two or even three Levels into the future.

Tracking is the basis of career planning.

In Chap. 8 of *The Healthy Organization* ten variables are assessed for their impact on career tracks, while in chapter 11 of *The Accountable Leader* I plot the track of an individual crossing from Level 2 to Level 8 over a career life time. In both cases the number of jobs in Levels 3 and 5 are shown to be most critical for a vibrant and successful career track.

We have also seen how the military rigorously track potential. For example, while writing this book, there was an obituary published of a successful General[44]

[44] General Sir Michael Wilkes, *The Daily Telegraph* 4 November 2013.

which illustrated how he reached a key Level 3 role (SAS Regiment) at age 37, Level 4 by age 40, Level 5 and then Level 6 Lieutenant General and then "a full General at age 53." Clearly someone who becomes a full General has been on the fast track. Looking at the example of General Wilkes' career it is also clear that the *quality* of the assignments chosen to stretch and test a leader is also very significant. For example only the very best of those on the fast track would be chosen to command an SAS regiment and that is unlikely to be his first role at that level.

Fieldwork in civilian organizations suggests three or four ages when it would be helpful to undertake a thorough assessment of someone's leadership potential, especially in the case of those assessed to be heading to the top of a very large organization.

- At age 30, "What *evidence s*uggests this individual could make Level 5?" I.e. are they on "Track 5?"
- At age 35, "What *evidence* suggests this individual could make Level 6?"
- At age 40, "What *evidence* suggests this individual might reach Level 7?"
- At age 45, "What *evidence* suggests this individual might reach Level 8?"

The next key question in each case is *what now needs to be done to keep that person learning and growing?* (This a key challenge for women who may leave for a while to have a family.) Not many organizations have eight levels of accountability thus very few leaders of that capability are required—or one suspects, are available. The objective data (evidence) emerging from comparing an individual's behaviour against the requirements of the relevant differentiating competencies helps sharpen the focus (and accuracy) of these discussions. Recall the example of the "eleven high potentials" in paragraph 8.4.1, reduced to two when the rule of differentiating competencies was passed over them for the first time.

5.8.7 Best Practice in World Class Companies

I wish to share some the best practice I have found in the civilian world to compare with best military practice. Generally it has been in the private not the public sector. I was asked by an international client to identify best leadership development practice in the world as a challenging benchmark. I approached six multinationals recognised as world leaders in their respective industries, known for their ability to develop international managers and build internal succession pipelines across the world.

5.8.7.1 The Findings

The companies' benchmarked revealed the following ten features:

- Their leadership development policy is closely *linked to business strategy*. For example they want the best people in critical businesses/countries to heighten leverage in performance both of the business and the individual (s).
- They take *a long term view* of their best talent; realising retention is best served by ensuring genuine challenge and learning, leading to personal growth.
- They have a *formalised approach*, which is consistently applied to identify talent, with top executives trained in the requisite process
- It is *owned* at the general management level *by the CEO* with the HR Dr's support.
- They seek out managers *early in their careers* who might have potential for top roles and general management.
- They have a built-in approach to the *tracking* of their best talent.
- These candidates are being given international experience earlier. *More managers are truly global* and the concept of the traditional "missionary" expatriate from a home country has broadened. For example, today a Thai studying at UCLA is likely to take her first job in Brazil rather than 'back home'.
- Formal learning via external and internal courses is part of the mix, although with some questioning of the effectiveness of the latter for general management. *Formal training/education is more effective outside the home base*; for top strategic talent.
- They are increasingly sensitive to and more assertive about the *management of diversity*.
- *The process is open* (not the personal details about individuals) and well understood throughout the organisation with individuals aware of their own career plans, which take account of their own aspirations and wishes.

The best civilian companies were highly committed to leadership development and spent a lot of time aiming to develop their people and plan their careers. There was unmistakable commitment from the top. They governed the processes having designed global systems to ensure consistency. But even the best did not quite match the rigour and robustness of the military approach to selection, assessment and development of the individual via a mix of line and staff assignments through a well defined pattern of battle echelon accountability. They generally did not have an objective system for identifying different levels of accountabilities complemented by an integrated set of differentiating leadership competencies. The differences between operational and strategic accountabilities tended to be blurred which blunted the effectiveness of their tracking programmes.

Interestingly the best civilian system I have worked in was adapted from the military. The UCMDS (Unilever Companies Management Development Scheme), which selected about 2 % of those it interviewed on targeted university campuses. It was modelled on the War Office Selection Boards for officer selection during WW2. The approach called for training of the senior managers attending the final selection days, working with Tavistock staff. The new recruits then had 2 years of rotational training and attended appropriate training courses. Further in-house international courses occurred aligned to Work Levels. Not unlike the approach outlined for the military officers as they crossed different echelons. The company ran Management Reviews each year to verify the quality of its promotion pipeline for its 20,000 managers worldwide.

5.8.8 Civilian Leadership Development: The Recurring Nightmare

The military approach is not perfect but it does have a good grasp on the leadership equation of matching a talented person to an appropriately challenging role. They also appreciate the need for different types of quality experience (tours)—boundary moves. Once the focus is upon a leader in an accountable role it is possible to draw conclusions about what makes for a great supervisor or battalion commander and so on.

It is probably fair to say that much of the stress felt in civilian organizations today stems not from new, fluid structures or fast moving technology with its focus in real time, but from faulty organization design spawning hollow jobs, both wasting and frustrating talent. This is de-motivating, undermines leadership development and personal growth opportunities are missed. Individuals move jobs too often without purpose. *That is the recurring employee nightmare in too many civilian organizations.*

The major leadership development shortcoming in civilian organizations is the focus on the person without a good understanding of the job context and its accountabilities. By way of contrast military organizations simultaneously study the person AND the job context within a level of accountability (the battle echelon). That arguably makes the difference between a good investment or a waste of talent and money - success or failure.

Some questions to ponder.

1. Leadership development requires:

   - An role with unambiguous accountability
   - A competent incumbent
   - A lean structure aligned to Levels of accountability

- A valid potential assessment framework aligned to those Levels
- Top management trained in the use of that framework

  How would you rate your organization on those five essentials and what actions would you suggest if necessary?

2. How are potential leaders identified: is the process reliable, consistent, robust, open and based on merit?
3. Which is the critical layer of leadership development in the organization—why?
4. Who is ultimately accountable for leadership development in your organization and what targets (e.g. cover by level) are set and measured to identify progress?
5. How does your organization benchmark against the 10 leadership development practices of the best companies?

Pillar 4: Experiential Learning

6

Theoretical knowledge is not enough. Mastering this practical art (of leadership) means developing qualities of mind and character which are shaped by training and guided by experience.
Helmet Von Moltke
On strategy 1871

The fact is our management schools do not generally hire people capable of teaching true managerial skill. The PhD is a licence to teach in a business school. That degree neither preselects nor trains for skill in pedagogy, ***certainly not of the experiential kind*** (my emphasis).
Henry Mintzberg p. 85 *(Mintzberg on Management, 1989)*

6.1 General

There in two nutshells, you have it. It is accepted wisdom that people learn best by doing, not talking about doing. I have called this chapter Experiential Learning to stress the importance of 'learning by doing'. It is also known as 'rehearsal training', practising before the real event. Military war games are a classic example, where the reality of war is simulated to gain insight into how participants react in situations of stress, which test leadership behaviour. They are taught by people who have led, who have been in the heat of battle. They *rehearse* the experiences they are likely to encounter in battle and *learn from experience*. Formal rehearsal training is not widespread in the private or public sectors although I will give some examples where this does occur. It seems rehearsal training is largely limited to operational levels—i.e. Work Levels 1–3, which is typically 99 %+ of an organization's workforce.

(continued)

B. Dive, *Mission Mastery*, Management for Professionals,
DOI 10.1007/978-3-319-25223-0_6

Strategic learning outcomes are harder to simulate although behavioural learning is possible at all levels. As Alaric Mostyn's research shows, executives at strategic levels are not always noted for teamwork, but this can be learned via simulation. In terms of career development the key form of experiential learning in both the military and best civilian organizations is delivered via a sequence of different learning assignments usually involving a change of job, orchestrated on the basis of an individual's development needs. This is known as career planning or 'tracking' in the best organizations, which may be facilitated with coaching of key individuals. Thus I will use the words *rehearsal and experiential* training interchangeably. It is important to bear in mind during this chapter Aldous Huxley's insight: "*Experience is not what happens to a man, it is what a man does with what happens to him.*" The challenge for an organization lies in orchestrating what happens to a person to ensure that person learns and grows to full potential.

6.2 Two Contrasting Approaches

Civilians, in contrast to the military, tend to learn leadership by listening to those in classrooms who, as a rule, have rarely led anything, *talking about how to lead.* It was really no surprise to learn in 2008 that so many of the failed leaders who floated as useless flotsam to the surface in the lakes of failure during the GFC were MBAs from Harvard and assorted business schools. Their domain of competence was Analysis in Wonderland.[1]

> *Our MBA programmes take people who have hardly ever made or sold anything and make damn sure they never will. And the most popular jobs of these graduates:* ***finance!*** *(My emphasis as this was written in 1989) Jobs where the abstractions of money, so compatible with the whole thrust of quantitative MBA training, shield them from the messiness of people and products.*[2]

Goodwin of RBS is now famous for his obsession with the colour of biscuits at his 'executive' meetings, the shape and colour of filing cabinets and his colleagues' ties, as pointed out by Ian Martin in his damning book (2013). This is hardly the stuff of a Level 8 leader. The Harvard Case study method has come under closer scrutiny following the financial debacle of 2007/08 where too many failed leaders were darlings of the MBA university circuit. Intellectual arrogance stroked by academic subservience is no test of general management. On the academic circuit Goodwin, for example, was lauded for his 'successful integration' of NatWest into RBS. Insiders told me some time ago it was never fully integrated and customers who could not access their current accounts for weeks in 2013 will vouch for that.

[1] A phrase first made popular by Albert Shapiro in 1977.

[2] Mintzberg op cit, p. 91

The civilian 'method' where inexperienced, pushy kids discuss what they would do as a general manager, having read 20 pages of a case study the night before, led in discussion by an academic who invariably has never run anything in the company being 'studied', stands in stark contrast to the military approach. In the latter instance officer cadets (even the title tells you something) having had some theory input are soon subjected to demanding tests of practical leadership supervised in the field by senior officers. Their decision making under pressure is studied, as planned by Moltke, who often attended field exercises himself. The contrast between the military and civilian approaches is stark.

We saw in the previous chapter that high potential military officers reached the top of Level 2 around age 32. My experience of civilian organizations suggests, revealingly, their high potential managers will be in at least Level 3 by then.

The CEO of Sony, Akio Morita, came to a similar conclusion over 25 years ago: "*Management, despite the work of Harvard Business School and others, is an elusive thing that cannot always be judged by next quarter's bottom line. A manager is measured by how that manager can organize a large number of people and how effectively he or she can get the highest performance from each of the individuals and blend them into a co-ordinated performance*".[3] Morita wrote in the 80s, a time when some academics were dining out writing about the success of 'Japanese Management'. How the likes of Moltke, Morita and Matsushita must have chuckled. Good management is not 'Japanese' or 'German': it is universal.

6.3 The Military Approach

It seems the Prussian reformers wanted to create an intelligent organization whose success did not depend on being led by a genius. Moltke made clear that his job was not just about strategy and setting direction but building an organization that would *spontaneously* act in line with the direction he set. He refined the General War School set up in 1810 as he had greater ambitions for it. He renamed it the War Academy in 1859. (Today it is almost de rigueur for civilian organizations to call their training centres, "Academies".) It had two purposes: one to act as a rigorous selection mechanism and second to develop a group trained in their professional skills who would behave in a similar way given a shared leadership philosophy. The aim being that one should not only know what was required in action but would also be capable of executing a mission once it was made clear, even when the leader was not present.

[3] Akio Morita et al. 1987, *Made in Japan*, p. 154.

In 1872 he had the General Staff running the Academy. He set up a course for high potential officers: the first of its kind with such a clear mission. Only the best could apply. They underwent a rigorous examination following which a small minority were accepted. It involved passing papers that focused on assessing the reasoning candidates used to reach solutions since the objective was to identify potential based on clarity of reasoning and decision-making ability.[4] The course aimed to develop professional skills rather than assess academic excellence per se. *More than half of the staff on the Academy were active General Staff Officers (the rest were university professors) to ensure the teaching was practical,* including the visiting of battle fields to study the terrain and options for attack based on analysis of the site. Moltke himself devised a final practical test of endurance and know-how designed to find out "what the officer in question was capable of doing in the field, not just the classroom". Those who were successful underwent a further 2 years of practical probation. During this period they had regular tactical map exercises to develop their prowess further. Moltke *was the senior tutor* and undertook two "staff rides" a year during which these high potential officers were subjected to war games "designed to develop powers of decision making in circumstances subject to friction." The focus was practical, preparing officers for the real thing.

This rehearsal training and experiential learning was unique and new.

Apparently Moltke considered this rehearsal training delivered through the War Academy was the secret to building the type of organization he needed. Its hallmark was to be top performance based on the exercise of individual initiative and willingness to take responsibility for an outcome once the mission was known. He knew this would not happen of its own accord. He took this so seriously that for over 20 years he personally supervised and was involved in the high potential programme. (Uniquely Moltke was Chief of Staff for an unprecedented 31 years: from 1857 to 71 for the Prussian army and 1871–1888 for the German Army. None of the other 30 Chiefs of Staff from 1808 to 1945 even remotely approached his longevity in post and influence.) He made it clear he expected his officers to identify what was required in a given situation and then act quickly and decisively. They were put into situations where they could practice (rehearse) and learn these skills. Independence of thought was expected based on reason and sound judgement and on at least one exercise the logical answer in the case study (as we might call it today) was to disobey an order. *Apparently he would not promote high potential officers who did not display the self confidence to be prepared to disobey an order on the appropriate training exercise.* Moltke was keen to see energy and enthusiasm among his officer and counselled his superior officers against being too critical

[4] Bungay *The Art of Action* p. 178 and 179.

of their juniors if a mistake was made based on logic and initiative. In 1888 he stated in the Field Service Regulations that:

> *All commanders must always be aware that an omission or failure to act is a graver charge than making a mistake on choice of means.*[5]

He was building a high performance culture, which we would recognise today as a learning organization.

The aim was to have someone who knows what to do and who can function independently of ongoing instruction once the mission is known. This is the ultimate example of distributive leadership in action. In an army this is more critical given one can expect to lose layers of management during a conflict. This has been anticipated with officers trained to operate at the next higher battle echelon (level of accountability) in a crisis. There are also clear guidelines for a situation where survivors are all the same rank. The person first appointed to that rank is expected to take charge and everyone else knows that.

The parallel situation in civilian organization is unexpected loss via resignation (s). Civilian organizations often make a meal of the (generally predictable) situation taking far too long to take action. The other mistake is the short sighted policy of cost reduction based on "no replacements". Corporate memory walks out the door with no planned response until a few years later someone wakes up to the fact there is a serious shortage of talent in a given promotion pipeline. I have seen this as a classic public sector response in a department favouring a "no redundancies" policy and therefore not replacing retirees. Skill levels in the core function eroded rapidly. It takes years to re-establish this expertise in an area of specialism that does not reside in the private sector and which cannot therefore be bought in the market. I have also seen a major multinational make the same mistake: but only once.

Bungay has suggested Moltke's approach, when used in a civilian setting, should be called 'directed opportunism'. I think it is more than that: I believe Moltke built the first true self sustaining large learning organization. This remains a major challenge for civilian organizations today, especially those that have a global footprint.

6.4 Civilian Initiatives

A number of civilian organizations have established something akin to Moltkes' War Academy for their high potential staff. Unilever has had for many years an international residential training centre at Four Acres in the UK running programmes for high potential individuals from across the world aligned to key

[5] Bungay op cit 180

levels of accountability. The company has recently opened another centre in Asia to recognise the growing importance of that region as over 50 % of sales now come from outside the Triad of the US, Europe and Japan. The CEO regularly appears at these programmes to add impetus to the "Unileverisation" process of its key executives, some of whom are given a key business problem to solve under the leadership of leading business professors known to have succeeded in the field. The approach tends to be a mix of experienced managers and world class academics. One case was the brief to improve innovation across the company. The initial programme was led by Professor Clark, who (with Professor Wheelwright) had successfully introduced a unique innovation culture in the US car industry. The principles were migrated to the consumer goods world triggered by a Four Acres programme aligned to a major business need. The participants were among those identified with potential for the top of the business.

Tesco has an academy in the UK which runs "Options" programmes for its high potential managers across the business. Both companies operate with Work Levels. This means they can align courses to key levels of accountability within the business. Both companies have processes to assess and then to confirm those with potential to move up to the next level of accountability. These individuals are then formally placed on high potential Lists. Thus someone in Work Level 2 with confirmed potential to move up to Level 3 would be placed on List 3, and so on right up to and including the top executive team. At the time of writing Tesco was suffering a leadership crisis. Part of this, in my opinion stemmed from the fact that some parts of the business had moved up a Level as a result of massive growth since 2000 but assessment of the jobs and individuals had not taken this into account as some of the relevant differentiating competency definitions were not updated. Thus some leaders appeared to be under geared for the responsibilities and challenges they faced. Hogan might say that under pressure their identities were exposed, some of which apparently were weak on character and integrity. Top management have taken strong action in the meantime aimed at redressing these shortcomings.

Since introducing Work Levels, BT has been aligning its training and development to Levels. Other companies, such as Shell and General Electric, are recognised for having well established central acculturation programmes fully supported by top management.

6.4.1 Rehearsal Training

In my experience rehearsal training is very rarely practised for distributive leaders in civilian organizations. This is not surprising given the approach to strategy in action is much looser in practice than the focus on mission in the military. The micro management engendered by scientific management and process re-engineering has militated against establishing a culture built on trust and the responsible use of initiative in civilian organizations. They have embedded a culture of control by measurement. It divides work into small steps which of themselves are rather meaningless. The focus is efficiency, doing (small) things right. Not effectiveness: doing the right (big, integrated) things.

This is in complete contrast to the philosophy and approach to leadership and work in the military. *Mission command fosters empowerment*. It aims to integrate tasks and encapsulates them as part of a total assignment (mission) the purpose of which is both understood in its own right and linked to the levels immediately below and above it. These provide a meaning and purpose that is invariably lacking in piecemeal civilian white collar work, which desiccates human motivation. Back-briefing is the thread which makes these connections in the military. It is rather difficult to impart a clear purpose and generate commitment in a hollow layer of management. This is why top down cascade initiatives tend to go awry in civilian settings.

The pervasive myth of twenty-first century civilian organisations is the belief that they have got rid of command and control cultures and have moved into the sunny uplands of empowerment.

The main obstacle to civilian organizations empowering their workforces and building a culture of trust is their inability to identify their levels of accountability with different and discrete decision rights. Hence the hollow layers of management. Trust is built upon clear accountability and its corollary, authority. The most commonly neglected skill areas are those relating to the management of people (selection interviewing, performance management, handling of grievances, meeting management, pubic speaking to mention but a few). Yet these are all areas ripe for rehearsal training and practice. It seems that some technical skill areas such as engineering, IT, finance, marketing and advertising are vehicles for rapid promotion but too often these 'managers' seem to be bereft of people management skills.

While the civilian world generally prefers preparing for leadership by talking about it, there are, nevertheless, some impressive examples of "experiential" or "rehearsal training" practised in a number of civilian organizations.

6.4.1.1 High Reliability Industries

Preparing for the unusual, isolated event is an imperative for high reliability industries such as aviation, nuclear power, chemical, petroleum, rail and marine where the probability of an event is very low yet the consequences can be horrendous. Probably the most impressive example is in the aviation industry. The industry has established that most air mishaps are the result of pilot error often accentuated by technical failures. Therefore much effort has gone into simulating the kind of situations pilots might expect to encounter. Aviation techniques include both aircrew training and airline emergencies, which could involve police and medicine—specifically trauma and paramedics. Those in nuclear power, chemical and marine industries all rehearse potential disaster scenarios. The air traffic service, rail and marine industries are moving more and more to the use of simulators (usually fixed-base devices using big screen technology to provide competent visual presentations) to provide experiential training. The training of pilots in full-motion simulators and the training of cabin crew, train drivers, bridge crews and air traffic controllers in fixed-base simulators all use scenario-based syllabi to create training and testing opportunities.

Many of these civilian organizations conduct "war gaming" scenarios. The very term "war gaming" is significant since it indicates the origin of the technique of experiential learning. The Police and Fire Services would appear to be set up on a military model including an overt rank structure but without having such a clear concept of battle echelons. For example in the UK, ranks 'at the top' of the police forces have been added in police forces (Deputy Constable, Assistant Chief Constable etc) over the years, which smacks of top down organization design. Having a very scenario-based response capability and routinely having to exercise those skills and protocols improves their ability to respond quickly and competently in rapidly changing scenarios. A concept of bronze, silver, gold leadership is often in place to help manage emergencies. This idea is used widely: for example I have analysed its application in a prison setting, geared to handle emergencies. Trauma medicine teams (in hospitals and paramedics in the field), also regularly practise a scenario-based response. Their leadership structure is more opaque—the members of the team know who is the Intensivist/Trauma Surgeon/Registrar/Anaesthetist/Nurse etc but these roles are not necessarily apparent to an outsider observing the team.

6.5 What Is the Purpose and Value of Experiential Training?

Clausewitz was a strong advocate of experiential training.

> *"The theorist is like a swimming master, who teaches on dry land movements which are required in the water, which must appear grotesque and ludicrous to those who forget about the water. This is also why theorists, who have never plunged in themselves, or who cannot deduce any generalities from their experience, are unpractical (sic) and even absurd, because they only teach what everyone knows—how to walk."*[6]

The purpose of "war gaming" in the military is to provide the opportunity for battle plans and responses to be tested as well as enabling individuals to gain experience in dynamic situations when the normal hierarchical structure is disrupted. So a typical war gaming scenario would include a senior person being "eliminated" from the scenario and the next most senior available having to take over the role. Given the nature of military conflicts this is most likely to occur

[6] *On War*, Book 1 chapter VIII, "Friction in War" p. 165.

during a period of confusion and uncertainty due to the "fog of war". Clearly civilian organizations do not face this imperative. Or do they?

Police, Fire, Trauma teams and even flight crews may face a similar situation; the loss of a leader at a critical time and the need for a junior person to assume the mantle of leadership. Hence the scenario training for these groups must include not only the expected and standard responses to a dynamic situation, but also include the recognition of changes in the situation and the development of a competent response. This includes a junior person having to take over the pivotal leadership role without warning and possibly when events are already uncertain and creating a high workload. Their training is designed to test the readiness of the organisation and the "emergency response team" to manage the scenario in accordance with their existing management plan and to subsequently modify the plan to correct deficiencies discovered during the training.

Air traffic, rail and marine training is primarily designed to practice the skill sets required to competently manage, respectively, the flow of aircraft, the control of a train or the control for a ship. While emergency scenarios are included the focus is on management of the emergency rather than the possibility that leadership may suddenly be passed to another person.

6.5.1 Implications for Leadership Development

Police and Fire, being close to a military model, use the role of a leader very overtly and expect to have to replace the leader at short notice in unpredictable situations. Medical teams routinely expect their leaders (the specialist consultant) to be present or to be available on short-notice should they be needed. The junior members of the team are expected to use their initiative within their knowledge base but the situations rarely actually develop leadership; rather they develop diagnostic skills. In addition, it is problematic to actually achieve competent scenario-based training because of the difficulty of providing bleeding and broken bodies!

Pilot and cabin crew training includes the development of leadership skills and the testing of those skills. There are two reasons why pilots and cabin crew may fail training: a lack of skills, knowledge and attributes to actually do the required job (fly the aircraft); and, a lack/ inadequacy of decision-making and/or command competency. The emphasis in the late C20th for pilots has turned to the "management" of the aircraft as being the crucial behaviour required and the assessment in the simulated scenarios is designed to allow this capability to be explored. The Captain clearly is expected to perform but the First Officer (FO) is also given the opportunity to practice command behaviours in the simulations. In flight, the FO would not normally manage an emergency situation; rather they would assist and be allocated specific tasks. In the simulator, under "command practice" the roles of Captain and FO are effectively reversed with the Captain allowing the FO to lead for the duration of the exercise. Thus the FO has the opportunity to develop leadership skills.

Similarly, Air Traffic Controllers, Police and Firemen all rehearse for the possibility of a subordinate having to exercise command during role play scenarios.

6.5.2 Use of Simulation in Commercial Organizations

Simulation is a well proven method for developing behavioural skills in commercial originations

6.5.2.1 The Case of Factory Supervisors

Some years ago I was involved in designing a programme for long serving factory supervisors. The company felt they needed to be brought up to date with the latest thinking on a number of aspects of their leadership skills and behaviour. The challenge was that the programme had to cover leadership, motivation, teamwork and planning. But most of these supervisors had left school without many qualifications and certainly had not sat in a class room for at least 30 years. They were used to action as they moved around their respective plants. Just the thought of a lecture or even interactive discussion would probably put them to sleep.

I recalled reading earlier about Coverdale training techniques, based on using **game theory**, as a method of teaching. Ralph Coverdale was a psychologist and management consultant in the 1960s and 70s who believed that skills could not be taught like knowledge, but rather had to be learnt from experience, which was the basis for his training approach. He was one of the first people that I am aware of, to talk about the importance of experiential training in a civilian context. So we knew we had to devise some activities that would challenge these supervisors both manually and mentally at different stages of the training process

The task we chose was straightforward. The participants were divided into three small teams and told they would be in competition with each other. So far, so good. Then we produced the materials for the game. They could not believe it. These consisted of three items: sheaves of balsa wood each stamped with a cut-out of a fighter plane, razor blades and plasticine.

The task was: "Build as many planes as you can in the next forty minutes. If they pass quality control by flying twenty feet past a measured target, they can be sold for $100,000. The team with the most money in the bank wins."

This caused quite some merriment with comments like: "This beats work"; "Can we take them home afterwards?"; "Am I on the right course?"; "How am I going to explain this to my shift?" Virtual chaos reigned for half an hour or so. After 25 min we gave a rain check on the "planes sold" to ramp up the sense of competition. It certainly raised the activity levels and the noise level went through the roof as "test pilots" jostled to get into the queue to test fly their planes and.if necessary start urgent price negotiations for scrap if their plane failed the QC standards. We then called 'time' and announced the results identifying who came first, second and third.

The real work came next. The question put to the course was: "You all had the same instructions, the same materials and yet your teams performed differently with many planes failing the QC test. Discuss why and explain how you would avoid this in future."

This was the illuminating part. Suddenly the hilarity subsided as these supervisors analysed why one team came first and one came last. They tumbled to the fact that the only variable was the players in each team. Therein lay the explanation for the performance of the team. Nothing else, there was nowhere to hide. Two teams realised then that "failure" could be explained only by examining their behaviour 'as a team'. This realisation made them uncomfortable as the supervisors' default approach in the factory had been to blame management when things go wrong. But this was a situation in which management could not be blamed. In fact in later courses we involved supervisors from factories in other non competing industries to help bring home the message that they can't always blame the managers above them, which was their standard response. They increasingly saw that they had a critical leadership role to play as the first layer of leadership in the company.

They all quickly came to the view that as these were (deliberately) unstructured groups a major problem was the lack of a leader. Hence they were slow to get organized and decide whether to specialise by dividing tasks or to let each member operate as a generalist. This was not discussed or assessed. The work process "just happened". They acknowledged they did not really have a plan. Their approach to the task was 'hit and miss' and even the winning team acknowledged their result was a fluke once they examined how they have behaved.

Their own conclusions were more instructive than a lecture on the same topic because they had experienced success or failure.

Their work methods were chaotic. When the time pressure was added in before the end two teams realised that in effect they then panicked. One team had not failed a QC test prior to the "time pressure" and then never passed one afterwards as they grew more frantic and less efficient. They put this down to no clear working system which, when coupled with the lack of leader and no plan, degenerated into near chaos. Teamwork was not evident and under the "time pressure" generated into every man for himself. We observers noted that the noise level shot up when we deliberately ratcheted up the competitive tension. We then had the insight to video the teams in future games so that they could then watch themselves and critique their own assessment of what actually happened.

They also realised that no one had thought about negotiating a "scrap price" for planes that just missed the QC mark. If one team had secured even half price for their failed flights they would have had the best result. Sharing of ideas was nonexistent as individualism prevailed with a vengeance. We could have run a session pointing out the importance of these issues but we knew this would have sent the supervisors to sleep. It was a far more compelling learning experience when they reasoned their way to these conclusions based on examining their own efforts. We were then in a position to discuss how these issues actually played out in the real work force.

So we next gave them a more complex task, which was to build a large tower of wooden Lego blocks with its base on a table but which had to reach the ceiling. Once again this was to be in competition. The results would depend on speed and quality of construction. Based on their recommendations from the first exercise they could now chose a leader and spend 45 min working out a plan for the tower and the allocation of work by the team members. The leader was to own the plan and any sketches that had been prepared.

Then once the teams declared they are ready we asked the leaders to change teams! That led to further interesting reactions which were valuable insights *based on their experience.*

The simulation techniques were working very well and people were queuing up to go on these "play-way" courses. There was a clear acknowledgement they were fun and participants were asked not to disclose the tricks to future participants. They all enjoyed checking on how the 'new' participants made out after the event. "How many planes did you sell etc." But more importantly the supervisors, some of whom were pretty jaded and cynical, took on a new lease of life as they realised the company was emphasising the importance of their contribution to the efficient running of the factory.

6.5.2.2 The Case of the Bank Managers

I next used a similar approach with a group of bank city branch managers. They were initially rather patronising about game-theory as they took their jackets and ties off. This of course was rather helpful as they generally performed worse than the factory supervisors. It was extra grist to mill now to ask "Why was that?" Given the simplicity of the tasks they knew they could not hide behind the technical skill of the factory supervisors. At first they were a little narked but increasingly tumbled to the real purpose of the assignments being given to them.

The "Tower Game" with the swapping of leaders was always dramatic. At that point the organizers were called some choice names. At which point they were asked: "Don't bank branch managers ever change jobs?" Now we were videoing the process, which proved to be very effective learning as people saw themselves in action. In one instance one of the participants was tapping a colleague on the head with a pencil to get his attention! When he saw this on the play-back session he was somewhat taken aback and had no recollection of doing that. This fact opened up a very helpful discussion about self awareness. A further refinement was to include some personality assessments (e.g. Myers Briggs) which make the self awareness discussion more penetrating and valuable for the individual(s).

On another occasion a bank manager, who had been chosen as a leader, froze at the moment he was to go to the new team. He walked over to his new team but stood transfixed for quite a while. In the meantime the team did not really notice the new leader who ostensibly had come with a new plan and took on a life of its own and implemented "their" plan not that of the new leader. This subsequently led to a key discussion about informal leadership and how to seek out and find natural leaders who could be developed. A role they now recognised was a key responsibility for a bank manager.

The bank manager who froze discussed his own behaviour with me separately. Until he looked at the video he had not realised the extent to which he was inactive and therefore not influencing his new team. We later re-played the video in private and stopped it at critical phases. This led to a constructive discussion about what he was thinking at the time, why this happened and what could be learned from it. Like a lot of managers in financial services he was a trained accountant but had had no training in interpersonal behaviour. He thought he was 'good with people'. He was comfortable and confident with customers but came to realise that he was usually in a controlling position where he was not under the kind of personal pressure that emerged in the case study.

It was clear that if he was to go further in the bank he had to deal with "friction" and pressure in a constructive way. He had assumed he would be fine in any people related situation. He admitted to being shocked by what he observed and said "This has been an incredible piece of insight and learning that I would never have guessed would come from such an exercise." We next mapped out the critical leadership skills he needed to focus on and develop. These two cases related to supervisors in WL 1 and branch managers mostly in WL 2. I will discuss below the Gemsasim case that can also be used very tellingly to analyse the *behaviours* of strategic management 'teams'.

The majority of organizations I have worked with tend to have weak meeting disciplines. This banking organization was no exception. But unlike many organizations they recognised the need for improvement. One of the cases we used was "The Hidden Agenda." The idea was to pick a topic—e.g. the location of a new airport. Participants would all have a briefing. All but two had different commissions to represent the views of a particular interest group. The remaining two had the same brief:

> You are not interested in the issue of the airport. You are attending because you have political ambitions. Behave in such a way that you will be elected chairperson at the end of the meeting.

Participants were told they could admit to their interest or brief if they wished.

At the end of the discussion the participants were asked: "What was going on at this meeting?" This was a case study to help sensitise people to be aware of the topics that were not on the table and to be able to sense and recognise that people have different agendas at meetings, which may or may not be overt. We then moved on to the dynamics of effective meetings.

I can think of one large multinational company that has successfully embedded a positive meeting culture that gets things done and which every leader is aware of. Decision making meetings require only one layer of management; namely the person who is accountable for ensuring the decision is taken. (This presupposes an organization knows its levels of accountability and who has the power to decide, which is not always the case.) In this company the accepted discipline is that operational meetings should typically take no more than an hour. The person chairing the meeting asks each person to state why they are at the meeting and what they expect/need to get out of it. Ideally this takes no more than 5 min—this means meeting membership should be small, kept to the essential players. Ten minutes before the end of the meeting the chair again asks each person to state what he or she gained from the meeting. This is often summarised as a view of "Bs & Cs"—benefits and concerns. It is a simple discipline, which means the working time in a meeting is about 45 min. It encourages focus and efficiency.

Hierarchy heavy organizations are notoriously prone to unending meetings with large numbers of attendees, who "need to be in the know", that resolve little. These are simply talk-shops and are a waste of time for most people. Probably the most inefficient meetings I have encountered are telephone conferences to accommodate people "working from home". It is little short of staggering how many people can be on the line. I have witnessed up to 50 on more than one occasion. The time management disciplines are chaotic as is the conversation since the chair cannot see who wishes to speak next. Repetition and circumlocution abound. These calls need more discipline and preparation than normal meetings.

The other source of make-work in hierarchy heavy organizations is the list of delegated authorities. The occupant of each layer is keen to have sign off authority so the spending limits are often too close together. They tend to be set on an arithmetic basis when geometric steps would be more effective.

Sometimes the bureaucracy is driven by the audit process. I once came across a situation in Africa where, because of previous loss of control problems, seven people, up to and including the CEO, had to sign off a process before it was cleared. I went to the CEO and said: "I see you have signed this. Did you read it?" "Well no, I didn't actually as I am very busy at present and I noted the CFO had signed it". So I went to the CFO and asked the same question. Same answer "as the chief accountant had signed it." And so on down to the first person in the chain, who answered: "No I don't need to worry as six others are going to check it!"

The introduction of legislation such as Sarbanes Oxley tends also to make-work. "We have to have this meeting/insert this new controlling layer, because of the new legislation." I have yet to come across a statute that legislates a new layer of management should be added to an organization's structure but the legislation is often interpreted as if it had. This is a potential extreme likely to affect financial services as currently people seem to think increasing regulation will solve the issues of defective strategy and ineffective organisation structure placing leaders in hollow jobs lacking accountability. The pendulum is in danger of swinging from too much risk to too much regulation and compliance, which is simply another way to further squeezing the accountability out of jobs.

6.5.3 GemaSim™

This is the most powerful simulation tool for assessing individual and group behaviour that I have come across. (The designers of GemaSim are two Swiss consultants, Werner and Andrea Naef, who previously worked for Swissair but who have been working out of New Zealand for a number of years specialising in

Human Factors training. They also work with NATO and many other organizations including hospitals around the world.)

Some of the most dysfunctional "teams" I have observed have been at the 'top' of civilian organizations variously called the executive team, the board etc. These teams are often made up of big egos that may have got to the top because they are the leading player or expert in their part of the organization.

GemaSim takes Game Theory to a whole new level. It uses a unique, sophisticated; modern IT based application. The application is designed to generate pressure—even stress—in a group situation. It is "played" on a lap top, in teams of four where each participant has a key role and their own lap top. The teams can also be placed in competition with other groups of four. These four players are interconnected and need to share information and work together otherwise failure is guaranteed.

The task is to fly into space (the laptops are configured as cockpits with realistic instrument panels and engine noise etc), achieve given objectives while completing a designated flight route and returning to base within a specified time. But the flights are subjected to unpredictable activities randomised by the computer programme. No two flights are the same. What has to be learned is how to behave under the pressure of the unforeseen while competing with others. The task to be completed is clear but the sequence of interference is not. The unexpected events test team coherence, self awareness and leadership.

Groups of 4–16 individuals form into teams of 4; each team representing a scientific space crew that takes part in a spectacular exploration of "quadrant X-578". Each team is aboard a small space ship that is being launched from a much larger space station that brought them to quadrant X-578. Once onboard their own space ship the crew members have to get accustomed to their own discrete working stations first. The crew members also need to work in pairs. Each member has a specifically configured work station available representing propulsion systems, task panel, experiment panel, control and indication elements. The operation of such a workstation requires the two crewmembers to develop an effective and efficient communication- and cooperation-style. But it is not only the pair of crewmembers that need to communicate and to co-operate, since both groups of crew pairs also have to manage their individual workload, to co-ordinate, to manage stress, to communicate, to manage tasks and experiments. Otherwise the team dynamic breaks down. All teams will have to cope with an increasing communication input (even overload) calling for decision making, time management and task completion within a given time frame.

Experience shows that in mastering all these challenges teams develop authentic behaviour patterns: i.e. they behave as they would in real-life. Individuals "play" their own part—which reveals how they behave under pressure at work. This is particularly so when the stress is ratcheted up.

Once back at the base station a thorough debriefing takes place including feedback, team dynamics' analysis, video feedback if required and individual reflections on one's own behaviour. The analysis is not judgemental only revealing. Sometimes additional insight can be offered by studying behaviour in the light of earlier personality inventories. That is what makes GemaSim an outstanding experience—the awareness that authentic behavioural patterns can be reviewed, modified and re-trained. New journeys can be then orchestrated to test learning, since the randomised nature of the journeys ensures totally a new experience each time.

GemaSim is based on research programs carried out in both the US and Europe. It has also been used in Australia and New Zealand as well as the US and Europe. The present version of GemaSim ™focuses primarily on seven core el elements that are fully explored plus another four el elements that are also discussed but not in the same depth.

Overview of the core training elements

- Teambuilding and development
- Leadership
- Planning and Co-ordination of task
- Information Acquisition
- Situational Awareness
- Workload Management
- Decision Making and Problem Solving
- Stress Management
- Conflict Management
- Error (Threat) Management
- Communication

The Rating Data of the programmes has been consistently high. For example using the average Likert-rating for each of the first seven items on the critique sheet—see Table 6.1—scores have been consistently high. Not only is the programme effective but people enjoy it. These scores are based on a programme run in the US, where the top score in each category was, “5”.

This is a rare case of a behavioural simulation that could be used with top executive strategic teams, who would consider it below their station to “play” with

Table 6.1 Average Likert-ratings for the first seven items on the GemaSim critique sheet

Classes	10–03	10–05	10–06	Item average
Critique item				
1. I used CRM[a] skills in this training	4.9	4.8	4.9	4.9
2. I felt I was challenged in this training	4.9	4.6	4.8	4.8
3. I learned from this experience	4.9	4.6	4.6	4.7
4. The training helped develop my CRM skills	4.9	4.7	4.6	4.7
5. I see benefit in this type of training	4.9	4.7	4.5	4.7
6. I enjoyed this type of training	4.9	4.7	4.1	4.6
7. I prefer this type of training over others	4.7	4.7	4.3	4.6
Overall class average	4.9	4.7	4.5	4.7

[a]CRM = Customer relationship skills

lego toys. GemaSim uses modern technology, which can ruthlessly expose the dysfunctionalities of top teams. The learning outcomes are basically the same, only the means are different. And today I would use GemaSim with supervisory leaders also.

6.6 Experiential Learning: Crossing the Strategic Divide

Most of these examples illustrate experiences in the operational levels of accountability—Levels 1–3. It is a moot point whether strategic roles are open to rehearsal training/experiential learning, except *maybe* for Level 4, in sophisticated war games. The essence of operational accountability and authority is ensuring existing resource(s) perform better. These are recognised as improvements in productivity, development of products and processes—the 'new and improved' beloved of marketers.

Strategic work is about more than just improvement. It is about identifying constraints and gaps in performance and resources. A gap in the market for example is an opportunity. It calls for the realignment of resources to meet perhaps a new or emerging social need. Driving the performance of existing people and assets is no longer enough. Strategic work cuts in at the fourth level of accountability. In a Level 5 organization the strategic work is quite heavy at Level 4 whereas in a Level 8 organization the strategic burden is lighter and more diffuse since there are another four layers of leadership above Level 4.

6.6.1 How Does Experiential Learning Prepare One for Strategic Roles?

Experiential learning is most commonly referred to as *on the job training*, although managerial leaders don't tend use that term for their training. As Morgan McCall (1988, 98 and 2002) has demonstrated in three books, it is also the basis of successful leadership development but it has a very patchy record in most civilian organizations. The most effective and proven form of experiential learning for strategic roles in civilian organizations is career planning based on *boundary moves, which as explained in Chap. 5:*

> *A boundary move takes an individual outside their comfort zone but not outside their learning zone. The aim is to stretch and broaden the learning of the incumbent.*

Strategic roles often entail general management responsibilities. The challenge is how to orchestrate the balanced experiential learning that will ease the move across the strategic Rubicon—Level 3–4. Most of us have encountered CEOs who have come up through only one line in the business: e.g. finance. It is difficult for them to develop impressive general management skills. The best preparation for general management is a blend of previous work in a number of different functions, geographies and/or 'business lines', which entail a steady but measured set of critical 'learning experiences'. In public sector organizations these might be different policy departments, different local authorities, hospitals, different regions and so on.

There is plenty of evidence to show that the best way to prepare the potential general manager is to ensure they have successfully worked in more than one testing learning situation. But 'lateral promotion' is not popular owing to the resilient and pernicious influence of multi-grade systems offering administrative "promotions"—(a change of label but not accountability). But it is not simply a matter of being in one job for a long time or having high intelligence because experience, no matter how carefully orchestrated, cannot compensate for a lack of innate mental horsepower. Both talent and blended challenges are needed to deliver the quality of experiential learning being espoused here to master the complexities of strategic accountability.

Genuine talent that lacks experience of more than one accountable role in more than one level of accountability is likely to result in a stunted and frustrated bonsai manager if working in a hierarchy heavy organization, which restricts growth and personal development.

6.6.2 The Critical Role of Boundary Moves

McCall, who arguably has done most work in the field to identify "the right stuff of executive development" also states that "*Potential is not the demonstration of acquired assets but rather is the demonstration of the ability to acquire the assets needed for future situations...In a world of rapid change, the real measure of leadership is the ability to acquire needed new skills as the situation changes*".[7]

Leadership development begins with experience but is driven by the mission and the organization's needs, which generate opportunities. We are now in a position to answer the question above about how and when to move from an operational role to one at a strategic level of accountability.

The answer is to move the person with *identified* high potential leadership capability through a sequence of testing *boundary moves.* There are typically seven of these.

[7] Ibid p. 5

Undertaking two or more boundary moves at the same time risks breaching the learning zone for all but the most talented individuals.

The 7 typical boundary moves:

1. A **change of function**, usually at the same Level and usually best done at an operational level of accountability, such as WL 2.
2. A **different learning experience at the same Level**, such as a turnaround or a start up or within the same function: e.g. a hypermarket manager moving to a turnaround situation in another store.
3. A **change of geography or country:** really critical for potential country managers and ideally orchestrated in Level 3 as a second or third role in that Level.
4. A **change from a line to a support role.**
5. A move to ***lead*** **a change project** (operational) or programme (strategic).
6. A move **from a field to a head office**/corporate role. Could also be to a support role: see no. 4 or a project/programme.
7. **A move to the next higher level of accountability: i.e. a real** ***promotion.***

The seventh move to Level 4+ can be risky ***if*** none of the other boundary moves have been used to build, expand and develop the leader's experiential learning base.

6.6.2.1 The Military Approach

As we have seen in the previous chapter the military services all have a rigorous and tested approach to the development of their officers and ultimately their generals. One has to be *identified* as a high potential officer who might be effective in future at the rank of general. Blindingly obvious you might say but the difference when compared to civilian organizations is that the military are aware, from years of experience, that there are age-rank-battle echelon alignments that need to be met on the path to becoming a general. For example it is known that a high flier in the army needs to be a major by age 32 to be on the path to the top. This is because they know their battle echelons and what experiential learning is needed to bridge the various opportunities presented along that path. Some individuals can progress very quickly and successfully—e.g. Eisenhower—but while flexibility is important it is dangerous to base leadership development programmes on the exceptions. A major aged 48 (in peace time) has not got time to complete that learning process since he will run out of both road and time for the necessary learning opportunities and is therefore very unlikely to become a 4* general—unless there is some sort of disaster in the meantime. In fact it is most unlikely the major would be still in the army at that age. Once an organization knows its levels of accountability (or battle echelons) it is then possible to plot realistic career paths. These are the vital experiential steps that enable personal growth given the right boundary moves at the right time *for the right reasons.*

Career planning is, or should be, a series of orchestrated experiences geared to heighten depth and breadth of learning in preparation for the next job, which could be at a higher level of accountability.

Some accountability levels are more important for personal development than others and it has been found that two or three jobs in those levels are essential stepping stones to success. In Chap. 11 of *The Accountable Leader* I plot the lifetime career of a manager who moved through eight Work Levels. He had three key roles in both Levels 3 and 5. Conversely I have seen that crashing through Level 3 in a short time actually undermines the chances of success in the higher levels. And we now know that one has to be well grounded in WLs 2 and 3 in the military via a number of different learning experiences—boundary moves. It has also become clear that skipping a level is a likely recipe for lack of success, as I have already mentioned earlier in this book.

Finally the military's ability to distinguish accurately between the value and importance of line and staff renders their leadership development both more effective and more complete. Civilian organizations are still beholden to methodologies of grading and 'quantitative' job evaluation systems that work against true leadership development. The result is many do not have a good grip on where their accountability levels reside and so cannot orchestrate optimal learning experiences for their high potential leaders across a blend of line and staff experiences. Too many civilian leadership development schemes are more akin to betting shops.

6.7 Strategic Experiential Learning in the Private Sector

Some years ago I worked with a company that had aggressive growth aspirations—I do not have permission to identify this company, since much of this work is considered a competitive advantage in its industry. **The strategy** set out the target areas for growth. The CEO was convinced it would be best if the new country or unit leaders came from within the existing business. He had invested much in embedding new values in the home operation and he wanted those driven across the Group. It was clear to him that buying talent on the market would not achieve that aim. But the majority of his top management had generally not worked outside the home country. The business did not have cadres of international management ready to take these new jobs. In fact the experience of the first few managers' chosen to be country managers was more than challenging. They had limited operational experience outside their unit. They were not accustomed to managing the political intricacies of doing property deals and the like in countries that did not always have similar standards of integrity to the home country, added to which these leaders invariably had little knowledge of support functions such as finance, legal, HR and IT. A number of these placements were risky.

The structures had been designed following the clarifying of the overall mission. The company had implemented Work Levels so we knew most of the relevant strategic roles were at or near Work Level 5. Thus we had to examine all the existing Level 4 leaders in the business to assess who might have potential to reach Level 5 within a defined but short time period. A problem was the company had only just refined its competency model and aligned it to Levels and top management were not yet fully au fait with how to apply it.

The challenge: how to plan the right experiential learning for future country managers across potentially Levels 4–6

In short this required the establishment of pillars 3 and 4 of Mission Mastery. The business was growing so even the core management's abilities were being rapidly stretched and extended. The major restriction for growing organizations is not money but the quality of their leaders, not all of whom can grow with the business. So we decided to set out to learn how the current crop of Level 5+ managers had learned over their careers to date. It became clear that a critical task was to capture the history and patterns of their individual experiential learning from the past to enable us to map lessons and create a blueprint for the future.

I therefore set out to interview a selection of the long serving, successful Level 5 managers "to learn lessons".

6.7.1 The Approach

I had earlier worked with Morgan McCall and George Hollenbeck on the research for their book, studying the development of top international executives.[8] I used some of their key questions in the interviews, such as:

- What has been the main source of your learning in this company and how did it influence your progress to your current level of responsibility?
- What and/or who were the catalysts of your development? What prepared you for your current responsibilities?
- When you think about your career and progress to general management, what events or episodes stand out in your mind—things that have changed you in some way and shaped you as an executive? What training did you get, was it appropriate and what did you learn from it (for better or worse)?
- Now think about someone whose career you have seen rise and fall; someone who was initially very successful as a manager and general manager, who was expected to continue to be successful—but who failed to live up to those

[8] McCall, M W Jnr, and Hollenbeck, G P (2002) *Developing Global Executives*

expectations. Without revealing the identity of this person please be prepared to discuss:

a. Why this person had been so successful prior to the derailment,
b. The flaws that were eventually his or her undoing,
c. The circumstances that lead to the derailment.

- What are the special challenges of having a boss who is from a different culture than yours? What about having direct reports from different cultures? How can managers be prepared for these situations?
- What in your view are the critical qualities and behaviours that enable general managers to be successful in this company? What behaviours will block progress?
- How do these behaviours manifest themselves in a manager who has potential to reach WL 5? How could you identify those qualities or behaviours?
- Finally, in your view what are the three critical things that are the "stuff" of successful general managers in this company? Can they be learned, trained and/or developed?

I aimed to interview a cross section of experienced managers then at the top of the business in the sample, particularly those who had had international experience. Thirteen key findings emerged.

6.7.2 The Thirteen Key Findings

Whether you are managing your own career or working in one of the best civilian organizations today, certain principles prevail.

- *Current General Managers had learned mostly on the job.* This would not change but these learning experiences needed to be less haphazard and more orchestrated than in the past for the learning to be more consistent and effective.
- Some formal learning is helpful, particularly if it outside the home continent in an international company and beyond the individual's historical cultural comfort zone.
- General management potential tracks/pathways can be detected when people are in their 20s. Many of those interviewed were in the equivalent of Level 2 jobs in their early to mid 20s and some in Level 3 by their late 20s. Therefore most of the General Managers needed in 8–10 years' time were already in this business, *and not just in the home country.*
- *Those with long service had tended to remain in the company because they had kept learning and growing as a result of changing jobs at key periods in their careers.*

High potential leaders tend to get restless as the gestation time for a real promotion is approaching. It seems the best leaders are aware of when they need a greater challenge.

- More than one person indicated they were considering options outside the company during this period, just prior to a major promotion. This demonstrated the importance of openness in career planning.
- There seems to be a series of fulcrum ages for development (around 30, 35, and 40 (*depending on the quality of jobs they have had in the respective Work Levels*) for assessing the progress of those *on track to reach general management at WL5+*.
- Current GMs were asked about the factors, which they perceived to cause **the derailment of GMs**, and they cited the following:
  - Inability to influence people over whom they did not have authority
  - Inability to build a track record, which delivered personal credibility
  - Lacking in intellectual curiosity, depth and clarity of purpose.
  - Lacking in emotional warmth and genuine interest in people.
  - Lacking the ability to build a team or contribute in a team.
  - Lacking successful results with external stakeholders
  - Lacking cultural sensitivity—often correlating with personal arrogance.
  - Lacking international experience prior to performing a GM role
  - Lacking a wide business experience.
  - Too few (or no) cross-boundary moves in career prior to general management.

  McCall also found that "*Insensitivity was the most commonly reported flaw among derailed executives in our research and was one of the sharpest differentiators between derailed and successful executives.*"[9]
- There was a strong consensus that **international exposure needed to start early in management careers,** if a bank of good potential general managers was to be available to support the company's growth strategy. An international development mindset was only slowly emerging. It was recognised that **Level 3 was the ideal time** to have an international move, especially if it was the second or third role in that level.
- It was felt that managers with Level 5 general management potential should have demonstrated all *or most* of the following:
  - a firsthand understanding of the business' core operations,
  - exposure to at least two business functions
  - international experience "sooner rather than later"
  - evidence of being able to learn outside their comfort zone
  - a good intellect, a clear sense of purpose and strong self organisation skills
  - a proven track record of managing people: "a cold fish is probably fatally flawed for general management"
  - evidence of being able to think strategically, "from a blank sheet of paper"

[9] McCall (1998) op cit p. 39

- evidence of being able to influence peers, e.g. through running a project where the authority to 'tell' is replaced by the need to 'sell'
- evidence of successfully building external relationships to achieve business objectives
- the ability to achieve results without doing excessive hours and/or working 'down' in the Work Levels of their direct reports.

This daunting list shows why it takes some years to nurture effective leaders.

Good leadership development based on experiential learning is an ongoing financial investment. It is not a cheap process or source of instant results but the payback can be a powerful source of competitive advantage. This assumes the organization knows its purpose, and reflects this with jobs in its structure, which have clear accountabilities and which are the basis for providing stretching learning experiences contributing to personal growth of individuals who live the values. That then results in a positive culture.

6.7.3 The Recommendations

I recommended the company take the following steps to improve the experiential learning and development of its strategic General Managers

- Potential General Managers must have provided evidence they really understand the business as a whole. They will need to have worked in more than one area, function or division.
- There must be evidence they practise the organization's Values
- They need to have wide business experience. They should have had a number of "boundary moves" across any of four levels of accountability, prior to appointment as a General Manager. Any combination of:
  - To another function,
  - To another division
  - To another country
  - To the Corporate Office
- They should have had at least three of the following *experiential learning assignments*:
  - Accountability for direct management reports
  - Accountability for a core line management department
  - Accountability for a "turn-around"
  - Accountability for a "start-up"
  - Accountability for a national or international project
  - Accountability for a though leadership role in Head Office
- Potential Country General Managers should have worked outside their home country at least once

- Potential Country Managers should have attended a formal general management programme outside their home Continent with an international focus
- They should have three boundary moves in WL 3.
- There must be evidence of above average brainpower and ability to set an agenda or direction and make effective decisions in tight situations in line with that. In other words, to think from first principles.
- It would help their personal growth to have a mentor, ideally someone whom they could choose.

In order to improve the leadership development and career planning, to help ensure the requisite bench strength and cover was in place differentiating competencies aligned to WLs were devised to sharpen the identification of the potential managers needed. The internal **training and development programmes** were designed to complement experience as requested by managers interviewed in the sample.

The most significant development to emerge from this project was the realisation that key boundary moves need to be planned early from WL 2 + for high potential leaders to both facilitate experiential learning and to ensure the best talent is motivated and retained in the business.

6.7.4 Reality Check

Now you might think that in the twenty-first century better progress has been made on issues such as training, international knowledge and skills transfer together with better career planning. A touch of reality makes for sober reading. In only 2006 a very thorough research undertaking came to the following conclusion:

> *The Jones Corporation (a hypothetical enterprise representing an amalgam of several multinationals known to us) addressed the problem of transferring knowledge and skills through expatriates typically drawn from the HQ country…top management remained wary of entrusting commercial governance to local managers. Expatriation has been used not only to control overseas subsidiaries but to provide career development for high potential (home) managers in support of corporate top management succession. The notion of a non HQ (nationality) board membership appointment has not been considered a remote possibility even if the candidate came from another English speaking country.*[10]

The research would seem to have focussed on UK and US companies. I have noticed even more pronounced biases in favour of home nationalities in French and Japanese companies.

[10] Perkins S.J. and Shortland S.M. (2006) *Strategic International Human Resource Management* p. 37

Consider further the following research reported in May 2015, giving an even more up to date and equally revealing insight into the reality of experiential learning in the UK:

> *The majority of business leaders will recruit external talent, rather than invest in the skills and development of the existing workforce, research has revealed. Despite 86 % of UK organizations identifying themselves as skill builders,* ***nearly a third (31 %) have no formal learning programme in place.*** *(My emphasis throughout) Furthermore of the 500 business leaders surveyed for the report from an online training provider Skillsoft—55 % said they are more likely to recruit externally to address skills shortages inside their organization.* ***Just 20 %*** *of businesses have aligned L&D programmes to organizational growth, despite the majority reporting an endemic skills shortage.*[11]

For those of you who plan to build your career by moving from organization to organization you just might end up tilting at windmills. The evidence suggests choice of employer is more critical than ever.

This chapter further reinforces the message of this book, that the military has long had an insight into how best to grow and develop the leaders it needs, which civilian organizations need to learn from and emulate as their record is very patchy in comparison.

Some Questions to Ponder

1. *Is experiential learning orchestrated in your organization or is it haphazard? What is the basis of a promotion?*
2. *Are key boundary moves identified and proactively managed to produce vital learning experiences for the best leaders?*
3. *If you have a 'leadership competencies' model on what basis is a 'promotion' calibrated: evidenced potential or is it simply based on good performance?*
4. *When people return from training courses, or learning programmes, what can you do to follow up and strengthen their learning through further orchestrated experience(s)?*

[11] People Management 01.05.15

Pillar 5: Culture

7

I would have loved to have achieved a flatter organization than we have ended up being. There are issues of almost cultural pushback. We're a very hierarchical country, so to have a very flat organization runs contrary to what the Indian wants to see. He wants to be better than the next guy.
Ratan Tata
Chairman Tata Group (This is the reply Ratan Tata gave to the question: "Are there things you wish you had done as chairman?" reported in Time magazine 14 January 2013 on his stepping down from the post of chairman of one of the world's great companies.)

7.1 General

The key idea of this chapter is the following: ***the culture of an organization is predominantly an output, not an input****. It is the output which stems from a clear mission, a healthy structure, objective and effective leadership development underpinned by sound individual assessment and appropriate experiential learning. If these are all positive, reciprocal influences then they will be mutually reinforcing and the culture will also be positive as a result. Conversely if even one of these pillars is faulty then the organization's culture will be undermined. Most writers on culture seem to think of it as some sort of psychological fire hydrant that can be sprayed all over an organization resulting in its general betterment. They portray culture as the lever to ensure sound strategy & structure, which guarantees outstanding leadership and a highly motivated workforce. But culture cannot thrive in a vacuum. If you cannot control the inputs you can't produce the desired output. This chapter*

(continued)

B. Dive, *Mission Mastery*, Management for Professionals,
DOI 10.1007/978-3-319-25223-0_7

will also briefly examine the makeup of military esprit de corps (culture) and contrast this with the ingredients of the culture of international success in team sport. The components of these cultures will be analysed for their potential application to civilian employment organizations. I will also explore the culture of a UK Bank that has been publicly criticised recently and critique the health of its other four pillars. This chapter briefly addresses the question of ***governance****, still a rumbling issue post the GFC.*

7.2 What Is Culture?

It is a question that has vexed many people and continues to do so. One anthropologist provides 11 definitions of culture.[1] Another author, reviewing the work of anthropologists, sociologists, psychologists and others, identified no fewer than 160 definitions of culture in circulation.[2] As Arbuckle (2010) wrote, "*For centuries the concept of culture has remained the subject of vigorous controversy: in fact anthropologists have never been able to agree on a single definition of culture.*"[3] This is patently a slippery academic path, which could lead to an unhelpful quagmire. I intend to limit my sources on culture to those who have written in an organizational context. In fact I doubt whether anyone has bettered Aristotle's suggestion that culture (ethical virtue or behaviour in contrast to intellectual virtue) is for the most part the product of habit. Fukuyama picks up that thread and sees culture in terms of inherited ethical habit.[4] He argues that trust is an inherent need of positive culture. I would argue there can be no real trust without clear accountability. Arbuckle would add that needs to be embellished with collaborative leadership. I agree.

In simple, pragmatic terms culture is 'The way we do things around here.' The challenge with culture is it is both "soft" and "hard". It is the soft behavioural element permeating an organization, which is not easy to grasp or measure reliably while also being the hard (difficult) thing to get right. For many line managers "culture" is fluffy stuff that they don't see as relevant to their challenges. It seems many HRDs make the mistake of going there first before the fundaments of Mission Mastery are put in place. It is of course easier to talk about "style, morale, organizational resilience" and so on, which is apt to spawn more meaningless initiatives. But this very lack of hard data and meaningful levers for managers to

[1] Clifford Geetz in *The Interpretation of Cultures*, pp. 4–5

[2] Ian Jamieson, *Capitalism and Culture*, p. 9

[3] Arbuckle, Gerald A (2010) *Culture, Inculturation, Theologians, A Post Modern Critique*, Michael Glazier Books. Chapter 1 of this book is the best summary of the development of the various threads of work on Culture over the last 140 years.

[4] Francis Fukuyama, *Trust*, p. 34.

work on simply generates indifference at best and hostility at worst from busy line managers. This is because culture is a consequence of the other four Pillars of Mission Mastery. Culture initiatives cannot overcome an accountability blancmange. And in their gut hard working managers know this.

Culture is a consequence not a cause. It is the end point not the start point: the outcome not the input.

Positive culture is an amalgam of tradition when built upon the sustained excellence of the first four pillars. I could quote countless blogs and comments from OD websites where people believe culture drives strategy, structure and leadership development. As we saw in Chap. 3, if a CEO has not really fathomed a clear strategy or mission for the enterprise, things quickly go awry or at best stagnate. My experience suggests most organizations do not have clear levels of accountability, which are the prerequisite of good performance. We also know from countless people-engagement surveys that ineffective structures correlate with low morale, lack of commitment. The outcome is a negative culture.

When the first four pillars are not robust a culture of no consequences is to be expected. Inertia is its manifestation. This will be illustrated in Chap. 9.

In one large international company in which I was working recently, the HRD was surprised to see employee engagement scores in the Latin American part of the company were low. "I wonder if that is a language issue" she mused. I replied: "I don't think so and I am not that surprised as there are twelve layers in that part of the organization." If there are critical shortcomings in the formulation of strategy and its partner strategy into action, coupled with a faulty organization architecture it is self evident that neither leadership development nor training is likely to be effective, no matter how much money is spent on both. This leads to individuals' lacking a sense of worth and/or purpose in their jobs. The resulting low "culture scores", typically unleash a flurry of improvements in hygiene factors to improve the culture scores. In reality there is a disconnect between what is actually happening and the cultural band-aids being applied. The cultural inputs are dealing with consequences and symptoms not causes. This in turn helps explain why "culture" has a bad press in so many organizations. As Tom Holland has pointed out, "The Romans judged their political system not by asking whether it made sense but whether it worked."[5] Busy line managers are no different.

[5] Holland, T (2003) *Rubicon: The triumph and tragedy of the Roman Empire* p. 24

7.3 The Military Approach

As there is greater clarity about mission, structure, leadership development, career planning and training in the military it is not surprising they have a well defined approach to culture. This is generally referred to as *esprit de corps* (literally 'the spirit of the body'): the common spirit existing in the members of a group inspiring enthusiasm, devotion, and strong regard for the honour of the group in pursuit of a goal. In other words: effective teamwork.

Having interviewed many senior officers they made clear their loyalty is to the monarch, not, by implication, to some public official/politician. This independence is nevertheless circumscribed with strong badges of belonging which also command great loyalty and affection as symbolically representing the regent. Sun Tzu long ago saw the importance of that. He was the forerunner in establishing what today we call governance. In a true democracy the head of the military cannot commit a country to war.

In the army, for example, a key focus is the regiment (a Work Level 3 unit) most reverentially manifested in the regimental colours, which represent the honour and traditions of a regiment. Hence each year in the UK, a regiment is chosen for the pubic Trooping of the Colour. The colours are usually laid up and displayed in a chapel, perhaps hanging from the rafters, when they have been replaced by new colours or when the owning regiment/battalion/Corps has been disbanded. In-service colours are held very safely and securely by the owning organization and will not ordinarily be let out of their custody. The rank of colour sergeant was established to designate those with *the honour and duty* of guarding the colours. For an established regiment with a proud history its battle honours are embroidered onto the flag. It is the spiritual manifestation of the achievements of that regiment, its proud history and the record of where so many of its forbears made the ultimate sacrifice. The flag and what it stands for used to be carried aloft into battle and soldiers lost their lives rescuing theirs or capturing the enemy's. The flag then is the embodiment of everything good these soldiers stand for and believe in: the team, not just the individual. Hence the telling phrase "wrapped in the flag." I was moved at my father's funeral in 2006 to see his coffin draped poignantly in the national flag, reminding us that he had previously volunteered and fought for his country, as his father, who lies in France, had done.

A regiment typically has **its own uniform**, recognisable colours and hat band. Some regiments become universally known for their fighting prowess and **tradition of excellence.** There also tends to be a pecking order among regiments, where over time some regiments have become more selective/exclusive and more famous. For example I found it revealing to read the motivation of the first man to win the VC in Afghanistan and why he was prepared to go to such lengths to win selection for the New Zealand SAS in the first place.[6] Similarly the motivation of another VC, John Kenneally, who during WWII, deserted his original regiment to join the Irish

[6] Little, A (2008) *Willie Apiata VC: Reluctant Hero.*

Guards he admired and how keen he was to mask his true identify to achieve his ambition.[7] People are always keen to join **elite organizations** such as the Paras. Not everyone is good enough to make the grade so to just be a member is a badge of honour in itself. The SAS has the added mystique of secrecy: unless you win the VC and your cover is blown!

The elite corps ticks all our Pillar-boxes: crystal clear mission, unequivocal command structure, top leadership development based on rigorous selection and rehearsal training coupled with a consciously crafted culture and tradition of excellence in the field. The one form of excellence that is supremely important in the military is **teamwork.** When the stakes are a matter of life and death being able to rely on your colleagues is of paramount importance. The Royal Marines don't apologise for their ambition to be the best fighting unit in the world. Mission command presupposes experiential training in teamwork at a level that rarely exists in civilian settings. Most units, especially elite units, have an established mantra "fight for the man at your shoulder". This drives a level of commitment that has been built up through shared adversity coupled with pride. As shown in Chap. 3 the military command structure is built around teams unfolding like a Russian doll: the squad, the platoon, the company, the battalion and so on. As one officer said to me: "*There is a great deal of academic work which points to the fact that whatever leads folk to enlist/volunteer, what makes them fight is not their nation, not their regiment, not their colours, not their company nor even their platoon but the men to their left and right with whom they eat, sleep, socialise and bleed.*" They are the key realities of teamwork.

7.4 The Civilian Approach

It is already clear that not too many civilian organizations are going to score highly on the demands of the Culture Pillar, given the widespread shortcomings that have already been evidenced across the first four Pillars. The strongest cultures in civilian organizations tend to be most evident in the sporting world. But, even there, sustained performance over a long period of time is the exception rather than the rule.

7.4.1 Schein's Contribution

Much that has been written on culture relating to 'what' it is, without being much help on how to build or embed it. Edgar Schein has written as extensively as anyone on organizational culture & leadership.[8] Indeed he is credited with inventing the term 'corporate culture.' For example he wrote about six Primary Embedding

[7] Kenneally, J (2008) *The Honour and the Shame*

[8] Schein, E (2010) Organizational *Culture and Leadership.*

Mechanisms, the first of which was "*What leaders pay attention to, measure and control on a regular basis, such as organization design and structure*." But there is no great insight into how that might be done and no guidance on how to choose the correct metrics. He defined culture as: "*A pattern of shared basic assumptions that the group learned as it solved problems of external adaption and internal integration that has worked well enough to be considered valid and, therefore, to be taught to new members as the correct way you perceive, think and feel in relation to those problems*." If that state is reached, it should then be habitual.

According to Art Kleiner, Schein talked of three cultures within an organization: Operations, Executive and Engineering.[9] He asked Schein why he did not develop this model. "Not enough time": Kleiner did not find that answer convincing. Schein clearly did not believe culture is uniform or homogeneous but cited the firing of the CEO of General Motors (Robert Stempel) as a case of a leader not reading and comprehending the internal culture. He saw tensions between these three cultures, especially the engineers (mainly IT managers) who want to design people out of systems rather than into them and who are not known for people leadership skills. Kleiner cited the former Intel CEO, Andrew Grove: "*Only the paranoid survive in Silicon Valley*". Schein was adamant that organizational culture is not monolithic and that to call P&G "cautious" or Microsoft "ruthless" is nonsense and that most blanket attempts to "change the culture" of a whole company are a waste of effort.

7.4.2 Fligstein's Contribution

Fligstein took a more generalist approach but his work was first and foremost an historical analysis of what has happened with the cultures of large organizations.[10] He noted that companies have changed their dominant culture a number of times during the last 100 years. He gave examples (US) to show that companies were initially monopolist, then manufacturing led, followed by marketing and currently finance (i.e. stock market driven). It would be nice if Fligstein and Schein overlapped but his model does not quite map onto Schein's operations, executive and engineering cultures.

So arguably there is no clear theory of how culture can be understood and *changed* in civilian organisations. Schein advocated a slow approach to organization change and it is clear, given the complexity and enormity of ensuring all four Pillars are aligned that this is an assignment to be calibrated in years not months. During an interview in 2002 he explained that cultural change takes a long time—25 years in the case of Procter & Gamble.[11]

[9] Kleiner, A (2001) "The Cult of Three Cultures", *Strategy & Business* 3rd Quarter

[10] Fligstein, N (1990) *The Transformation of Corporate Control*, Harvard U P.

[11] Edgar Schein interviewed by D.L. Coutu (2002) in 'The anxiety of learning' *Harvard Business Review*

7.4.3 One Company's Contribution

One approach in a global company, which was more impressive than most was written up recently showing how it linked OD, Lean Six Sigma and Project Management initiatives together.[12] The focus was on mission: to help GlaxoSmithKline "execute strategy brilliantly". It also gave an extensive overview of relevant academic work which, on the face of it, was impressively laced into their programme. The links were extensive but it was not clear quite how they played out in practice. The missing elements in terms of Mission Mastery seemed to be any work on organization structure and leadership development. There was reference to training of internal consultants and line management. Imperfect structures lacking clear accountability could have been a major drag on this initiative and that does not seem to have been considered. So an initiative that was far better than most in the "behavioural area" had a major gap in its design and implementation in terms of Mission Mastery. This might help explain the company's embarrassing leadership failures in China during 2013.

7.5 Culture in Sport

One area where the impact of culture is most evident in a civilian setting is national sporting teams. Although rather different to an employment organization there are clear factors, which seem to drive success. Some teams are consistently more successful than others. The few that are successful over a long period of time have a pronounced culture, which fuels that success. It is worth considering the best to see what can be gleaned from their cultures, their esprit de corps.

It is very difficult to gain *international dominance in a team sport* and therefore greatness in a particular sport is very rarely achieved over a long period of time. (For this reason I have not considered the results of national teams such as in US baseball "world series" or their basketball, and grid iron teams. There are no international benchmarks for these sports although aspects of team culture may be similar.) Individual sportsmen and women count their supremacy in short time periods. Teams on the other hand have the potential to dominate their sport for years on end and that is worthy of closer study. But perhaps not surprisingly the numbers of these internationally dominant teams can be counted on one hand.

7.5.1 The German Football Team

In football Germany are the current (2014) world champions. A mantle they have held previously but not regularly since the first world cup in 1932. Some say that is

[12] Alexander J and Huggins M (2012) A new Prescription for Improving Business Performance at GlaxoSmithKline, OD Practitioner Volume 44 No. 4

because football is very competitive as shown by the fact that four different teams have won the last four world cup tournaments. Interestingly the same holds true for rugby, where four different countries have won the last four world cup tournaments prior to 2015.

7.5.2 Australian Cricket Team

In cricket Australia has just won the 2015 cricket (50 over) world cup. Ever since the end of the nineteenth century the Australian cricket team has consistently been the team to beat in that sport. They fielded the greatest cricketer in the nineteenth century, Victor Trumper and the greatest cricketer in the twentieth century, Sir Donald Bradman. (At the battle of Monte Cassino in 1944 General Freyberg used the code "Bradman is batting" to signal attack, based on the fact that the Germans were not cricket aficionados.) The Australians have built up an aura which is today embodied in their cricket cap—the "baggy green". (The shape of the Australian cap is different to every other country's cap, which helps make it unique and therefore "special.") It has a symbolism for the players redolent of a regiment's colours. They make a ritual out of awarding a rookie his first cap as it symbolises the history of Australian achievement on the cricket field for over 100 years and that in turn epitomises the tradition of great achievement, success and *teamwork* which the new comer is expected to recognise, be aware of and not only match, but eclipse. The totem pole of long term success is a slippery one but as sportsmen know, form is temporary, class is permanent.

Historically the Australian cricket team is noted for playing to win and win at any cost. What is more it expects to win wherever in the world it is playing. The idea that in an away-from-home venue a draw is a "good result" is considered the mindset of losers.

7.5.3 The New Zealand Rugby Team: The All Blacks

In 2013 the England rugby coach, Stuart Lancaster, rated the All Blacks the best sports team in the world over the last 100 years. It has dominated international rugby with a sustained win rate close to 80 % that no other international sports team has matched for such a long period. It is somewhat unique in being universally recognised by its moniker "The All Blacks": not the name of the country. The first team to the UK, in 1905 lost one game in 35 while the next team in 1924 won all 32. So the legend was born. At the end of 2014 the All Blacks had won 40 (95 %) of their most recent 42 games, the majority away from home. The German world champion football team and the Australian cricketers both won 25 (62 %) of their last 42 games in the same period.

So what epitomises the culture of a successful team?

7.5.3.1 Ritual Symbolism

A key part of success is building a successful heritage and establishing symbols that both evoke and capture that tradition. The baggy cap is the symbol for Australian cricketers. They get only one and some look very tatty on the heads of 'old timers' who have played in dozens of tests under a burning sun. That in itself is a status symbol.

The black jersey with the silver fern is the iconic symbol for the All Blacks. It is simply referred to as "the jersey".

A symbol is "any reality that by its very dynamism or power leads to another deeper reality through the sharing in the dynamism of the symbol without any further explanation."[13] In 2013, the eminent rugby writer Paul Ackford, himself an ex international, wrote in the Times, somewhat mystically about the three layers of Zen "*The third is more complex and more ephemeral. It involves buying into a concept, playing for 'the shirt' which enshrines a sense of history and national identity, tacitly acknowledging those who have gone before and those who follow*".[14] That is what the regimental colours, the baggy green or the black jersey are about. The current All Black captain put it this way in his recent book[15]:

"This jersey will show up the frauds, the imposters. It'll squeeze those who look for short cuts. You won't last in this jersey if you are not prepared to do the things you need to do to fill it."

The black jersey has a mystical status probably no other jersey approaches. It symbolises the team. The All Black culture is a team culture. Although down the years they have had many individual stars they all know the team comes first. And the ritual afforded the awarding of the jersey deliberately emphasises the cult of the team. Great care is taken to reinforce the pride of receiving the jersey especially that first jersey, often given out by a famous former All Black. Each player knows he must not let down the high standards set by those who have played before him. Ironically journalists often write about the "myth of the black jersey." Unfortunately they are thinking of a 'myth' as a fairy tale or untruth, whereas any anthropologist would point out that myths are narrative symbols that bind a group together. The unfortunate journalists are naively feeding the real myth!

Another important piece of the All Black bonding process is the haka—the challenge—performed at the start of a game. It was first performed against Wales in 1905. At the centenary match in 2005 the Welsh alickadoos—a derogatory term

[13] Arbuckle G.A. (2013). *Humanizing Healthcare Reforms* p. 25

[14] Saturday 26 October 2013.

[15] McGee, G (2012) *Richie McCaw the Open Side*, Hodder Moa, Auckland

for bumptious officials—made a grievous cultural mistake. They refused to allow the performance of the haka on the field, an insult to any country from Oceania, each of which has a similar tradition. (All Pacific Island nations have their own challenge. It is part of their cultural heritage, part and parcel of who they are. Perhaps only the clans of Scotland would today have a comparable tradition, which is felt at the singing of "Flower of Scotland" when Scotland plays a rugby test match.) This of course incensed the All Blacks who could be heard performing the haka with a vengeance in their dressing room prior to coming out on to the field. For the record they dismantled the local team 41-3: an appalling hiding for a test team. Insulting someone's culture is one way to guarantee a heightened performance from them.

One of the tenets of the All Black culture is: "You are an All Black 24 × 7." To let down the jersey on or off the field is the worst sin a player can commit. It is also why they do not write newspaper columns when still playing. Criticising a fellow player in public is counter cultural. The touring management also give a lot of thought as to who rooms with whom on tour and when, which is deliberately aimed at building team culture and instilling the right ethos. No cliques, no favourites. Strict codes of dress are laid down as are disciplines about punctuality all aimed at reinforcing the culture of being an All Black.

7.5.3.2 Excellence

One of the key things the All Blacks strive for is to be the best at all times. Of course they do not always achieve that but the *Mission* is uncompromisingly clear. Often when interviewed after a game they have won comfortably the captain will make a comment such as: "we have some things to improve and to get right." They are constantly looking to improve their game to a level other teams cannot match. *Innovation* and thinking ahead of the potential opposition is part of that search for perfection. Aristotle was a firm believer in the virtue of practice to achieve excellence.[16] During 2014 I was in the office of the leading doctor in the New Zealand sports foundation, Ruth Highet, and was struck by a small saying on a carving behind her desk: "Success in life is proportional to your pursuit of excellence." She ministers to all sports and is one of those proud of the fact that she is a member of the country which, on the basis of population, has won more Olympic medals in more sports than any other. The culture of excellence there affects more than just rugby.

Having failed as coach to win the Rugby World Cup in 2007, Graham Henry, when re-applying to the New Zealand Rugby Football Union (NZRFU) to become coach of the All Blacks through to 2011, outlined his mission as follows:

[16] *Nicomachean Ethics* trans W.D. Ross p. 331

"Talent rarely beats brains at international level." He explained his trio of coaches would ensure that on the field the All Blacks would strive to take the initiative. ***"This means taking the high ground in the contest and playing the game at such a tempo and skill level that the opposition finds it difficult to compete."*** *He said this would be based on self-belief honed by in-depth preparation and organization as well as positive reinforcement of the player's execution in relation to this high tempo, highly skilled game. Add huge defence that would reflect the steel of the players in both individual attitude and pride they had in the team and you had the total package.*[17]

This is a clear articulation of the mission behind wearing of the black jersey and an unequivocal statement of excellence to be attained. In essence: 'We aim to win every game playing a quality of rugby no-one can match'. Idle boasting you would say until you see the subsequent record. He supervised 106 All Black games from 2004 to 11 for a win ratio of 85 %.

In that one statement you have:

- A clear mission: win every game. Respect the opposition but aim to outplay them in every facet of the game.
- Organization and structure He went on to construct a player leadership team of seven led by the captain
- Leadership development—he started his tenure by removing seasoned players, especially those he judged were not the positive influence he demanded of the team.
- He appointed a new captain and brought in young blood. Henry had only two permanent captains in his eight years. The All Blacks have a tradition of exceptional leaders (captains) starting with Gallaher in 1905. Many have been knighted over the years.
- Rehearsal training—sportsmen train and train and train to inculcate the "tempo and skill level" required. The All Blacks are known to focus on both physical and mental skills. They set out to be better than everyone else and to *execute* better than anyone else. It is not by accident they win so often. *And they do not buy talent from elsewhere to paper over the cracks.* Their coaches generally come up through the ranks (experiential learning) to develop and hone their skills.
- Note also Henry's career development as a leading coach. He had a number of key *boundary moves* along the way. He worked at many different levels starting at the bottom with schoolboys. A resilient winning culture cannot be built in a couple of years.
- The culture is clear: loyalty to tradition and the jersey (the team) and what has gone before coupled with discipline and respect to maintain its unique standing

[17] Howitt, B (2012).

in the international game. That means winning and winning well but not at the expense of good sportsmanship. The unspoken need is to innovate and stay ahead of the opposition who will analyse your strengths. The stated aim is to keep them in "catch-up" mode. (In 2013 a British journalist crept into the All Blacks training room and noted the statement: "We want to dominate world rugby". This was written up as boastful: the hapless journalist missed the whole point. I suppose he would also think the Royal Marines, who aim to be the best fighting unit in the world, equally arrogant! He clearly did not understand that excellence calls for a constant raising of the bar.

Graham Henry was knighted after winning the World Cup in 2011, having been chosen best international coach of the year on five occasions across 2005–11. Over his 40 year career he coached 562 games for an 83 % success rate at all levels.

7.5.3.3 Mindset

The forgoing helps breed a tough mindset in order to deliver against that mission. The All Blacks know what they are about and what is expected when they go on the field. Their fans and the nations' journalists expect them to win every game. That creates immense pressure. The All Blacks also have a mind skills coach who helps ensure they can handle the pressure. Interestingly they are so proud of this they will not even talk about it and they do not go into detail in public, clearly seeing what they are doing currently as a source of competitive advantage not to be shared. It stems from the fact that they are expected to win wherever they play. Securing only a draw away from home is a failure. In the last 10 years or so the All Blacks have lost one of their 45 tests played in Europe and it is no secret the team was laid low with the norovirus the day of that loss.

7.5.3.4 Study of the "Opposition"

The All Black management also study and analyse their opponents looking for weaknesses in opposition players that could be exploited. As Ritchie McCaw noted in the Epilogue to the book on Graham Henry "He spent hours reviewing videos, analysing, looking for that little something that would give his side the edge"[18]:

7.5.3.5 Innovation: "Brains Beats Talent at the Highest Level"

It is one thing to analyse the competition, but it is more important to have innovations up your sleeve that catch the opposition off guard. This calls for careful study of the laws of the game that are always changing. Being first to implement with skill before the opposition have realised what can be done. At the skill level the major challenge is designing new set plays and moves to take the opposition by surprise. And then to "put those in the locker" as opposing teams plan to counter them and think up new options and surprises in their place. Then to reintroduce them when least expected to gain advantage. In short, one must constantly raise the

[18] Howitt R, op cit p. 303

performance bar. The try scored to win the 2011 World Cup was just such an example.

7.5.3.6 Teamwork

What really matters is not the performance of the individual stars but the performance of the collective.[19]

Teamwork is the sine qua non of world class team, to state the blinding obvious. How to achieve that state of nirvana is not so obvious. The captain of the All Black World Cup winning team of 1987, David Kirk, shared his thoughts on the nature of "World-class teams" in 1992.[20] His article focussed on two groups of insights that he called "Signs of greatness" and "Qualities of greatness".

The Leader

Not surprisingly Kirk then describes the critical role of the leader. In essence it is to "strike the balance between belonging to a group and remaining an individual." New Zealand is an egalitarian country where recognition is the corollary of achievement. It is not who you are that is important, but what you do and have done. This may explain why so many All Black captains have been great individual players in addition to being outstanding leaders. There is no room for passengers in world champion teams like the German footballers, the Australian cricketers or the All Blacks.

7.5.4 In Summary

The spin-off of this strong culture is clear. The NZ Sevens men's team has won the international series for 11 of the last 14 years. The women have similarly successful in both 15 s and 7 s. The coaches of eight rugby nations are currently, or have very recently been, New Zealanders: Ireland, Wales, Scotland, Canada, Japan Fiji, Georgia and Australia. England tried to recruit one in 2011 but he turned them down.

The essence of the overlay to a powerful culture boils down to the pursuit of six soft things that are hard to develop and even harder to deliver.

- Ritual & symbolism
- Excellence
- Mindset
- Analysis of the competition
- Innovation
- Teamwork

[19] Bungay S op cit p. 183

[20] Kirk, D (1992)

So how do these six soft things play out in the civilian world of employment organizations?

7.6 Civilian Organizations

How do you deliver these six dynamics of culture in a leading international organization such as BT, DHL, Genus, Tesco, or Unilever? Similarly how can this be done in the largest Whitehall Departments or one of the largest Local Authorities? Although I am taking it as read for the moment, it is absolutely vital that the first four pillars are already in place.

We are now moving onto the next phase.

7.6.1 Ritual and Symbolism

The military have identified the Regiment as the focal point for "the colours", and the sense of loyalty that goes with that. But this is not the same for the whole army. Civilian organizations could do the same but there is one big stumbling block. The regiment/battalion is at the third level of accountability when the army is in the field, but few companies know where Level 3 cuts into their leadership hierarchy.

"The symbol" for a company could be its logo (but not its brand). But that is rather ethereal for the person at the front line and difficult for public service organizations, although not impossible. Plus the company logo is a two edged sword when things go wrong as they did for BP in the Gulf of Mexico.

More likely to be common to a given organization is its set of values—if they are known *and practised.* "Values are embedded in myths. They are action oriented priorities and beliefs shared by members of a culture about what they consider to be good or desirable."[21] Most organizations have a list of values, which at times are paid only lip service. But these could be the symbols people can relate to and identify with.

But the real trick seems to be to focus on leaders at Level 3 across the organization. These are typically general managers of key operations, likely to lead around 1000 full time staff but as I noted in elsewhere "discretion has to be used" because these numbers *depend on the nature of work being done at the front line.*[22] These are the managers who lead a significant call centre, development laboratory, distribution centre, factory, hypermarket, oil refinery, regional office, tea estate or sometimes a small country operation. These leaders can make symbolism clear and real in practice. I describe in Chap. 5 of *The Healthy Organization* how empowerment and use of symbols (feedback) worked in a factory in the US, where the top job was WL 3. People at and near the front line can identify with

[21] Arbuckle G.A. (2013) op cit p. 33

[22] *The Accountable Leader* p. 150

"their" unit and see the level of performance being attained. They can also recognise teams within that infrastructure provided its hierarchy is not unduly cluttered. It seems this (encompassing the first three levels of accountability) is what Schein had in mind when he spoke of the culture of "operations". A tea plucker in Kenya's Kericho highlands will not readily identify with the company's total African operations let alone the corporate office in London. *An effective culture has to be localised.*

7.6.2 Excellence

Excellence does not just happen; it has to be made to happen.

The advantage of the Level 3 unit is that it has clear directives and typically about five or six clear key performance indicators (KPIs) that can be easily measured. The "unit" knows what is required at each level. It is where the practice of values becomes concrete, observable and measurable. The training required is predominantly skill based for concrete tasks where feedback is clear and unequivocal. The standards of excellence are agreed and measured be they specified in terms of quality, quantity, cost, time and/or service driven. We now know that Level 3 managers are the backbone of high performing organizations. Conversely an institutional weakness at Level 3, as will be shown in the next chapter, is seriously debilitating for any organization. We also know, as illustrated in Chap. 5 that the mix and number of accountable roles, combined with time spent in Level 3, is a key determinant of individual development and success in higher levels of accountability. Finally the number of level 3 jobs is the litmus test for establishing whether an organization has grown (or has clear plans to grow) to a further level of accountability overall.

Although distributive leadership (at all levels) is important for success, it is clear that attempts to build an excellent culture will stand or fall on the quality of Level 3 leaders across an organization. I described a situation in Chap. 2 where a company had severe compression in Level 3. I would not recommend buying shares in that company! Furthermore, as that case study showed, it is also important to have good strategic managers at WL 4+—Schein's "executive culture" Those at Level 3 would, in my view, be at the top of his "operations" culture.

7.6.3 Mindset

This is a corollary of clarity of mission. It is the "no excuses" culture. I have just been reading the history of a smallish but successful Winery Group called Villa Maria. The owner, George Fistonich, gave his wine makers a clear mission: "Make the best quality wine possible". As he had more than one company he set the winemakers in competition with one another. The measurable goal was clear: "We want to be the most awarded (with gold medals) wine company in the country."[23]

The mission was clear. The mindset required was unequivocal. The selection and leadership development of winemakers was rigorous and supportive. (Over the years a number of the Villa Maria wine makers have gone onto success in other companies.) The goal, at the time of writing has been consistently achieved over a number of years. Excellence equals "top quality", the symbolism is "gold medals and international trophies" and the mindset is: "Be the best winemaker." The by-product is profit and commercial success not to mention great pride and satisfaction.

7.6.4 Analysis: Know the Competition

Most organizations we work with have a plan or idea of what they want to achieve. This is often broken down into great detail. Sometimes the environmental scanning is the weakest part of the plan. It is often amazing how little companies think about the competition or have detailed knowledge about their key competitors. They are the predictable source of "friction" but companies seem to plan as if there will be no reaction to their initiatives.

It is quite common in military strategy to set up decoys to divert enemy (competitive) action. The second battle of Alamein is one case in point. I have seen this done only once, successfully, in business. Some years ago PRC was planning to launch of a new type of toothpaste in the Philippines where they were no. 3 in the market behind Colgate Palmolive and Procter & Gamble. The CEO, Clive Butler and his marketing director, Peter Dart, decided to first launch a standard but decoy product, which caused the two competitors to jump all over it and spend a lot of promotional money ensuring it did not succeed. It was a deliberate diversion. Secretly in parallel, in a separate blacked out location, ignoring the local advertising agency, known to leak like a sieve, the team planned the new and real launch, based on a clear technical advantage at the time: a laminate tube. It was hugely successful, helped by the fact that the two competitors could not quickly match the new technology and they had spent most of their promotion budget "blocking" the decoy.

7.6.5 Innovation

Management innovation is often stalled in the breach. One reason being the lack of an effective innovation process (an example is given in the next chapter) and another being confusion between development and research.

[23] See Tyack, K R (2012) *The Winemaker* p. 170

Most innovations (covered under the DMA Element of Change) are development: Level 3 modifications of a product, process, service or system that already exists. These are very important and are the life blood of the "new and improved" marketing initiatives. (Note the finding in Chap. 3 by Chan Kim, W and Maugorgne, R that 86 % of innovations are only line extensions.) Changes based on research depend on some form of invention or discovery based on a new connection between existing categories of knowledge or even new knowledge. These are manifest as first in the industry, first in the world changes.

It is important to clarify whether an innovation laboratory is being set up for development or research otherwise confusion can result. (In Chap. 5 of *The Healthy Organization* I provide a short set of Work Level definitions for a research laboratory.) Innovation also fails on occasions because the individual is seen to be more important than the team. Although not part of my concern in this book, this is manifest at times in universities where teamwork is undermined by academic jealousy.

Once again the key level of accountability is at Level 3. Managers at this level are accountable for continuous improvement year on year, the driving of operational productivity and therefore development.

7.6.6 Effective Teamwork

Effective teamwork is an ongoing challenge in civilian organizations. It is an obvious need that everyone can agree upon but, it seems, few can orchestrate and deliver. Given the weaknesses already highlighted in Chaps. 3–5 this is not altogether surprising. When boundary moves and career planning is haphazard teamwork inevitably suffers. This is partly a systems issue as people chase the rewards that stem from grade-promotions, meaning invariably time-in-job is too short to develop both the individual and the team being led.

As David Kirk argued above, in Sect. 5.3.6 on teamwork, the quality of the leader is all important. And as Alaric Mostyn's research revealed in Chap. 4, too many 'top teams' are not teams at all. A lot of his consulting time is spent on endeavouring to improve the performance of top executive teams.

Another initiative of questionable value is the so called management bonding session where key managers are taken offsite to a remote location to share time and activities together. The aim allegedly is to improve teamwork. It is not altogether clear how roughing it in the jungle with different levels of colleagues will achieve that unless very insightful selection of the teams takes place. As Kleiner[24] wrote "*There's always been a frustrating fragmentation problem to solve somewhere (called the 'stove pipe' or 'silo' problem). Although corporations like to talk about cross functional co-operation, people don't work well across professional cultures. They probably never will.*" This thought seems to have led to Schein's

[24] Op cit (2001)

insight about "the three cultures". Thus operators see people as valuable team members, executives see people as expendable resources and IT engineers see people as troublesome nuisances. Teamwork within these 'silos' is probably easier to tackle (even though evidence suggests it is rarely optimal in IT), than across these cultures. It is not obvious how avoiding tarantulas in a jungle achieves that.

Schein makes clear that leadership is the key to his list of key determinants of behaviour in organizations. What leaders pay attention to, show what they care about in word and deed, what they reward, ignore, punish and who they promote and why. These are the things that give force to innovation, teamwork, a sense of belonging and values. He seems to be focusing not so much on what drives culture (the four Pillars) but what embeds or conversely undermines it. Key in that would be systems of selection, promotion, reward coupled with protocols for every day routines such as meetings, charters, statements and plans. (Note also Moreau's comments in Sect. 8.3.1 below.) Leaders set the design and systems but if they do not build in clear accountabilities they are likely to undermine all their efforts to model and demonstrate a desired culture.

But to state what should now be obvious: if the vertical elements of organization design are lumpy then attempts to build effective cross functional teamwork are well nigh impossible. The horizontal linkages are distorted as people with no decision rights block the progress of those colleagues in a network of lateral roles who do have them. The intended straight lines of a neat organizational lattice will degenerate into wavy squiggles of muddled accountability.

Note these factors of success reflect the DMA Elements.

Faulty organization design on the vertical axis is, I believe, the main reason why teamwork is often poor in civilian organizations.

7.7 Cultural Implications for Management

The assumption underlining management accountability is a line manager is held to account for the design and/or delivery of a service, policy, product or result that can be assessed in terms of quality, quantity, time and cost. In well led organizations there is a realisation that there is no such thing as a perfect plan or strategy. The challenge in a dynamic environment is constantly seeking alignment between plans, behaviours and results or outcomes. The one certainty is that there will be "friction" between intent and delivery. To quote Murphy's law: "If things can go wrong they will", or as General Meckel wrote in 1877: "Every order that can be misunderstood, will be."[25] It is the task of a manager to cope with this inevitable turbulence to ensure the journey from intent to outcome is not disrupted leading to a gap in performance.

[25] Bungay, S op cit p. 71

The essence of line management therefore is adjustment to inevitable but often unpredictable variances to plan and therefore the delivery of change and continuous improvement, which is usually measured in some form of productivity enhancement. This can only be done if the manager in question has control over the levers of change. This is often not the case in many organizations I have studied, being manifest in lack of authority for people (e.g. recruitment) and money (budgets).

If managers are not given ownership of the levers of change the result is a culture lacking trust, which undermines commitment. It is disconcerting how many top managers do not grasp this fundamental point, especially when there is an obsession with cost cutting.

When faced with deviations from plan and poor ensuring results, the danger for top management is falling into one or all of the friction traps identified in Chap. 2: (the knowledge trap, the alignment trap and the effects trap) resulting in more detailed information and analysis, more detailed instructions to the field and more detailed controls. That is likely to degenerate into micro management, undermining empowerment because a leader is likely to be working in the team's decision space. When line management accountability is not clear this vicious organizational circle constricts improvement. More confusion and delay are the predictable outcome as managers have to revert to more (often hollow) layers above them for a green light to progress. Increasingly this 'progress' is apt to focus on a process or input, not on output or results. Sclerotic structures feed on themselves slowing the heartbeat of the organization.

When managers lack resource accountability they are not true line managers. As indicated in Fig. 2 of the Introduction, leaders should have freedom on the 'how' assuming the appropriate training and knowhow.

7.8 What Causes a Negative Culture?

If culture is an output, then what causes it to fail? The Financial Times asked in April 2013: "What does it take to change the culture of a British Bank for the better?"[26] It was commenting on a parliamentary report into the downfall of HBOS and a report on Barclays' failed culture by the city lawyer, Anthony Salz. It concluded:

[26] Editorial 6/7 April 2013

> *"The standing of bankers will improve only when the quality of decision making is better and they have a less hubristic view of their (own) value. On the latter point in particular, much work is needed"*

There has been evidence of significant cultural failure in some banks since 2007. There has been a lack of relevant controls in the face of high bonus possibilities, skewed lending practices and old fashioned greed. There are also the macro issues, such as Clinton's misguided repealing the Glass-Steagall Act and setting up Fanny Mac and Fanny Mae to lend dollars to people who could not repay their loans, which in turn triggered the subprime fiasco that infected the Western financial system. But that is not the focus here.

Integrity is often a casualty of success.[27] My colleagues and I have consulted to a large number of banks since 2003. They were all scarily over managed, with many unaccountable layers of leadership. There was consistently a clear leadership vacuum in middle management. The one exception was a new bank just starting up. But even there, given many of its managers came from unaccountable structures in other financial services companies, they were keen to replicate those structures in their new bank.[28] Collusion based on self interest in the sector was quite noticeable. I well remember one HR department did not want us to reveal our findings about numbers of unnecessary jobs since that would affect the promises the CEO and CFO had made to the city *and of course their bonuses. That in turn would affect internal relativities and rewards including those of the HR department!*

7.8.1 What Led to Barclay's "Toxic Culture?"

Following the departure in 2012 of its CEO, Bob Diamond, triggered in the end by the dishonesty behind the Libor scandal, his successor Antony Jenkins bravely commissioned the city lawyer, Anthony Salz, to examine its practices.[29] He then did so under four separate headings.

Culture Salz found evidence of reluctance among staff to escalate issues of concern. He wrote: "*There was also in some parts of the group a sense that senior management did not want to hear bad news.*" He concluded that the bank needed to establish a set of shared values across its various business lines, and that the bank's senior leadership team should be responsible for demonstrating and promoting these standards. He also called for the bank to "look beyond" financial performance

[27] See Barbara Tuchman op cit p. 125

[28] Tesco Bank

[29] Paid almost £18 m in 2011

when considering new hires, to assess cultural fit and to reinforce this with induction programmes.

He found reference to the opening of a bottle of Bollinger for another banker in exchange for attempted Libor manipulation and suggested that the bank "fully investigate other areas where similar issues could have occurred." The clear implication being, he felt they had. He concluded, that a culture had developed within the bank that "some people have termed 'too clever by half', even arrogant and aggressive". This is a key but subtle point linking back to Schein's insight above. The top made the culture clear: it was one where what leaders signalled and meant, rather than what they wrote was: "Do anything that makes a buck." Salz called for more open collaboration between the banking industry and its regulators. He also called for bankers to spend 2 years working for the regulator, and vice versa, to recognise the value of good regulation for both sides. Creative boundary moves!

Regulatory and Tax Matters The review said it had "observed a tendency for Barclays to test the interpretation of rules and regulations rather more strongly than would have been expected." It highlighted Protium, a 2009 off-balance sheet structure used by Barclays, as something that "exemplified Barclays' corporate character at the time." In classic legal understatement, the review found that Barclays "may have underestimated the reputational effect of its dealings with the tax authorities, which have been another source of damage to the bank's reputation".

Compensation Salz found that Barclays' remuneration systems over-emphasised short-term financial performance and "tended to reward revenue generation rather than serving the interests of customers and clients". Pay should also be linked to group performance, not individual business unit performance, and should avoid potential conflicts of interest. Significant bonuses should only be paid in the case of strong performance across all dimensions of a balanced scorecard which appropriately weights risk, values, and other non-financial elements. During this period, although the share price fell, the pay of the CEO, Bob Diamond, still went up. It seems it is rare for so called variable pay to ever go down.

Leadership and Governance Salz found that when Barclays promoted Diamond to the role of chief executive in 2010, it did not adequately consider other candidates. He found that when the focus turned to weighing him against a short list of external candidates, it was decided that only one should be interviewed. He wrote: "It is possible that too much weight was given to Diamond's considerable achievements in building a leading investment bank and not enough to the different challenges of leading a UK institution such as Barclays, with an important retail customer base, and in an environment of low public trust and enhanced scrutiny." The review found that the challenge process between the board and the executive committee of the bank was "not as effective" as some interviewees would have liked.

The Rise of Investment Banking From its "edgy underdog" years in the late nineties and early noughties to its post-Lehman Brothers stature as a leading global investment bank, the report noted the rapid growth—almost from scratch—of Barclays Capital relative to the rest of the group's businesses. Barclays Capital lacked history, which gave its leaders a chance to "define their own cultural context". But its differing characteristics compared with other businesses meant that "despite being part of the Group and benefiting from a lower cost of funds supported by a single credit rating, and retail inflows, the investment bank tended not to recognise the relevance of Group and was never likely to adopt its culture."

Its leadership by a "stable, close-knit team" brought continuity and experience to Barclays Capital (BC) but those interviewed told the review team "this made it hard for others to inject challenge". (It will be pointed out below in this chapter, that a strange decision had been taken whereby the head of BC was given charge of developing the bank's top 100 leaders, when he had only "provincial" experience of the bank as a whole. This was not a wise or normal approach to leadership development and Salz also highlighted his lack of comparable experience in retail.)

It is important to note that the culture in the bank at this time *was very strong and strongly reinforced—but it was wrong!* Weaknesses among the four pillars, as shown below, contributed to this debacle.

The review added that: "Many of our interviewees told us that while some members of Barclays Capital's top team inspired and valued loyalty, the team disliked bad news. This all combined to create an environment in which leaders were rarely effectively tested or challenged, contributing to a sense of ambiguity about what was considered right and wrong."

In 2013 Barclays Bank was publicly castigated for its toxic culture. I had consulted to the bank prior to the GFC and was in a position to consider the robustness of the four pillars and their contribution to that culture.

7.8.2 Assessment of Barclays Against the Five Pillars

7.8.2.1 Strategy

As I have remarked above in Chap. 2, the strategy just prior to the financial crash was to be one of the top five banks in the world. This led to the rather simplistic approach to put the Dutch bank Amro in play as part of its global ambition. But as invariably happens in these situations, the company that puts a takeover target into play is rarely successful. Barclays' CEO was incredibly lucky that RBS also did not have a sound strategy either and set out to trump his offer. So, somewhat fortuitously, Barclays was saved from disaster.

Its strategic pillar was not sound.

7.8.2.2 Organization Structure

Although there were serious issues in organization design this became the strongest pillar based on work done initially by Gary Dibb with help from others such as my colleagues Adam Pearce and John Bruce Jones. A set of OD structure principles were devised called the Barclays Organization Structure Principles (BOSP). Although these empowered HRBPs to enter further into strategic OD discussions with line manager clients there was still the issue of deciding how many layers were justified. My colleague, Adam Pearce, used to be the Head of Organization Design in Barclays and he convinced the CEO in 2004 that the bank at that time justified no more than eight layers of hierarchy. He demonstrated that they had eight layers in their senior executive grade alone, which was a shock to the CEO. The result of this hierarchy heavy situation meant that over two thirds of its employees were too far removed from the top of the business. They were below layer 8—taking the CEO as layer 1. Over a period of 2 years Adam helped to significantly improve that situation, with strong backing from the CEO and members of the top Operating Committee. As in most organizations it was not the jobs near the front line that were at risk but those in the unnecessary layers in middle to top management. These were very expensive roles so the cost implications, not to mention the impact on empowerment and customer service, were significant. In one piece of fieldwork we found eight layers that all claimed to be in the customer escalation line.

There were a number of important OD projects, which Adam and I worked on together, such as those in Barclaycard and in Africa, under the aegis of Gary Hoffman and David Roberts respectively. (It was Gary Hoffman who later called us in to help him turn around Northern Rock.) We trained 100 HR managers together in OD principles and techniques such as DMASS. The challenge at Barclays became increasingly complex since while needing to de-clutter middle management structures the bank began to pursue ambitious growth targets. Staff numbers doubled in the period from 2003 to 2008. This combination of events added greatly to the accountability, organization design and leadership development challenges.

Although structure was the strongest pillar, and much good work was being done, it was not yet as robust as it needed to be across the whole group in the run up to the GFC.

7.8.2.3 Leadership Development and Training

Given their strategy ambition for growth, top management realised leadership development and career planning was a vital adjunct to this ambition. When I was first called into Barclays by Adam, the organisation design task had already been coupled with the bank's leadership aspirations. What I heard from his leadership development peers was something like: "Our results are pretty good, but not quite as good as some of our key competitors. This suggests our leaders are not as good as theirs." There did not seem to be an embedded culture and approach to leadership development and career planning that matched the international growth aspirations.

The assumption seemed to be: "Our strategy is clear but we are not so clear on the quality of our leaders." We quickly showed the structure was too rich with many hollow jobs. The problem then for the leadership development ambition of the company was, you cannot fail in a hollow job with no decision rights, but you can't succeed either, which encourages political behaviour and undermines effective leadership development.

It is virtually impossible to accurately assess leadership capability in a hierarchy heavy organization. The likely result is stunted bonzai managers.

The truth was Barclays did not know how good (or how bad) its leaders were and was hampered in finding out given its unwieldy structure. Another problem appeared at this stage. Usually in a global company the CEO takes direct charge of managing the top 100 jobs and people in the organization, covering reward, potential assessment and career planning. The best CEOs spend more than 20 % of their time on this critical task. But at the time the CEO of Barclays had passed this task to the Head of the investment bank (Diamond). Varley may have been grooming Diamond to take over as CEO, but it was a most uncharacteristic step for an incumbent CEO to take and a huge risk, given his aggressive growth strategy and drive to recruit the 'best bankers in the world'. Added to which, as Salz noted, Diamond did not have wide experience of the whole Group. Harold Stieglitz pointed out over 50 years ago that one of the five "hard core reserved responsibilities of a chief executive is succession development."[30] The Barclays CEO was perhaps confusing delegation with abdication, an issue I return to in chapter 9.

Accountability for executive leadership development is a CEO accountability that should not be entrusted to anyone else, let alone outsiders Board members are "insiders" in this context.

Given the agreed importance of leadership across the bank if it was to deliver on its strategy, the bank set out to identify the best 100 managers given their ambition to achieve greater international market domination. They employed an approach called 'top grading', which generated a lot of unsettling churn as people deemed not good enough were moved out of the business and new comers were brought in.

Gopalakrishnan has noted the gap in many organizations between intent and delivery ('friction') in the field of leadership development, "which calls for a structured planning system".

[30] Stieglitz's 1962 paper reprinted in (1972) *Organization Structuring* ed. E.H. Frank p. 307

Developing management succession requires a sequence of protecting, nurturing and pacing. This is observed in Nature.[31]

Assessment of training was not part of my brief so it would not be appropriate to comment further. But overall the strong impression was:

The pillars of "nurturing" leadership development (and training perhaps) were not as strongly embedded as they needed to be. It is possible that the bank's bold ambition led to an indigestible upsurge of pressure in the workload of the first three shaky pillars.

7.8.2.4 Culture

Salz was scathing on the topic of internal culture but of course the horse had bolted by the time he visited the stable. But, as I have already argued, culture is an output not an input. It builds principally on the quality of the first four pillars. So given some shakiness in at least two of those pillars it is self evident the bank would struggle to generate a positive culture.

During this time the bank embarked on an aggressive drive to *rapidly* recruit 'the best bankers in the world'. What seemed to be overlooked is the fact that 'best' is completely dependent on the *best fit to the new job* being offered. Even the 'best' cannot perform to their best in an unaccountable role. The risk of such a talent strategy is it was apt to water down the good culture that existed in some parts of the bank. In 1 year, as I understand it, about a quarter of the senior executives in Barclays were moved on. Whilst the people who replaced them might have been talented, my sense is they came from many different major competitors. In some cases the new recruits at or near the top, seemed to bring in a whole teams from their previous company. That approach raises important questions about the prevailing values: but leaving that to one side, the speed of the process was not conducive to creating positive cultural integration. It was not a case of "protecting, nurturing and pacing" talent.

Salz had little to say about the first four pillars, which also tends to illustrate how the true drivers of culture are still not really understood.

Consider the following anecdotal evidence and note the significance of the role in question. Around the time of the leadership review a new person was put in charge of HR. He was something of a maverick whose exploits came to be covered in the local press as he was known to kick staff members' bags if they displayed a competitor's logo or cut off managers' ties during a meeting with key suppliers if he did not like the supplier's performance. One morning he deliberately jumped over the security barrier as he entered the building via the ground floor foyer on his way to his office on the 20 something floor. Once there he rang down to have the security

[31] Gopalakrishnan, R (2007) *The Case of the Bonzai Manager* p. 115

guard, who did not stop and challenge him or check his identify pass as he hurdled the security barrier, reprimanded!!

Cultures don't go rancid overnight. Key elements of Barclays Pillars of Mission Mastery had been deficient/partially deficient for some time. While it is critical to have all Pillars in sync to achieve Mission Mastery, only one has to be seriously deficient to cause a major wobble in the equilibrium of an organization and therefore its culture. Its strategy had been exposed over the Amro bid. Neither its structure nor its approach to leadership development and career planning were completely effective or appropriately dovetailed across *the whole Group*. Indeed not surprisingly, with the wisdom of hindsight, these factors taken in conjunction with what seemed to be not an unduly strong board probably contributed to the choice of an unsuitable CEO who quickly failed in full glare of the footlights. Indeed a dangerous "culture" in relation to reward was also becoming more evident by then. Prior to his retirement Varley spoke of the need to pay the market rate when justifying the high pay of some of his executives. The issue of good performance seemed to be slipping off the agenda.

Ambitions for helter-skelter growth and the snaring of the 'best bankers in the world' became the victims of hubris. But encouragingly, the signs are Barclays' new leadership is stepping up to the plate but culture change of this magnitude takes time. In 2015, the CEO of Philips, Frans van Houten, admitted that since taking up his post in 2011 he had been on a "transformation journey" to address under performance admitting he had spent 4 years up to then, striving to change the company's culture to make it more agile, fast moving and collaborative.[32]

7.8.2.5 Impact on HR

Something rarely commented on has been the continual loss of good HR managers from Barclays over the last decade. Good companies always lose some high quality managers. In fact low management turnover can be a sign of a sleepy culture that is blind to poor performance. But the number of Barclays HR managers who have left and prospered elsewhere is close to remarkable. Even more interesting is the fact that they meet informally to keep friendships alive. A toxic culture fuels the departure of the best people who know they have marketable skills.

For example many of Adam Pearce's former bosses and colleagues, have asked him into their new companies to "ply his trade" that they admired in Barclays. These include, Gary Hoffman at Northern Rock, Pavita Walker at Lloyds Banking Group, Allan Fielder at Toronto Dominion Group in Canada, Valarie Scoular at Aegis Media, Paul Fretten at the Cabinet Office and Mark Wells at Experian.

[32] The Sunday Telegraph 19 April 2015.

7.8.3 The Issue of Governance

The quality of governance is the one over arching issue that affects the interplay of the five pillars. The knee jerk response to organizational failure is more control and/or legislation, which closes the stable door after the horse has bolted. The effects trap. Many so called "systemic" failures are misnomers. The Enron failure stemmed primarily from the auditor (Andersen) not following their own internal governance procedures set up to clear their audit reports. Any auditor will tell you, neither their systems nor laws will overcome collusion. The resultant Sarbannes-Oxley act spawned plenty of bureaucracy and warm feelings but did little to avert the GFC.

In its aftermath of the GFC there is a distinct danger the pendulum is swinging towards too much regulation. Now the danger is an army of people with limited practical understanding or experience of the entities they are to 'control'. For example, when I was working with a new bank the regulator insisted it have a job evaluation system. The bank in question had moved beyond that to install Work Levels, but the regulator was locked into its limited, historical view of the universe and did not seem to understand how grading systems have contributed to excessive pay in the industry.

7.8.3.1 The Military Approach to Governance

In 2003, Gary Moreau argued post the Gulf War (when NATO first used mission command) that the military approach to governance had much to teach business.[33] He noted that the military define specific rules of engagement (the mission) for "*all levels in the organization to follow. Front line personnel are given authority to act. There is no need to clear their decisions through a committee or to call HQ for authorization If you are the captain on a ship and the admiral happens to base his command from your ship, nevertheless all decisions outside the fleet's mission are ultimately your call. The same applies in the cockpit of a plane where the ranking pilot has unquestioned authority on matters that do not compromise the overall mission. There are no such constraints on CEOs. If they are on your ship they are likely to dictate everything from rules of engagement to the items on the menu in the cafeteria.*" If that sounds farfetched recall the example in Chap. 2 of a CEO at the helm of a WL 8 organization who decided the shape of the filing cabinets in head office and the colour of wafers at his meetings.

Moreau was concerned about the excessive consolidation of CEO authorities that result in excessive power. He argued that power is the fuel of corruption and the war in Iraq and elsewhere demonstrates that authority does not have to be absolute in order to be effective and efficient. Greater delineation and compartmentalisation of power within the corporation is needed, in his view, especially in matters controlling advancement, compensation and job retention. "*These governance*

[33] Moreau, G (2003) What the Military can teach corporate-governance reformers, *Across the Board*. p. 31ff

functions should report to the board chairman, not the CEO…to ensure greater objectivity." Note *he was writing 5 years before the explosion of the unbridled greed that contributed to the GFC*. Sadly a number of board remuneration committees have proven to be ineffective, despite their governance brief. This performance gap in civilian governance has not yet been fully overcome but it is intriguing that Moreau saw part of the answer in the military model, 12 years ago, which is an implicit endorsement of Mission Mastery.

7.9 Culture Is Universal

Although international organizations and countries have their different cultures subpar behaviour is always possible, for a variety of reasons. Consider the following:

7.9.1 A Culture Failure in Japan

The Olympus culture failure, which occurred in 2011, when they dismissed their whistle-blowing English CEO, is also dramatic especially since it led to an 82 % fall in the share price. It seems to have been a case of collusion and weakness of leadership at the highest levels of the company.

When dismissed, CEO Michael Woodford revealed he was ousted because he raised questions about $1.5 billion of questionable payments made during four previous acquisitions. The company at first tried to brazen it out but had to admit these had been used to hide losses going back two decades. He found he was challenging Japanese corporate culture where "harmony" trumps all else. "*The country needs thorough reform*", he said.[34] "*My view is the thing that is profoundly wrong in Japan is the cross-shareholding, which returned after WWII.*[35] *Culture was based on notions of consensus, and harmony (so praised as 'Japanese management' in the 1980s*[36]*). Now everyone tends to own each other so it is taboo to criticise another company and you never sell the stock. Managements can stay unless they go into liquidation, no matter how incompetent they are. That creates a culture of sycophancy and yes men.*"

Woodford's disclosures led to, Tsuyoshi Kikukawa resigning his positions as chairman, president, and CEO on 26 October 2011—only 12 days after he took on the CEO role himself. He had a combination of roles that would not meet basic governance standards in the majority of Western economies.

---

[34] The Sunday Telegraph, 13 November 2011, p. B9.

[35] The Americans were supposed to break up the Ziabatsu arrangements from before WWII.

[36] Pascale, R T and Athos, A (1981) *The Art of Japanese Management*, Victor Gollancz, London.

Clearly this is a case where the issue of culture and poor governance can be larger than a single company. Garratt has flagged that these issues invariably stem from ineffective governance and poor leadership at the top of organizations.[37]

Wherever it occurs, a negative culture inevitably spells failure in the end because the underlying bastions (the four pillars) have started to disintegrate.

7.9.2 The Influence of National Culture(s)

Now let us return to the quote of Ratan Tata at the beginning of this chapter, to consider to what extent an organization's culture may be captive to the national culture. It can be a factor as the Olympus example illustrates but I believe there is a tendency to overplay the significance of national culture in the context of organization design, accountability and leadership. It is also interesting to note that Gopalakrishnan, who summed up his insights about lack of empowerment in "*The Case of the Bonzai manager*", was also a senior executive in Mr. Tata's team when he wrote that book.

I first went to India in 1982. Yes, it is a very hierarchical culture stemming in part from the caste legacy but that does not seem to be the root cause of its unwieldy bureaucracies. (Low cost labour and the desire to spread employment are two factors not to be underestimated.) Much of the country's bureaucratic mindset and organizational failings are laid at the door of the Indian Civil Service (ICS), with its armies of "Assistants to" and "Deputies", which are said to be an earlier legacy of the British Civil Service that have since migrated into private sector organizations. One key reason stemmed from a pay cap in the ICS. In 1982 the top salary that could be paid to a director in industry was 72,000 rupees p.a. (hardly $10,000 then). This was because the top rate in the Indian Civil Service was 72,000 rupees, which had not changed since Independence in 1947. India became a republic at the beginning of 1950. This in turn led, over time, to a veritable explosion of fringe benefits, such as flats, cars, drivers, bearers, cooks, education allowance etc as managers tried to keep up with the cost of living. These were also very critical status markers which in turn reinforced the importance of (excessive) hierarchy. Fringe benefits undermine a performance culture, since everyone gets the benefit irrespective of the quality of their contribution. Rajiv Ghandi courageously opened Indian markets to the world of global competition but the previous culture was by then also well embedded in the national mindset. So in that sense Mr. Rata is correct. Interestingly he took over Tata during the new 'Rajiv epoch' so he inherited the dead hand of the hierarchical status-driven legacy. As we have already noted Schein advocated "slow, thorough and gentle corporate initiatives" in order to succeed with a change in culture. Mr. Tata's instincts seem to take him in that direction.

[37] Garratt, R (1996)

Unilever introduced Work Levels around the world in 1998, including Hindustan Lever (HLL), their very successful Indian company. Earlier field work there using the Work Level approach had already highlighted structural shortcomings and over layering that needed to be addressed. The approach was adopted by the CEO, Dr. Ashok Ganguly and in fact a number of managers who later left HLL took the philosophy with them. A couple (including Gopalakrishnan) went to the Tata Group and aimed to introduce a version of Work Levels there. I was asked to audit this approach in 2005 and pointed out a couple of flaws in the approach that needed to be redressed if it was to be fully effective. Mr. Tata clearly recognised the overall problem. He had the company tackle it but it seems progress has not been as good or as quick perhaps as he would have liked. Change in a huge organization is not straightforward but as Tata now operates around the world it must not let the legacy of a previous Indian culture hold it back. I work with a consultant in Japan who has the same challenge with a number of Japanese companies wanting to be "less Japanese" and more effective in international markets.

7.9.3 So, Is Accountability Only a Western Concept?

When introducing Work Levels in Unilever I travelled the world introducing the logic and approach in different countries. I well remember running a workshop in Singapore, where I was getting a lot of resistance to the idea of one layer per Work Level. "You must realise Asia is different. It is very status conscious and this approach will not work in this part of the world". Then it dawned on me after some time that only the expatriate Europeans were talking in this forum. The Asians, as is often the case, were keeping their powder dry in front of their "knowledgeable" Western colleagues. I then asked my Asian colleagues for their thoughts.

The Japanese pointed out that in Japan there was a national set of titles, which were usually on business cards indicating who should bow lower, assuming the two executives' companies were of relative equal worth. These titles such as: kakaricho, kacho and bucho for example were well embedded in the national psyche. In discussion it became clear that kakaricho broadly equated to a WL 1 supervisor, kacho to a WL 2 manager, bucho WL 3, honbucho WL 4 and so on. In fact it was becoming apparent that we could use the Japanese nomenclature to delineate the levels in Japan. The Japanese were very comfortable with this idea as they had long thought their approach was superior to the Gaijins' (foreigners') job evaluation systems!

The Koreans had a similar system. In their case Ju-yim was akin to a supervisory Level 1 role, Dae-ri WL 2 and Cha-jong, WL 3 and so on. My concern was the Koreans had, over time, inserted too many instances of the title "deputy" which is often the harbinger of a hollow job. This meant they tended to have two titles per Work Level, which was not such a good starting place.

The Indians as already noted have a social caste system but it does not seem to have migrated directly to the work place. But they still tend to have a plethora of empty job titles such as "Assistant to", "Deputy", "COO" and so on, which denotes a heavy cultural baggage as Mr. Tata experienced.

In addition I had heard the Chinese have had an understanding of "levels" for about 1000 years, led I initially thought by someone called de Lixue. Two friends, Michael Donnelly in China and Hiroo Inoue in Japan helped me track down this material. *De Lixue* was a school of philosophy led by Cheng Yi (1033–1107).[38] There is an authoritative translation of his writings by Thomas Cleary.[39]

Cheng Yi's model of thought for inner design is organized into hexagrams. He refers to "six lines of organization" as follows:

- The first line = workers, artisans
- The second line = educated and skilled people
- The third line = lower and middle management
- The fourth line = upper managerial levels
- The fifth line = Central directorate
- The sixth line = the emeriti.

He applies this specifically to the army which he describes as having "5 lines" of "leadership".[40] Cleary claims that Konosuke Matsushita was profoundly influenced by Cheng Yi.

I am not arguing that Cheng Yi introduced five levels of accountability but there is evidence that over 1000 years ago the Chinese recognised that a clearly delineated hierarchy was essential for the essential functioning of the state, built on a study of the tenets of Confucian ethics. Interestingly it seemed flat by today's standards. It was also clear that other Asian countries recognised the importance of sound hierarchy being broadly influenced by the same philosophies. For example it is claimed that: "In medieval Japan, it was the Zen Buddhists who imported and disseminated the teachings of Cheng Yi. In the early C17th Cheng Yi was selected by the Japanese Shogunate to be the official ideology."[41]

Christianity by way of contrast offers little insight into the issue of effective depth of hierarchy, although the "hierarchical" Catholic Church is very (too?) flat at four to five layers. The five working layers being: Parishioner—(Priest)—Parish Priest—Bishop—Pope. An interesting span (of ~4000!) for the pope but I guess he would claim his boss gives him more help than most! Titles such as Monsignor, Archbishop and Cardinal are not strict hierarchical layers being more akin to the role of supporting military ranks or leaders with only primus inter pares

[38] There are two systems for rendering Chinese names in English, which does not make searching history for key players as easy as one might think. One system is the Wades-Giles system and one, now more official, Pinyin. In Pinyin this individual is Cheng Yi and Ch'eng I, according to Wade-Giles,

[39] Cleary (1995) *Tao of Organization, The I Ching for Group Dynamics.*

[40] Cleary op cit p. 16.

[41] Cleary op cit p. 223

co-coordinating accountability within a given country for example. Although Papal Nuncios appear to have disproportionate lateral influence e.g. in the selection of bishops, it seems the conference of all bishops is taking on a more official role as a collective. But my take is the structure does not seem to afford perfectly workable accountability, as recent events would appear to illustrate.

In the Singapore workshop it was the overconfident Westerners who were ill informed and jumping to all sorts of conclusions based on *their* perceptions of Asia and possibly the fact that *they* had grown up in over layered structures where status was an inbuilt obsession. I have already shown in Chap. 4, that the Persians, Greeks, Romans and Mongols understood the value of flat, accountable structures, peopled with talented people mostly selected on merit. There is nothing new under the sun.[42]

7.9.4 The Issue of Status

Culture is often confused with status and I am yet to see a country that does not have and cherish status norms, which typically distort hierarchy. US management tend to believe there are no status demarcations 'in the land of the free' but the facts suggest otherwise. For example: the normal nomenclature in a US management hierarchy for "exempt" staff (Non exempt are unionised and can consist of 2–4 layers of employees.) is typically: manager to director to vice president, to senior vice president, to executive vice president to COO, to President to Chairman. Given *at least* two layers of "non exempt" (but often more) staff, that presupposes ten layers of hierarchy at least. No company justifies ten layers but the cultural nomenclature of titles drives US companies towards hierarchy heavy structures. Akio Morita, the CEO of Sony seemed to notice this when he remarked: "Generally, in the United States, management's attitude toward the labour force and even the lower-level executives is very hierarchical, much more so than in Japan."[43]

Culture can make it difficult to delayer as the predictable question from managers moving to a flatter hierarchy will be: "How will we get promotion?" The culture of administrative "promotions" (change of grade) is embedded in many organizations. And that could be what Ratan Tata ran into when he saw the need for change. The answer is to change the nature of the debate—refer to Chaps. 5 and 6 on leadership development and 'boundary moves'. The 'what' of promotion is about learning, growing and developing—Gopalakrishnan's "protecting, nurturing and pacing"—the 'how' is via boundary moves.

> *It is then vital to have the right means to accurately identify the relevant levels of accountability and a reliable set of differentiating competencies to choose the right people for promotion. That is the core leadership message of this book and this chapter has aimed to emphasise the critical role a positive culture plays in this process.*

[42] Ecclesiastes 1:9.

[43] Morita et al. (1997). *Made in Japan* p. 181.

Since organizational culture is predominantly an output, then if only one or two of the pillars of mission, structure, leadership development and training is damaged the culture is undermined and any ensuing change assignment can be enormous. That helps explain why so many cultural change programmes fail in civilian settings and why Schein suggested that most blanket attempts to "change the culture" of a whole organization are wasted efforts. Change needs to be digested in bite size chunks. It seems many civilian organizations embark on a cultural change programme without having analysed the four pillars, which helps to explain why they inevitably run aground.

Some Questions to Ponder

1. How would an outsider describe the culture of your organization?
2. What behaviours would you see if you had a winning culture?
3. If culture is an output what are the healthy driving factors in your organization?
4. If your organization has a set of values, are they clearly lived out at all Levels? If not, why not?

Mission Mastery: The DMA Solution Set 8

The search for an optimum number of management levels is generally held to be a futile search for a holy grail
P. Kettley [(1995)
Is Flatter Better? Delayering the management hierarchy.
The Institute of Employment Studies report 290, p. 13]

8.1 General

If the search for an optimum number of management levels is a 'futile search for a holy grail', then one response might be to think 'any old structure will do'. But if it is not a 'futile search', if there is a way of establishing the 'optimum number of management levels' for a particular organization, and if having the wrong number of management levels has harmful consequences, then the belief that the search is 'futile', encouraging the acceptance of bad structures, can do enormous harm. In this chapter I aim to answer three fundamental questions to prove the search for an "optimum number of management levels" is not only possible but essential. What is the DMA Solution Set (DMASS)? Where did it come from? How can it be applied? I wish to show it is a set of universal, flexible principles that can be applied to any employment organization that exists for a purpose. (A partnership is not an employment organization in this context.) It is a real solution to a real business challenge. In short ***it is not a futile search for a holy grail***.

B. Dive, *Mission Mastery*, Management for Professionals,
DOI 10.1007/978-3-319-25223-0_8

8.2 Decision Making Accountability

The underlying thread throughout this book is the importance of accountability and a set of concepts I have built over time to help identify it. They are encapsulated in what I have called Decision Making Accountability (DMA). They have been written about elsewhere (*The Healthy Organization* and *The Accountable Leader*) but as they drive Mission Mastery I think it will help to spelt them again out in some detail. The 'DMA Solution Set' arose out of that very 'search for an optimum number of levels', and it consists of a number of clear and flexible principles that can be used in identifying what levels of management an organization needs to meet its mission effectively: to make use of these principles appropriately, is to have a way of seeing, very clearly, not simply what "management levels" are needed, but why; and it is to have a way of clarifying what sorts of things you would expect the people, operating at those levels, to be doing.

So, to prove the search for an "optimum number of management levels" is not only possible but essential for best in class leadership development, I plan to answer three questions.

- **What is the DMA Solution Set?**
- **Where did it come from?**
- **How can it be applied?**

8.3 What Is the DMA Solution Set?

DMA aims to characterise the discrete and individual decisions which any individual makes in their job within an employment organization that exists for a purpose. It maps accountability. DMASS is a 'Solution Set' because it is not an inflexible approach offering the same one-size-fits-all answer on every occasion. It is based on a set of universal principles that can be flexed and tailored to meet and fit any employment organization's design needs.

An individual's decisions should be different from those of the people who report to him or her (not because their team is not allowed to take those decisions but because the members of the team do not yet have the knowledge and/or requisite experience to make the appropriate response) and from those to whom they in turn report. Similarly the person in the layer above should be taking decisions that are adding value to the larger team and so on. This is the key to effective decision making and individual empowerment in an accountability hierarchy and is the basis of distributive leadership. A job that cannot meet that stipulation has no right to be in the structure.

8.3.1 A Healthy Organization

The aim is to ensure people have jobs with discrete decision rights, which meet customer needs, reflect the organization's mission while ensuring their work makes a difference, enabling them to learn, grown and develop. This is the basis of empowerment and personal satisfaction. Such decision making is the life blood of a healthy organization and lays the foundation for organization design, leadership development and sound reward management.

A healthy organization is one which meets it mission, satisfies its customers while simultaneously enabling individuals in it to learn, grow and develop in line with their abilities.

Healthy organizations are based on the five pillars of Mission Mastery. Developing this health metaphor further, the layers of hierarchy, known as the spine of accountability, can be likened to vertebrae in a spine. The wrong number of vertebrae damages the central nervous system. It is the same for organizations. The wrong number of layers disrupts the decision making process, leads to ineffectiveness, which is de-motivating, wasting both talent and money.

Although we live now in the information and technology age, neither information nor technology builds trust in organizations. As Fukuyama has reminded us:

> *When the information age's most enthusiastic apostles celebrate the breakdown of hierarchy and authority they neglect one critical factor, trust. Trust does not exist in an integrated circuits or fibre optic cables. Trust is not reducible to information.*[1]

Trust emanates from clear accountability. As explained in Chap. 7 on Culture, trust is a facet of that 'softness' that needs to be underpinned by a hard, empirical reality, which is both difficult to identify and master. Clearly defined accountability is that reality. DMASS identifies that appropriate accountability, which is essential to ensuring that work is challenging, satisfying and aligned to personal capabilities and therefore which leaders can be trusted. Trust is a rich concept with different dimensions: there is a 'trust' related to 'ability to do something', and another trust related to 'will to do something' and there are aspects of personal honesty and integrity that are all relevant. These are all the obverse of clear accountability.

The DMA Solution Set is based on one simple question.

Are you adding value to the customer, the patient, the consumer, the constituent and the work of your colleagues?

[1] Fukuyama, F (1995) *Trust the social virtues and the creation of prosperity*, p. 25

If the answer is "yes", then this becomes the basis for effective organization design, leadership development and reward management. In short everything to do with the management of people. *DMASS is therefore a conceptually integrated framework, based on the simple idea of adding value to others.* In this it is unique as many HR systems are only administratively linked but not conceptually integrated, which is a fundamental weakness. Their "integration" is at best an artificially forced fit.

8.3.2 Where Did DMASS Come From?

Some 30 years ago I was global head of organization for Unilever. I was trying to find the answer to some very simple questions to help build an organization that was at the cutting edge of world class organization design. These questions were:

How tall should the company be?
How many layers of management were justified?
Was the (global) company too tall or too short?
How would you know?
How could you find out if you did not know?

Answers were not readily available. In fact no-one seemed to have *a mental reference frame* that could reliably provide the answer

8.3.2.1 Consultant Contributions

I thought consultants must know the answer. They of course were keen to sell their packages and ideas on organization but these all focussed only on the horizontal axis of organization design. Namely—do you organize by function, customer, market (business) geography, or project? But this was not enough as my mentor, Roger Roes, and I had spent 10 years bottoming out these questions and already knew the answer to those issues. But this was only half of the picture. Once again no-one offered a robust frame of reference or proven set of principles to assess the 'height' of an organization.

It was by now clear to me that the two axes of organization design, the horizontal and the vertical *had to be in a dynamic equilibrium.* If they were not balanced, organizations became dysfunctional. It was also becoming more obvious that the key driver of this balance was the vertical axis *not* the horizontal, which was the preoccupation of consultants. When given an OD assignment they favoured working from strategy to (top) structure and then top down to the customer. I was getting evidence that organizing top-down led to a tendency to unconsciously build in *span breakers* and I still see that happening today most of the time as a result of consultant interventions.

***A span breaker** is a job that adds comfort to the boss but does not add value to the customer of the work of other members in the team.*

No-one seemed to be working from the customer inwards and building back up from the front line. This led to another major insight. Once the top two layers have been established it is important to work bottom up from the most junior role at the front line. This is because working up from the front line patient or customer, is the surest way to plot whether each job in a chain of command or spine of accountability has discrete and different decision rights, which add value and move work forward. In other words decision rights which differ from the jobs below and those above. So another key message crystallised:

The key is to work from the customer into the organization to plot whether all jobs are adding value.

8.3.2.2 Global Companies

For a number of years I was chair of the New York Conference Board's Council on International Organization, which included leading OD Directors/Vice Presidents from about 30 of the world's leading multinationals. Interestingly many of these great companies were convinced they had to de-layer and were charging ahead. When I asked the likes of Don Kane at General Electric (his boss, Jack Welch, was called 'Neutron Jack' as a result of his de-layering efforts at that time), Tom Liptak at IBM, Chris Wheeler at 3 M, Henk Cliteur at Philips or Basil South at Shell for some insight into the logic underpinning their approaches it was clear they were experimenting often at the behest of the then new process re-engineers. They admitted that sometimes they had to re-insert a layer that had earlier been removed because things "started to fall over." *It became clear they were not working with a tried and tested method* and yet these were all leading companies with arguably the best OD managers in the world. Most other companies were simply driven by the accountant's knife in the name of "down with hierarchy." At the Conference Board I worked closely on these challenges firstly with Alan Janger and then Robert Kramer, the most knowledgeable researcher on the organization design of multinational companies I ever met. Robert also researched the size and shape of headquarter organizations of global companies but even his insightful work was not providing the clear answer I needed.

8.3.2.3 Academic Contributions

In parallel I was scanning what existed in the academic world covering the work of Miles' Network organizations, Galbraith's five star model, Bridger's pentagram, and Mintzberg's seven basic types of organization. They were empirically based and along with some popular consultant packages such as the McKinsey 7S model, all conceded "structure was important" but none of them had any significant insights into assessing the height of hierarchies. The fundamental issue remained unsolved as it still is today for many civilian organizations.

In this search I came across some interesting work being done at Brunel University on 'Strata' (Jaques) and 'work-levels' (Rowbottom, Kinston and Billis). Jaques' described work in varying time dimensions and focused on the different mental qualities individuals needed to operate at different strata. He and Stamp studied the maturation of individuals through what they called cognitive levels of capability. As far as I could ascertain they argued, somewhat controversially, that individuals matured along fixed development curves based on innate ability. They made an intriguing connection to organizations, arguing they should somehow reflect this capability of individuals and so posited the reasonable idea that organizations should also consist of a corresponding number of levels.

I arranged for Stamp to demonstrate the CPA methodology. It did not allay my key concern. In addition to the above shortcomings it presupposed organizations had only six levels and it was already my strong hypothesis that Unilever had more than six levels of accountability. (It was then a conglomerate of ~300,000 people, selling in 200 countries with a firm infrastructure in 100.) This also suggests the validity of CPA remains questionable today since a great number of organizations on the Forbes top 500 around the world have more than six levels of accountability. For example over a 2 year period we were working in a company I assessed as a light Level 7, which was around the top 20 % of the FTSE 100, but the bottom 10 % of the Forbes 500. I have subsequently observed that Brunel consultants continue to work with a fuzzy line between WL 1 and WL 2, which means they are seriously prone to pitching lower levels too high and in that process they quickly 'run out of road'. There is also a tendency to say: "This is a level 2 capable person therefore the job is Level 2". The rigour of DMASS organization design would indicate the job is Level 1 even though the person subject to a different assessment might be capable of working at a higher level. In a well designed organization the job and an individual's capability (the two templates) should be aligned to better ensure optimal motivation and performance.

This Brunel model of strata was based on what was called the 'time span of discretion'—how long it took an individual to complete a task. It seems Jaques originally stumbled onto this idea when he endeavoured to explain "felt fair" pay rates. In fact one of his colleagues told me he elaborated the time scales influenced by pay differentials in the UK when working at Glacier Metal Company with Wilfred Brown in the 1950s. One of the trade unionists there suggested these differentials seemed to align to the time it took to do a job, and Jaques started from there. Jaques later called his set of concepts "Stratified Systems Theory". Being a psychoanalyst he was particularly interested in how people had to think (problem solve) at different strata in an organization. I did not find this logic entirely convincing, since having conducted executive pay surveys around the world in the 1970s and 80s, I knew the pay progression market rates of Brazil and the US for example were very steep while those in Ireland, New Zealand and Sweden were much flatter. I could see this approach based on UK 'felt fair' pay rates was not going to work in a company which had different pay for managers across 100 countries. The pay in India bore little objective relationship to that of South Africa or Japan.

The work that really interested me was that of Jaques' colleague Ralph Rowbottom and his co-workers who were starting to look at the issue of organization design in terms of levels. They too rejected the validity of time span for organization design.

> *"Time measures are not in our experience, easy ones to use in detailed organization design or problem solving. And the theory offers no very clear picture of the actual quality of output or end product required in work or how it varies from level to level"*.[2] (Or from industry to industry, which could also be different as I subsequently discovered.)

They coined the term 'expected work' and their approach moved away from a focus on the job holder to exploring the substance of the job. Although this was another step forward, it was still rather mono dimensional and there was no convincing empirical work beyond what was called 'work-level 5' in only the UK, where their work had been done principally in parts of the NHS. In addition they were not crystal clear on the critical issue of where Work Level 2 cut into a hierarchy, although they called it 'management'. Thus were their 'work-level 5' roles reliably calibrated? There was lack of clarity over the substance of a 'decision level' and an 'organization level'. These academics still referred to both layers of hierarchy and decision levels as "levels" or "strata". This was more confusing than helpful. But there was something in this approach that whetted my appetite. I invited Rowbottom to work with me in Unilever but he had just retired and suggested I contact his colleague David Billis who had helped him, which I did. He made clear why they considered time-span inadequate for reliably assessing "work-levels" as the basis for organization design. Time Span was based solely on the *longest task* in a job. This often proved impossible to confirm. Furthermore the measurement of the longest task seemed to entail endless definitional debate. They concluded time could not be considered as the sole determinant for organization design.

Unilever at this time was a conglomerate in a number of different industries. It was becoming clear that different industries operated with time nuances reflected by realities such as whether they were labour intensive (plantations and tea estates), capital intensive (chemicals) or knowledge intensive (research laboratories). It was also clear that Jaques' theoretical time frames became increasingly unreliable the higher the strategic work in an international setting. Additional assignments since then in other industries have reinforced this finding.

[2] See *Organization Design the Work-Levels approach* (1987) p. 23.

DMASS is the result of fieldwork across more than 30 years, 70 countries and numerous industries covering over a million employees.

A Side Project

During the 1980s I was working around the world on reorganizations being aligned to new core strategies stemming from the challenging economic realities of the 1970s. At the same time I started also to work a side project aimed at getting more insight into the problem of 'how high should the hierarchy be in a global organization with ~300,000 employees?' I decided to ask top management two questions:

- What decisions do you take that your team cannot take?
- What decision do you take that your boss does not also take?

After conducting this fieldwork over about 4 years across some 40 countries I could see that seven clear themes were emerging again and again about the kinds of decisions people took and in which areas—money, people, systems, ideas, customers, suppliers, governments, pressure groups and so. Some could make changes others could not. Some solved simple concrete problems, others solved more abstract problems. Some worked across a significant international network while others were more local in focus. Some scientists worked on development of existing products and processes while others did research that called for new connections between existing knowledge and science and a few for invention and discovery. Many worked on short term plans, some on longer term horizons. The overall patterns seemed to be universal, abstracting from the country in question and/or the type of business. Looking back I can now see Unilever at the time was a perfect research laboratory for testing organization design principles. At that time it was a conglomerate with different types of international businesses, with different time lines, with significant presence in over 100 countries and a management workforce of 20,000 who were moved seamlessly across these businesses and countries as part of the company's leadership development policy. Most decisions were taken in operations—ensuring existing resources perform better—and some were strategic—trying to answer questions such as 'are these the right resources, in the right location' and so on?

It was clearly emerging that there were seven decision areas or zones in which people consistently took key decisions. I distilled these into the **Seven DMA Elements**. They form the mental framework which is the basis against which any job can be assessed. *By identifying the decision(s) someone legitimately takes, irrespective of any qualifications they may or may not possess,* it is possible to assess whether *the balance of accountability is operational or strategic.*

This fieldwork also helped crystallise in my mind the difference between a **Level** of accountability that reflected a certain set of decisions and a **Layer** of hierarchy that reflected the architecture of an organization's structure. More importantly it crystallised how the interplay of Levels and Layers made up the building blocks of the organization's architecture.

DMASS is a theoretically robust set of organization design principles that emerged from fieldwork, which was conducted in numerous countries and different cultures taking into account varying types of business over about 4 years in a search for a real solution to a real business problem.

8.3.3 Layers and Levels

The distinction between layers and levels is fundamental and lies at the heart of the thinking underlying this book.

The Levels of accountability have to be identified before the layers of hierarchy can be clearly established.

- **A Level of accountability** *is a decision making zone with discrete and individual decision rights, which differ from those of the levels above and below.*

  The level is constant across an organization, in that the quality of decisions to be made, are essentially the same in terms of accountability, whatever the function, or type of job. *Leaders in that level must add value to the customer front line and the work of others in their team otherwise their jobs are not justified.* The total number of levels varies between organizations of different sizes, complexity and geographical reach.
- **A Layer** *is a job in the structure of an organization, which resides within a single level of accountability. All jobs across the organization within that level have comparable decision rights.*

  The term 'level' describes the character of the actual decision making involved in a job. The term 'layer' describes the position of a job, in a hierarchy formally apparent in a structure chart, showing who reports to whom. A job is a 'layer' as part of that hierarchy comprised of reporting relationships, formally recognized by the organization. If a particular job is a 'layer', then the job to which it reports is the 'layer' above: the boss of the individual in a particular job. So, the reporting relationships formally recognized by the organization—determining who is the boss of whom—make up a hierarchy comprised of 'layers'. I am in a layer; my boss is in the layer above; the boss of my boss is in the layer above, and so on.

  A layer is both part of a vertical spine of accountability (commonly referred to as a 'reporting chain') and part of a horizontal axis across the structure of an organization. It is the hardware of the organization. If there

(continued)

are no discrete, distinctive decision rights in a role there is no 'space' for that layer within the level of accountability.

That a job is in a certain layer, with a layer above, does not of itself guarantee that the difference between the layers will be reflected by a difference in the actual decision-making associated with the jobs in those layers: that is, an individual, in an organization that is not well designed, could have a boss tasked with taking decisions that are not qualitatively different from that individual's, and that do not add value therefore to the work of that individual.

In a healthy organization, additional layers of hierarchy reflect increasing, cumulative complexities, which call for decisions of higher quality.

The Golden Rule of DMASS: ***Only one layer of leadership is needed per level***

- **Compression** occurs when there are two or more layers of leadership within one level of accountability. It means two or more people are working in the same decision space and therefore are not each adding value to their direct reports. There are occasional situations—where the front line is above Level 1—where the compressed lower role might not be a leadership role.
- ***Compression is the opposite of empowerment.***
- In order to reinforce this empowerment message we refer to change programmes that remove non-value adding layers as providing leadership **Space to Lead (S2L).** This term was invented by my colleague, Adam Pearce when he was head of OD at Barclays. It has also been the umbrella term at other companies such as BT, DHL and Severn Trent Water.

Layers are counted down from the top line of the organization. The role of CEO, for example would be layer 1.

Levels, on the other hand, are counted up from the most junior role at the customer/patient front line, often, but not always, at the first Level of accountability.

A number of organizations that have implemented various aspects of DMASS refer to levels of accountability as Work Levels. I will use the terms 'Work Levels' and 'levels of accountability' interchangeably throughout. The most junior role is usually Level 1 depending on the nature of the work being done—but sometimes the front line can be higher than Level 1. This can be the case with highly skilled professions that have strict, internationally recognised gateways of training coupled with experience before members are 'licensed' to practice: e.g. as a solicitor, chartered accountant, certified engineer. If, though, a person needs to show 'Level 2' capability to qualify in certain professions, that person may not, on entry to a particular organization, be given a role where that capability is put to use: that person may not be given accountability to match that professionally certified capability. One of the problems with the newer professions of HR, IT, Supply Chain, Social Services for example, is the lack of internationally recognised and shared standards of professional excellence as exist in medicine, law, engineering or accounting. The decision rights are not clearly and consistently defined hence some "professionals" may have Level 1 accountability notwithstanding certain qualifications. *It is not the qualification that drives a Work Level but the decisions a person is held to account for.*

Accountability is not shared—teamwork is—and it necessarily involves rewards or sanctions. *Accountability entails consequences.*[3]

Unclear accountability degenerates into a culture of no consequences which leads to organizational inertia: an example is provided in Chap. 9. The pervasive disease in many organizations I have encountered is the tendency to build in more hierarchy than is needed. This is why "hierarchy" often has a bad name since the negative effects of too much hierarchy are widely experienced: it is what many now understand by "bureaucracy". It has become a pejorative term:

A "*bureaucracy*", *in that sense, is an organization that is disconnected from its purpose, customer and performance - usually because it is massively overlayered.*

The Level of a top job can vary according to the size and complexity of the organization in question and therefore its justifiable infrastructure of roles. Indeed it is an open question whether a level 9 organization exists and/or is manageable or whether individuals exist who have the capacity to successfully manage such a large, complex entity. (Eisenhower, as supreme Allied Commander towards the end of WWII may have been **temporarily** operating at Level 9, although it is a moot point whether he truly managed huge egos such as Paton and Montgomery.)

8.3.4 How Is DMASS Applied?

Clear accountability and the concomitant authority is a pre-requisite of a high performing organization.

[3] Klatt B et al (1999) *Accountability: Practical tools for focusing on clarity, commitment and results*

Applying DMASS identifies the total number of levels of accountability in an organization, which possess discrete decision rights, from the customer front line to the CEO. Since only one layer of leadership is needed in each level of accountability, this is the key to effective organization design. This in turn can also establish the platform for leadership development, career paths and reward. The key aspects of the process are covered below in Sect. 3.4.

8.3.4.1 Personal Accountability

Personal accountability occurs when an individual is answerable to a higher authority for work, resources (people, money, systems and knowhow), outcomes, service and/or results that can be measured in terms of quantity, quality, cost and/or time

Personal accountability is not shared and it necessarily involves rewards or sanctions because true accountability entails consequences.

Hierarchy is reflected accountability resulting from the response needed to manage increasing complexity. The challenge is to identify what is necessary and appropriate for a particular organization.

8.3.4.2 DMA Principles

The DMA approach to organisational design is based on three key principles:

- All organised work, managerial (level 2+) or non-managerial, falls into a hierarchy of discrete accountability levels, called **Work Levels** reflecting decisions of increasing complexity in a more extensive environment.
- At each Work Level, the balance of major tasks will align to the assigned level. So while a job might have a mix of decision rights the balance should fall within the same Work Level. Wide variation suggests there could be compression in the spine under review.
- Each Work Level requires one and only one layer of leadership. (There are a few situations where a job or layer in Work Level 2+ could be a specialist without a direct report and so would not be a leader in that context.)

8.3.4.3 The DMA Elements: Uncovering a Job's Mission

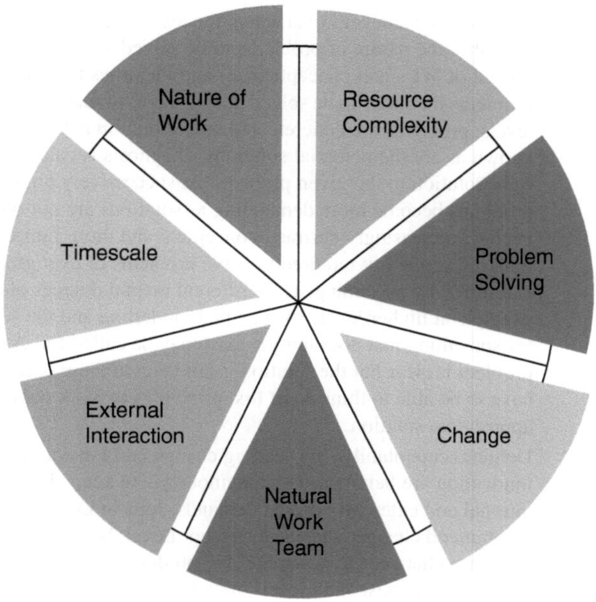

The DMA Solution Set enables the assessment of roles and the decisions taken, against seven key Elements or decision making zones.

Nature of work	*Refers to the mission of the job.* It focuses on the core reason for the existence of a particular job (its purpose) and where it differs in essence from those above and below. The nature of work becomes more complex at each successive level. It describes what the organisation expects the individual to do in the role to which he or she has been assigned. It defines the essence of their accountability for a distinct area of work. When the purpose of the job is clear it can be described in one or two sentences. Following that it is then possible to focus on the 5–6 critical tasks the incumbent is held to account for and whether these activities differ from those of the jobs below and, in due course, the job above.
Resource complexity	Each ascending Level requires authority to manage an increasingly complex resource mix. This Element defines accountability for resources: people, technology, money (expense and capital budgets), systems and decisions that need specialist know-how. The first critical divide occurs between Level 1 and Level 2. Leaders in Level 1 are supervisors[4] who support managerial leaders in WL 2+. At level 2 there is a major leap forward as managerial leaders are held to account for deciding (or at least having a veto) who comes into their team, what they will do, set their goals, assign appropriate authorities, assess performance, coach and recommend on what basis people should move out of the team: e.g. on promotion.

(continued)

[4] Many terms are used to describe Level 1 leaders: *front line managers, team leaders, night shift managers, superintendents, section leaders* and so on. In the military, non commissioned officers, warrant officers, petty officers.

	Roles in ascending levels are accountable for an increasingly extensive and complex array of resources.
Problem solving	All roles, at whatever Level, entail the resolving of problems. This Element describes the nature of problems to be solved at each level. The great insight of WLs is it conceptualises and identifies the different quality of problems that need to be solved at each layer of management. At the lower levels, problems are concrete and operational in nature. The problem is known as are the potential solutions. Diagnosis is called for to match the right solution to the given problem. At successively higher levels, problems become more demanding as solutions are not obvious and become increasingly abstract, conceptual and more future oriented. The thinking capability required to solve problems of ever greater complexity is referred by psychologists as different mental degrees of abstraction. For example at higher levels (4+) mental modelling and the selling of an idea for something that does not yet exist may be called for. At these levels the problem is clear but the solution is not yet. On these occasions job holders have to be able to think from first principles to work out a totally new and appropriate solution.
Change	Defines accountability for leading change and innovation—change and innovation are being used synonymously—to keep abreast of changing internal and externally driven demands. Jobs in Level 1 can only recommend change whereas jobs from Level 2+ are expected to drive and authorise change: for example drive productivity improvements. Whilst creativity can exist at all levels, not all levels are *accountable for ensuring that innovation actually takes place* or that creative ideas are implemented. At the lower levels (up to Level 3) innovation involves further developing, modifying or improving something, which already exists. This process is commonly recognised as *development* and is the life blood of marketing innovations for example At the higher levels, the jobholder may be accountable for break-through or first in the industry changes and the integration of resources to ensure that identified innovations are implemented quickly and effectively to gain a completive edge in the market place or to provide best in class service based on research. This is likely to call for new linkages in knowledge (*applied research)* or rarely the discovery of new knowledge (*blue sky or pure research*). This would result in a world class invention of Nobel Prize proportions. Note that without clear accountability for resources (people, money, systems) managers lack the levers to make change(s). A key reason why some organizations become noted for their inertia results from unclear accountability for resources. Thus their managers cannot initiate or make meaningful change happen.
Internal collaboration	Refers to the lateral collaboration (literally *"co labore"*, to work with, not just liaison) with peers within and across the organisation, which is needed to complete certain key tasks en route to meeting shared objectives. It refers to the peers whose cooperation is needed in order for the individual to be successful in his or her job. In short, their networks. This accountability is about influence without formal authority although in some cases an incumbent may possess the authority of expertise. The job incumbent does not have the authority to tell their colleagues what to do (unless in a formal audit role) but must win them over and elicit their support. This calls for influencing skills and the ability to persuade colleagues who may have different priorities to co-operate on an

(continued)

	unexpected task. In the lower levels, individuals collaborate with others to deliver outputs that tend to be localised. In the higher levels, individuals collaborate with others to deliver outputs that may call for international or even global collaboration. Near the top of the organization this may require working in a wide network right across the total organization.
External collaboration	Not dissimilar to Internal Collaboration but the focus is now outside the organization. Many organizations exist to serve a need in society which entails interactions with patients, customers, suppliers, constituents and significant external organisations such as political bodies and pressure groups. The substance of these links can be simple or complex, rare or frequent and the nature of these interfaces flows from the accountabilities sketched out in the previous five Elements. In the lower levels, roles have clearly defined external contacts, such as specific patients, suppliers, customers and/or players in the local community. Up to and including Level 3 external contacts tend to be reactive, responding to someone making a demand upon the organization. An appropriate response to the external demand then has to be orchestrated. At the higher levels, the external environment may include national, regional or international organisations, which may have a significant impact on business results and which may need to be proactively managed to ensure the best outcome for the organization. This external network is likely to involve the leaders of national and international bodies such as the IMF, World Bank, UN, E.U., the media and so on. Their agendas could be inherently hostile to the organization e.g. Greenpeace, calling for proactive work to ensure the best overall result for the organization is achieved.
Accountable timeframe	Focuses on the time it takes to complete the balance of the work outlined in the previous six Elements. Clearly the greater the complexity uncovered the longer a series of tasks take to be completed. This can be driven by the increasingly extensive infrastructure of resources and the time taken to deliver comprehensive change programmes together with that needed to build up both effective internal and external networks that are seen to bear fruit. The task here is to assess when the impact, outcome or result of the majority of the decisions of the jobholder will be known and recognised as completed. For significant break-through of first-in-class change the journey would be from initial concept, through the securing of relevant capital to delivery and proven outcome. Accountable timeframes can range from minutes in some front-line jobs to many years at the highest echelons. These time frames are typically set by the boss in at least the next higher Work Level. Accountable timeframes can be difficult to pin down but the key is often found by referring to the internal planning, project cycles and budgetary processes operating within an organization, which are normally reflected in the other six Elements. Assessment of changes completed by the role holder is another reliable indicator of an accountable time horizon. One needs to beware of long time lapses, which amount to queuing: e.g. a lawyer waiting (years) to get a case heard in the court. That type of delay is dead time which does not register as true accountability. It is important to identify what an individual is really held to account for: preparing a brief is relevant: waiting for the (inefficient) court is not.

8.3.4.4 Assessment of the Work Level

The assessment aims to identify *the value added quality of the decisions taken across each of the seven Elements.* It is not a quantitative method endeavouring to measure the different Elements and awarding a score, as is common to job evaluation methods. It is important that a given job has a consistent pattern of outcomes across at least six of the Elements. If it does not, this could result in what is known as a 'rainbow' effect: e.g. level 2 on some Elements, level 1 on others and one at level 3. This pattern is often a precursor to compression—remember the assessor is coming up the spine of accountability from the front line and may be sailing into compression—two or more roles in the same level of accountability. In these situations the accountabilities tend to be very erratic with evident overlap and duplication.

Why can an Element not be represented in a job? This is because there are some jobs that may have no external interaction: e.g. a financial accountant with no work outside the organization, hence that job cannot resister on external collaboration. But judgement may be necessary because if, say, a customer sales advisor has no accountability under External Collaboration this would be very odd and would suggest something is awry in the structure since the thrust of a sales role should be to work outside the company, or perhaps the title is a misnomer.

Since the DMASS approach is not quantitative a WL 3 job combined with a WL 3 job to create a new job does not result in a WL 4 role because the qualities of decisions have not changed (but it might well result in an overloaded WL 3 job). This logic can reveal that combining some jobs is not sound organization design. For example, one well known European retailer decided to have some store managers run up to three outlets instead of one. This was a cost saving measure. Although the job evaluation system awarded a higher grade to the new job, the initiative failed because it was an unrealistic organization design, which created an accountability gap in too many stores since for great periods of time the manager was in a car rather than a shop.

While it is important to assess whether the job controls a budget, the size of that budget does not determine the Work Level unless there is an inherent mismatch or inconsistency where it is too small to be effective. E.g. if a manager with 200 staff has a budget of only $15,000 this would be an accountability inconsistency since the money is not aligned to the 'accountable' staff numbers. The task then would be to find who does have that accountability.

While size of staff infrastructure does not drive the Work Level outcome directly it is relevant and taken into account because the larger and more complex an organization becomes the more likely a more extensive infrastructure of jobs is required. The 'infrastructure' covers all the jobs in a manager's department: his or her direct reports and their direct reports and so on. It is the infrastructure that affects the nature and quality of the decisions that need to be taken by the leader and the level of accountability which is then detectable across the seven Elements.

WL Misconceptions

As WL implementation spreads sometimes misconceptions appear. For example in 2014 a manager of an earlier client wrote:

> Many roles at the front line are now more technical, requiring better qualified people, who would be considered WL 2 when the principles were introduced in the 1990s.
>
> If the old principles for determining roles at WL 1 are applied then it will be almost impossible to build a manageable infrastructure.
>
> At that time the hypothesis was that post graduates performing professional (e.g. Finance and Legal) roles would be operating at WL 2.
>
> Therefore applying the methodology in its purist form will manifest itself in compression in WL 2 as people are more qualified today.

Not one of these statements is correct.

They seem to have been written by someone with a job evaluation mindset used to a system giving "points" for qualifications. *Work Levels reflect accountability and the quality of decisions taken in a given job, not exams passed.* (Notwithstanding the fact that the gateway to certain established professions such as medical, may require a statutory mix of qualifications and experience, where entry is typically at the top of WL 1 for a short period, which is very similar to the development of officers in the military.)

I have already noted the nursing profession is prone to promote people into higher grades and new layers simply because they have passed some exams, which is not a sound organization design principle or practice. While it is true that the nature of work in a given level (mostly level 1) can change over time and even be eliminated in this fast moving digital world, the principles of accountability remain constant even if structures have to be re-calibrated to match a new organizational form, which might require fewer layers for example. As I demonstrated in *The Accountable Leader,* one of the great OD shortcomings in the twenty-first century has been the replication of failed twentieth century blue collar organization design, whether in the Triad or the BRICs.[5]

As people learn more and develop, their talent might be under-utilised.[6] It is not uncommon for the tectonic plates of accountability and capability, described in Chap. 6, to be misaligned as a result of faulty assessments. The matching of talent whether qualified or not, with an appropriately accountable assignment, is an ongoing challenge for top management in civilian organizations. In practice the two often become rather tangled, which it seems can then give rise to misconceptions about the nature of accountability levels.

---

[5] See Chap. 5.

[6] Recall the earlier reference to the work of Crawford, M (2009)

8.3.4.5 The Work Level Definitions[7]

Assessing jobs against the seven key DMA elements facilitates classification into a number of discrete accountability levels. The critical changeover from predominantly operational work to predominantly strategic work occurs at Work Level 4. It is important to note that the weight of strategic accountability at Level 4 will vary depending on the number of value adding layers above—e.g. where the top role is WL 5 the WL 4 role will have a clear balance of strategic work. In a WL 8 organization that will be more dilute. This is why we strongly suggest organizations have their own set of WL definitions to accurately reflect the precise accountabilities in their organization (It also makes writing general definitions in a book quite a challenge!).

Operational work (Levels 1–3) is concerned with the efficient use of given resources to achieve defined KPIs—such as service levels and outcomes, cost budgets, staff ratios and performance constraints or interpretation of policy within clear guidelines or precedent. Strategic work (Levels 4 and above) is concerned with the identification and resolution of gaps in resources and maximising gaps (opportunities) in the market place to ensure better performance.

Careful assessment of a job against the seven DMA elements will establish the accountability level for that job. There is, however, one additional factor, which should be taken into account when deciding whether or not a job should be placed on the vertical spine of accountability.

The line jobholder is the 'Boss', who is individually accountable for the performance of subordinates at lower levels.

It is the line job, which is justified as a value-adding layer on the spine of accountability.

Jobs which add value but do not form part of the management spine of accountability, are termed 'Support Jobs' (known as Staff jobs in the military). The most common such job is the supervisory leader in Work Level 1, who does not have the accountability of the level 2 leader for budgets, recruitment and performance management decisions, system design and/or specialist know how. The supervisor recommends to a manager in WL 2 who decides on critical resource questions. At WL 2 the manager has the authority and right *to intervene* to take action and ensure appropriate delivery and/or change, whereas at WL 1 the authority of a supervisor or case worker is limited to *liaison* within the accountable boundaries, guidelines, plans and precedents set by management in WL 2+.

Supervisory support jobs may be required in WL 1 when, for example.

[7] When working for a client we craft a manual set of definition tailored to the organization in question, if required.

- There are very large numbers of people who need to be led by a manager in WL 2
- People in a sizeable team are widely dispersed geographically well beyond physical line of sight
- There are multi-shift operations requiring a continuous presence and oversight
- There is a need for someone to step-up and "hold the shift" or "hold the shop" for a defined, short period involving seasonal work for example.

Specialist support roles can occupy any level up to the CEO. They are often 'zero span' managers who could be high powered specialists, a world authority even, if in a strategic WL. Normally experts are required when:

- There is a need for essential, specialist capability or know-how, which is not otherwise available in the line or elsewhere within that team: e.g. an HR manager in a factory of 750 people, who may also manage HR team members in WL 1.
- Thus a support manager to a boss in the higher level could also be a line manager of the specialist staff needed in a lower level, e.g. WL 1.

Unlike supervisors in WL 1 these specialist roles are not an intervening layer within a level of accountability as they report directly to the manager being supported in the level above. This is because the four conditions that call for a supervisor within a level do not apply as a performance constraint from WL 2 and above.

8.4 Work Levels Applied to a Global HR Network,[8] Levels 1–3

Hierarchical, value-adding levels of accountability in an organization reflect increasing complexity of work. Each successive Work Level therefore requires decisions, which are broader and qualitatively more demanding.

The example of the definitions which follow is based on an HR network in a global company, covering only the first three levels of accountability. Each step upwards on the spine of accountability in an enabling business function like HR demands an increasing depth of specialist know-how, and a more extensive and comprehensive response to its environment. The example only goes up to Work Level 3: a small number of HRD roles in large, complex, global companies could reach Work Level 6.

8.4.1 Work Level 1: "Demand Response"

Resources, policies, systems, processes and procedures are given. They underpin the destination which is pre-defined by people in higher Work Levels. Problem solving is circumscribed by case precedent within policy guidelines. There is no

[8] Assuming presence in ~100 countries and/or with staff of 100,000+

accountability for change in the destination or output required—the *what*—but there may be some discretion about the *how* or the means to get there, as long as the means deployed locally do not cut across formal processes or procedures defined at a more comprehensive level. In that sense the output is prescribed. So changes are likely to be driven by others at higher levels. The jobholder will be accountable for adapting to change, responding quickly and making suggestions for improvement. Customers, internal or external, are generally defined by bosses in higher levels as is the potential interaction with them. Accountable time frame is up to about 3 months.

Key support roles can sometime be required in Work Level 1, such as supervisors who are the first layer of leadership. Their primary role is to train and supervise staff while supporting a manager in level 2 to manage large numbers shift work patterns and/or people working in different locations. WL 1 roles can require HR supervisors but as the numbers in HR are generally not great this is not common.

Some staff will be individual contributors (more specialised) in the technical space high in WL 1. In these cases, which are likely to require a considerable degree of skill (and training), they should report to a manager in WL 2. While their individual contribution can be clearly defined by the manager, there may well be some flexibility as to the choice of techniques to be used to deliver the response being demanded. However, any such local discretion must respect wider functional policies and guidelines such as those needed for example to run a shared HR services across the organization.

8.4.2 Work Level 2: "Diagnostic Response"

Work at this level in any function could entail accountability, as a WL 2 manager, for WL 1 subordinates. However, an important issue for HR is sometimes truly expert front line professional work, can commence at WL 2. Truly expert professional work has clear entry requirements, whilst technical work high in WL 1 does not. At WL 2 it is based on a body of recognised theoretical knowledge that requires study, meaningful work experience (around 7 years in combination) and "certified permission" to practice: e.g. medicine, law, engineering and finance. This knowledge enables the WL 2 expert to penetrate and assess the underlying causes of specific cases.

In general WL 2 Managers will usually be accountable for a team of Level 1 staff. In these cases they are responsible for recruiting the team, setting objectives, varying their jobs, shifts or locations of work, delegating work, identifying training and development needs for individuals, managing performance, coaching, managing the relevant succession pipeline and for delivering against all of these responsibilities within an agreed cost budget and time line. Problems are discrete, non-routine issues requiring analysis and the drawing of conclusions based on knowledge and experience to judge what is appropriate from a range of possible options.

The essence of WL 2 work is to assess a range of known potential solutions to a given problem based on significant previous (professional) knowledge and/or experience and to judge which is appropriate in this particular situation.

Decision making at this level is a matter of exercising professional judgement (i.e. judgement acquired through the assimilation of the requisite professional knowledge via experience and/or training over a period of several years) on particular problems, identifying what output should be aimed at in given cases. The challenge can often be a matter of identifying, from a number of possible solutions known in advance, which solution would be best adapted to the particular situation or case. Unlike Level 1, *the output for this case is not defined in advance*: the Level 2 manager, working from a general idea of what is desirable, must define and decide the particular output or solution to be aimed at *based on a diagnosis of the facts presented.*

Whilst most enabling functions also have some frontline roles in Level 1, other front line jobs could be at Level 2 in legal, engineering, finance, auditing, IT and HR. The problem with IT and HR is the absence of tight entry requirements and universal international recognition as to what constitutes the profession. So if a job is said to be an HR Business Partner a further key question is "What is the business, the level of the audience being partnered, the context and *what decisions are called for*?" Much of HRBP work is liaison that depends upon personal credibility, such as between the internal clients being partnered with and central HR teams. But liaison is only a light form of accountability, which does not entail authoritative (based on requisite know how) decisions over the network in question.

The nature of any apparent professional "casework" also needs to be thoroughly probed and understood. It is usual in some organisations for Technical staff in high WL 1 jobs or even supervised staff lower in WL 1 to refer to "casework". For example, in a Local Authority, "casework" is a term that is often used to refer to "social work directly concerned with individuals, especially that involving a study of a person's family history and personal circumstances". Such case work is undertaken on a day-to-day basis by qualified Social Workers in WL 1 jobs with oversight from more experienced Social Work managers in WL 2 (and higher), ensuring that the key decisions are taken by professionals at WL 2+ even though the cases are *owned day-to-day* by trained Social Workers in WL 1. Thus, whilst we refer to "casework" in our definition of WL 2 (and as you will see also in our definition of WL 3), we are using the term specifically in the sense of particular problems—whether relating to an individual or more likely an organizational unit (WL 3)—the complexity of which requires a truly expert professional diagnosis in order to judge the appropriate output to aim for. The key consideration is: "What decisions can be taken by the individual doing the case review?" "What *intervention* is called for by the Level 2 professional?" Not all "casework" has these WL

2 characteristics. This is the key question to be considered in the case of determining the WL of an HRBP.

At Level 2 the manager can initiate change within the upper boundary set by frameworks and systems which handle the flow of existing processes, policies and systems which govern the appropriateness of individual responses to customers, patients, or suppliers. The job holder is expected to *and authorised to* make changes and improvements in the performance and delivery of existing resources (people, money, systems) processes and activities within the context of the annual plan, budget and policy guidelines. This is not the case in WL 1.

Experts and professionals at this level such as HR BPs would be expected to collaborate with peers in comparable roles across the organization. The key point to note *is the absence of authority in most such horizontal relationships* other than that stemming from the credibility of the individual's knowledge. Formal, certified, professional knowledge, such as that needed by a GP or a lawyer, is not as self evident in HR or IT. Assessing these latter roles can therefore be challenging.

Outside the organization HRBPs could well be engaged in sourcing discussions with suppliers of candidates, learning solutions or services. A Level 2 manager could be responding to trade unions and/or local politicians about implementing changes in legislation. Once again the key is to isolate what decisions the individual can take in these domains as this will help separate liaison from collaboration.

Typical time frames would be 6 months to a year. The WL 2 managers should be accountable for a budget, particularly when accountable for staff in WL 1. *Depending on the nature of the WL 1 work,* a WL 2 manager could lead around 150 staff supported by a number of supervisors. Some with seasonal work patterns could have more at times, most would have less. HR specialists would typically lead very small teams or might indeed have no subordinates.

8.4.3 Work Level 3: "Integrative Response"

The WL 3 managers is accountable for achieving continuous improvement in performance, cases solved, cost reductions to improve performance and profitability together with driving increased productivity. They would typically be held to account to manage their operation within an agreed cost budget, which might also entail managing projects and possible capital expenditure. Level 3 managers manage, integrate and optimise a flow of interrelated problems that need to be prioritised, balanced and resolved using the resources of the team. They will need to use analytical skills to identify patterns and trends in the performance of KPIs and will put plans in place to improve performance in e.g. underperforming districts as part of a region.

The response now is beyond responding to specific situations requiring (WL 2 managerial or professional) judgement and the matching of solutions on a case by case. The requirement now is to envisage the needs of a continuing sequence of situations that must be understood in the context of an integrated system, unit or geographic area. This calls for *a systematic or integrated provision of service.*

Now the challenge is to understand the linkages between events and cases that were treated at Level 2 as separate, unique situations. Is there a discernible pattern emerging or any significant trends?

At this level, the challenge becomes more a matter of dealing with a number of problems as part of an integrated whole or at least in connection with one another, with the aim of achieving continuous *year-on-year* improvement (in costs, performance, quality, people and system outcomes). *The manager has to juggle resources to get the best overall result for the unit or department.*

Resource management becomes increasingly complex. Accountability for capital budgets can cut in at WL 3. A classic example being the true project manager who has control of the people joining and leaving a project, the budget expenditure and the time line of the project. While management of performance is a key accountability of the WL 2 manager people now entails more rigorous assessment of potential of those people who could move up into WLs 2 and 3 in due course, Often the WL 3 manager cannot always be physically present to assess subordinate work and has to rely on data to assess situations, analysing patterns and trends that identify priority areas for investigation. This calls for scanning a series of activities and evaluating the existence of or quality of linkages between situations and people, recognising patterns and significant trends in performance that require intervention. Problems to be solved are more challenging but still largely concrete and operational.

It is at this level that the balance of skills required can start to move from 'professional expertise' only, to include 'general management', such as in the case of directly managing a professional practice of WL 2 experts. Thus people skills, project skills and productive time management *across sections likely to have conflicting objectives* become increasingly called for. Weaknesses in these general skills could limit further promotion unless in a highly specialised area. Where professional knowledge/expertise is central to the role, the knowledge must be of a high order—involving a familiarity with the latest (international) developments in a particular specialist profession—such as a consultant surgeon.

The Level 3 manager is expected to *modify* existing ways of working, which amounts to *development* of existing products/services on the innovation spectrum, together with improvement in the performance and delivery of existing resources. It is at this level that *the focus of change shifts increasingly from the individual to the organizational* with meaningful *advisory contributions* to policy and strategy being expected.

An HR specialist in WL 3 in a global company is essentially concerned with developing (modifying and improving) procedures (a system within an HR discipline) which set out how future WL 2 work is to be carried out. *The Level 3 manager is expected to both manage and develop that system.* For example a specialist WL 3 ER manager in Europe would be expected to have significant specialist knowledge (e.g. national IR legislations such as in-depth knowledge of TUPE in the UK or Works Councils in Continental Europe) to perform the key tasks. It is not ideal to have WL 2 posts in a Head Office as they cannot usually add sufficient value/knowledge/experience to the field. Thus distinctive jobs in the head office of an international organisation typically emerge at level 3+. An example might be a direct report of a group specialist role. Group wide specialist roles, such as pensions, learning and development, would typically be in WL 4. Specialist jobs at the centre are expected to add value to the field: it is not really possible to do this in jobs below WL 3.

The focus of the jobholder is upon the present, with significant contribution to the future, which involves being consulted on, or involved in, developing policy and strategy. This contribution to policy and strategy is expected at WL 3, but accountability for deciding on which policy or strategy option to go with, rests at WL 4+.

The cadres of WL 3 managers constitute the backbone of a successful organization. They are the general managers who know what works and what does not. They are well positioned to make suggestions about how to overcome shortcomings they have observed as they are still close to the operations. In more people intensive organizations they can manage around 1500 people (again depending on the nature of work at the front line) typically running hypermarkets, distribution centres, factories, refineries, call centres and tea estates.

At WL 3, the future in the sense of next year is as important as the present, i.e. this year. The organizational network could well involve HR roles in other divisions and other Group HR departments. External relationships are likely to be predominantly national but could be international. The operating mode is essentially reactive: crafting the best response to external pressures. They would be expected to have an external network that reads the pulse of the local (and perhaps the international) environment on key people issues, so that they can guide their organization appropriately. The accountable time frame is up to 2 years. Within that timeframe the role holder is expected to signal developments and make a sound contribution to plans for the next year.

8.4.3.1 Strategic Work Levels

Definitions would also be crafted for Levels 4+ depending on the nature of the organization in question. But the nuances can vary more than for levels 1–3, hence it would be misleading to suggest exactly the same definitions fit every large, complex organization. Furthermore the key professions vary in different organizations. The nature of work and their accountabilities in a hierarchy of tax advisors in a large government revenue department would be fundamentally different to those of engineers in a large ship building company, even though both professions could reach into WL 4 and above. The general principles of accountability would nevertheless apply in both cases.

For example the definition of a Level 4 role that is the CEO of a Care organization would be quite different for a Level 5 bank where the Level 4 roles are members of the top executive. In both these cases strategic accountabilities would predominate. But at the other end of the spectrum Level 4 roles in a Level

8 organization would not be heavily accountable for strategy. This would occur mostly at Level 6+. Thus the Work Level definitions need to be flexed to match the realities of a given organization otherwise it can be misleading and over simplistic to provide 'universal definitions' for Work Levels 4+. They will always need to reflect the realities of the organization being reviewed.

8.5 DMA Leadership Model of Differentiating Competencies

As explained in Chap. 5, most "competency" models do not differentiate between the requirements of different levels of accountability. They are not therefore reliable indicators of potential for higher leadership positions. The power of the DMA Leadership model is the alignment of an individual's behaviour and performance to a given level of accountability. The individual is assessed in and against the requirements of a meaningful context. A DMA competency is defined as:

> A *set of behaviours, which ensure an individual's performance is effective when calibrated against the demands of a given level of accountability.*

These behaviours will result from the individual's unique mix of qualities, values, attitudes, motives and abilities, underpinned by certain transferable management skills. The individual's behaviour at a given level of accountability can be assessed in terms of the *consistency* with which these behaviours are demonstrated and observed.

The DMA Competencies are "Differentiating" because they also help to identify who has potential to move to the next higher level.

8.5.1 Characteristics of the DMA Leadership Competency Model

The seven Work Level Elements identify the decisions that need to be taken at each level. The *Competencies indicate how one should behave (think and lead) when making those decisions.* They summarise the standards of effective performance at each level of accountability. They can also be used to identify behaviours that are not up to standard, which can then form the basis for an individual development programme.

They are further used to identify who to promote to the next level. The approach calls for consideration of the requirements of the job(s) at the next level of accountability and then seeking evidence, by considering the relevant competency definitions that a person can progress to that level.

8.5.2 DMA Competencies Aligned to the Work Level Elements

Seven elements	Six differentiating competencies
• Nature of Work (& Timeframe) • Resource Complexity • Problem Solving • Change • Natural Work Team • External Interaction • Timeframe	• Setting Direction • Leading Resources • Analysing and Decision Making • Driving Change • Influencing Colleagues • Managing the External Environment • *Values driven,* ***non differentiating competences*** *such as, "passion", "energy" "Commitment".*

Successful behaviours are cumulative; meaning that at higher levels managers should already be demonstrating the required behaviours from lower levels.

8.5.3 How to Apply These Differentiating Competencies

Let us assume we are working in an organization where the top position is at Level 5. Positive behaviours and negative behaviours can be listed across all levels from one to five. Some clients do not like to publish negative behaviours—their argument being people need positive reinforcement and the negatives come from the reverse of the positive definitions. The problem is that at higher levels the most common de-railer is an inability to work effectively within a network of peers. In these cases it is essential to specify the unsatisfactory behaviours and give evidence to support the assessment. An individual should score well on all the positives. But it is equally important to check also against the negatives, which in some cases will more than offset the positives. For example, a low score on *Influencing colleagues* would undermine a level 3 manager otherwise looking promotable to level 4 notwithstanding a number of positive ratings.

The way to use these Competencies is as follows: for a manager currently in level 3, look at the level 3 positive characteristics to confirm (s)he is a good level 3 manager. Check the level 3 negative definitions to confirm the overall assessment picture for that individual is well balanced. The presence of one or two negatives, could point to development needs going forward. They will also help confirm why a manager may not be ready for promotion. This is critical for those whose ambition can be getting ahead of their current contribution.

To check whether the manager in a Level 3 role has potential for level 4 accountability, then look at the level 4 definitions and ask, "Is there any ***evidence*** that this person shows the positive level 4 characteristics against each competency?" Summarise that evidence, then check the negative definitions for level 4. Does this strengthen or weaken the case for level 4 potential being confirmed?

8.5.4 Benefits of Applying a Differentiating Competency Model

The model will enable an organization to:

- Communicate clearly to jobholders those behaviours, which are required for top performance at their respective Work Levels.
- Identify priority competency development needs for individual managers in their current or likely future roles.
- *Identify individuals who, at their current level, are demonstrating behaviours, which indicate they have potential to move to the next higher Work Level.*

The DMA differentiating competencies are designed for use by line management. However they can also be used in conjunction with external assessment. Psychometric tests would also plumb the areas of *Resilience and Energy*. These latter behaviours do not change per level of accountability but they should be present in every effective leader. (A case study illustrating this approach is set out in Chap. 10 of *The Accountable Leader*.)

8.5.4.1 An Example of One Differentiating Competency

An example of one differentiating competency designed for in a financial Organization Northern Rock, where the top role was WL 5, is set out below.

First competency: Setting direction

Definition	*The capacity to set the direction and deliver plans over time, which are aligned to the needs of a defined context of accountabilities.*
Related DMA elements:	**Nature of work** Stems from the purpose of the role and defines where it differs in accountability from those above and below. **Time frame** Focuses on the time over which the impact of the majority of the decisions of the jobholder will be felt.
Range	Short-term operational → Long-term strategic
	Low level → High level
Positive differentiating behaviours	
Work Level 1	If a team leader/supervisor: • Works within short term prescribed objectives of up to 3 months. • Reports back on progress against these plans, highlighting variances, but not accountable for setting them or changing them.
Work Level 2	• Sets, communicates and holds team members in level 1 accountable for delivery against realistic but stretching, short-term operational objectives. Personally accountable for objectives of up to 12 months. • Continuously reviews and acts to remove obstacles to ensure progress remains on track.
Work Level 3	• Balances potentially conflicting sub-goals or the objectives of sections within a unit or department to ensure an integrated set of results for the unit or department as a whole. • Identifies trends, patterns and priorities for performance improvement and contributes to policy and plans for the year ahead, as well as the current year.
Work Level 4	• Leads a key function or activity within the bank, and given an authoritative understanding of the bank's future needs in that area, sets achievable milestones for direct reports of up to 2 years ahead. Personally accountable for objectives of up to 3–4 years ahead.

	• As an Executive Director of Northern Rock, establishes relevant specific objectives and direction derived from the strategic intentions of the Board while also contributing to that strategy and future aspirations.
Work Level 5	• As CEO, takes the lead in charting the future destiny of the bank, aiming in the short term to successfully ride out the demands of the TPO (Temporary Public Ownership) and ensure the conditionalities of the Government's emergency loan are successfully met. • Demonstrates ability to deliver ST plans, explore numerous options while ensuring there is a robust LT strategy post TPO to guarantee the bank returns successfully to private ownership with a secure future.
Negative differentiating behaviours	
Work Level 1	If a team leader/supervisor: • Is personally disorganized. • Too often misses deadlines that have been set by management.
Work Level 2	• Spurs self and team members to action but without a clear sense of direction and well-conceived objectives. • Ignores or fails to identify and remove obstacles to progress.
Work Level 3	• Tolerates and does not resolve conflicting objectives within and/or between subordinate managers at the expense of overall departmental or even bank performance. • Is overwhelmed by detail and fails to identify negative patterns and to act on the causes of poor unit or departmental performance.
Work Level 4	• Concentrates on short-term issues and immediate results to the detriment of longer-term objectives. • Unable to work up a concrete plan of action from an idea or produce a solution to a new problem.
Work Level 5	• Struggles to maintain a balance between short-term achievement and setting long term direction for the bank. Is prone to hold too many meetings, which are not well time-managed and which tend to be counterproductive and tie up too much of key board members' time as a result.

This approach is then applied with each of the remaining Leadership Competencies. This approach is a demanding, systematic and reliable assessment of an organization's leadership talent. The secret is to keep the process simple. The summary of the competency assessments should be no more than one page backed up with short examples providing evidence for the recommendation. Ideally these assessments should be discussed by the relevant top team chaired by a "grandparent" two levels above those being recommended for the high potential list. The aim is to arrive at a consensus based on factual evidence, not simply opinion(s). Once everyone in the top team understands the competencies and how to apply them (this also assumes a sound knowledge of the various Work Levels) the establishment of robust lists of high potential leaders becomes easier. Some companies refer to those in WL 2 with *confirmed* potential for WL 3 as a "List 3" manager and so on.

It is then possible to identify *cover*—the number people in WL 2 for example with confirmed potential for WL 3 within say 5 years, expressed as a percentage of the total of number of jobs in WL 3—throughout management. Inevitably more work is then needed to mine the degree of cover by function, geography and increasingly by various minority groups.

These managers make up the bench strength of high potential leaders

This process becomes the basis for personal development and the mapping of relevant career paths. For example it is possible to plan moves for a young accountant across a mix of financial jobs at different levels of accountability to ensure he or she emerges in the role at the top the function with the relevant expertise and experience to be successful. This can be orchestrated over time by a series of *boundary moves* as explained in Chap. 5.

8.6 Finally a Word About Spans of Control

The span of control refers to a leader's direct reports.[9] It is sometimes referred to as a span of management or span of leadership. If a Chief Engineer has 5 direct reports in a department of 50, the span in that case is 5 not 50. There has been much written about "the ideal (universal) span". There is really no such thing but that does not mean there is no such thing as "the right span" in a given situation.

There is a persistent tendency for people to speak of an ideal of six. This seems to be grounded on a misunderstanding of some work done by a mathematician, Graicunas in the 1930s, who argued that a leader could not manage more than six people *if their work is interlocking*. This was a theoretical calculation that apparently had no or limited empirical basis. But interestingly the proviso of interlocking work has been forgotten over time and the "ideal span of 6" is seemingly embedded in the management psyche.

The fundamental problem with the work of the classical theorists, such as Urwick and Graicunas, was this: ***they were arguing for both a limited number of layers and limited spans of control. But they are mutually exclusive objectives.***

My colleague, Adam Pearce, has done some pioneering work on spans based on a data bank of over half a million job holders (stemming for ~30 projects) including the relationship to their leaders. The average span of control in this sample is 6.6. *But note: over 90 % of these civilian organizations were over layered. This figure emerged* ***before*** *they had improved their structures.* Improvements of between 5 and 14 % are often feasible in my experience. Even though well short of the ancient military organizing principle of the 'ten' it does suggest average spans of

[9] Spans can get be nuanced and therefore confusing; Do they refer to actual heads in roles, full and part time staff (making up Full Time Equivalents—FTEs), seasonal staff, agency staff/temps and so on? I am referring throughout to the number of jobs/heads as part of the establishment, in the budget.

~7.5+ are feasible in most medium to large civilian organizations. That of course does not mean everyone has a span of ~7+. Spans will vary depending on the complexity of work being done but the work at the front line of many organizations is still quite straightforward—often aided in fact by new technology—e.g. the new 'picking technology' exploited in Distribution Centres run by Amazon and DHL. Thus spans still tend to be conservative. If someone has never managed more than four direct reports it is easy to understand why they might think six is "impossible." This is almost a standard reaction of many CFOs for example. A reason often given for not being able to increase spans is the bureaucracy of the performance management process that calls for detailed quarterly assessments and interviews of all front line staff. In such cases it is indeed probably the performance system that first needs review. I can think of one bank where staff at the front line complained in the engagement survey of a 'lack of performance feedback.' The bank then used its detailed management system for the performance assessment of its most junior staff, which indeed was overkill. It placed a lot of emphasis on assessing potential yet less than 5 % were ever promoted from the front line and the factors being "assessed" were not relevant. But the point here is the spans of supervisors were constricted as a result of a daft HR policy.

8.6.1 Influence of Layers on Spans

I mentioned earlier that the horizontal and vertical axes of any organization design need to be in balance to establish an optimal structure. Given their focus on the horizontal dimension of organization design it is not surprising to find so many consultancies obsess with spans of control. It is a simplistic way of encouraging companies to widen their spans to save money.

But the driver of effective organization design is the vertical NOT the horizontal axis. The number of layers drives average spans of control, not the other way round, set in the context of the type of work being done. An organization might have an average span of seven, encouraging the manager with a span of eight to think his or her structure fine. But experience indicates that the section in question could still be over layered to the point that the average span there should be 10+ because of the type of work done at the front line. See Fig. 9.2 in Chap. 9 for an example. Thus increasing an average span by 0.5 but leaving excessive layers in place is spurious OD. Furthermore:

> ***Spans and layers studies undertaken without insight into the appropriate number of levels of accountability are dangerous.***

Consultants peddling a 'one size fits all' solution to "spans and layers" (even the order in which they use these terms betrays the basic misunderstanding of the dynamics involved) such as '8 × 8' (an average span of 8 coupled with 8 layers) are a menace. I actually heard the CEO of one of the biggest banks in the world recently proudly explaining how a US consultancy helped him reform the bank so that "we now have only 8 layers and *everyone* (my italics) has eight reports". It is a bit worrying when the head of a bank does not understand the concept of "average".

8.6.2 Is There an Optimal Span?

The answer is, in general terms no, but in specific terms, yes. But at the risk of sounding like a lawyer, it depends on the individual circumstances of the case. Using the initial work done at Lockheed written up by John Child,[10] who also examined the pioneering work on spans of Woodward, Barkdull and Stieglitz, I have constructed a guide for managers, which looks at 11 variables to help decide the appropriate span for a leader in a given context. Managers find this particularly useful as it illustrates why and how optimal spans can be different. For example the span of a CEO and a supervisor leading the front line are invariably among the wider spans in the organization. The problem is when the *average spans* in middle management are around 3–5 this invariably correlates with hierarchy heavy structures. Table 4.1 in Chap. 4 provides a compelling example: imagine my chagrin when a few years later the head of this organization was knighted!

Adam Pearce and I have also discovered that there is a strong relationship between the percentage of lowly graded jobs and the average spans that can be achieved. This is because the lower grades indicate the work is less complex and not 'interlocking'. An example could be a call centre where average spans in excess of 12 would be par for the course. The staff are working within very clear guidelines and precedent (WL 1). Whereas in some corporate departments, such as legal, the spans could be justifiably lower than the overall average given the nature of the work where more than one person could be working on separate aspects of the same case. In this situation the work is interlocking and could be sequential in that person B cannot start their work until person A has finished. This work pattern requires much closer supervision and tends to require more highly graded staff given the type of work involved. Indeed in some departments the front line might even be at WL 2. In these cases a span of between three and five might be more appropriate.

But generally managers are too conservative in their thinking about the number of team members that can be led. While some spans are considerably higher than others on average nevertheless it has invariably been the case in the fieldwork I have done that ALL the average spans of control can usually be improved. Thus just because the span of one department is wider on average than others or even higher than the average for the organization as a whole it does not mean it cannot continue to improve, as the line of best fit indicates in Fig. 8.1.

In this example 95 % of the jobs are in the lowest grades, indicating the type of work being carried out is on balance, not highly skilled. This reveals that the

[10] J. Child (1977) *Organization: a guide to problems and practice*, p. 58ff.

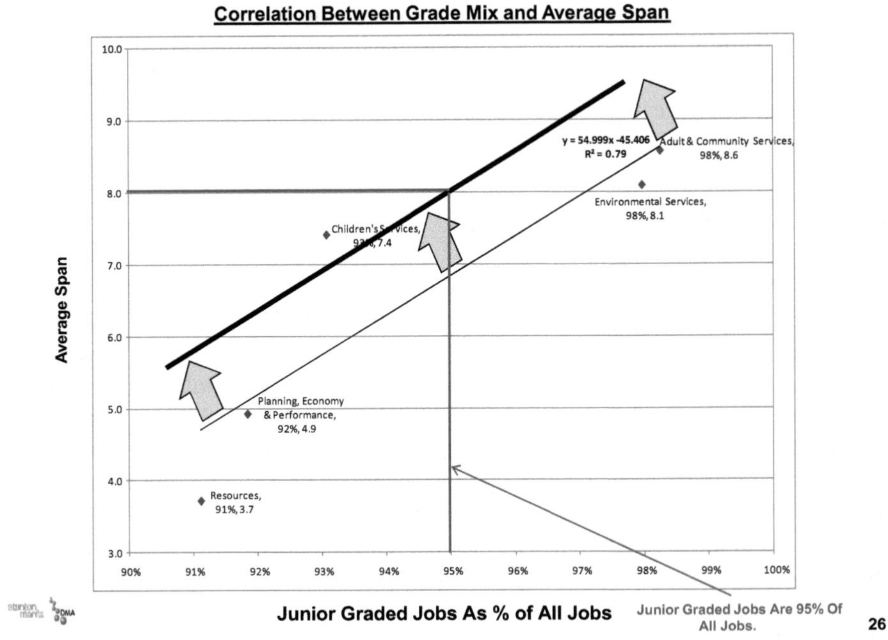

Fig. 8.1 To help this organization reach a higher average span overall, some units must average more to offset those with higher graded staff

average span figure is conservative. The line of best fit shows the current average of just under seven should be raised to eight and that in this case that necessitates each of the key departments in the sample all improving their averages, to varying degrees. Without this insight this case might have been considered, incorrectly, to be healthy. It shows that the figures are different based on the quality of work being done at the front line. In other words not every section or department needs to reach eight.

8.6.3 Identifying the Right Span

Calibrating the right span of control requires very careful analysis. *It cannot be done reliably without first identifying the total number of levels of accountability in a given organization.* Since we now know that there can be only one layer per level above WL 1, we then have the basis for the maximum number of layers, which is "up to one more than the total number of Levels." Thus if the top job is at Level 5 there can be up to six layers of hierarchy. This is because if there are many staff in the Level 1 front line then supervisory leaders will be required in Level 1. In other words there are two layers possible in WL 1: the front line and the supervisor. As indicated in Sect. 3.4.5, there are three reasons that necessitate the role of the supervisor in WL 1: very large numbers of front line staff to be led, wide geographical spread or shift work. Above Level 1 there is scope for only one leader (or layer) per level: one each at WLs 2, 3, 4 and 5 in this case, since those three reasons do not apply. Hence up to six layers in total. For a level 6 organizations up to seven layers are feasible and so on.

8.6.4 The Layers Are the Key

As already indicated the number of layers drive the average span for the organization as a whole. The requisite layers once established provide an insight into the necessary average spans of control that are required. The linkages are as follows:

- The Work Levels dictate the number of layers needed.
- The total number of layers required drives the optimal average span of control that can be achieved.
- The guideline is as follows:

The Average Span of control should equal *at least* the total number of layers.

One of the findings that seems to be emerging consistently from fieldwork is the average span seems to correlate with at least the available number of layers needed. Thus an organization which has a top job at WL 5, should achieve an average span of at least six (because there can be up to six layers). An organization with a top job at WL 6 should have an average span of seven and so on up to WL 8. This is a new insight that might become a helpful guideline but which at present probably needs more empirical backing before it can be said to be a valid principle of organization design. Notwithstanding the need for more work it suggests:

Work Levels are the key to layers and layers are the key to spans.

But too often the diktats about layers and spans are guesswork and dangerous especially if they are driven by the accountant's knife not the OD laser. This is why 'spans & layers' so called guidelines often (rightly) have such a bad name.

The DMASS principles provide the insight into the number of layers an organization justifies and the average spans that are feasible, which establishes the right platform for the selection, growth and development of leaders.

9 An Absence of Mission Mastery: A Case Study

Whatever was required to be done, the Circumlocution Office was beforehand, with all public departments in the art of perceiving—HOW NOT TO DO IT.
Charles Dickens (*Little Dorrit,* Chap. 10, Containing the whole science of government, p. 126)

9.1 General

I have argued thus far that clear accountability is a pre-requisite of a high performing organization. In addition I have argued that to attain Mission Mastery all five Pillars need to be robust, manifest in a clear mission, an effective structure of jobs with discrete decision rights, leadership development aligned to levels of accountability coupled with experiential learning often in the form of boundary moves, all of which combine to generate a positive culture. I have also established that military organizations, practising Moltke's mission command, consistently outperform their civilian counterparts in the field of leadership development. The focus of this chapter is a case study of a civilian organization: the British Civil Service in which the Pillars of Mission Mastery are not robust. This contributes to a performance gap. The findings are based on extensive field work—about 500 interviews at all levels across this organization. Each of the five key pillars is examined in some detail and their shortcomings exposed. The result is at times a dysfunctional, de-motivating work place, which adds up to a culture of no consequences. Good work is not well rewarded and poor performance is not sanctioned. Reasons for a culture of inertia were identified 50 years ago in the Fulton report and continue to be noted, but have not yet been fully redressed. The reasons for this will be analysed in this chapter.

B. Dive, *Mission Mastery*, Management for Professionals,
DOI 10.1007/978-3-319-25223-0_9

9.2 A Case Study: The British Civil Service

I have already singled out Barclays Bank as a recent example of a negative culture emanating from some weaknesses in its Pillars. However it does appear to be getting back on its feet under new leadership, notwithstanding more heavy fines in 2015 for misconduct. The organization reviewed in this chapter is the British Civil Service. Eddie Knox, later a famous Punch editor, commented after 18 months in the service: "*The first duty of a civil servant, I gathered, was to decide at what date he would take his holidays, the second to decide at what time he would have his tea.*"[1] What causes this inertia caricatured by influential writers such as Dickens and Knox?

It is of course an over simplification to state the civil service is a single organization. It is in fact a generic term for a federation of departments (or organizations) expected to maximise what could be called a loose form of professional leadership. But that is also the case with any large organization especially one that straddles many countries and of course leading a federation in one country is not more difficult than running one across numerous countries. I have consulted to public service organizations in other countries and noticed similar situations where at times "words speak louder than actions". Even the pope, in December 2014, castigated the Roman Curia as: "Infected with careerism, scheming, greed and spiritual Alzheimer's."[2] You might ask: if public officials are so ineffective elsewhere why single out the British Civil Service, especially when anecdotal evidence suggests international bureaucracies are worse? (It is also important to point out that many of the shortcomings mentioned in this chapter are also prevalent in a number of private sector companies as shown in Chaps. 4 and 7.) The reason is the following: I have not undertaken extensive fieldwork in these other public bureaucracies, whereas I do have a large data base of material on the civil service, which is more than anecdotal hearsay. My team and I also trained departmental staff who undertook a similar number of interviews. Their findings were consistent with ours. As it is a large federation of organizations with over half a million employees the issues highlighted below are significant and not untypical of very large organizations.

The analysis in this chapter is based on work, which cover a 5 year period from 2007. We studied nine organisations across Whitehall [The six consultants who carried out the work on DMA Consultancy (DMAC) projects were Brian Dive (9 assignments), Adam Pearce (8 assignments), Bernard Dive (7 assignments), Peter Dugmore (5 assignments), Martin Pierce (1 assignment) and Charles Seaford (1 assignment)]. This work covered a population of 180,000 jobs across Whitehall. Many improvements were made as a result of these projects but as I signed confidentially agreements the areas of work we studied and the actions subsequently taken must perforce, remain anonymous. The focus is to provide an

[1] Fitzgerald P. (2002) *"The Knox Brothers"*

[2] See Pope Francis' Christmas message, 22 December 2014.

illustration of what life is like *in any civilian organization* that has too many layers and is hierarchy heavy. Pilkington wrote in 1999 that "There have been significant managerial reforms that have revolutionised the structure and functioning of the civil service since 1986."[3] Notwithstanding that assertion an examination of its five Pillars reveals certain fundamental inadequacies remain.

The analysis underpinning previous work tends to be strong but implementation continues to be patchy. My contention is there are some very clear reasons for this that have not been thoroughly addressed as yet.

9.3 An Assessment of the Five Pillars of Mission Mastery in the UK Civil Service

It is now clear that if a civilian organization is going to meet the Mission Mastery gold standard then all five key Pillars need to be strong. Let us now assess the CS against those five criteria, looking at the CS through Moltke's telescope—he was famous for having a very powerful telescope to observe matters in the field.

9.3.1 Pillar One: Mission

As we now know, Moltke's auftragstaktik starts with a clear statement of mission. That is the trigger point for the development of a learning organization: one that *implements* policy and strategy. If that is not clear from the outset an organization will first flounder and then probably founder. So how clear is Whitehall's mission and how well is it implemented?

On mission the besetting sin across Whitehall stems largely from the lack of clear accountability at the top, essentially between politicians and senior civil servants.[4] There is clear doctrine—Ministers are responsible for policy, civil servants for implementing it—but the reality of day-to-day life in practice not so clear. It seems some top civil servants have become almost timid and afraid to speak truth unto power—and indeed heads could be chopped off for doing so. (Somewhat ironical given Charles the first was beheaded outside Whitehall Palace.) Today's reality at the top has been described to me as 'a conspiracy of muddle-headedness'. This materialises into uneven and ineffective policy processes. Examples would include hastily hatched manifesto 'commitments', or a desire to massage today's headline that has to be turned painfully into policy. And yesterday's "policy" goes into limbo. This means the mission is at times ephemeral, uneven, and erratic, as the essentially political or symbolic are pursued with zigzagging enthusiasm often to satisfy a particular lobby group. Change, of course, is not unique to government

[3] Pilkington C. (1999) *The Civil Service in Britain Today,* Manchester University Press p. vii.

[4] Whitehall is shorthand for the government departments that historically have been based in and around the location of the former Whitehall Palace.

departments. It is a "constant" of work in the twenty-first century. But some organizations orchestrate their response better than others.

Central government departments typically see their mission as the production of policy in line with the political manifesto of the government of the day. This means that to be effective their role needs to be one of successful innovation and implementation. Most people interviewed, from the must junior grade to Senior Civil Servant (SCS) in departments based in London, described the purpose of their job simply as "contributing to policy".

9.3.1.1 A Constraint on the Delivery of Mission

Civil servants are quick to point out "We are not accountable for policy. That is the preserve of politicians." True, but they are responsible for 'policy into *effective* action'. We could not detect a consistent or crisp mission against which these "advisors" were held to account. In fact accountability for the innovation process behind policy development seemed to be opaque, unclear, tortuous, bordering on chaotic at times. Few engaged in policy development, whether near the coal face or the minister's office, seemed to be crystal clear about what was required of them or were noticeably satisfied with their work. We could not detect a consistent approach across Whitehall, based on the departments in which our projects took place.

This is in contrast to best private sector practice where the innovation process for ideas, policy, products or services is usually clearer. Many companies employ something akin to the innovation funnel set out in Fig. 9.1 which is based on the pioneering work done by Wheelwright and Clark of the Harvard Business School in the car industry, initially. For example almost 20 years ago Unilever developed their innovation work into a disciplined network, which was rolled out globally and installed with rigorous project training to enhance the quality, speed and

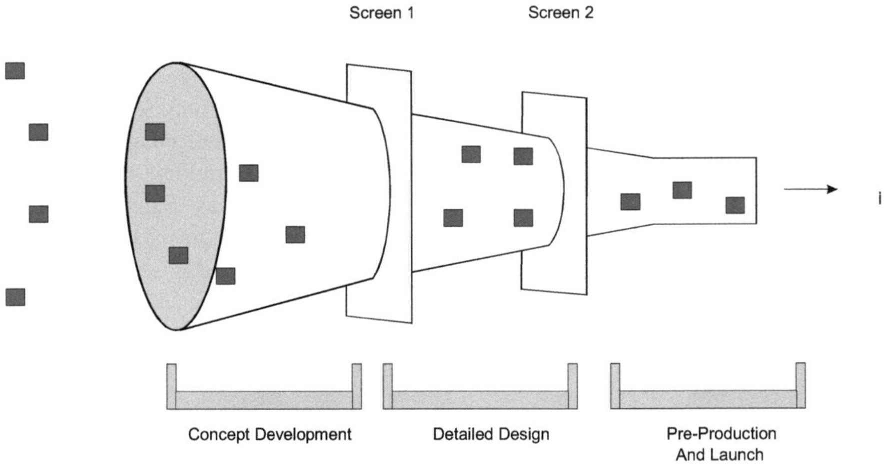

Fig. 9.1 The funnel

effectiveness of its innovation and speed to market. This was described in some detail by Dr. A. Ganguly, previously the R&D Director at Unilever.[5]

This figure is a very simple illustration of how a pipeline of ideas or initiatives (the squares) moves through the various phases of discussion, assessment, rejection, support, prototype/draft to launch. What is important in this process is identifying who owns the funnel or pipeline and furthermore who owns the screens or gateways. This is where the no/go decisions are made, which then indicates how resources will be allocated or reallocated. In a think tank environment these resources could be know-how, money, people and *time*.

Accountability to stop something is very important in a well disciplined, Innovative organization.

This is culture that is foreign to Whitehall. It seems initiatives and projects can meander on indefinitely in Whitehall. A Permanent Secretary (a 'CEO' of a department who could be in a job at Level 5, 6 or maybe 7 in a handful of cases), would own the total (departmental) funnel and should ensure the pipeline is healthy with active ideas, and policy projects coming through in line with the policy of the government of the day. But while a competent "funnel owner" is not necessarily the inventor or discoverer of all the new ideas and policy insights he or she would be accountable for ensuring only the right matters of worth come into the funnel in the first place. Then that appropriate resources are deployed in such a way that the funnel is part of a productive and successful process. "Launch" in this case, would be the hand off to the minister even though policy experts in the funnel may also interface with ministers as required based on their expertise.

We could not detect clear gateways in the process of policy development that are unambiguously owned at a consistent level across Whitehall. Lines between Green and White papers seemed to be blurred and confused more often than not. Indeed given the lack of clear line management accountability, the overlap, duplication, bypassing and confusion we observed was not totally unexpected.

In summary there does not *seem to be* a *clear and consistent policy production process across Whitehall, nor clear, transparent accountability for its various stages. Although there appear to have been various efforts to improve over the years and some departments are probably better than others, something (politics?) always gets in the way.*

9.3.1.2 A Disconnect Between Policy Work and the Field Work

There is a tendency in Whitehall policy departments to split the formulation of policy from delivery. The great majority of civil servants we interviewed who "contributed to policy" were rarely accountable for delivery or work in the field. They generally had little or no operations experience. The closest they seem to get

[5] Ganguly, A (1999) *Business-driven R&D: Managing knowledge to create wealth.*

to the field is "to inform people in local authorities etc on the interpretation of the policy." The formulators of policy generally did not seem to visit the field while crafting new policy. Indeed they invariably expect "the field workers" to come to London, rather than the other way round.

There's a profound cultural point here that the top of the civil service is—whatever the rhetoric—more concerned with looking up to ministers and handling the immediate than in looking to long term delivery. The former is where the brownie points are to be won.

Time management is consistently an issue. Everything tends to be "urgent" and reactionary (given the twenty-first century desire of politicians seeking to spin daily headlines), which disrupts ongoing work or causes much of it to be left in limbo. People are "busy" but wheels do not seem to gain sufficient traction. I was requested by a senior civil servant to produce a report: "You have done more work on the structure of the civil service since the Fulton Report so it would be very helpful to have your findings."[6] I provided an extensive summary and after a month's silence I had to check to see whether the report had been received. "Yes, thanks but we are busy with pension negotiations at the moment." I never did get a formal response even though I was asked to produce the report. Yet, given the wage freeze in place at the time it was an unparalleled opportunity to do some fundamental strategic thinking about the grading and accountability problems first highlighted in the Fulton report and not resolved satisfactorily since. As I have noticed in the private sector, excessive layers of management seem to drive the tactical rather than the strategic, which means the latter is largely neglected and/or given insufficient thought and time. And yet *the raison d'etre of these departments is thought leadership!*

This contrasts with the behaviour of the better strategy and policy makers in other organizations such as the military where a staff officer with no experience of the line (and vice versa) would not get very far in the promotion stakes. We saw in Chap. 2 that one of Moltke's great insights was identifying how "operations" can link the top and the front line of an organization. This connectivity is not obvious in Whitehall where initiatives come spinning out of the government of the day, as it lurches in a new direction. The danger is this shotgun approach to policy making generates organizational whiplash in the lower reaches of a department, disrupting delivery. While politics is undoubtedly a factor, sudden change is not unique to Whitehall, but the apparent lack of rigour and discipline in the Whitehall process of policy-into-effective-action and the tendency not to remove or reallocate jobs in the resource portfolio when government policy moves in a new direction; helps explain the feeling of "hamster management" repeatedly reported back to us. It has also contributed to a situation where the number of *senior civil service jobs grew 43 %*

[6] See Sect. 3.2.1 below.

from 2000 to 2010.[7] Peter Drucker is one who has argued that genuine innovation needs a disciplined approach.[8] The hierarchy of scientific knowledge and discovery (and innovation policy formulation) is not based purely on serendipity.

So, in the light of the above, how does the civil service perform against Moltke's the three strategic traps than can undermine mission and its delivery, identified in Chap. 3?

9.3.1.3 The Knowledge Trap

This is the trap stemming from the desire for certainty. It fosters a search for more and more information at the expense of making a decision.

Knowledge is important as a basis for sound policy work. There is a concern that this respect for knowledge is also being undermined as 'knowledge owners' are moved around too much and too frequently in the civil service–in the great chase for grades. This is another outcome of ineffective career development and planning: see further comment below under leadership development, Sect. 3.3.

But the respect for knowledge, theory and discussion in some quarters seems to have become an end in itself. *There tends to be an inbuilt proclivity to constantly seek more information and 'data' rather than risk a decision.* For example, when describing how the DMA approach builds data based on interviews starting from the 'front line' we became enmeshed in a long and rather meaningless discussion with senior departmental management about what constitutes the front line in a policy department. This is a straightforward organization design issue but this discussion finally thought it might be at grade 7—around Level 2. The fact that this group was ignoring people in about six grades lower down (i.e. *most* of their people) seemed to be a blind spot.

9.3.1.4 The Alignment Trap

This is the trap stemming from the desire to see plans put into action but when actions fall short there is a tendency to enter into more discussion and issue new and more detailed instructions.

There seems to be great caution to accept results that signal shortcomings, which logically suggest corrective action. It was not uncommon to encounter discussions

[7] In 2009 the Government sought a "25 % reduction in the senior Civil Services". Early in 2010 it was shown the number of jobs had actually gone up: see Source: Senior Salaries Review Body reports: 2006 (Table 1.3), 2007 (Table 2.1) and 2011 (Table 2.1).

[8] Drucker, P.F. "The Discipline of Innovation", *Harvard Business Review,* November-December 1998

about the need for “more guidance material” when outcomes were “disappointing” and challenged the status quo. For example, when presenting findings of DMA Probes in a department the approach quickly turned to questioning the statistical reliability or validity of straightforward activities. “Is the sample large enough”, “do we need another survey” *rather than* “What have we learned so far and what needs to be done?” There seems to be a tendency to baulk at the prospect of committing to action. Civil servants are apt to circle back and say “But are we sure? Do we need more evidence? Has there been enough consultation?” Sometimes these are fair questions, but not on virtually every occasion calling for action. *Even when alignment exists there is a tendency to question it rather than act.*

9.3.1.5 The Effects Trap

This is the trap stemming from the desire to see actions achieve the planned outcomes. When this does not happen the tendency is to impose more detailed controls, more metrics and more measurement.

The civil service has some of the best and most extensive employee engagement survey material of any organization I have worked with. Worryingly the scores reveal the same issues persistently recur. There is overwhelming data highlighting areas for improvement but, “a certain shyness of action prevails”.

Effective metrics need to be set in the context of a clear strategy in a truly accountable organization. Otherwise they can be misleading and/or positively unhelpful. It is critical to measure the right things. A recent shattering example was the case of Stafford hospital’s record of failed leadership in 2008 as it chased government of the day’s metrics about central administrative targets and cost controls rather than patient welfare in its desire to become a foundation trust. It lost sight of its mission and measured the wrong things. Many patients died as a result.

Some HR managers in Whitehall will cite metrics about how well their appraisal system is working. The fact that the engagement surveys illustrate again and again that the performance management system is not working well seems to be ignored as long as the paper work comes in on time. During this period the item in surveys: “Poor performance is not well managed” was regularly scored in the 30s—out of 100. The civil service has tumbled into the effects trap since it collects more and more input metrics on the same themes but rarely seems to take discernible corrective action.

The civil service mission to implement and innovate effectively in the field of government policy seems to be hamstrung by lack of conceptual clarity and rigour together with an absence of clear accountability notwithstanding the fact that it is never easy to measure the causal impacts of policy work in any organization.

However ***the mission pillar is defective****. Moltke would be worried already by these initial observations.*

9.3.2 Pillar Two: Organization Structure

As has been flagged in Chap. 4, effective organization design is invariably suboptimal in civilian organizations. This is also not helped by the fact that Moltke did not treat issues relating to structure and therefore people could be forgiven for thinking he did not think it was important. Nothing could be further from the truth. He realised the command structure he headed was effective. It did not call for major reworking or redesign. Thus even the serious student of his work could be forgiven for thinking he did not pay attention to organization design.

This is the potential trap in understanding mission command for the unwary.

Unlike civilian leaders he did not have to: the problem was solved long before his time. He focussed on improving leadership behaviour within a sound structure.

It means the issue of structure and unambiguous accountability is rarely given appropriate attention. One feature of the current civil service system is it disjointedness. Recently 'joined up policy' making has become a buzz phrase but even so too many of the budgetary, power and organisational structures of Whitehall militate against joining up. Radical efforts to think about 'Total Place' (the different flows of money into one place, or even single families—e.g. housing, education, health, social care) have not got very far. The current 'difficult issue' is integrated health and social care.

The lack of single point accountability in the civil service is a major contributing factor in my opinion—see next paragraph. The desire of politicians to keep the service "weak" is a corollary as they can then happily divide and rule.

There appears to be quite a long standing awareness that the structure of the civil service including its Whitehall departments and Arms Length bodies (ALBs) is not effective (In my limited experience this is less a problem with ALBs). Many papers acknowledge the problem but have been unable to remedy this shortcoming in the last 50 years. ***The fundamental problem is no one civil servant can really drive change*** in the civil service despite the mirage of titles that include "Head of the Home Civil Service." Home Civil Service means the Foreign Office is not included. Until 2010 the job had two other responsibilities: Secretary to the Cabinet and CEO of the Cabinet Office. Following the retirement of that Head of the Civil Service in 2010 the job was divided into three! The structure has changed again more recently but there is still no role with single point accountability for even the Home Civil Service.

There is still no-one with executive single point accountability for the performance of the CS.

So there are two issues here that need resolution: an accurate analysis of the problem with a defined solution and the presence of someone with the authority to make it happen. As recently as April 2103, at a Parliamentary hearing on the service the top two civil servants, *who then shared two of the three elements of the previous job of head of the home CS at the time*, stated in answer to a question from the chair, Bernard Jenkin, "*The model is working*." They were not asked to provide any evidence to back up this assertion.

9.3.2.1 The Fulton Report

The last extensive and impressive formal review of the "Structure and management of the Home Civil Service" begun in the 60s, became known as the Fulton Report. It concluded there were too many layers of management in the Civil Service: "At least 7 organizational levels in administrative work" and that spans of control "are very narrow, usually only two or three." A span of control, reflects the number of staff reporting directly to a person in the next layer of the hierarchy. Excessive layers of bureaucracy tend to correlate with small spans of control—although we have found exceptions in the CS where some departments with straightforward work at the front line have both wide average spans and yet are still over layered, which is counterintuitive. The Fulton Report was also critical of what it labelled the "cult of the amateur generalist" and it was also critical of the grading system, or "system of classes" that prevailed at the time. "The present system of classes is a major obstacle to the proper application of the principles of accountable management".[9]

What Has Happened Since the Fulton Report?

In the 25 years post Fulton, there was little noticeable improvement in the effectiveness of the civil service organization structure. This was not from lack of effort by the Efficiency Unit. Its impressive "Next Steps" initiative was the next significant reforming report, finally released in 1988 given the usual machinations of key mandarins and politicians.[10] The key proposal suggested breaking off the executive functions of government into structures where they could be run as the needs of the task to be delivered dictated rather than political expediency. This gave rise to executive agencies that became known as Arms Length Bodies (ALBs).

Over time the looseness of Whitehall accountability was further evidenced as ALBs—which is the generic term for any organisation at arms length from a core Whitehall Department—came to embrace Non Departmental Public Bodies

[9] Fulton Report, paragraph 213.

[10] Improving Management in Government: *Next Steps* Report to the Prime Minister (1988) compiled by Kate Jenkins, Karen Caines and Andrew Jackson

(NDPBs—quangos), executive agencies and a few other forms. A study by the Institute for government showed that there was no rhyme nor reason for these different structures—they had just grown up. "Another hole in the accountability bucket, dear Lisa."

Today there seems to be more confusion in the landscape about 'bringing back bits into government'. One of the key authors of "Next Steps", Andrew Jackson, drew my attention to Professor Peter Hennessy's law of political propinquity: "The nearer a delivery function is to the politicians the more likely it is to be messed up". The ongoing tinkering with the NHS over the years seems to be an ongoing example of this law. An organization network with over one million employees is a major organization design challenge, likely to be well beyond the ken of a politician and most senior civil servants not schooled in the vagaries of successful organisation development. The record suggests that in this domain Fulton's "enthusiastic amateur" is given full rein in the twenty-first century. The consequences continue to be predictable.

In 1993 a more limited report by John Oughton, the then Head of the Efficiency Unit, called for "leaner and 'flatter' management structures through the removal of unnecessary management layers in Whitehall departments." These concerns were yet again addressed in a somewhat oxymoronic White Paper of July 1994 entitled: "Change and Continuity." One of the seven major proposals was: "There should be the development of a 'leaner and fitter' service by removing unnecessary layers from the hierarchical management structures."

What is significant here is that on more than one occasion in the last 50 years the extensive and pervasive shortcomings of the civil services have been recognised. But other than exhortations to "remove unnecessary layers" *no-one clarified what they meant by "unnecessary", how to identify these offending layers and more importantly, how to redress what the White Paper referred to as "excessive management levels."* Confusion over "levels" and "layers" added further grist to the mill of muddled thinking, although as this book illustrates that issue is not limited to the public sector. Lack of accountability has been an endemic problem in Whitehall for decades. It is time civil servants were empowered and given *space to lead.*

The Civil Service Reform working paper of March 2009 noted that "The Civil Service has further to go if it is to adapt in the way articulated by the Cabinet Secretary and senior leaders and apply the earlier ambition of Excellence and Fairness".[11] The great achievement of Northcote &Trevelyan in the nineteenth century was the introduction of selection based on merit. Unfortunately the current belief that an individual in or with potential, for grade 6 for example, can do virtually any grade 6 job, illustrates Fulton's cult of the amateur generalist is alive and well in some quarters. We have seen some examples of arbitrary minority quotas that have not been thought through and which also tend to muddy further the waters of accountability, robust succession planning and selection on merit.

[11] "Excellence and Fairness", Cabinet Office June 2008

There has been no discernible improvement in either the efficiency or the effectiveness of the civil service structure in the ~50 years since Fulton even though the shortcomings have been recognised again and again.

9.3.2.2 Current Structures in Whitehall Continue to Be Ineffective and Inefficient

The ineffectiveness and inefficiency of the organization structure of the civil service has been widely recognised. *Ineffectiveness* means a structure is suboptimal in terms shape and layers whereas *inefficient* means there are more jobs than needed even if the depth of hierarchy is appropriate. Ineffective structures waste talent and money whereas inefficient structures are unnecessarily expensive.

Indeed the time seems ripe for a more fundamental review of Whitehall's mission and structure in its entirety as the value of many departments and therefore their very existence is questionable but that is beyond the scope of this chapter. My brief did not include reviewing the appropriateness, mission, shape and number of Whitehall departments and their various offshoots; hence this chapter is limited to assessing the effectiveness of what exists.

The Whitehall departments studied ***all*** *had some seriously suboptimal structures. Some of the drivers, e.g. the approach to grading, are widespread and entrenched in the civil service's DNA. The implications are far reaching since this defective Pillar completely undermines the possibility of establishing effective Mission Mastery in the civil service at present. This has far reaching consequences for the people working in the organization and the quality of service(s) the public expects as part of their social contract.*

Hierarchy Heavy

In June 2007 I attended two sessions of senior civil servants working with the Cabinet Office, who identified major issues of concern over 2 days of open ended discussions. A key item on the agenda was concern about the 'excessive growth' in SCS roles since its introduction in 1996. The analysis was superficial as causes were not identified and therefore solutions were not forthcoming.

A proposition to "cap the SCS" in the light of this uncontrolled growth and affordability issues was discussed by both groups, but rejected as a possible solution. It was not felt that central control is the answer for a dynamic organization, which must respond to the changing needs of its current environment. There was a concern evident in the above about central control (by the Cabinet Office) from the departmental representatives. But there also seemed to be *surprising confusion over the difference between delegation and abdication* and how these two concepts are playing out across Whitehall. Despite much discussion and the identification of a clear problem, *no actions were agreed.*

The lack of knowledge about organization design principles and the concomitant challenge of how to deliver the change management needed was something of an eye-opener. Since 2007 DMAC has conducted organizational reviews in nine departments. The Layers and Spans findings for seven, set out in Fig. 9.2 illustrate the extent of the over layering. The key question is:

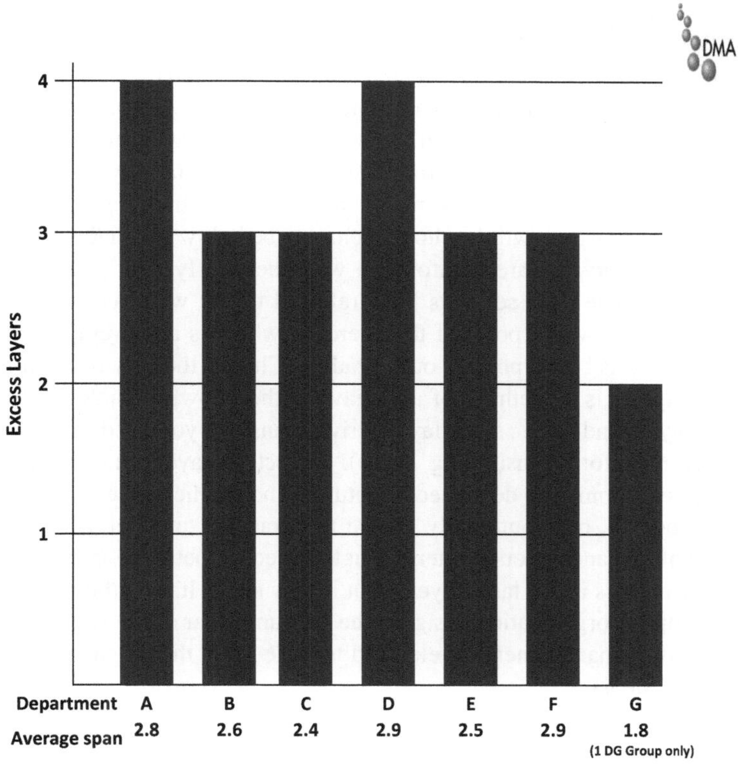

Fig. 9.2 Excess layer in seven Whitehall departments

Why has this recurring problem not been redressed when its existence is well recognised?

These departments ***all*** had cases of too many layers of management, given their assessed levels of accountability. Having worked with private sector organizations of comparable size to the largest Whitehall departments, average spans were more likely to be two to three times those in the CS. Policy departments should be nearer to five on average and those with significant delivery operations nearer to eight. *This suggests Whitehall departments are both unnecessarily costly and wasting talent.* It is a devastating mirror reflecting widespread lack of accountability. The causes are common and demonstrate unequivocally that lack of accountability is the issue and no amount of fine words can fudge that reality.

This data also illustrates why there has been little productivity improvement since Fulton: there are still too many jobs and layers of management in the Whitehall hierarchy reflected in average spans of control that remain far too low.

9.3.2.3 Whitehall's Chronic Structural Deformity Has Not Been Redressed in 50 Years

You might ask: why this emphasis on layers and spans? Firstly it is because I am not focussing on the shape of the departments (that is a "given"). Secondly because they are the unforgiving hardware that relentlessly expose an organization's culture and these shortcomings reflect hazy to nonexistent accountability, which in turn undermines empowerment, performance management, training and leadership development all of which will be shown below to be below par in the civil service. It suggests civil servants are comfortable with the "fluffy stuff" but avoid what really matters. Some civil servants have referred to my work as 'just spans and layers' missing the whole point of the exercise, which is about empowerment or 'Space to Lead' (As I have pointed out already in Chap. 8 the very order of the term 'spans and layers' is something of a giveaway: the knowledgeable OD manager focuses on layers and spans, since layers drive spans and you need to know how to identify layers before considering spans). Defective layers and spans are the unforgiving symptom of a deformed structure. Finding the cause, let alone doing something about it, has continually eluded the grasp of civil servants. There has been plenty of talk and papers written about the need for better people management and better structures in the last 50 years but reality keeps hitting the accountability buffers. To repeat: organization design is the fulcrum Pillar of Mission Mastery and without it people management is relegated to little more than a gavotte on twitter and the social media.

The other Pillars cannot be established if the architecture is flawed. That is the abiding problem in Whitehall that still has not been addressed nor redressed.

Twenty years after Fulton it was reported that those leaving the civil service felt "They had little personal responsibility and saw little prospect of getting more as they rose through the hierarchy. Chains of command tend to be too long".[12] In other words there had been little to no progress even then! The shorthand that exposes this endemic failing is the presence of too many layers and overly narrow spans of control. It has been highlighted again and again. That is the easy task of course but until this debilitating flaw is repaired the best intentions and more written reports amount to 'sound and fury signifying nothing.' *Thus I don't apologise for demonstrating how deep this malaise is across Whitehall, how damaging it is and how little it has changed in 50 years.* The big question is what is blocking the change needed? Is it lack of knowledge, lack of competence, lack of courage or a combination of all three?

[12] Next Steps: Detailed Findings paragraphs 52 and 53.

Department A

This department was studied in depth and had a total of seven discrete levels of accountability. It was one of the largest in Whitehall. As only one layer of leadership roles was needed in each level of accountability *up to* seven layers of leadership could be justified.

But it had twelve.

This is illustrated in Fig. 9.3. This excess hierarchy impacted negatively on the average span of control, which in this case is 6.8. Although this is the best average I have found in Whitehall, in this case it should be at least eight. This does not sound much but it is very significant in a very large organization with tens of thousands of employees.

Department A was both over-layered and under-led.

De-layering will shift all the respective average spans of control. It is quite worrying for example, to see relatively small *enabling functions* of specialists with 9, 10 and 11 layers. By way of contrast the large *core operating units,* although over layered, have relatively good average spans in this example reflecting the fact they involve large numbers of people under their control, who are engaged in relatively straightforward work at the front line. This is reflected in the high percentage of people in low grades. This fact also demonstrates the danger of focussing only on average spans. Intriguingly these over-layered sections of the department have spans that are ahead of the average but their spans are still suboptimal. Thus even the 'best' units needed to improve *given the nature of the work they were doing at the front line.* In other words:

> *Counter intuitively sections with spans above the average target can also be over-layered depending on the nature of their front line work.*

Following this analysis the department in question is now taking some steps to improve the effectiveness of its *overall* structure.

As is illustrated by the target lines of best fit in Fig. 9.4 below *all functions and units have to improve,* in order to meet an optimal structure of "8 × 8": i.e. up to eight layers of hierarchy with an average span of control reaching at least eight. *Note, "8 by 8" is NOT a one-size-fits-all solution.* It is the answer for a particular organization, department A in this case, once its levels of accountability had been identified and the nature of its frontline work understood. At that point, and only then, is it possible to indicate the appropriate total of leadership layers possible (bearing in mind the Golden Rule: "only one layer of leadership per level of accountability") and a sensible average span target.

Figure 9.4 is taking the analysis of layers and spans a stage further using insight introduced to me and his clients by Adam Pearce. Although the average span for the department as a whole, which at 6.8 is the best we have encountered so far in

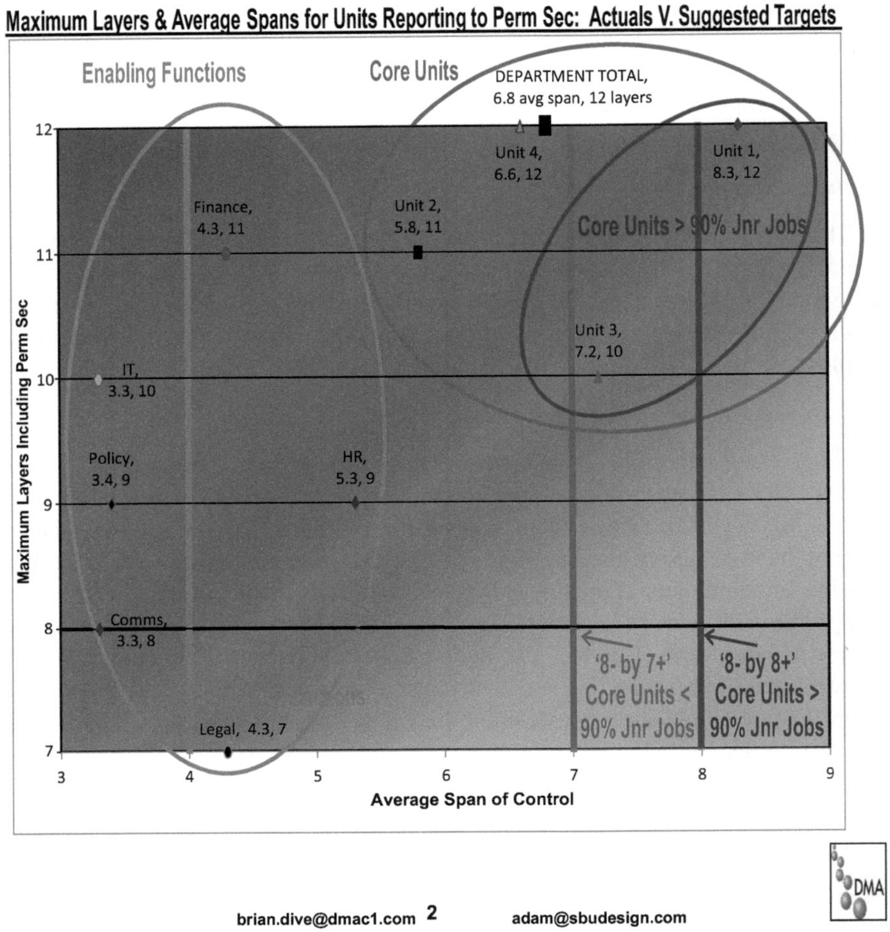

Fig. 9.3 In this example all units could have up to eight layers since the top job (permanent secretary) was WL 7. Enabling functions' average spans could be 4–5 and core units 8+ if >90 % of jobs are in junior grades. Maximum layers and average spans for units reporting to Perm Sec: actuals Vs. suggested targets

Whitehall; it still has up to four layers too many in places. This is primarily why these spans can be improved. It also shows why focus on spans only is not a reliable indicator of structural efficiency and effectiveness. But the picture of this department is not monochrome and therefore different spans and layers are appropriate in different parts of the department. The front line work varies quite widely across the various enabling functions and core units. This is reflected in the percentage of roles

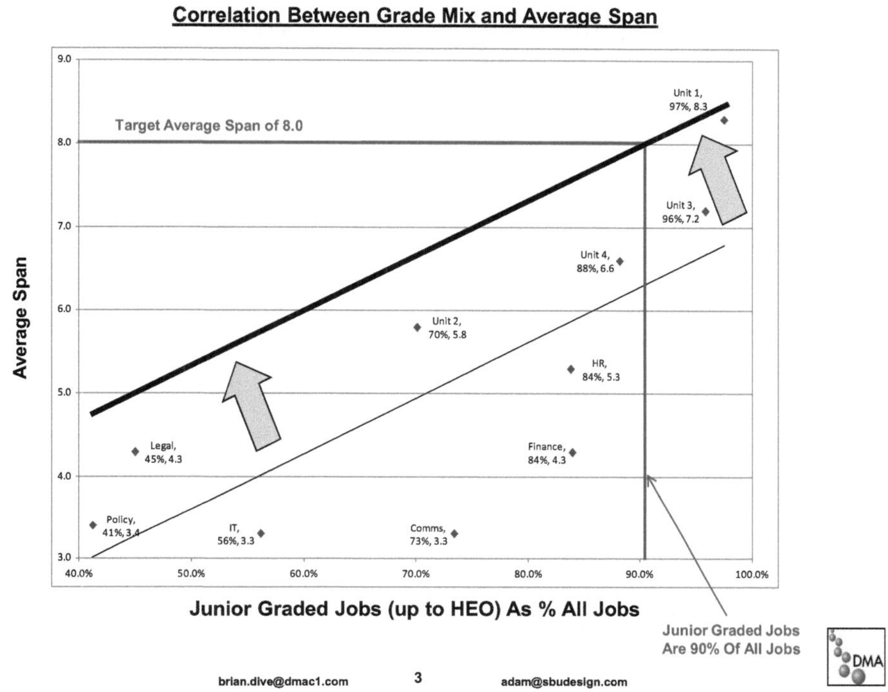

Fig. 9.4 Line of best fit for overall improvement in structure. Units with over 90 % of jobs in junior grades should aim for an average span of over 8.0 to offset units with a senior grade mix. But, no top unit in this organisation should have an average span less than 4.0

up to and including grade HEO. Grade HEO is relatively junior.[13] ***In theory***, the higher the grade the greater the work complexity entailed. But as we will see below—see Fig. 9.5—in this chapter these grades do not align neatly to accountability, which is another very significant problem in the CS.

The key finding is the enabling functions and the operating units ***can all improve*** *their ratios of average spans and total layers to move the department down from 12 layers to a maximum of 8 and from an average overall span of control of 6.8 to in excess of 8.*

Units in Department A with over 90 % of their jobs in junior grades (from AA up to HEO) should aim for an average span of more than eight to offset units with a more senior grade mix. Given the different types of work in the various Director General (DG) Groups the grade mix varies. Higher average spans correlate with lower grades. This is because the lower grades signify (or should signify if the job grading is reliable) that the work is less complex but grade drift often undermines a

[13] The civil service lowest grade is AA (Administrative Assistant). The progression is then to Admin Officer (AO), Executive Officer (EO), Higher EO, Senior EO, G7, G6. Then through to five Senior CS (SCS 1–5+) grades: 12 in all. Each department can flex the grades below SCS since the latter only are "controlled" by the Cabinet Office

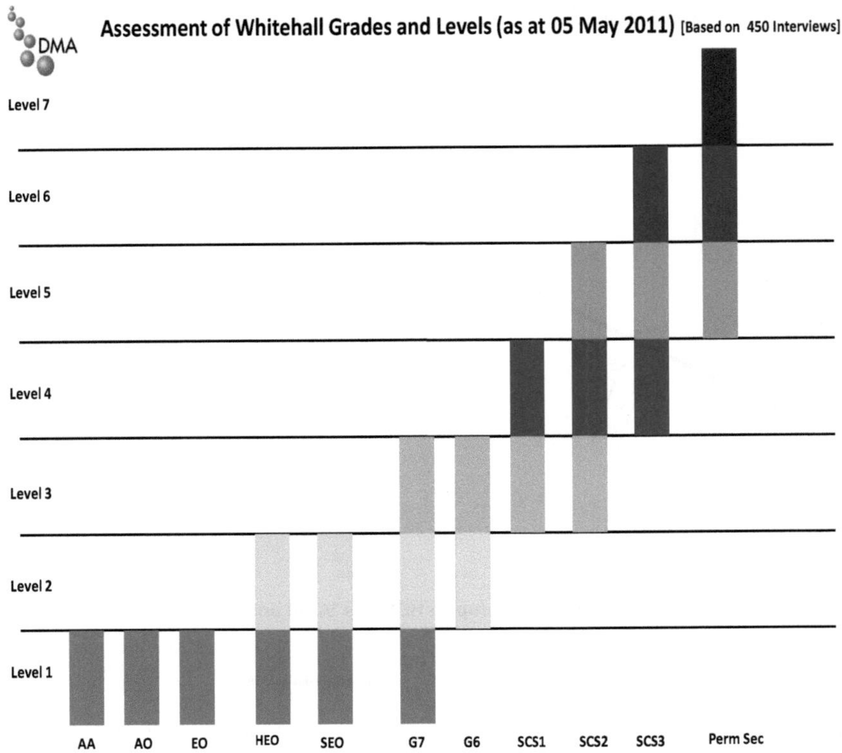

Fig. 9.5 Assessment of Whitehall grade and levels (as at 05 May 2011) [based on 450 interviews]

situation like this, even further. Thus Unit 4 with 97 % of its jobs in lower grades can achieve an average span in excess of 9 whereas the policy unit with only 41 % of jobs in those grades can achieve a better span than the current 3.4 but probably only to between 4 and 5, not as high as 8. Although this might seem a small improvement, in a large department the unnecessary cost has been estimated to reach 7–8 figures.

Why has there been so little productivity improvement since Fulton?

9.3.2.4 The Fundamental Issue: A Lethal Cocktail

Clear Accountability is essential for high performing leadership. But the civil service does not have a reliable way of identifying clear accountability. I once questioned an ex civil servant about the many "talk shops" encountered in Whitehall and was told: "You must understand civil servants are very busy: it is a matter of accountability". "Or lack of it" I thought. It had not occurred to him that lack of accountability feeds "busy-ness" and the hamster management, which seemed to be his pride and joy.

The civil service has developed a lethal cocktail mix, which has three ingredients. One is its inability to calibrate accurately the accountability of jobs and hierarchies. Two its approach to grading jobs is flawed. Three the governance process has collapsed.

Talented people get very frustrated when someone else is working in their decision space.

9.3.2.5 CS Grading and Broken Governance

Post Fulton the civil service has modified its grading systems on more than one occasion but they have not solved the disease of over-layering. Indeed as I have pointed out, grading systems bedevil organization design, contribute to over layering and undermine leadership development if not restricted to their real purpose, which is to establish equitable pay. The organization design work of the civil service has been undermined by an almost slavish reliance on too many hierarchical grades for too long, added to which the governance of the system seems to have collapsed. It is the silent assassin lurking behind much that is sub optimal in Whitehall, adding to the confused and diluted understanding of mission and its delivery. Some are dismissive and say: "Grades are not that significant in the scheme of important things." But they are the manifestation of the basic issue which persists: a lack of accountability and the lack of a reliable mechanism to identify it.

The civil service currently has at least 12 grades available. Our fieldwork demonstrates that this tends to result in very long reporting chains since, in practice; often each grade tends to report to the next higher grade. Chains of 'one over one' and 'one over two' are more the norm than the exception. Since there is an embedded *grade culture across Whitehall*—civil servants are known to state their grade before their job title when introducing themselves—all of the grades tend to be used, which helps explain why virtually all the departments studied can have about 12 layers of hierarchy when the most they could possibly justify is 8, and then only in a handful of the largest departments. Most can justify up to seven layers, some only up to six.

> *The gradist culture remains rampant and debilitating today, despite claims to the contrary—usually by senior civil servants. Perhaps work does not always pass up through all the layers everywhere—**if that is really so then what are all the layers of the departments in figure 9.2 doing**? It is insultingly clear that work is not structured according to accountable tasks against which performance and potential, in some cases, can be assessed. The mindset of 'every grade a layer' persists, which drives heavy hierarchies and undermines clear and effective career paths, because there is no established way of assessing accountability in the civil service.*

CS Grades Are Disconnected from Accountability

In order to judge how many layers of leadership are required in Whitehall we first need to identify how many levels of accountability exist within a given department.

This is because, as is now clear, *there should be only one layer of leadership aligned to every level of accountability. Once the Level of the top job is established together with that of the front line the organization design answer for the vertical axis is clear.* On the basis of the field work that has been done since 2007 it is clear that a handful only, of the largest, most complex departments in Whitehall have seven discrete levels of accountability. It would also seem that a significant number of Arms Length Bodies (ALBs) might justify four or five levels of accountability, based on our work to date, taking into account their different scope, size and the nature of their 'business'.[14]

By way of reference, a four star general in the Army could be at the seventh battle echelon (or level of accountability), when in the field, depending on the size and complexity of the military command in question. The FTSE 100 would typically span companies with five to eight levels of accountability although not many would be Level 5 or Level 8. We have never encountered an organization with more than eight levels in total as yet and indeed it seems one with more than eight might well be unmanageable, added to which would there be anyone with the capability to manage it? We have worked in four of the ten largest companies on the Fortune 500 (ignoring the largest Chinese organizations) including the largest, Wal-Mart. None seems to have more than eight levels of accountability. Therefore, none seems to justify more than nine layers of hierarchy. Less than 0.4 % of jobs in large private sector organizations that I have worked with are at strategic levels of accountability. Those said to have strategic accountability in the civil service (i.e. those in SCS grades) amount to ~0.8 %, which begs the question: "Are they all really strategic?" Fieldwork conducted in policy departments has shown that SCS1 roles are consistently in WL 3 not WL 4, which would be strategic.

Figure 9.5 illustrates the link between Whitehall grades and levels of accountability.

This unforgiving diagram *illustrates the widespread inconsistency of grades across Whitehall departments: the greatest lack of alignment I have seen anywhere in 50 years.*

Take Grade G7 as an example, the first of the management grades. Figure 9.5 illustrates G7 has emerged from fieldwork in different departments in *three different levels of accountability: levels one, two and three.* If the CS grades were reliably calibrating accountability they would align to one level not three. As the figure above shows all the management grades straddle TWO to THREE levels of accountability. This suggests a major flaw in the underlying logic of the job evaluation system, lack of meaningful governance in the application of grades across different departments or, it would appear, a combination of both.

[14] My experience of ALBs is limited, but based on our work in Local Authorities we have found a few have six levels of accountability. I am not aware of an ALB the size of Birmingham City Council for example, which is the largest in the UK.

Figure 9.5 demonstrates unequivocally that the governance system for grading jobs in Whitehall is broken and totally inconsistent because all "management" grades straddle more than one level of accountability!

As illustrated, this applies even for the role of Permanent Secretary, which covers three levels of accountability across Whitehall.

There is no consistency within or especially, across departments that I have detected.

All seem to be replete with their Christmas trees of Deputy Directors, Directors, Director Generals and sometimes two or even three layers of Permanent Secretaries. Evidence suggests that given the collapse in governance, grades are often awarded to pay a given salary, especially for external recruits, rather than being based on a rigorous assessment of the job's responsibilities. Hence inconsistency of grading abounds, which in turn leads to faulty organization design and parochial leadership development.

Faulty organization design means the CS leadership development platform has more holes in it than an emmental cheese.

From G7 (notionally WL 2) and above this inconsistency is widespread. Staying with G7 as an example: we have found roles outside London where the incumbent role has de facto Level 3 accountability managing hundreds of people; while in London it could be in Level 1, in a highly paid IT role for example. This seems to be because pay outside London is lower so "a G7 is enough." The evidence suggests pay drives grades not a true evaluation of accountabilities. In reality there is a widespread tendency not to use the formal job evaluation systems, including that for SCS roles under the supervision of the Cabinet office.

Jobs in Level 3 are the backbone of a successful organization. As highlighted in Chap. 6, fieldwork has established that time spent and number of jobs discharged in Level 3 is vital for successful performance in Levels 5 and above. Conversely even highly talented people who are crashed through level 3 within a year have a history of failure in the higher levels.

Yet, as can be seen from Fig. 9.5, SCS1 roles (particularly in London), are also in Level 3 along with some G6s and a few G7s. The civil service does not know its tactical apex from its strategic elbow.

There is a major technical shortcoming in the evaluation of Whitehall grades since two job evaluation systems are in play, which produce results that overlap within a single level of accountability—Level 3.

A system called JEGS is used to evaluate jobs below the SCS, i.e. up to G6. These are known collectively as "the delegated grades". Another system called JESP, which came into being in 1993, is used to assess jobs only in the SCS. A logical thought would be: "Then combine the two systems into one." On the face of it that seems the logical solution but the internal approaches of the two systems are different and suffer the inherent problems of job evaluation systems as discussed above. Neither assesses accountability.

They could of course both be superseded by introducing Work Levels across Whitehall, but that was not my brief as "the grades were a given" in all of the DMAC reviews. But it is apparent that if a Unilever can use Work Levels to calibrate pay for 20,000 managers across 100 countries in many different types of businesses, (capital intensive, labour intensive, and knowledge intensive such as research laboratories and the international corporate office) the pay problems of the civil service 'management' in only one country are hardly insurmountable.

The civil service has an institutionally broken spine of accountability in Level 3! Yet jobs in WL 3 should be the backbone of a high performing organization.

This is a unique and seriously debilitating organization design feature, with clear and worrying consequences for leadership development.

A number of senior civil servants vented their concern about the uncertainty and blurring of the differences between G6, SCS1 and SCS1A. In the light of what we now know, that was not surprising but they had no reference frame to explain how to unravel it. That was significant. There is great confusion caused by the application of the two grading systems. Large, complex jobs accessed via JEGS can only get into G6 as that is the 'top of the range.' Thus many big operational jobs accountable for over a thousand staff, especially outside London, can be assessed only as G6 as part of the JEGS regime. In accountability terms they are invariably in Level 3, where SCS1 jobs generally also reside! The bottom of the JESP system, SCS1, consistently emerges in Level 3 in London policy departments. This grading demarcation does not reflect a reality of different accountability. It could mean for example, a G6 manager running a large prison could report to an SCS1 in London, who has worked only in the "head office" of a policy department.

Both jobs would be in Level 3, with the G6 institutionally compressed, resulting in flawed organization design, constraining the career development of the prison manager.

The SCS seems to have emerged in the 1990s, partly in response to the white paper *Change and Continuity* aiming to reduce layers of management. It apparently recognised the need for strategic leadership in the CS and consultants introduced a new job evaluation system to recognise and identify these new roles. The number of SCS jobs has increased markedly ever since.

There is no doubt the civil service needs strategic leadership but unfortunately JESP does not reliably identify where strategic accountability cuts in.

To compound the problem it was decided to call SCS1 roles "deputy directors", thus a single director can have many deputies! I have consistently found across all organizations around the world that titles like "deputy" are not infrequently status titles for somewhat hollow jobs. In local authorities in the UK, the awarding of the term "deputy CEO" can justify a pay rise. Thus it is not unusual to see more than one deputy in a top team. When pay drives organization design in any civilian organization, problems arise.

The major cause of this broken spine of accountability across Whitehall is the existence of two grading systems, which overlap in Level 3, neither of which reliably assesses accountability.

And yet one of Fulton's significant recommendations had been to get rid of the then two grading (class) systems and "Install unified grading between the administrators and professional groups." I am not making this up!

Department B

But the problem is not just at Level 3. As Fig. 9.6 illustrates many G6 roles in London have emerged in Level 2, often compressing G7 roles also in level 2, where management accountability should start. This was the case in at least four major departments of those studied. This means there are usually three grades, G7, G6 and SCS1 variously squeezed into two Levels leading to compression in either Level 2 or Level 3.

DMAC interviewed 75 people in a range of jobs and found 14 G6 leaders not adding value to G7s.

Summary of DMA Interview Findings in Dept B

	PS	SCS3	SCS2	SCS1	G6	G7	SEO	HEO	EO	Total
Level 6	1									1
Level 5		3								3
Level 4			10							10
Level 3				12						12
Level 2					14	13	1			28
Level 1						3	6	9	3	21
Total	1	3	10	12	14	16	7	9	3	75

Grade-related compression in Level 2: generally G6s compressing G7s, but also with one case of a G7 in Level 2 compressing an SEO job in Level 2, *outside London.*

brian.dive@dmac1.com adam@sbudesign.com

Fig. 9.6 Work Level 2 compression of G7 and G6 roles in Department B. DMAC interviewed 75 people in a range of jobs and found 14 G6 leaders not adding value to G7s

Not surprisingly this confusion also spills over into the roles of DGs and permanent secretaries.

An illustration this compression in Level 2 is set out in Fig. 9.6.

But most worryingly of all, the CS does not seem to be aware of its flawed approach to identifying accountability, which is undermining the effectiveness and quality of its organization design, leadership development and career planning.

By way of contrast the military approach rests on firmer foundations. Battle echelons establish organisation architecture. Ranks anchor pay. Officers are on the same pay as a rule and the ratio from OF1 (second lieutenant) to OF9 (4* General), is typically 1:7. *Moltke did not confuse accountability, organization design, pay and rank in the Prussian army*, thus he would struggle to comprehend the muddle and confusion in the CS and he would not understand why it has not been resolved when it is so obviously undermines performance and delivery, not to mention leadership development.

9.3.2.6 Lack of Single Point Accountability in Whitehall

The most important and over-riding principle of effective organization design in any employment organization is single point accountability (SPA). This means one person is held to account for the performance of the organization. In the private sector the CEO is clearly held to account for the performance of his or her total organization and is therefore one higher level of accountability than the most important direct report(s).

The CS does not have a true Chief Executive Officer

"Next Steps" pointed out almost 30 years ago: "The the centre of government is fragmented.—There was no single voice of authority."[15] At the time we were doing our work the 'top job' was that of Head of the Home Civil Service who enjoyed what was described to me as the "accountability of consensus". I was told this means that when all the departmental Permanent Secretaries/CEOs (~40) agree on an issue, then the "Head" can tell them what to do! When the incumbent retired the job was divided into three! One of the three posts was that of 'top civil servant', which was described by a government minister (E. Pickles, 14 November 2013) as "entering a snake pit. That job is the nearest thing we have to being a member of the Tudor court. There are two doors—one leading to the throne room and one leading to the scaffold." This lack of single point of accountability also existed in a number of major departments: one had three Permanent Secretary roles. The inefficiency and overspend in these departments was predictable.

Since then, a CEO has been appointed to run the 'back office' with what seems to be a brief to build a central infrastructure pooling 'corporate resources/services' across departments. This is a sensible and sound initiative, which many well run

[15] Next Steps—Detailed Findings paragraph 38

large organizations have implemented. It is however counter cultural to the baronial fiefdoms of permanent secretaries who are past masters at filibustering any initiative they don't like. But what I don't know at the time of writing is how well the structure of this new initiative is aligned to its mission and whether the structure is really effective.

Notwithstanding my earlier comments, the military are not perfect in this regard as there are examples of peacetime grade to grade reporting (4* to 4*) in individual services, which is a harbinger of murky accountability. I was asked to look at the structure of the Navy with its array of admirals. The number of ships in the fleet has shrunk so much (from ~900 in WWI to less than 40 today) that it is likely the Navy could have shrunk a level of accountability and therefore may not require the leadership of a four star officer, let alone two. Now that could set a cat amongst the military pigeons if correct [The role of Chief of the Defence Staff, the professional head of the armed forces and principal military adviser to the Secretary of State for Defence and government in the UK is a also 4* General serving as a temporary primus inter pares[16] leader of the military in peace time. The role is not in a higher level of accountability than the other 4* generals. Apparently this lack of SPA leads to some interesting expenditure decision discussions (trade-offs) around aircraft carriers versus the best in class fighters versus safest troop carriers and so on. Not surprising perhaps the procurement section of the MOD is not noted as a paragon of best practice, let alone effective organization design. The same type of primus inter pares top structure seems to prevail in the US military based according to C. Powell].

Implications of the Lack of Single Point Accountability in the Civil Service

Although "Pace" is espoused as one of the critical "4Ps" of the civil service, the current lack of SPA means the civil service will struggle to be a fleet footed organization noted for quick, decisive and cohesive action. I once asked a minister why he did not favour a civil service with single point accountability. "We don't want it to be too powerful." When I pointed out that New Zealand and a number of Scandinavian countries do have single point accountability in their corresponding public service organizations he replied: "But they are small countries." There is none so blind as he who refuses to see. Others point to issues about constitutional difficulties given 'independent secretaries of state'. So, how is it other democratic countries have found solutions *when they wanted to?*

> *The culture of the CS seems to favour, "discuss, debate and record" not "decide, act and review": this is nourished by the lack of SPA.*

Given the heavy structures diluting accountability this is not altogether surprising. Apparently the service works best when there is a clear consensus

[16] First among equals

among the forty or so Permanent Secretaries/CEOs that they will then do what the Head of the civil service suggests. As this consensus invariably does not fully exist or only exists after a great deal of time consuming discussion, policy dilution, and political manoeuvring, initiatives for improvement are easily filibustered.

Some would argue that the lack of real progress since the Fulton, "Next Steps" and "Change and Continuity" are classic cases in point since the lethal organization design fault lines uncovered by Fulton and others still exist.

The government departments show just how dysfunctional a structure can become when there is no one with the authority to build and maintain an effective architecture that holds leaders to account as the basis for good performance.

This all leads to the following conclusion about the organization pillar:

Organization design in the CS is an accountability blancmange. The second Pillar of Mission Mastery is also defective, which explains the ongoing hobbling of its performance.

9.3.3 Pillar Three: Leadership Development in the Civil Service

Leadership development was Moltke's forte. It is Whitehall's foible.

Ineffective structures and the lack of any reliable measurement or identification of accountability combine to undermine leadership development. A major criticism of leadership development in Whitehall is that fact that it is still the preserve of the mandarin class who see life through a political and policy lens not a delivery lens. Not surprisingly the process is prone to politicisation. As we have just seen, the clear manifestation of this is the flawed approach to grading of jobs, which undermines leadership development. The classic manifestation of weak grading governance is grade creep in an organization that is not growing in real terms.

9.3.3.1 Grade Creep

The number of CS jobs grew by 1 % from 2000 to 2010.[17] But the number of SCS jobs grew by 43 % (1299 jobs) during the same period.[18] This represents compound growth of 3.6 % per annum. The "Smarter Government" initiative in December 2009 aimed to cut SCS costs by 25 % in 3 years. The SCS growth in 2009 was 1.4 % and a further 1.9 % in 2010.

Although the SCS 1 roles have grown the most in absolute numbers, SCS 3 roles have grown the most in % terms. From 2003 to 2010 the surge was 50 %.[19] This

[17] Source: Public sector employment Quarter 4 2006 (14 March 2007) and Quarter 4 2010 (16 March 2011).

[18] Source: Senior Salaries Review Body reports: 2006 (Table 1.3), 2007 (Table 2.1) and 2011 (Table 2.1).

[19] Source: Senior Salaries Review Body reports: 2003 (Appendix B) and 2011 (Appendix B).

growth amounts to unprecedented grade drift for the number of top jobs in a large, mature organization not enjoying organic growth. As noted at the outset of this chapter this was already a concern being expressed in 2007, based on the numbers available then, which went up to only 2005. There does not seem to be any evidence that the SCS increased productivity by 43 % during the same period. Since 2011 there has been some reduction but it has not come anywhere near redressing the unjustified inflation since 2000, despite uninformed political comment about "cuts". The unprecedented grade drift in SCS jobs further undermines leadership development as managers drift into and out of hollow jobs. Leadership is not nurtured in jobs with straw accountabilities.

If, as I have argued, an effective structure is essential for successful leadership development then if is self evident that the civil service's threadbare organization platform is not a basis for exemplary leadership development, which has become politicised as a result.

Far too many management "promotions" in Whitehall are really only an administrative change in label (the grade) not a real change of accountability or genuine leadership development.

9.3.3.2 Grade-Rank Misalignment: CS Versus the Military

Military Officers are regularly transferred into Whitehall (usually the MOD). There is an official alignment in Whitehall of civilian grades to military ranks. Apparently the basis of the alignment was struck over 20 years ago, to help decide the accommodation status of civil servants attending military staff college programmes. Not surprisingly given this 'logic' our fieldwork found the two systems are not well aligned. When I pointed this out in a report I was actually instructed to remove that finding, so no corrective action ensured. One recurring outcome means military personnel are demoted 'into the civilian office'. For example I interviewed a high calibre Lt. Colonel (equivalent to level 3) just back from leading a regiment overseas, who had been "promoted" to a level 2 civilian desk-job. This is not exemplary leadership development. Constructive boundary moves from line to support or vice versa would not normally recommend or involve a demotion for a high potential person. But this reality is masked by faulty 'grade alignment'.

9.3.3.3 Counterfeit Line Management

There is a widespread virus in the CS culture that believes "I must have at least one person reporting to me so I claim line management experience at my next job interview." This false premise is a key driver of many over layered structures and small spans of control, especially in Whitehall policy departments and *ironically the "line management" referred to is counterfeit*, as are the "leadership" opportunities it spawns. It also explains the ongoing cultural acceptance of tiny spans in Whitehall, first questioned by Fulton.

Given the lack of true line management in junior and even middle management roles civil servants' leadership development is hamstrung as a result. We have advocated in more than one policy department that the default setting for grades AA to SEO in London (typically in WL 1) should be that they all report directly to at least a G7 role (in WL 2).

Most civil servant leaders do not sufficiently own the levers of change: the seven DMA Elements outlined in the previous chapter.

Concerns about lack of empowerment frequently emerged from interviews, particularly from those who had some taste of the private sector. Typical comments we encountered, included:

"Managers don't have authority to hire their own teams: they are given people."
"Line managers cannot award differential salaries for their team members."
"Performance management is very weak to nonexistent."
"Line managers don't have financial accountability."
"Line managers in the civil service lack authority to change things."

In other words, they are not line managers in WL2+. This has helped feed a culture of "no consequences".

9.3.3.4 Decision Rights

Our findings demonstrate that time and again civil servants do not have appropriate or sufficient decision rights to deliver the basic requirement of their job. We typically illustrate this using the Decision Rights Matrix similar to that set out in Chap. 4—see Fig. 4.3—as this is a dramatic way to highlight lack of accountability.

9.3.3.5 Leadership Development: "Pass the Parcel"

The appraisal of performance in the CS is not noted for being honest, courageous and accurate. No one pretends that is easy but the CS seems to have largely side stepped this critical management accountability. As one, ex private sector manager confided: "After a time in the role I decided, for good reason, to discipline a former performance category 1 (top rating of a 5 point performance scale) person, who reported to me. Firstly, people nearly fell off their chairs. Secondly the disciplinary meeting had, by process, to be 7 days in the future. How bonkers is that? This policy hardly encourages line managers to use the disciplinary process. And from the reactions to my action it was clear there was not much history of doing such a thing in the department."

Another manager confided he had been "given" a known poor performer to manage. When I asked "Why did you accept that person if you knew he was a poor performer?" The revealing reply was: "I was told it was good for my development as a manager (this was the *first time* he had had a subordinate!). If I rate him 4 (on a 5 point scale where 1 is best) as he deserves, he will go to a Tribunal. I have been warned by HR that the union will point out that he has been rated 1 or 2 by his two previous managers. They will argue *I am the problem* and he will win his case. Or I will have a 'bullying manager' case, or if a BME (Black or minority ethnic) a claim of racial discrimination." He then said revealingly:

> *I have learned how to play performance management here.* ***I will pass the parcel*** *by rating this individual a '1 or 2' performer. That way I get rid of the problem as people are always changing jobs and chasing grades.*

When I mentioned to the relevant Permanent Secretary that I felt he presided over a career planning system of 'pass the parcel' he was sceptical and politely said: "I think that is a little unfair." (Even when challenging someone, civil service language tends to be somewhat understated.) I then gently reminded him what HE had told me in his own interview, which had gone something like this:

Q "What do you do if one of your direct reports is not up to the performance standards of the job?"
A *"Well, I had an example recently, so I got rid of her."*
Q "What did that involve?"
A *"I managed to move her to another department!"*
Ah-ha. . ...!

9.3.3.6 Performance Management in the CS

> *Once an organization becomes disconnected from performance it degenerates into a bureaucracy in the pejorative sense—a culture of no consequences.*

Evidence suggests civil servants' performance is often not accurately assessed nor the assessments rigorously scrutinised. *There are no noticeable consequences* for senior mandarins who, with little fear of losing *their* job or being exposed for poor people management, are cushioned from exposure within over-managed structures. It is very difficult to identify good or bad performance in an accountability blancmange.

The most recurring result of staff engagement surveys in Whitehall is the entrenched score of ~30 % or below relating to performance management, particularly "The management of poor performance." Even the SCS surveys paint the same picture *and they are the leaders of the civil service.*

True line management accountability presupposes the manager must have a say (at least a veto, when there is a central recruitment/leadership development process) over who comes into the team, what they do in that team, how they are assessed when they should be moved from the current job and on what basis. The manager is also accountable for the training, coaching and development of the team member and decides (initially) on what basis the person should leave the team, such as promotion. Otherwise a manager cannot truly be said to be held to account for his or her team.

This fundamental premise of people management is not discernible in Whitehall.

9.3.3.7 Assessment of Potential Is Not Reliable

Since the service does not have clear structures of well defined accountabilities the chances of having a fair, reliable and valid way of assessing potential are not great. Promotion in the civil service is largely a matter of gaming the grading system. Career paths across the top 2 layers of the 40 or so departments are haphazard and said to be "political". This is because the top jobs (graded 'Permanent Secretary') could be anything from Level 4 to Level 7—as illustrated in Fig. 9.5 above, showing how the same grade and title therefore can straddle up to three levels of accountability. These represent huge differences in accountability calling for widely differing capabilities of the job incumbents. Yet these are precisely the levels of accountability, which in the military covers the echelons of one to four star generals and for which they have rigorous leadership assessment and development programmes. The career path to First Sea Lord in the Royal Navy is not the result of a lottery or political jiggery-pokery.

The Whitehall leadership development problem is accentuated by two design shortcomings: an inability to identify levels of accountability and the lack of a robust competency model aligned to the levels of accountability. Promotion is calibrated in grade movement and performance management, i.e. skill mastery in the existing role. But performance alone is not a guarantee of promotability. The best maths teacher does not make necessarily the best school principal. Something more than a knowledge of maths is now required. There is apparently some assessment of the top 200 mandarins using outside consultants but these assessments are done in an accountability vacuum, not aligned to the requirements of the next array of jobs in higher Levels.

9.3.3.8 Quality of Career Planning

"The military and the best companies put a lot of effort into developing leaders for a number of reasons. They need to prepare the next chief executive, and the one after that. The company of the twenty-first century needs leadership in depth and it must train its leaders to cope with the constant change they will face."[20]

This was the first premise of Moltke's approach to training since wastage in the field had to be anticipated and prepared for.

There is a corresponding need to enhance the mapping of career paths across specific DG roles in combination with different Permanent Secretary roles—the equivalent of Moltke's generals. For example should a Level 4 DG in a functional area be moved next to a Level 5 DG role in the same speciality or a general management role, such as Permanent Secretary of a small department at Level 5?

[20] Wind and Main (1998) op cit p. 107.

And so on. In recent years the succession planning in Whitehall has looked very haphazard for a federation of organizations that suffer very few resignations among the top levels. Over a relatively short period the jobs of a half dozen plumb departmental permanent secretary posts (seen as equivalent to CEOs) became vacant, as a result of retirements: so nothing unforeseen or unexpected, except in one case where serious illness was a factor. All were jobs that senior civil servants would aspire to. Yet apparently there seemed to be a surprising dearth of good candidates. A contributing factor to this apparent dearth is the fact that civil servants change jobs too frequently in the lolly scramble for grade enhancement, which works against the development of deep skills and/or general management experience via planned boundary moves, as espoused by Moltke and evident today in the military and leading civilian organizations.

As the quote from Wind and Main at the top of this section illustrates, multinational companies and the military would regularly plan career moves at this level up to 3–5 years in advance in order to both be prepared for the unexpected and to prepare potential incumbents. They are also acutely aware that placing someone on a potential list is not a self fulfilling prophecy. Life is full of the unexpected. A number of those organizations familiar with Work Levels create "Lists" of candidates with potential for the next level of accountability: e.g. 'List 5' for those with confirmed potential for WL 5 and so on. The concept of calculating the percentage of necessary "cover" for the next level of accountability seems to be unheard of in the CS. *Meaningful and effective* career planning is not evident. The example in the previous paragraph of six of the top eight jobs in the CS, all being in play at virtually the same time is something a well run leadership development scheme would *plan to avoid* especially given the cause in this case was predictable retirements, not unexpected, unplanned or regretted resignations.

At about the same time the so-called top civil servant job (Head of the Home Civil Service) also became vacant, again as a result of a known and therefore well flagged predictable retirement. Apparently, we are led to believe, there was not one suitable candidate: (Why didn't the CS head hunt for an external high quality candidate, which any well run organization would do, if caught on the hop? It seems the service believes a top quality leader 'from outside' could not adapt to their culture. Others would argue that is precisely why they need a proven outsider to stir the waters of cultural inertia.) The military's career planning ensures it is never caught on the hop at this level. Why? Simply compare the health of the military's respective pillars with those of the civil service where a job already lacking single point accountability was further divided into three. Apparently there was not one suitable internal candidate for the top job: a direct result of flabby career planning in an unaccountable organisation. Sadly, in light of the shaky pillars of Mission and Organization Design already described in this chapter, this outcome is not altogether surprising.

Let's face it, Moltke would have never understood how a large organization such as the British Civil Service could have such a haphazard, wasteful, inefficient and ineffective approach to leadership and career planning, unless of course it was on its way to Jena.

The career planning and leadership development pillar in the CS also appears to be very shaky if not broken.

9.3.4 Pillar Four: Experiential Training

By now Moltke would be worried about the quality of training since it he would fear it would be a combination of wasted time and money, given the defects already uncovered in the first three pillars. He might well turn his horse around and head back to barracks wracking his brain on where to start the transformation needed.

Experiential training does not seem to feature significantly on the civil service training agenda. There has been a lot of emphasis of late on acquiring skills, perhaps in reaction to the recurring criticism of the "gifted amateur" ethos that still prevails in parts of Whitehall. Yet the central Sunningdale training centre, set up in wake of Fulton, was closed in 2012 even though the 2002 government apparently authorised a deal with de Vere's to run it for 30 years. Furthermore these skill programmes seem to have proliferated and do not appear to be joined up across Whitehall. This seems to be a further case of falling into the 'alignment' trap stemming from the lack of a CEO with Single Point Accountability.

I could not detect a consistent approach to the analysis of training needs across Whitehall. At the time of writing the top HR job was also double hatted with that of DG role in a department. This might suggest either a paucity of talent and/or an accountant's approach to cheaper organization design. Double-hatting two jobs across two levels of strategic accountability in a large organization is not noticeably successful in my experience. Skills training is important in a well run organization but it is limited to performance *in an existing level.* Yet some obvious skills and the necessary training are consistently overlooked in Whitehall. The best organizations I have worked with have identified the 8–10 skills they need to run their organizations and therefore which need to form the basis of their training programmes. No-one in Whitehall has shown me the basis of the skills needed to run the machine of government, some of which are unique (e.g. tax officers) nor how training needs are undertaken and then what corresponding courses are laid on or how the promotion pipeline is calibrated. In fact a number of DGs recognise this is a shortcoming but did not have budget accountability to undertake a rigorous study to provide a way forward!

Take just one example: the lack of financial training.

9.3.4.1 Financial Accountability and Training in the CS

One of the shortcomings undermining the practice of good management in the civil service is the endemic lack of budget accountability and financial training for managers in Levels 2 & 3, who make up 90 %+ of its managerial leadership.

This is a major source of "friction" holding back the management of change and productivity across Whitehall. Given the role of Permanent Secretary is also described as the departmental Accounting Officer and is responsible to Parliament for the correct and efficient use of the departmental budget it is surprising to see budget accountability is so weak within departments. Orchestrated financial training is also thin on the ground*; indeed it is only in very recent times that departmental Finance DGs were expected to have a financial qualification.*

Despite attempts in the early 90s to improve financial management in the CS it seems budget accountability has rarely migrated below the level of Director, which can be many layers above the front line. This means that junior and middle management are not appropriately empowered. The 'no need for a budget' mindset is deeply entrenched. At a recent departmental workshop I was told "You need to change your definitions (of Work Levels) about budget accountability as they are wrong! They do not apply here."

It would be too embarrassing to reveal the name of that department.

Consequently junior and middle management in the CS are invariably not held to account for budget or project expenditure, resources or deadlines. Spending is not their concern and certainly does not affect their performance rating. We noted for example a G6 manager working on a multi-million pound project, blithely taking on consultant resource at four times the cost of an equivalent civil servant in the same role. The reason given was "The HR processes are interminably slow and they will come up with someone at the grade of the job totally unsuited to the skill requirements. They would select eleven goal keepers for a football team." So, instead of a G7 doing the work an external consultant was immediately available, but at an excessive annual cost compared to an equivalent the civil servant. *The G6 manager was not accountable for any aspect of the project budget so cost was not a consideration for his performance assessment.* The incidence of project over-runs exceeding budgets is the stuff of legend across Whitehall because there are rarely any noticeable consequences for the managers involved. *This project subsequently joined the list of technology failures in the Whitehall dustbin and nothing was ever implemented despite expenditure north of £10 m.*

Civil servants are apt to argue their work cannot be subject to targets. But as one chancellor (Nigel Lawson) said: "You don't need targets. You just need to know how much you are spending and whether or not you are providing a good service."[21] Unfortunately politicians don't realise just how far from that simple reality the civil service has drifted. We have been told more than once by civil servants that the introduction of budgets for junior and middle managers will only add to bureaucracy. It will if badly managed! We have also been told that "our managers have not been trained to handle budgets." (Well, train them!). But the same managers are then expected at director level to suddenly manage a budget of some millions of pounds without having had any significant previous budgetary experience or training. It is no surprise that politicians bemoan the financial incontinence in their departments.

---

[21] Stevenson, A (2013) *The Public Sector Managing the unmanageable*, p. 54

9.3.4.2 Training

Although we were not briefed to study the training programmes it is clear there was a myriad of "skills" courses that were uncoordinated and did not enhance performance in an orchestrated way. Experiential training had huge gaps in the light of weaknesses in performance management and financial accountability. Training in the assessment of potential in an objective and reliable manner does not seem to exist. This is not helped by the loss of grading governance and the cultural reluctance to appraise performance (and identify training needs), let alone attempt to accurately assess potential.

Time spent in a single job seems to be too short across Whitehall, especially in senior roles. This militates against the performance and development of top quality, appropriately experienced leaders. Turnover in key jobs does not appear to be well managed—during this critical period I dealt with three directors in the same job in the Cabinet Office in just 3 years (it took 6 months to appoint the third—from within—after the departure of the second incumbent.) Other organizations have learned that rapid changing of jobs by junior and middle management quickly undermines their key functional skills.

9.3.4.3 Capability Reviews

A relatively recent initiative (2005) that seems to be aimed at enhancing delivery via better training and management of people has been the introduction of departmental Capability Reviews. They seem to have been introduced to assess the performance and overall quality of the people and people practices within different departments. Departments' capabilities are assessed against ten variables. This is clearly a very good initiative although the process of assessment may not yet be that reliable, as different people do the reviews across the various departments and the basis of their selection (and competence therefore) is opaque.

One of the variables, relevant to this chapter, is "Develops clear roles, responsibilities and delivery". Since this bears directly on organization design and effectiveness, I examined the results of 21 Capability Reviews across a 3 year period.

There were five possible assessment outcomes of a review:

- Strong
- Well placed
- Development area
- Urgent development area
- Area of serious concern.

Only one department was considered "strong".

A mere two were considered "well placed."[22]
Fourteen were "Development areas"
Three were "Urgent development areas"
One was an area of "Serious concern"

So while the Capability Reviews are a source of further information about weakness of organization structures and leadership across Whitehall, there is a worry that the application of the assessment criteria may not be internally consistent yet and follow up seems sketchy. Implementation and 'follow up' is not the stuff of legend in Whitehall. Another key variable assessed was: "*Manage Performance*". Two of these same departments were rated "Strong" and seven "Well placed." Now if only three are strong/well placed on "Clear roles and responsibilities" it rather unconvincing that nine could score so highly on performance management and that none fell into the categories of "Urgent development area" or "Area of serious concern." This is just one revealing and worrying degree of inconsistency.

Moltke's assessment would probably be: "Good initiative, well begun but now let's now raise our game and deliver some genuine improvements."

Given the weaknesses of the first three Pillars and top civil servants' lack of experience in organization design, change management and the development of leaders, it would be surprising if the civil service was a bastion of world class training, whether experiential or theoretical. It is not.

9.3.5 The Fifth Pillar: Culture

Seniority trumps know-how in the Civil Service.

Prior to unfurling Auftragstaktik, Moltke's army had been victorious at Koniggratz but even so he detected shortcomings. He would be very restless about the civil service's record in the field.

Given the weaknesses already flagged in the first four pillars it is entirely predictable that the civil service would have a flabby culture. Culture is a frequently used term in Whitehall but confusion rather than enlightenment tends to reign. To cite just one instance: in one rather addled document the Department of Health mentions 'a culture of waiting',[23] 'a culture of reporting',[24] 'every care setting will encourage the culture',[25] 'continuing to drive a culture of greater patient safety',[26]

[22] One of these departments had been studied by DMAC, who came to a less favourable conclusion.

[23] Department of Health (2004) *The NHS Improvement Plan: Putting People at the Heart of Public Services*. p. 11

[24] Ibid p. 21

[25] Ibid p. 27

[26] Ibid p. 31

'a culture responsive to change'.[27] All of which led Gerald Arbuckle working on *Humanizing Healthcare Reforms* to explode: "What perplexity. I sympathise with Raymond Williams' frustration: 'I don't know how many times I've wished that I had never heard the damned word'."[28]

Permanent Secretaries are encouraged to consult with their managers when making changes. A laudable management practice in principle. But given the unclear accountability we have exposed in Whitehall over the years, it also ensures not too much happens too quickly because not many civil servants are fully empowered to drive through change or to take any decisions that could lead to change(s) even assuming they would wish to in the first place. The death knell of many initiatives at the meetings of Permanent Secretaries is: "We must now go and discuss this with our colleagues who also need to consult their ministers. . .." That is well rehearsed code for the cognoscenti: 'This initiative is heading for the long grass.'

Trust thrives in a positive culture. But trust is a consequence of clear accountability in an organization that exists for a purpose. A culture of excellence is the combined outcome of a clear mission, effective structure, aligned leadership development coupled with experiential training as we saw in Chap. 7. These ingredients are not demonstrably present across the civil service. Talk of collaborative leadership in such a setting is largely a pipedream. The loss of grading governance is just one example encouraging political behaviour distorting the culture of the civil service. Indeed it is a moot point whether there is anything approaching a coherent culture across Whitehall, notwithstanding *the word* gets a lot of airtime.

Many departments had crafted values and spent a lot of time in consultation about them. At least one department has "Accountability" as one of its values but accountability remains at best only a word across the civil service, not a set of practices. The department in question was consistently over layered and its management disempowered: "accountability" was no more than a word on the wall.

The same is the case with culture. Although it was noted above that organization design is a leadership competence (Chap. 4), it is not greatly in evidence across Whitehall. Given the impact of a spendthrift government up to the GFC, the civil service has subsequently had to undertake major internal change programmes but skill in organization development of this magnitude is not an arrow in the quiver of the average senior civil servant. I have seen senior civil servants placed in charge of key organization design projects based on their grade equivalence with the job, not relevant knowhow, expertise or experience. The gifted amateur ethos that concerned Fulton still prevails in some quarters.

9.3.5.1 Engagement Scores Reinforce the Same Message

Work in the private sector has revealed a persistent correlation between low staff engagement scores and stultifying management structures that eviscerate the

[27] Ibid p. 63

[28] Arbuckle G.A. 2013, p. 23

substance and challenge of jobs, which are then devoid of purpose and accountability. There is overwhelming evidence that people want to have jobs with a purpose that enable them to make a difference, at all levels in an organization.[29] The Civil Service has an impressive commitment to measuring employee engagement scores across Whitehall. These are both helpful and revealing, but the recurring shortcomings seem to be mostly ignored in practice.

Low scores in engagement surveys noting inability "to manage poor performance" are a regular feature across the civil service. There is similar criticism of the "Inability to manage change" and the "quality of leadership". These items consistently score in the region of 30 %. Even the SCS engagement survey is similarly critical of line management performance—and yet *they* are the leaders of the civil service! In one department there were disquieting indicators from a most recent last survey. Key reactions were noted in one of our reports as follows:

> "In grades AA to G6 the ratings for 'I feel the organization as a whole is managed well' ranged from only 11 to 18 %. Those for, 'I feel change is well managed' ranged from similarly low scores of 8 to 12 % and for 'Poor performance is dealt with effectively in my team' from 30 to 42 %. The lowest overall average Engagement Index (35 %) is registered by the HEOs. All grades below G7 (In principle Work Level 2 managers) average below 40 %. Even the G7s and G6s are below 50 %—44 and 47 % respectively. The best scores came from a sample of high fliers (50 %) and the SCS (59 %) and yet the latter are among the top 1 % of CS leaders. These are most disquieting scores." A well run organization would be mortified with any engagement scores below 50. An average around 75+ would be what the best would expect.

These widespread low scores are consistent with comments from the interviews of incumbents in the same department, such as:

> My greatest problem is:
>
> "Getting a decision"
> "Getting a quick decision"
> "Mostly having to go up many layers in the line"
> "Decisions are just imposed centrally"
> "Too many layers which increase ambiguity".
> "We have a policy culture, rather than an empowered culture"

These are comments from different individuals but only from those in jobs G7—the equivalent of WL 2 in principle—and above who are supposed to be among the key leaders. When coupled with extensive low engagement scores they dramatically illustrate that *the lack of accountability and empowerment is both widely felt and recognised by staff.*

---

[29] Bains, G et al (2007) *Meaning Inc: the blueprint for business success in the 21st century*

9.3.5.2 A Confused Approach to Centralisation and Delegation

CS understanding of "centralisation" seems to be confused between that of sound delegation within clearly defined principles, which can be flexed to meet the needs of a given department, and that of abdication, which lets departments do what they like.

Drucker argued in 1964 that an effective structure needs both a strong centre and a strong periphery.[30] This does not seem to be the case in the civil service. The breakdown in job evaluation governance is a case in point. The number of "competency" systems and skills' courses would appear to be going in the same direction. The two combined are actually undermining robust leadership development and the culture of the civil service. Organization Development (OD), or in this context Mission Mastery, is a complex process linking strategy, organization design, leadership development, experiential learning and culture. Its cultural synapses seem to have fused and short circuited in the civil service.

The lack of effective OD leadership across Whitehall—and political interference—seems to be a major source of "friction" in the building of a robust cultural identity.

The civil service is not always clear when and how to delegate. There is an aversion to "central control", already evidenced in the first discussion of senior civil servants referred to in paragraph Sect. 3.2.2.1, which seems to be quite widespread and largely misconceived. There is a culture of "we must do it to ourselves", otherwise, it is implied any initiative from above will not work. This seems to have fostered a wasteful philosophy of "let a thousand consultative flowers bloom".

If there are not sufficient clear principles providing boundaries and guidelines from the centre delegation can degenerate into abdication whereby departments are left to their own devices to the detriment of overall performance and cohesion of the federation. The broken governance mechanisms of delegation, such as the overlapping job evaluation systems and faulty organization design illustrate this point. The outcome has been a loss of OD governance, grade and cost drift, inequitable reward practice, contributing in turn to inconsistent performance management and likely underutilisation of talent together with an erosion of real leadership. Departmental engagement (or lack of engagement!) scores on these items consistently tend to reinforce these impressions.

[30] *The Practice of Management* p. 187

Given the lack of clear accountability, weak performance management, and confusion about capability to do a job, it is clear that generally there seems to be abdication and lack of leadership espoused in the name of "delegation."

The original OD approach in the civil service concentrated on work and organization architecture, initiated rather oddly in the Treasury in 1949. The aim of that Staff Inspection (establishment control) was "to promote a higher level of efficiency".[31] The stated objectives were:

- To establish that the work is necessary
- To ensure that the organization is both economical and conducive to efficiency
- To ensure that the numbers are adequate but not excessive
- To ensure that the grades are right.

Staff inspection was to offer the "benefits of a consultancy service to line managers as an aid to management efficiency." This service seems to have become dislocated and fragmented after 1981. There would appear to be four key reasons for the loss of OD expertise in Whitehall.

The first probably was the *growth in the bureaucracy* surrounding the large numbers of Establishment Officers conducting endless reviews of grades and work. Experience in other organizations would indicate this is prone to be an inflationary process as the pressure of internal relativities invariably results in grades drifting upwards

Secondly the *work on grading appears to have moved* to Personnel (subsequently HR) departments that "controlled" grading through the JEGs job evaluation system. Senior Civil Servant grading was passed to the Cabinet Office which introduced the JESP job evaluation system in 1993. They are not obviously joined up and now overlap in Level 3.

Thirdly *the grading system has been allowed to wrongly migrate into the space of organization design and leadership development*. In the Civil Service, as elsewhere, the short cut to obtaining a higher grade is to add a layer into the hierarchy.

Fourthly *the faulty premise underpinning the JEGs and JESP*. They are quantitatively based, factor rating systems, which do not calibrate the value adding nature of different decision rights across Whitehall. They do not identify accountability. In fact it is possible *they have contributed directly to the disempowerment of junior and middle management over the years*. Thus the two grading systems do not now meet the four objectives of the original staff inspection system. And even if they were fused into one system evidence from

[31] An Introduction to Staff Inspection Its origins, aims and practice, HM Treasury June 1983

other civilian grading systems suggests it would not overcome the problems identified in pillars 2–4.

9.4 An Assessment of the Civil Service Against the Five Pillars

As already demonstrated the civil service currently has serious weaknesses in each of the five key pillars needed to achieve Mission Mastery. As I wrote this chapter at the beginning of 2015, The *Financial Times* revealed a report on the NHS management, completed 2 months earlier, had been put on the 'back burner of the back burner' as it describes NHS management as "totally shocking". The report has not been published as yet.[32] Having worked in some Health organizations I was not entirely surprised. On a more positive note, Arbuckle noted, based on his experience of healthcare leadership in New Zealand, Australia, Canada, the US and the UK:

> *Paramodern leaders in healthcare have distinctive qualities, for example, inspired by its founding story they are collaborative, committed to accountability, financially competent, imaginatively proactive, courageous, appreciative of the different gifts of their colleagues and committed to the importance of storytelling as a way of binding people together in a common mission.*[33]

That is the blueprint: a huge change journey for the NHS. If P&G (an organization of ~130,000 employees took 25 years to change its culture, according to Schein) the NHS being a loose federation with over one million employees represents a daunting change challenge. But it IS possible. Another simple, but telling comment from Arbuckle that reflects Fulton: "*In my experience of healthcare systems, the failure to clarify roles is a source of unnecessary turmoil and frustration.*"[34] An opaque structure that totally undermines personal accountability and development tends to lead to a negative, bullying culture. My experience provides evidence of that in public healthcare organizations and although the NHS is not strictly part of the Whitehall machine, it is driven *and funded* by the Department of Health.

The *One HR* project has increased that function's cost ratios and brought it more into line with median private sector practice but even this assignment has taken a good 3 years or so. That attack on *quantity* is a really good start, but as this chapter demonstrates, there is much more to be done on the *quality* of people management in Whitehall.

Finally, there is a convenient belief in the civil service that it is "managing the unmanageable" and that "For managers in the public sector democratic accountability can make it harder to do things quickly or less attractive to take risks". It is further argued "Political accountability softens the demand for managerial

[32] June 2015

[33] Arbuckle G A (2013) *Humanizing Healthcare Reform* p. 172

[34] Ibid: p. 177

accountability."[35] No doubt that is what some civil servants think, but it seems to be a universal tendency for people to oversimplify the work of others while exaggerating the complexity, importance and difficulty of their own challenges. I well remember a senior civil servant saying to me: "*All I would have to do in Wal-mart is stack shelves and make a profit. My job here is much more difficult than that and can't be measured.*" She was taken aback when one of my colleagues replied: *"I have not seen one person in this department I would wish to recruit to source fresh fruit and vegetables from twelve different countries, mostly in the southern hemisphere, get them quickly through UK Customs in bulk, have them repacked into small retail packs meeting stringent quality demands, then arrange overnight delivery to hundreds of stores up and down the country, knowing the product has a shelf life of only a few days while needing to meet a target wastage rate of less than 3 %".*

The root cause of all the people management problems in the civil service stem from an inability to assess accountability. And yet the Fulton Committee Report put its finger on this very issue 50 years ago.

"One guiding principle should in our view govern the future development of the Civil Service. It applies to any organization and is simple to the point of banality, but the root of much of our criticism is that this is has not been observed. The principle is: *look at the job first.*"

So if the civil service has been told ad nauseam what is wrong, that the issue is the accountability of the job, why has no one emerged with the courage and competence to implement this obvious message?

I hope the answer is now clear.

Finally how would Moltke's assess the civil service? I suspect his overall verdict would be something like:

"This organization remains largely unaccountable. It needs to focus on overhauling its approach to mission, organization design, leadership development and training, if it is even to commence the journey towards Mission Mastery. To do that it needs a courageous leader, enjoying single point accountability, who has the ability and determination to implement the above."

This overall challenge is daunting and more than one person has asked me:

Do you really think it is possible?

I believe it IS possible, but it needs a Moltke.

[35] See Stevenson, A (2013) *The Public Sector Managing the Unmanageable*, pp. 11 and 41

An absence of the first four Pillars in the Civil Service has led to a culture of no consequences. The mantra of Dickens' Circumlocution Office: 'HOW NOT TO DO IT' is still recognisable. Or in other words: the shortcomings Fulton identified in the Civil Service almost 50 years ago have still not been fully redressed. Dickens might say, 150 years.

Some Questions to Ponder

1. Having assessed the performance of your organization against the five Pillars in Chap. 1, is your assessment a "pass" or a "fail"?
2. Would you say your organization is close to the British Civil Service?
3. In other words is your organization in the foothills or on the road to the peak of Mission Mastery?
4. What is the first and most important action you feel needs to be undertaken?

Mission Mastery: Building a Learning Organization in Which There Is Space to Lead

10

A leader moulds and communicates a task-oriented mission. . .which gives direction to the work of others: if the leader fails to provide that mission . . .the strategies to realise it and appropriate accountability structures, the group becomes confused and de-energised.
G.A. Arbuckle (2013 *Humanizing Healthcare Reforms*, p. 166)

10.1 General

It is now clear that Mission Mastery consists of five Pillars that need to be implemented as 'a package'. I will summarise some of the approaches different organizations are taking/have taken on their respective paths to Mission Mastery. This will hopefully help answer the question: "How should I go about this in my organization?" Clearly an organization with an unrealistic strategy linked to a flawed structure and haphazard leadership development process faces an enormous challenge. A transformational change is a slow, complex process that cannot be put to bed in just 6 months. It is a significant culture change programme that needs to verify resilience of the four variables (the Pillars), in a logical sequence. For example if leadership development, potential assessment and experiential training need to be introduced this will not work if any organization design shortcomings have not been redressed first. The most common failings seem to be unawareness of the key variables involved and the assumption that culture change is an input, such as a few million $ on the training budget, that can be controlled, while underestimating the complexity and inter-linkage of key activities and the

(continued)

B. Dive, *Mission Mastery*, Management for Professionals,
DOI 10.1007/978-3-319-25223-0_10

time needed to achieve the change. One or all of these may contrive to de-rail the transformation initiative. Awareness of the need to implement Mission Mastery is merely the first step.

Finally the three questions posed in Chap. 1 are revisited and answered at the end of this chapter.

10.2 The Path to Mission Mastery

As the quote at the top of this chapter suggests, the quality of the CEO or top executive leader in a civilian organization is the key to achieving Mission Mastery. He or she sets the mission and has the overview and authority to embed the other four Pillars. Every learning organization needs its Moltke. The transformation he helped to bring about is encapsulated in Eckhart Tolle's insight:

Failure lies concealed in every success and success in every failure.

That is an apt summary of the journey the Prussian Army took from its heady success under Frederick the Great, to humiliation at the hands of Napoleon to meting out the same medicine to the French 64 years later, only to meet defeat again as the German army in the twentieth century. An ambition to attain Mission Mastery deserves better than failure but that can be the outcome if it is not well planned and sustained by good leadership at all levels. It should follow a logical sequence, which calls for thoughtful orchestration and usually takes more than a year to complete, even in a small organisation. It is important the staging posts and the final outcome being sought are clear from the outset. The five Pillars are the staging posts and planning how to implant them is the key to success. They are best tackled in the logical sequence of the chapters in this book, starting with mission and structure as they are the bedrock pillars, but some such as leadership development and training, can be managed in parallel. Underpinning the whole implementation process is a communications strand, equal in importance to the five Pillars in ensuring successful delivery, ownership and commitment by all those involved and affected. In Chap. 9 of *The Healthy Organization*, I explain in some detail the five phase model that enables the mobilisation of change in any organization. In my experience, communications is the one item that most often is short changed, its importance and the effort needed underestimated, which can then undermine the whole transformation undertaking. I worked with one global company that spent seven figures on communications materials and training on a journey that took 3 years to reach successful completion.

10.2.1 Reasons for Change

10.2.1.1 A Change of Leader

Cleary there must be a sound rationale for wanting to change an organization. Organizations undertake change for various reasons, some more valid than others. One of the most common reasons is a (sometimes necessary) change of chief executive. This often leads to a shake up at the top of the organization to "improve performance". But as is now clear, tinkering only with the top structure is not enough if the organization is unhealthy. In Chap. 8 I gave an example of a bank that wanted to improve its performance relative to its competitors but which poisoned its culture in the process. The ambition was sound but the process was not because the initiative did not connect all five Pillars. Mono-facetted initiatives inevitably to run into the sand. The bank seemed to be recovering from its toxic culture but recently shocked people with the ruthless, public firing of the CEO noted for his ethical qualities. The chairman's 'explanation' for this callous act was nothing short of gauche. The fear is this highhandedness seems to signal a return to the "bad ole days".

10.2.1.2 A Burning Platform

Sometimes, as with the case of the Prussian Army in 1806, there is a burning platform that cannot be ignored. This helps commitment but undirected enthusiasm is not the answer either. The plan might not be perfect, as Moltke would concede, but a plan or what I am calling a road map is needed. The recent GFC caused a number of platforms to catch fire. Many reactions were driven by real concerns but tended to degenerate into a simplistic cost cutting initiatives often done in ignorant haste. The five Pillars were not joined up, which is not the route to Mission Mastery.

10.2.1.3 Internal Reorganization

On other occasions the catalyst for a review of the effectiveness of the structure comes as a result of a strategic decision to organize the business in a completely different way.

An example of that was the decision in September 2014 taken by Royal Philips to divide the group into two international businesses: one for healthcare called Health Tech and the other for Lighting. According to CEO Frans van Houten, the split will allow both companies make "*the appropriate investments to boost growth and drive profitability, ultimately generating significantly more value for our customers, employees, and shareholders,*" with an estimated total market worth more than 100 billion euros (US$128.6 billion). This sort of change can be controversial and difficult to implement since it is not immediately self evident how dividing a company necessarily improves efficiency. Focus on the five Pillars would be really essential in such a case.

10.2.1.4 Building for Growth

A common reason for embarking on a major change initiative in the private sector is a desire to facilitate planned growth. This might be the result of a takeover or simply via a 'new, more aggressive strategy'. This is a positive reason but as we saw in Chap. 3 it is no guarantee of success in itself. It is of course a non threatening narrative for employees and a good story to share with the outside world but a disarmingly large number of these growth initiatives founder. This can be because the inter-linkages of the first four Pillars are not thought through, are neglected or most often the leader is not aware of what really needs to be done to lead a holistic change initiative.

This type of initiative invariably starts as the outcome of 'strategy changes' which can be intellectual exercises carried out in isolation by the top executive not engaging their people at the appropriate stages. I have seen this occur when intelligent managers are promoted swiftly without having had the benefit of planned boundary moves that would equip them for the top job. Sometimes new problems emerge in the transformation process, such as growing the right quality of new leaders, quickly. I described earlier the challenge Tesco had in Korea with a very ambitious, but successful, growth strategy. The challenge was not so much building and financing ~50 hypermarkets in a short time but finding *quickly* the local managers to run them. *The quality, number and potential of Level 3 managers is the turn-key to successful organizational growth.* This critical talent cannot be bought en masse from the market, despite the seductive whispers of head hunters. The move across the operational (level 3)/strategic (level 4) Rubicon is particularly challenging and many civilian organizations stumble at this fence.

10.2.1.5 The Need to Down Size

The converse of the above paragraph is the need to 'down size'. This is often driven by external factors such as an economic recession and/or government policy. These cycles tend to recur with regular monotony. Following the easy growth of the '60s I can recall the oil shocks, spiralling inflation and growing international competition (especially Japanese at that stage) in the '70s that led to very difficult times in the '80s. The catch cry was "return to your core business" and 'downsizing' first entered the management lexicon. Sadly these eventualities provoked more ham-fisted than inspired organization change initiatives driven by a focus on costs. Further recessions at the start of the 90s and again early in twentieth century caused further organizational turmoil accompanied by initiatives to 'outsource' and 'offshore' in the name of 'better customer service', when the transparent motive was cost reduction. In *The Accountable Leader* I described how the resultant white collar 'call centres' were endemically over layered and customer service deteriorated. The latest of these buffeting waves came with the recent GFC, which for the first time had a significant impact on the public sector as the national debt of many countries in the so-called developed world spiralled out of control.

10.2.1.6 The Need for Sound Organization Development Know-How

OD learning through these recurring incidences of 'lean years', has remained surprisingly superficial. Many leaders still do not have a reliable, tried and tested mental framework to drive through what are often necessary changes to ensure the mission continues to be delivered as envisaged by an engaged, high performing workforce in structures affording them Space to Lead. In difficult times it is astounding how many top international companies responded to the organizational challenges of the day by getting rid of their OD managers! I first noticed this trend in the US in the 90s and it was around this time that the term "OD" there seemed to become limited to simply "learning and development". Notwithstanding that, or maybe because of it, widespread knowledge on how to grow and develop people in a dynamic, stimulating environment is not widely evident today. A classic example is the decision often taken during a recession to freeze recruitment as people resign or retire. By 2015 this was finally recognised by the National Audit Office in the UK as a mistaken approach denuding the talent pipeline in the public sector.[1]

Nevertheless a blue print does emerge from observing what some of the best leaders and their organizations are doing when confronted with these challenges. They respect their people at all levels. They appreciate that the demands of the digital age or the need to work in pods, does not replace the need for clear accountability. Their aim is to build an organic learning organization in which people are *clear* about what is expected of them, that ensures their work has *meaning* and they know they are *trusted.* In short they are truly engaged in a vibrant and rewarding working environment.

10.3 What Are Some of the Best Doing?

I have worked with a number of civilian organizations, which are well down the path to Mission Mastery. Their experiences might help serve as a guide on how to tackle any future transformation assignment in your organization as it moves towards becoming a learning organization. It is important to note that they undertake a holistic change affecting all five Pillars, not just one or two.

Let us review their approaches for lessons and potential insights

10.3.1 Strategy

Their common starting point has been a review of their strategy. In most cases in the private sector that has been a plan to grow but not always. More recently others have been forced into a reappraisal of their strategy as a result of major changes in the economy leading to declining profit, or frozen and reducing budgets as a result of government policy changes. This might lead to outsourcing and/or divestments or changes in the delivery model of care, for example.

In one case the arrival of a new CEO led to a fundamental review of the global strategy, which reflected particular opportunities in the BRICs (Brazil, Russia, India and China) and the need for a fundamental review of the underperforming business in Europe. The company also felt it had some technological advantages as a result

[1] 5 June 2015.

of its investment in R&D, which indicated it had a unique opportunity to gain market share in a way that was unlikely to present itself again. The outcome was a carefully thought out but more aggressive strategy which, although considered feasible, placed a number of new challenges on the three pillars of structure, leadership development and training, not to mention recruitment in what were then under resourced geographies.

10.3.1.1 "2020" Reviews

Recently more than one client has been working on a "2020 Strategic Review", over and above the annual planning process, which have been very thorough and wide ranging. These typically boil down into a small number of key 'strategic thrusts', which set the priorities for action over the next 3–5 years. These new strategic thrusts are usually around 6–10 in order to get maximum focus and support. One of these strategic thrusts invariably leads to a reappraisal of the effectiveness of the organization's structure to ensure it is strategy-enabling, competitive and within the new cost envelope set by the relevant governance body, whether that is a board of shareholders or government policy.

10.3.1.2 The Importance of Good Governance

Sometimes the journey encounters 'friktion' from unexpected quarters. In one case I have been involved with for some years, a public sector organization in Europe was badly affected by the GFC and the subsequent undermining of the country's finances. This prompted a radical review of its activities driven by government withdrawal of some funding and a national change in policy affecting the services being provided. This led to a fundamental and urgent rethink of the strategy and operating model under the heading of "The 2020 Journey." Given the dependence on a government strapped for cash, the manoeuvrability options were very restricted: for example the recruitment of new young staff and the paying of salary increases were ruled out for the foreseeable future while underperforming staff were protected. This stymied the revitalisation effort, which tends to be a factor with public sector initiatives that are often more tactical than strategic. Mission Mastery is strategic.

10.3.2 Structure

In each case I have worked with recently these strategic initiatives called for changes to the structure (both at the top and in the lower echelons) in order to ensure appropriate alignment to the strategy. It is a key step that needs to be led by the top executive as Kessler and Kates pointed out:

> *Organization Design is a leadership responsibility—not a consensus activity. Design decision making should not be delegated.*[2]

[2] The Foreword, 2010, *Learning Organization Design.*

But the fly in the ointment is not too many top leaders are greatly knowledgeable in how to build an effective target structure that is healthy and tightly aligned to the strategy, featuring the right number of layers and realistic spans of control dovetailed with the top two layers. This still tends to be a major vulnerability that can undermine a transformation programme. There are two aspects to consider here.

10.3.2.1 The Top Structure

In more than one case the review of strategy led to a fundamental change to the top structure. For example the first global company mentioned above that had ambitious growth aspirations, moved from a geographical structure to one based on global lines of business, as this had been identified in the strategy as the best way to capitalise on its growth opportunities. As the company was implementing Work Levels at the same time this meant we had to assess each of the jobs in the top two layers prior to embarking on a review of the new organization structure. Some of this work could be done quite quickly behind the desk combined with interviews of key managers currently in posts that did not fundamentally change: e.g. the CFO. The next stage was a 'bottom up' review process to help refine the number of jobs and accountability levels needed in the target organization.

Another global company with over 100,000 employees changed its operating model following its strategic review, leading to significant changes in the top two layers of the business, to start with. Our work had demonstrated that there was compression at the top of a continental region and the indications were that this was an issue in other parts of the world as well. Thus one of the major strategy initiatives in this case was to complete a full review of the structure in over 50 countries to ensure they were all Work Level compliant in support of the new strategy. This resulted in planned reviews under the umbrella of an empowerment initiative (Space to Lead) for the business as whole. Given this was a large, complex organization it then called for an extensive training programme, of which more below in Sect. 3.3.

The national organization mentioned in Sect. 3.1.2 changed its top structure as a result of a change in strategy. Once the strategy was signed off by the board, I started working with the CEO to help design the top two layers as some realignment was needed given the new strategy coupled with the fact that the current top structure was partly over layered. This in turn called for a fundamental realignment of the geographical divisions, which in turn impacted some key enabling roles and the removal of a COO span breaker role. The individual concerned was assigned to a new role so the change was completed without anyone losing their job. This organization embarked on a well planned journey. Following planned assessment a number of incumbents were placed in new roles in the top structure which was flatter and more effective. Both Work Levels and Differentiating Competencies were introduced together with more training to add momentum to the journey. But the organization has not been allowed to recruit new employees, being expected to tolerate and live with poor performance while working within a steadily declining budget. This turns out in most cases to be false charity akin to 'window seating' in

Japan.[3] This organization has been hampered by external governance, which has been short sighted and ill informed seemingly bereft of anyone with experience of successful organizational change. This has become the major source of 'friktion' blocking key productivity efforts. Sadly, as the economy picks up, this organization is now starting to lose key staff.

10.3.2.2 Effective and Efficient Structures

Effectiveness relates to the vertical dimension of structure, efficiency to the horizontal axis. It is possible to have too many jobs on both axes and although clarifying effectiveness tends to highlight inefficiencies the converse does not necessarily apply. Once the link of structure to strategy has been completed and the shape of the top two layers have been agreed the next step is to ensure the planned target structure is completely effective and efficient. This is reflected in having the right number of layers and appropriate spans of control based on building up from the front line to link back with the top two layers once the total number of WLs needed has been identified, affording one layer per level above WL 1. It is also important to check functional structures are not over specialised and divisional structures not subject to unnecessary duplication both of which result in too many jobs.

In one large international company the structural review highlighted issues of confusion over centralisation/decentralisation, between corporate office and the respective divisions. This had built in unnecessary duplication, over specialisation, unnecessary cost and frustration. The analysis showed that the balance between customer facing roles and support roles across the business was also out of kilter, with far too many of the latter. Delegations of authority were not clear and contributed to lack of empowerment and further confusion. A thorough WL analysis over a couple of years helped clarify these issues which in due course led to a change in the operating model. But as can be seen, this is not a 5 min job since poor structures feed ineffective processes, which can be made worse for example, by a CFO obsessed only with "controlling costs" taking away power from the periphery but leaving eviscerated divisional structures and processes in place. Any fool can cut costs in an international organization: the question is do they know when to stop and why?

10.3.2.3 The Trap of Too Much Top-Down Organization Design

The most common mistake I encounter following a strategy review is the building of a new structure top-down to the front line. It seems to be based on a mistaken understanding of Chandler's dictum that 'structure follows strategy'. It does, but going beyond the top two layers seems to invariably result in more layers of leaders than necessary. The offending roles are usually span breakers, there for the comfort of the boss but not adding value to the customer or the work of the team(s) below.

[3] Japanese organizations often don't make poor performers redundant because of 'life time employment'. They are stripped of real work and left to sit by the window: a form of public humiliation, which is worse than redundancy in my opinion.

An example of this tendency to focus unduly on the top of an organization was a speech on 28 May 2015 by Martin Wheatley from the Financial Conduct Authority, entitled "*Debating Trust and Confidence in Banking.*" He outlined compliance changes being made in banking. He made much of a new "Accountability regime" being insisted upon for banks. "Even Victorians had arguably a more nuanced understanding of personal accountability". The FCA has produced a heavy tome to support this initiative, but it is focussed only on the top of the organization. I gave an example in *The Accountable Leader* (p. 187), of a bank which in places had five layers too many some of which were just below the top layers, a failing that in my experience is not uncommon. Focusing only on the top layers does not solve the problem of unaccountable structures. Moltke would see this FCA initiative as: "Aiming at the right target but the sights need better alignment."

There is a widespread tendency for strategy consultants to build down to the third layer on their assignments, which I have found on more than one occasion hosts a number of non jobs, which then stymies further effective organization design. Once the top two layers are agreed and the number of accountability levels available has been identified then the design becomes more straightforward and not prone to building in problem jobs from the outset. The reason being it is much easier to plot value adding decisions when coming up from the customer or patient. Conversely it is almost impossible to assess the contribution of a role if you do not know what decisions are being taken below it. Top management confidently tell you what SHOULD BE going on "down there", whereas those at and near the front line tell you what IS going on. The two are rarely the same.

10.3.2.4 The Organization Design Process

This organization design step in the journey can be done by the CEO working alone with help from an OD manager/consultant or by the entire top team assisted by a consultant for both process and content but chaired by the CEO. I have done both over the years but prefer the latter. The former is quick in the design phase but commitment is low and this makes implementation sluggish at best. The latter approach takes some days and needs a skilled chairperson and consultant. The process can be difficult to manage but clear guidelines help. I have found it is most helpful not to discuss individuals or even existing jobs when constructing a zero based (Greenfield) target structure. The people issues come soon enough but the task can be made too difficult by bringing in the people implications too early in the design process. I often find that when a top manager is proposing a 'strange job' it is invariably because they have a person in mind and are intent on manufacturing the right outcome. This is why agreed "rules of the game" are important to help the chairperson guide a constructive discussion. The design may need to be modified later because of people shortcomings but that discussion should come after the optimal design has been agreed. The relevant action plans can be agreed as necessary, as I found when conducting a review with Chesebrough Ponds in the US.

The key building blocks at this stage of the process, given the top two layers are established, as are the number of WLs available to be filled with jobs (layers) and the business "givens" which together drive the optimal design. An example of a typical "given" would be the number and location of factories in a supply chain whose target structures need to be built into the overall structure, the location of the head office, and so on. I find this is the more effective of the two approaches. The major advantage is rigorous and fair debate can be provided for and strong commitment to the outcome is the more likely. That in turn facilitates implementation, which is then smoother and quicker. (A similar process of involvement is recommended for a strategy review, which can involve more leaders since job security is not likely to be a major distraction initially.)

10.3.2.5 Filling the Jobs in the New Structure

This is where the difficult work starts as the people implications to changes in strategy and structure emerge. Much of the work on strategy and structure up to this point is largely a matter of planning and considering options. Now the reality of who can do what job starts to bite. It can be quite a challenge deciding who should do which jobs if the structure has fundamentally changed. This is even more so if the current appraisals of performance and potential of existing staff have not been done with any rigour in the past and therefore are not a reliable or defensible basis for selection. It is also the time when the vulnerabilities of the new strategy and structure may start to crystallise if the quality of people is a concern. This of course can be a catch 22 situation if people have previously been in hollow jobs in the 'old' structure in which they have not been able to display their true qualities or if the quality of HR management in the organization is below par.

10.3.3 Leadership and Experiential Training

Consideration of these issues and changes can lead to the identification of extensive training needs and possibly even a major overhaul of the performance management system, which may have been exposed in the discussion about who fills/is selected for which job during the review process in Sect. 3.2.4. I have been involved in cases where this has occurred. However the assumption here is people management has been sound to this point and does not pose a major obstacle to the implementation of a new strategy and/or structure.

One of the things that can be done while the reviews of the strategy and structure are taking place is a rigorous quality check on the quality of all current staff. Then on the basis of what information is available, rank the potential candidates against the likely jobs/vacancies at each Work Level. Sometimes, once the WLs are clear, I have crafted a manual of Work Levels definitions for the particular organization and another for Differentiating Competencies' (see Chap. 6) to help a CEO and his/her team assess/choose candidates for the roles in the new structure on a consistently objective basis.

10.3.3.1 Differentiating Competencies

If the organization does not have a set of Differentiating Competencies aligned to Levels, since it may not have implemented Work Levels previously, the design of an appropriate set of definitions can be done in parallel with the organization design work, once a set of bespoke Work Level definitions have also been agreed. (As has been explained in Chap. 6 it is vital the competencies are aligned to the seven DMA Elements in the levels of accountability otherwise they cannot reliably differentiate.) The next step would be to train key top managers in the understanding of both the WLs and the application of the Competencies. In that way assessments of the existing staff can also commence in an open and objective fashion while the issues connected to the strategy and possible new structure are being worked through.

Sometimes in those cases where the performance has not been well managed in the past I have advocated external assessment of candidates for key roles. This helps demonstrate the process of selection is fair and objective. It is of course critical that the assessors can evaluate individuals against the requirements of accountability levels. The candidates' assessments are shared with them (including those who may not be chosen for the key jobs), which helps form individual development plans. This can be important if individuals' training needs have not been consistently identified in the past. Depending on the scale of the change and the quality of the candidates this process alone can take some months even though the desire is to move a quickly as possible.

10.3.3.2 Identifying (New) Career Paths

Once the levels of accountability are agreed for the respective parts of the organization then it is possible to work with the top leaders to plot likely future career paths across these levels relevant to each part (function, department, line of business or unit) of the organization. Some organizations identify the 8–10 fundamental skills the organization needs to be successful and use that as the basis for assessing individual training needs. These key skills areas often referred to as job families: e.g. Finance is likely to be a critical basic skill needed in the organization, which is also a job family made up of sub sets of skills such as management accounting, treasury, financial management, tax, audit and so on. This sets the groundwork for future boundary moves (explained in Chap. 6) and 'dwell time' in a given WL to facilitate personal growth and development. This then becomes part of the ongoing people practice in the organization once the strategy and structure Pillars are firmly in place.

10.3.3.3 Training

The osmosis process of transformational change calls for extensive training particularly if and when WLs are introduced as part of the journey. Assuming the field work has been done and the bespoke definitions unfurled—as referred to at the top of this section—then a number of activities may be advantageous especially if an organization does not have a rigorous, reliable approach to identifying training needs.

Appreciation seminars of 3–4 h are usually required for all distributive leaders to give them an appreciation of what the change is about, why it is necessary, what has been decided to date (e.g. the top two layers) and an outline of the logic of the accountability process that is going to be applied to the new organization. It gives leaders a chance to challenge the process and the logic as well as helping them to feel comfortable with the logic that will impact on both their jobs and their personal development in future. In large global companies, that has involved presenting to ~250 top managers to start with, usually broken down into country groupings. In some cases I have helped draw up communication packages, which these key line managers then in turn present to their respective teams. This ensures the key managers are seen to own the process and the key messages are consistently delivered. The local presentation may be then made in the local language to a wider audience, which greatly helps the overall osmosis process. Sometimes it also helps to have key manuals translated to help greater comprehension and commitment to the changes being introduced. Where these seminars have been short changed implementation issues surface further down the track.

Workshops may be needed for those who are going to be the implementers and guardians of the process going forward. More than one large international company has produced 'work books' with helpful organization and job design templates that could be variously applied around the world. This can be very helpful when there are units that are similar in purpose but vary in size and complexity and therefore WL: such as distribution centres, retail stores, bank branches, care homes, factories and call centres. They can also plot when and how a country or unit might grow into a higher WL as a result of changing infrastructure: e.g. mapping any significant growth of WL 3 roles.

Training managers within an organisation so they can undertake further organization design work is another key step particularly if implementing levels of accountability. This can be done also via workshops that are a combination of theory and case studies geared to ensuring this can be done by a client's own managers. I have trained up to 150 in one global company, ~100 in another, ~50 in another and ~5 in another. Size and geographical spread are key factors as well as the policy of the organization in question. For example some organizations want the process to be owned by the HR function, which is then trained accordingly. In other cases a mix of line managers and HR managers are trained to carry out the work. This design work is not straightforward so ideally the candidates on these workshops should be at least WL 3.

Once leaders have been trained it is important to ensure the implementation work is consistently applied so *Quality Assurance workshops* are arranged to ensure this takes place. These are also important learning opportunities to share lessons learned and discuss new roles inserted since the change began. It also helps widen understanding of the "how" of the new organization.

Another key activity has been producing *templates and guidelines for the accountability profiles* of common roles across an organization with guidelines on roll out issues. These profiles, based on the seven DMA Elements (see Chap. 8) should be no more than one or two pages maximum. This helps ensure implementation can proceed as quickly as possible, exponentially not just sequentially.

10.3.4 Culture

As indicated in Chap. 7 a positive culture outcome will take place if the first four Pillars are revitalised and well integrated into the organization. Following the formulation of the strategy, DMASS is the golden thread which can tie together the other Pillars. Thus it is very important to give thought to the holistic osmosis process that will embed an understanding of the transformation throughout the organization.

10.3.4.1 Communications

This can be achieved via training options in Sect. 3.3 above but most companies have, in addition, focussed very much on the *Communications* challenge as the critical adjunct to a transformation programme. The key question that needs an answer for each and very individual in the organization is: "What's in this for me?" The quality of communications is the oil that overcomes the grit of friction that is inevitable in any comprehensive organization change process. Relevant communication packages need to be crafted for the different layers and sections of the organization together with training where needed.

Most of the major programmes have tended to have a battery of materials starting with an overview message (which may be written, a video by the CEO or video conference etc) explaining the **what** and the **why**. Potential changes to the top structure for example, will dictate the pace that is feasible for the relevant communications. The **how** is covered in materials focussing on the mechanics of the new approaches to organization design (e.g. WL definitions), reward, and leadership initiatives (e.g. Competencies), complete with guidelines on how to redesign role profiles as and where appropriate complemented by the appreciation seminars and workshops referred to above. Today organizations are also able to make great use of their Intranet and social media to keep people up to date with roll out activities and planning, ideally led by a programme director/vice president.

10.3.4.2 Programme Director[4]

Once the strategy process is underway—and in some cases there may not be a specific strategy review needed—it helps to appoint a programme director (with a team as appropriate) to lead the implementation of Pillars 2–5. This was the approach variously adopted in very large companies such as Unilever, Tesco, BT, and DHL Supply Chain for example. The programme director typically has project managers leading the various threads of the programme. This could include leaders to respectively cover the WL implementation, issues around reward, performance management (e.g. new differentiating competencies), training and communications (including employee relations, dealing with Works Councils and unions when necessary). The overall orchestration of this work in a large organization calls for careful tuning and those

[4] Usually at least WL 4 in a very large organization, which is typically a "director" in Europe but a vice president in the Americas and parts of Asia.

functions are best led by full time project managers who may need to be in place for 2–3 years depending on the scale and extent of the transformation.

10.3.4.3 CEO

It goes without saying that the person who makes or breaks any transformation programme is the CEO who at times has to be quite hands on leading the work on the first three Pillars. It is vital that person is seen to own the programme and known to be committed to its success.

10.4 The Three Key Questions

At the end of the first chapter I posed three critical questions about the leadership transformation of the Prussian army.

- *Firstly, what was the essence of that process, which remained secret for so long?*
- *Secondly, can it be replicated in twenty-first century civilian organizations?*
- *Thirdly, is that leadership secret, which emerged some 100 years ago, still relevant?*

Let us take each of those questions in turn.

10.5 The First Question

What was the essence of the process, which remained secret for so long?
It was the difference between trying to control chaos rather than trying to exploit it.

As is now clear, the process started as ***Aufragstaktik*** in German in 1870, which become ***mission command*** in NATO around 1987. It consisted of a clear mission (auftrag) but Moltke realised there was no such thing as a perfect plan: implementation would always encounter 'friktion' that had to be overcome. The friction would be manifested by gaps in knowledge, alignment and outcomes that had to be proactively managed. He broke this down into an understanding of *What, Why and How*. Great emphasis was placed on training of officers initially, later all troops, so that they understood their role in the process, which was in essence a cascade of *What* and *Why* from the top echelons down to the soldier at the front.

A new and unique feature of the cascade was the fact the senior officers focussed on the *What* and *Why* but did not move into the *How* space. Their enemies remained enmeshed and bogged down in the old way of describing the '*How*' in great detail. This rarely if ever worked. It added up to the difference between trying to exploit chaos—mission command—and trying to control chaos—reliance on the 'master plan'. 'How' was the domain of their team members—*who had been trained* in the relevant skills and techniques to carry out their mission. A mission was defined as *"a task with a purpose"*. Underpinning the cascade was a new mechanism:

back-briefing. Back-briefing required the junior officer in the interaction having to summarise back to the relevant superior officer his understanding of his brief. And so on down the chain of command, or spine of accountability. This avoided the well known communication glitch whereby a message, according to the old chestnut, could leave the front as "Send reinforcements we are going to advance" but having passed up the ranks, arrived at HQ as: "Send three and four pence we are going to a dance." Mission command enshrined two way communications with a clear discipline that removed "noise" from the process.

The next key component in mission command was the effectiveness of the Prussian/German command system, their organization structure. It had clearly established battle echelons, which were soundly constructed and therefore could be taken for granted. Ironically, in the military this was not an inherent advantage as their enemies operated under virtually identical principles of organization design. ***This is NOT the case in civilian organizations where much organization design is largely guesswork.*** It also means the civilian organization that does master the challenge of effective organization design enjoys a major completive advantage given the widespread poverty of thought in this area.

What was also different with Moltke was the rigorous standard of officer selection and training in his armies. Standard were high, unlike their enemies who often had generals of questionable intelligence who scraped through their officer training once the buying of commissions was stopped. This resulted in *different leadership behaviour*. Once the mission was clear the Prussian/German officer was trained to use his initiative. His enemy was not: he was hamstrung by the philosophy of a high command that meddled in the 'How', going into great detail, which became irrelevant once the first shot was fired in anger. This invariably resulted in decision paralysis in the both army and navy but not the air force which tended to be more individual and opportunistic by nature, which therefore demanded initiative. Although both sets of armies practised war scenarios, those supervised by Moltke himself were more demanding both in type and the behaviour being rigorously assessed. His were more subtly constructed to test leadership, based on the following principles:

- The basis of leadership are the mission and the context (accountability level)
- The mission and the context call for a decision
- The decision should pursue a clear goal with all means available
- The key refinement of leadership is recognising in a fluid situation the time and circumstances, which may call for a new decision.
- A leader must grant his team freedom of action provided it does not compromise his intention
- But they must not make a decision which is his accountability

In other words the culture was consciously geared to exploiting opportunities resulting from competitive chaos.

10.6 The Second Question

Can mission command be replicated in 21st century civilian organizations?
Yes, as Mission Mastery: the thesis of this book.

I have endeavoured to make the case throughout this book that mission command can be migrated to civilian organizations, where it could be known as Mission Mastery. I see Mission Mastery as the civilian version of Moltke's *auftragstaktik*, but as I stressed at the outset of this book I am not arguing that civilian organizations should become military clones. This is because there is nothing in what I have defined as the five Pillars of mission command, which are exclusive to military organizations. It is just as important, if not more so, for civilian organizations to perform at the top of the curve in the fields of:

- Mission
- Organization architecture
- Leadership development
- Experiential training
- Culture

But the reality is most civilian organizations that I have encountered over ~50 years continue to have *significant performance gaps in each of these areas*, especially the last four, which explains why so many do not deliver their mission over the long term. Time and time again the stumbling block is the quality of managerial leaders. But in fairness this is because they are often in hollow jobs in over cluttered structures reporting to straw bosses. This is most likely to degenerate into a culture of politicking and bullying increasingly overlaid with some well intentioned but unhelpful legal initiatives, quotas and/or management fads. Structural deformity is depressingly widespread in civilian organizations where unless it is overcome they cannot hope to achieve Mission Mastery.

Most civilian organizations are still unhealthy. Returning to health is the first imperative en route to Mission Mastery.

It is also clear a structure of mangled accountability completely undermines attempts to train effective cadres of management. Ideally training experiences and programmes should be aligned to the relevant Levels of accountability. They can be dovetailed with the demands of different contexts reflecting different Levels. Similarly they should set the context for experiential learning and boundary moves. We also know that key Work Levels, such as 3 and 5 should entail a series of critical job experiences for those with potential to reach WL 6+. The military seem to understand this and their career building moves are impressively orchestrated with that in mind. Civilian organizations need to be able to emulate the best military lessons without firing a gun.

Chapter 9 outlined what can happen in a large organization that has defective or missing Pillars. The outcome is a culture of no consequences. It has to build/rebuild a firm phalanx of the five Pillars in order to be successful. This can be done in parallel but it is not easy. Logic suggests Mission and Structure first and changing the latter can be a huge task in a sizeable organization.

10.7 The Third Question

Is that leadership secret, which emerged some 100 years ago, still relevant?
The fact it remained secret for so long proves how powerful it is.

I would hope that the case to embed Mission Mastery in the twenty-first century is now accepted. Indeed it is hard to see, in my view, how a civilian organization that is seriously deficient on one of some of the five Pillars will survive and be successful longer term in the twenty-first century. We are constantly told that the big challenge is the mastery of technology and an ability to adapt to a changing world. Technology is not the major threat as those who live by technology tend to be outflanked and disappear as a result of new technology. However the only constant in today's economic, political social world is change and "the only stability possible is stability in motion."[5] The real problem is not movement or change, but movement without meaning. Leadership is about providing that meaning, which starts with clarity of mission aligned to the appropriate context. That anchors people, enabling them to contribute with confidence and appropriate passion in what otherwise might appear to be chaos.

Clear accountability is the bedrock that enables the building of trust needed to have "stability in motion." Mission Mastery can help deliver that. At the risk of repetition, it consists of the following characteristics:

- A clear **mission** communicated to the whole organization
- A clear **structure** with layers of hierarchy aligned to levels of accountability
- **Leadership development** process based on differentiating competencies aligned to levels of accountability providing robust evidence of potential
- Career planning and development based on **experiential learning** built around seven clear boundary moves which lay the basis for personal growth and development
- The outcome if the first four pillars are well embedded is a **positive culture**, which gives meaning to people and which is a principal task of leadership. It is built on the practice of back briefing across the whole organization.

[5] Gardner J.W, cited by Robert H Waterman (1987) *The Renewal Factor*, p. 213.

The latter takes longer to embed than most people think; although I am not entirely convinced that Schein's claim of 25 years for P&G's cultural change is actually very helpful in this context. I remember visiting the P&G HRD in Venezuela who was tearing his hair out because HQ in Cincinnati had mandated "remove two layers" form the local company. This was an example of a simplistic North American-centric philosophy: "*We* have two layers too many so every country in the world must have two layers too many!" It was evident a small operation such as that in Venezuela did not need to remove two layers of management. A missing layer is as detrimental to decision making accountability and business performance as a layer too many.

10.8 The Challenge of Cultural Change

Implementing the answers to the three questions above will require a change of culture in an unhealthy organization. This is a tough challenge. Many managers underestimate what is involved and how long it will take. Too many CEOs think it is simply a matter of a few 'town hall speeches' and "everything will be OK.". How wrong can they be? It is reminiscent of the "War will be over by Christmas", which dogged the thinking at the beginning of both WWI and WWII. While I doubt a change programme needs to take more than 10 years in a large organization it is likely to take about 3–5 years, which would tend to align with the tenure of a single CEO. In 2015 the recruitment firm Robert Half reported that the average tenure of a FTSE 100 CEO was 5 years 2 months.[6] Then a re-launch and so on: "stability in motion".

Bungay's comments about embedding mission command are rather sobering:

"We have to recognise that the cultural soil out of which mission command grew is the hardest factor to reproduce and may act as a constraint in transferring it into some organizations".[7]

Bungay again: "*The Germans worked on their culture for decades. The Bagnall reforms (moving to mission command) have still not been totally anchored in the organizational behaviour and working practices of the British regular army. Anecdotally it is generally accepted that mission command is more deeply rooted in the Special Forces.*"[8]

Bagnall saw the need and opportunity in 1985–88 when he was Chief of the General Staff and Bungay was writing in 2011, which rather supports Schein's viewpoint that culture change is slow. It is slow because for civilian organizations it

[6] The Daily Telegraph 20.05.15.

[7] The Art of Action p. 82.

[8] Ibid (2011, p. 82).

is likely to need a review of strategy, structure and leadership training and development. No small undertaking. The difficulty of embedding cultural change is further borne out by Bose who describes that the American general George C Marshall had noted that over planning stymied the efforts of Generals Grant and Sherman during the Civil War. So in the 1920s he initiated a new dynamic approach to leadership training more akin to the spirit of aufragstaktik that became known as the 'Benning Revolution' (named after the location of the Infantry School at Fort Benning) changing US military training "to force officers to think on their feet and learn how to lead in dynamic situations".[9] Bose also notes "Marshall left the execution of clear orders to the divisional and company-level officers". Yet American generals were still over planning and providing far too detailed instructions during WWII—e.g. the high flier, Mark Clark at Monte Cassino."[10] Marshall had not perfected his approach with Moltke's feedback loop as the way to avoid the three traps outlined earlier.

When undertaking change many organizations seem to become impaled on one of two horns of the dilemma: either they underestimate the complexity involved or they over complicate it. In 1967 Larry Greiner identified six Phases in the "Dynamics of successful organization change."[11] The military have a clear purpose, sound structure and aligned career development for their leaders and yet still mission command in their case, has apparently not yet registered everywhere in NATO or the US army even though the top leadership have recognised its importance. This explains why Moltke's preoccupation became *training* in which the military invests an enormous amount of time and effort, compared to civilian organizations who tend to train in a context-vacuum. Bungay argues the Royal Navy probably has the more ingrained approach to mission command—recall the detailed description in Chap. 2. The message is clear. The mere recognition of the need to move towards Mission Mastery by those at the top is not enough. Indeed initiative can be hampered by others: recall the experience of Sir Keith Park in the Battle of Britain, mentioned in Chap. 2.

10.9 What WAS This Journey About Then?

I have been trying to pick the brains of those who turned a failing (military) organization into what I believe was probably the first large organic learning organization in the Western world and whose collective behaviour could become self sustaining even in the absence of the leader. I have touched on what the military do well in the production of leaders, which is now known in NATO as mission

[9] Bose op cit, p. 36.

[10] See Harper (2005, p. 252).

[11] See Greiner L *Patterns in Organization change* Harvard Business Review May/June 1967.

command.[12] I argued that a study of what the military does, reveals five key ingredients in their approach, which I have labelled "Pillars". They all need to be present to help ensure success. I outlined an organization where that is not the case: the British Civil Service, which has spawned a culture of no consequences. The type of change effort needed to be successful was highlighted briefly earlier in this chapter.

The aim of the book is to help civilian organizations successfully migrate the five pillars of mission command into their own domains. That is the basis of what I have called Mission Mastery. The closing of the performance gap is an all embracing culture change.

10.9.1 A Quick Overall Recap

Firstly an organization needs to have a clear mission, sense of purpose and direction. In Chap. 3 I highlighted the need to *execute* that mission or strategy. The mere statement of a strategy does not guarantee implementation and that is usually because either the organization's structure or leaders (often both) are suboptimal. Once a strategy or direction is set it is important to expect "friction" or resistance as competitors react to any new initiatives. I described how to avoid three traps that can occur within an organization, undermining implementation of the mission.

Secondly in Chap. 4 the central importance of effective organization architecture was emphasised along with the comment that virtually every civilian organization I have encountered is hierarchy heavy with too many hollow jobs lacking clear, discrete decision rights. Military organization design is effective, established and very clear, *in the field,* notwithstanding built-in buffer stock in the equivalent of WL 2, which ensures a robust platform for leadership development and career planning. Moltke knew his structures were fundamentally sound and proven and did not require further study or comment. This is invariably *not the case* in civilian organizations.

Thirdly Chap. 5 spelled out that once the structure and the platform of real jobs with clear accountabilities is in place then reliable leadership development and career plans can be mapped out. I pointed out though that it is vital to have a means of assessing individuals' potential to move up another level of accountability. Most so-called competency models fall short on that requirement because they do not *differentiate* the behaviours needed at the next higher level of accountability. This adds up to a double fault, imperfect structure and erratic selection, which makes leadership development and career planning much more open to chance. That in

[12] Bungay writes that the Israeli army now "also has it own version of mission command." Op cit: p. 82.

turn is prone to lead to a politicisation of the promotion process since objectivity has become an imposter.

Fourthly the way to cope with "friction" is to engage in rehearsal training, practising the right way to succeed. Chapter 6 pointed out that leaders have to be trained so they know how to exercise initiative and loop back to their leader to ensure they are on track. Examples were given highlighting the importance of rehearsal training (or war gaming in the military) such as simulation, which tends to be neglected in civilian organizations. The reinforcement of this process of planned experiential training via careful career planning was shown to be the next vital component in the personal development of leaders. The importance of utilising the possibilities of seven separate boundary moves was highlighted.

Fifthly the focus turned to the importance of building a positive culture in Chap. 7. This is almost a holy grail for many organizations' OD managers who seem to favour a 'cart before the horse' approach. Starting a change process by "addressing culture" in isolation is not likely to succeed. This is because the problems affecting the other four pillars need to be addressed first. *Culture is an outcome not an input.* It does not drive strategy, structure and leadership development even though I have seen that idea enthusiastically promoted by 'culture vultures' on OD websites. The toxic culture at Barclays was analysed against the five Pillars.

Chapter 8 outlined the background to the DMA Solution Set which is the shadow behind Mission Mastery.

Chapter 9 described in some detail what happens in a "Culture of no consequences" when key elements of Mission Mastery are absent and/or defective. Although the example was from the public sector examples could equally have been given form the private sector.

So does that all mean I think that the application of Mission Mastery is the only way great leaders can be produced? No, it does not and I am certainly not claiming that.

Many companies have been producing great leaders for many years without any knowledge of the tenets of mission command let alone Mission Mastery. Just as a number of military commanders naturally practised mission command such as Nelson, Slim and Freyberg to name but three, without being trained in its tenets. This would also apply to outstanding entrepreneurs, such as Matsushita, Tata, and Watson who innately practised the rudiments of Mission Mastery.

Indeed it could be argued that Mission Mastery simply amounts to the systematisation of what the naturally gifted leader does intuitively.

10.9.2 Relevance to Current Thinking on Leadership

Much of the talk and literature today is about the "emergent organization" where "agility" and "innovation" are said to be key features. But agility and innovation cannot "emerge" from a cluttered organization strewn with hollow jobs. Organization design has a critical role in mediating the effects of work demands—which need to create space for discretion, autonomy and personal growth. Self managed teams are re-entering the management lexicon of some theorists as the part of a new dispensation. It is quite feasible to provide for "self directed teams"—that is not new—as long as they work within clear, agreed accountability and authority limits. Good leadership affords them maximum autonomy but here is the rub. If junior management ranks are stacked with non value adding jobs of straw bosses there is not enough accountability space for "self directed teams" to function. Empowerment is hamstrung in the breech. Social scientists and economists selling the merits of empowerment for individuals and teams without due consideration of the accountable context of a job do us a disservice.

In 2014 *Raconteur* published a lift out in *The Times* on *"The Agile Business."*[13] The new 'enthusiasm' according to Dan Matthews, seems to be: "It is time to drop the business plan and get 'adaptive'." Not a bad idea, but Moltke got there over 100 years ago! The problem in 2015 is still faulty organization design in many civilian organizations and no amount of platitudes about "fast data, "nimble clouds" and "an agile landscape" will resolve that. Worse, this design shortcoming is still not generally recognised meaning real individual growth continues to be hamstrung and too many people do not understand why.

Another concern today I highlighted is the "lack of trust" in civilian organizations. Hopefully by now it can be seen that the secret to building trust and high performing teams is *clear accountability at each management layer peopled with competent people.*

The key point here is few civilian organizations have *embedded* their approach to leadership and personal growth in a way that is comparable to the military. Although they have different missions there seem to be very few civilian learning organizations. This stems from the fact that invariably they do not know their key levels of accountability. In nautical terms they are holed below the water line.

Many managers in civilian organizations, especially at or near the top, are seemingly unaware of the possibilities afforded by what I have called, Mission Mastery. They risk continuing to waste human talent. *That is the real leadership challenge of the twenty-first century*

It is also why I wrote this book.

The Question to Ponder
*What is the **one thing** your organization needs to do **right now** to remove any "friction" between the goal of Mission Mastery and its implementation?*

[13] Raconteur 14.10.14.

Acknowledgements

A book like this does not write itself. Many people have contributed both directly and indirectly to this material over the years. Looking back there were key influences on my career. My first boss, Colin Gray, launched my international career and Roger Roes was an outstanding mentor in the field of international organization design, who first whetted by appetite for this topic, while working with him in The Netherlands on various international assignments. Another key influence was Robert Kramer, previously senior researcher at the New York Conference Board, whose knowledge and understanding of the structures of international organizations was without peer in my experience.

Colleagues who have worked with me on a large number of projects since I founded my own company include Adam Pearce, John Bruce Jones, Bernard Dive and Peter Dugmore. We have worked together in four of the world's largest organizations, across many industries as well as both central and local government in a number of countries. In fact most of my clients have been in the private sector. The principles and approach outlined in this book stem from extensive fieldwork.

I am indebted to Alaric Mostyn, who gave me access to his research into the factors that ensure some companies grow faster and more successfully than their competitors. I refer in the book to the turnaround of Northern Rock: the key person who invited Adam and me into the bank was the CEO Gary Hoffman, with whom we had earlier worked when he was CEO of Barclaycard. The extensive work we did across Whitehall started with an introduction by Paul Fretten (ex Barclays) to Christopher Johnson in the Cabinet Office and then especially his successor Dusty Amroliwala who orchestrated a number of key introductions to HRDs and Permanent Secretaries across Whitehall. Our introduction to work in local government came initially though Rob Whitehead, then CEO of what is now the Local Government Agency working with John Bruce Jones. We undertook major assignments in a number of different Councils as a result. Subsequently the LGA manager, Suzanne Hudson, has run a number of projects with John Bruce Jones' oversight, while Ann Donoghue and Bernard have worked with me on the transformation programme of a care organization in Ireland.

A number of people have helped me by generously reviewing various drafts of the text and making most helpful suggestions and corrections of fact. Bob Henderson was most insightful on Chaps. 6 and 7 given his wide experience of

B. Dive, *Mission Mastery*, Management for Professionals,
DOI 10.1007/978-3-319-25223-0

both the military and the commercial worlds. Professor Paul Gifford of SOAS was particularly helpful when reviewing the early drafts as were my colleagues John Bruce Jones and Adam Pearce. Gerald Arbuckle, himself the author of about 20 books, was most supportive when I shared an early manuscript with him. Keith Rowland examined the manuscript from a North American perspective offering shrewd advice. Others who made particularly helpful suggestions on the text included, Andrew Jackson, Mike Samuels, together with Janne and Kate Pender. Their very helpful advice is much appreciated.

I particularly wish to thank my son, Bernard for his contribution. Not only has he worked on many assignments as a DMA consultant but his previous editorial and publishing experience meant he was in a particularly strong position to make constructive comments on the text, which were a great help. And of course I could not have written this work without the support of Anne and Lizzy who put up with my being locked away trying to put the draft together, even when on holiday! Their support and encouragement continue to be invaluable.

Professor Stephen Perkins, the Dean of Business and Law at London Metropolitan University kindly introduced me to Samuel Idowu at Springer, which led to the securing of the contract to write the book. Last but not least I wish to acknowledge the very warm and professional support I received form Christian Rauscher and Barbara Bethke at Springer. Their advice and patience ensured the quality and the sequencing of the ideas and chapters in the book became more robust and coherent. I am immensely grateful for their very professional support.

Many friends and colleagues have helped in the production of this book but ultimately I am accountable for any errors or shortcomings you may detect. Notwithstanding those, I hope you enjoy the read.

Brian Dive
London 2015

Appendix: On Strategy

Politics makes use of war to achieve its aims. It has a decisive influence on the beginning and the end of a war, and indeed reserves the right to raise its aspirations during the war's course, or to content itself with a more modest outcome.

As things are not fully determined, the aspiration of strategy can only ever be to achieve the highest end it can with the means available. It is therefore best if strategy works hand in hand with politics, working toward its goals, but free to act quite independently of it.

The first task of strategy is the assembly of forces, the initial deployment of the army. This involves the consideration of a whole range of disparate political, geographical and national factors. A mistake in the initial disposition of armies is almost impossible to make good during the course of a campaign. However, there is plenty of time to consider these arrangements, and—assuming that the troops are prepared for war and the transportation system has been organized—they have to lead unfailingly to the intended result.

Things are different, however, in the next main task of strategy: the military use of the available resources, in other words operations.

Here, our will very soon encounters the independent will of an opponent. If we are ready and willing to take the initiative we can constrain the enemy's will, but the only way we can break it is through means of tactics, through battle.

However, the material and moral consequences of every major battle are so far-reaching that they almost invariably create a completely different situation, a new basis for new measures. No plan of operations can extend with any degree of certainly beyond the first encounter with the enemy's main body. Only a layman could imagine that in following the course of a campaign he is watching the logical unfolding of an initial idea conceived in advance, thought out in every detail and pursued through to its conclusion.

Whatever the vicissitudes of events, a commander will need to keep his mind fixed unwaveringly on his main objectives, but he can never be certain beforehand which paths offer the best hopes of realising them. Throughout the campaign he will find himself forced to make a whole series of decisions as situations arise, which no one was able to predict. This means that the successive acts of a war do not follow a premeditated design but are acts of spontaneity guided by military judgement. Every case is unique. It is all a matter of seeing through the fog of uncertainty in

B. Dive, *Mission Mastery*, Management for Professionals,
DOI 10.1007/978-3-319-25223-0

which every situation is shrouded, making an accurate assessment of what you do know, guessing what you do not know, reaching a conclusion rapidly and then vigorously and unwaveringly following it through.

While trying to calculate on the basis of one known and one unknown factor—you own will and that of your enemy—you have to take into account a third set of factors, which are completely unpredictable. They include the weather, outbreaks of illness, railway accidents, misunderstandings and errors of perception: in short, all those influences on events that we ascribe to chance, fate or divine providence, but which human beings neither create nor master.

Even so, this does not mean that the conduct of war is completely blind and arbitrary. The balance of probabilities is that the sum of all those chance events is as much to the detriment or advantage of one side as the other and the commander who in each case issues directions, which are at least sensible, even if not optimal, stands a good chance of success.

It hardly needs saying that to do this, theoretical knowledge is not enough. Mastering this free, practical art means developing qualities of mind and character, which are shaped by military training and guided by experience drawn from military history of from life itself.

When all is said and done, the reputation of a commander rests on his success. How much of it is in fact down to his own effort is very hard to say. In the face of the irresistible power of circumstances even the best man can fail and by the same token it can shield mediocrity. That said in the long run, those who enjoy good luck usually deserve it.

Given that in war, once operations begin, everything is uncertain other that the will and dynamism of the commander himself, there is absolutely no practical value in rules of strategy and systems based on generalised doctrines.

Archduke Carl[1]considers strategy to be a science and tactics an art. He believes that the "science of high command can determine the course of military affairs" and that the only place for art is in executing strategic designs.

General von Clausewitz on the other hand says: "Strategy is the use of battles for the purposes of war." Indeed strategy provides tactics with the means of beating the enemy and can increase the chances of victory through the way in which it directs armies and brings them together on the battlefield. On the other hand, strategy builds on every successful engagement to exploit it further. In the face of tactical

[1] Archduke Charles of Austria was an accomplished commander who fought with success against Napoleon and wrote guidelines and insights based on his experience in the field.

victory the demands of strategy are silent—it must adapt to the newly created situation.

Strategy is a system of expedients. It is more than science it is the application of knowledge to practical life, the evolution of an original guiding idea under constantly changing circumstances, the art of taking action under the pressure of the most difficult conditions.

Helmut von Moltke (1871)[2]

[2] Bungay op cit pp. 245–248.

References

Adair, J. (1979). *Action centred leadership*. Hampshire: Ashgate Publishing.
Adorno, T. W., Frenkel-Brunswik, E., Levinson, D. J., & Sanford, R. N. (1950). *The authoritarian personality*. New York: Harper and Row.
Alexander, J., & Huggins, M. (2012). A new prescription for improving business performance at GlaxoSmithKline. *OD Practitioner, 44*(4), 4.
Arbuckle, G. A. (2010). *Culture, inculturation, Theologians: A postmodern critique*. Minnesota, MN: Michael Glazier Books.
Arbuckle, G. A. (2013). *Humanizing healthcare reforms*. London: Jessica Kingsley Publishers.
Bains, G., Bains, K., Anciano, D., Anderson, J., Bains, R., Encombe, J., Garner, C., Javitch, M., Kinley, N., Pelunsky, C., Robinson, R., & Rowe, K. (2007). *Meaning Inc: The blueprint for business success in the 21st century*. London: Profile Books.
Band, J. (n.d.). Admiral Commander in Chief Fleet. *Mission command: A view from the Fleet Battlestaff*. The Royal Navy.
Beevor, A. (2012). *D-Day: The battle for Normandy*. London: Penguin Books.
Bennis, W. (1989). *On becoming a leader*. Reading, MA: Addison-Wesley.
Bennis, W., & Nanus, B. (1985). *Leaders the strategies for taking charge*. New York: Harper and Row.
Bett, M., et al. (1995). *Independent review of the armed forces' manpower, career and remuneration structures*. London: HMSO.
Bevan, J. (2002). *The rise and fall of marks and spencer*. London: Profile Books.
Blake, R., & Mouton, J. (1964). *The managerial grid: The key to leadership excellence*. Houston, TX: Gulf Publishing Co.
Blake, R., & Mouton, J. (1969). *Building a dynamic corporation through grid organization development*. Reading MA: Addison-Wesley.
Bloch, S., & Whiteley, P. (2003). *Complete leadership*. London: Pearson Education.
Boal, K. B., & Hooijberg, R. (2000). Strategic leadership research: Moving on. *The Leadership Quarterly, 11*(4), 515–549.
Boam, R., & Sparrow, P. (1992). *Designing and achieving competency*. London: McCraw-Hill.
Bose, P. (2003). *Lessons from the great empire builder: Alexander the Great's art of strategy*. London: Profile Books.
Boyatzis, R. (1982). *The competent manager*. New York: Wiley.
Brown, W. (1971). *Organization*. London: Heinemann.
Bungay, S. (2000). *Most dangerous enemy*. London: Aurum Press.
Bungay, S. (2001). *The most dangerous enemy a history of the battle of Britain*. London: Aurum Press.
Bungay, S. (2002). *Alamein*. London: Aurum Press.
Bungay, S. (2011). *The art of action: How leaders close the gaps between plans, actions and results*. London: Nicholas Brealey Publishing.

B. Dive, *Mission Mastery*, Management for Professionals,
DOI 10.1007/978-3-319-25223-0

Bungay, S., & McKinney, D. (2003). Mission leadership. *Ashridge Journal*, Spring, 4–9.
Burns, J. M. (1978). *Leadership*. New York: Harper & Row.
Burns, T., & Stalker, G. M. (1961). *The management of innovation*. London: Tavistock Publications.
Campbell, A., Goold, M., & Alexander, M. (1994). *Corporate-level strategy: Creating value in the multibusiness company*. New York: Wiley.
Chan Kim, W., & Maugorgne, R. (2006). *Blue Ocean strategy: How to create uncontested market space and make the competition irrelevant*. Boston, MA: Harvard Business School Press.
Chan Kim, W., Maugorgne, R., & van der Heyden, L. (2003). *General failings in mastering leadership*. London: PWC/FT.
Chandler, A. (1962). *Strategy and structure*. Cambridge, MA: MIT Press.
Chandler, D. (1966). *The campaigns of Napoleon*. London: Macmillan.
Charan, R., Drotter, S., & Noel, J. (2001). *Leadership pipeline: How to build the leadership powered company*. San Francisco, CA: Jossey-Bass.
Charlton, G. (1993). *Leadership the human race a guide to developing leadership potential in Southern Africa*. Kenwyn: Juta & Co.
Clark, A. (1961). *Donkeys*. London: Pimlico.
Cleary, T. (1988). *Translation of the Tao of organization by Cheng YI*. Boston, MA: Shambhala.
Collins, J. (2001). *From good to great: Why some companies make the leap and others do not*. London: Harper Collins.
Connor, R. J. (2015). *It's about time*. Fleet, UK: Emp3 Books Ltd.
Cook, J. M. (1998). *The Persians*. London: The Folio Society.
Cooper, C. L. (Ed.). (2005). *Leadership and management in the 21st century*. Oxford: Oxford University Press.
Covey, S. R. (1989). *The seven habits of highly effective people*. London: Simon and Schuster.
Craddick-Adams, P. (2013). *Monte Casino Ten Armies in hell*. London: Arrow Books.
Crawford, M. (2009). *The case for working with your hands or why office work is bad for us and fixing things feels good*. London: Penguin.
Czikszcentmihalyi, M. C. (1991). *Flow: The psychology of optimal experience*. New York: Harper and Row.
Darling, J. R. (1999). Organizational excellence and leadership strategies: Principles followed by top multinational executives. *Leadership and Organization Development Journal, 20*(6), 309–321.
Davies, N. (2012). *Vanished kingdoms the history of half-forgotten Europe*. London: Penguin Books.
Dawson, D. (2001). *The first armies*. London: Cassell & Co.
Day, D. V. (2000). Leadership development: A review in context. *The Leadership Quarterly, 11* (4), 581–613.
De Geus, A. (1997). *The living company*. London: Nicolas Brealey.
Dive, B. J. (2003a). How to design a healthy regional headquarters. In *Regional headquarters roles and organization*. New York: The Conference Board.
Dive, B. J. (2003b, July-August). When is an organization too flat? *Across the Board*.
Dive, B. J. (2004). *The healthy organization: A revolutionary approach to people and management*. London: Kogan Page.
Dive, B. J. (2008). *The Accountable leader: Developing effective leadership through managerial accountability*. London: Kogan Page.
Dive, B. J., & Wright, C. (2011). The leadership equation. *Bedford Centre for Innovative Leadership*.
Dixon, N. F. (1976). *On the psychology of military incompetence*. London: Pimlico. Published January 6th 1994.
Dixon, N. F. (1994). *On the psychology of military incompetence*. London: Pimlico.
Donaldson, L. (1995). *American anti-management theories of organization*. Cambridge: Cambridge University Press.

Donnelly, M. (2000, The year of the dragon). *Two essays on China*. People's Republic of China: Self Published.
Drucker, P. F. (1969). *The practice of management*. London: Heinenamm.
Drucker, P. (1964). *The practice of management*. London: Heineman. Republished 1989.
Drucker, P. (1998, November-December). The discipline of innovation, *Harvard Business Review*.
Dupuy, T. (1977). *A genius for war, The German Army and general staff, 1807–1945*. Englewood Cliffs, NJ: Prentice-Hall.
Emery, F., & Trist, E. (1965). The causal texture of organizational environments. *Human Relations, 18*(1), 21–32.
Faulkner, N. (2015, May). Park the man who won the Battle of Britain. *Military History*, (58).
Fields, N. (2009). *The Roman Army of the Principate 27 BC–AD 117*. Oxford: Osprey Publishing.
Fisch, G. G. (1963, September-October). Stretching the span of management. *Harvard Business Review*.
Fitzgerald, P. (2002). *The Knox Brothers*. London: Flamingo (Haper Collins).
Frank, E. H. (Ed.). (1971). *Organization restructuring*. London: McGraw-Hill.
Franks, O. (2003). *Introduction to mastering leadership*. London: FT/PWC.
French, D. (2000). *Raising Churchill's army*. Oxford: Oxford University Press.
Fukuyama, F. (1995). *Trust—the social virtues and the creation of prosperity*. London: Penguin Books.
Fukuyama, F. (2002). *The end of history and the last man*. New York: Perennial of Harper Collins.
Galbraith, J. R. (2000). *Designing the global corporation*. San Francisco, CA: Josey-Bass.
Galbraith, J. (2010). Foreword. In G. Kesler & A. Kates (Eds.), *Leading organization design: How to make organization design decisions to drive the results you want* (p. 336). New York: Wiley.
Ganguly, A. (1999). *Business-driven R&D: Managing knowledge to create wealth*. London: Macmillan Press.
Gardiner, J. A. (2014). *Music in the garden of heaven*. London: Penguin.
Garratt, R. (1996). *The fish rots from the head: The crisis in our boardrooms*. London: Harper Collins.
Garratt, R. (2003). *Thin on top*. London: Nicholas Brealey.
Geetz, C. (1973). *The interpretation of cultures*. New York: Basic Books.
Goffee, R., & Jones, G. (2003). *The character of a corporation*. London: Profile Books.
Goldsworthy, A. (2003). *The complete Roman Army*. London: Thames & Hudson.
Goleman, D. (1999). *Working and emotional intelligence*. London: Bloomsbury.
Goold, M., & Campbell, A. (2002). *Designing effective organizations*. San Francisco, CA: Jossey-Bass.
Goold, M., Campbell, A., & Alexander, M. (1994). *Corporate-level strategy*. New York: Wiley.
Gopalakrishnan, R. (2007). *The case of the Bonzai manager*. London: Penguin.
Gordon, A. (1996). *The rule of the game: Jutland and British naval command*. London: John Murray.
Gratton, L. (2004). *The democratic enterprise: Liberating your business with individual freedom and shared purpose*. London: FT Prentice Hall.
Gray, C. F. Group Captain DSO, DFC & Bar (1994). *Fighter Patrol*. Auckland: Moa.
Greiner, L. (1967, May/June). Patterns of organization change. *Harvard Business Review*.
Grint, K. (2005). Twenty-first-century leadership—The god of small things: or putting the 'ship' back into 'leadership'. In C. L. Cooper (Ed.), *Leadership and management in the 21st century*. Oxford: Oxford University Press.
Handy, C. (1997). *The hungry spirit*. London: Hutchison.
Hardy, H. (Ed.). (2001). *Isaiah Berlin liberty*. Oxford: Oxford University Press.
Harper, G. (2005). *Kippenberger: An inspired New Zealand Commander*. Auckland, NZ: Harper Collins.
Hastings, M. (2013). *Catastrophe Europe goes to war 1914*. London: William Collins.
Herodotus. (1996). *Histories* (G. Rawlinson, Trans.). London: Wordsworth Classics.
Hogan, R. (2007). *Personality and the fate of organizations*. Princeton, NJ: LEA Publishers.

Holland, T. (2003). *Rubicon: The triumph and tragedy of the Roman Empire*. London: Abacus.
Holmes, R. (2003). *Wellington the Iron Duke*. London: Harper Collins.
Howitt, B. (2012). *Graham Henry final word*. Auckland: Harper Collins.
Huff, A. S., & Moeslein, K. (2005). An agenda for understanding individual leadership in corporate leadership systems. In C. L. Cooper (Ed.), *Leadership and management in the 21st century*. Oxford: Oxford University Press.
Hughes, D. J. (Ed.). (1993). *Moltke on the art of war*. New York: Ballantine Books.
Jamieson, I. (1980). *Capitalism and culture: A comparative analysis of British and American Manufacturing Organizations*. London: Gower.
Jaques, E. (1989). *Requisite organization*. Arlington, VA: Cason Hall &Co.
Jaques, E., & Cason, K. (1994). *Human capability*. Arlington, VA: Cason Hall & Co.
Jaques, E., & Clement, S. D. (1991). *Executive leadership*. Arlington, VA: Cason Hall & Co.
Kakabadse, A., & Kakabadse, N. (1999). *Essence of leadership*. London: International Thomson.
Kaplan, R. E., & Kaiser, R. B. (2003). *Detecting excess too: A quantum leap in 360 ° assessment*. Presented at the 9th annual leadership development conference and 6th annual coaching and mentoring conference produced by Linkage Incorporated, San Diego, CA, September 18, 2003.
Kaplan, R. E., & Kaiser, R. B. (2006). *The versatile leader make the most of your strengths without overdoing it*. San Francisco: Pfeiffer.
Kaplan, R. S., & Norton, D. P. (1996). *The balanced scorecard: Translating strategy into action*. Boston: Harvard Business School Press.
Katzenbach, J. R. & Smith, D. R. (1997, November-December). The myth of the top management team. *Harvard Business Review*.
Keegan, J. (1994). *A history of warfare*. London: Pimlico.
Kelly, S. (2003). *The hunt for Zerzura: The lost oasis and the desert war*. London: John Murray.
Kenneally, J. (2008). *The honour and the shame*. London: Headline Publishing Group.
Kennedy, C. (2002). *Guide to the management gurus: The best guide to business thinkers*. London: Random House Business Books.
Kesler, G., & Kates, A. (2011). *Leading organization design how to make organization design decisions to drive the results you want*. San Francisco: Jossey-Bass.
Kettley, P. (1995). *Is flatter better? Delayering the management hierarchy* (Report 290). The Institute for Employment Studies, University of Sussex.
Kinston, W., & Rowbottom, R. (1989). Levels of work: New applications to management in large organisations. *Journal of Applied Systems Analysis, 16*, 19–34.
Kirk, D. (1992, December). World-class teams. *Mckinsey Quarterly*.
Kladstrup, D., & Kladstrup, P. (2001). *Wine and war*. London: Hodder and Stoughton.
Kladstrup, D., & Kladstrup, P. (2002). *Wine and war: The French, the Nazis and France's greatest treasure*. New York: Hodder and Stoughton.
Klatt, B., Murphy, S., & Irvine, D. (1999). *Accountability: Practical tools for focusing on clarity, commitment and results*. London: Kogan Page.
Klein, G. (1997). The current status of the naturalistic decision making framework. In R. Flin, E. Salas, M. Strub, & L. Martin (Eds.), *Decision-making under stress* (pp. 11–28). England: Ashgate.
Kleiner, A. (2003). *Who really matters: The core group theory of power, privilege, and success*. New York: Currency/Doubleday.
Klemp, G. O. (1998). *Leadership competencies: Putting it all together*. Boston: Cambria Consulting.
Kling, A. (2010, Spring). The financial crisis: Moral failure or cognitive failure? *Harvard Journal of Law and Public Policy*, *33*(2), 507.
Knight, K. (Ed.). (1977). *Matrix management*. London: Gower.
Kraines, G. A. (2001). *Accountability leadership*. Franklin Lakes, NJ: Career Press.
Kramer, R. J. (2003). *Regional headquarters roles and organization*. New York: The Conference Board.

Kramer, R. J. (2005). *Global leadership*. New York: The Conference Board.

Krause, D. G. (1996). *Sun Tzu: The art of war for executives*. London: Nicholas Brealey.

Kressler, H. W. (2003). *Motivate and reward*. Hampshire: Palgrave MacMillan.

Lala, R. M. (2004). *The creation of wealth—The Tatas from the 19th to the 21st century*. New Delhi: Penguin Books India.

Landes, D. (1998). *The wealth and poverty of nations*. London: Abacus.

Lawford, J. (1977). *Napoleon the last campaigns 1813-15*. London: The Book Club Associates.

Likert, R. (1961). *New patterns of management*. New York: McGraw-Hill.

Little, P. (2008). *Willie Apiata–VC–The reluctant hero*. Auckland: Viking.

MacGregor, D. (1960). *The human side of enterprise*. New York: McGraw-Hill.

Mant, A. (1997). *Intelligent leadership*. St. Leonards, Australia: Allen & Unwin.

Manz, B. (1989). *The rise and rule and Tamerlaine*. Cambridge: Cambridge University Press.

Martin, I. (2013). *Making it happen: Fred Goodwin, RBS and the men who blew up the British economy*. London: Simon Shuster.

McCall, M. W., Jr. (1998). *High fliers: Developing the next generation of leaders*. Boston: Harvard Business School Press.

McCall, M. W., Jr., & Hollenbeck, G. P. (2002). *Developing global executives*. Boston: Harvard Business School Press.

McCall, M. W., Jr., Lombardo, M. M., & Morrison, A. M. (1988). *The lessons of experience*. New York: Lexington Books.

McGee, G. (2012). *Richie McCaw the open side*. Auckland: Hodder Moa.

McGrath, R. G. (2013). *The end of competitive advantage*. Boston: Harvard Business School Press.

McGregor, D. (1961). *The human side of enterprise* (p. 480). New York: McGraw Hill.

McMorland, J. (2005). Are you big enough for your job? Is your job big enough for you? *University of Auckland Business Review*, Spring edition.

Meier, C. (1998). *Julius Caesar*. London: The Folio Society.

Mintzberg, H. (1988, June-July). Crafting strategy. *Harvard Business Review*.

Mintzberg, H. (1989). *Mintzberg on management*. New York: The Free Press Macmillan.

Mintzberg, H. (2003). *Managers not MBAs: A hard look at the soft practice of managing and management development*. San Francisco: Berrett-Koehler.

Moorehead, A. (1988). *Gallipoli*. Norwalk, CT: Easton Press.

Moran, L. (1945). *The anatomy of courage*. London: Constable.

Moreau, G. (2003, September/October). What the military can teach corporate-governance reformers. *Across The Board*. The NY Conference Board.

Morita, A., Reingold, E., & Shimomura, M. (1987). *Made in Japan*. London: Fontana/Collins.

Mortimer, I. (2008). *The perfect king: The life of Edward III father of the English Nation*. London: Vintage.

Mourkogiannis, N. (2006). *Purpose*. Hampshire: Palgrave MacMillan.

Mulgan, J. (1967). *Report on experience*. Auckland: Blackwood and J. Paul Ltd.

Nibly, H. (1984, February). Leadership versus management. *BYU Today*.

O'Toole, J. (1995). *Leading change*. New York: Ballantine Books.

Ouchi, W. G. (1982). *Theory Z*. New York: First Avon Printing Company.

Paret, P. (1976). *Clausewitz and the state* (p. 202). New York: Oxford University Press.

Pascale, R. T. (1990). *Managing on the edge*. New York: Simon & Schuster.

Pascale, R. T., & Athos, A. (1981). *The art of Japanese management*. London: Victor Gollancz.

Paterson, T. T. (1972). *Job evaluation*. London: Business Books.

Perkins, S. J., & Shortland, S. M. (2006). *Strategic international human resource management: Choices and consequences in multinational people management*. London: Kogan Page.

Peters, T. J., & Waterman, R. H., Jr. (1982). *In search of excellence*. New York: Harper & Row.

Pettigrew, A., & Fenton, E. (2000). *The innovating organisation*. London: Sage.

Pilkington, C. (1999). *The civil service in Britain today*. Manchester: Manchester University Press.

Popper, K. (2002). *The open society and its enemies* (Vol. 1). London: Routledge Classics.

Reddin, W. J. (1970). *Managerial effectiveness*. New York: McGraw-Hill.

Reese, T. J. (1996). *Inside the Vatican: The politics and organization of the Catholic Church.* Cambridge, MA: Harvard University Press.
Rhind, D. (2005). Herding cats or Luxuriating in talent? Leadership and management of universities. In C. L. Cooper (Ed.), *Leadership and management in the 21st century*. Oxford: Oxford University Press.
Rowbottom, R. (1977). *Social analysis a collaborative model of gaining usable scientific knowledge of social institutions*. London: Heinemann.
Rowbottom, R. W., & Billis, D. (1987). *Organizational design the work—Levels approach.* London: Gower.
Rowbottom, R., Hey, A., & Billis, D. (1974). *Social services departments: developing patterns of work and organization*. London: Heinemann.
Sandel, M. J. (2012). *What money can't buy—The moral limits of markets*. London: Allen Lane.
Schein, E. H. (2010). *Organizational culture and leadership* (4th ed.). San Francisco: Josey-Bass.
Senge, P. (1992). *The fifth discipline: The art and practice of the learning organization*. Sydney: Random House.
Shapiro, A. (1977, February). What MANAGEMENT says and what managers do. *Interfaces.*
Sheffield, G. (2010). *The chief: Douglas Haig and the British Army*. London: Aurum Press.
Stevenson, A. (2013). *The public sector: Managing the unmanageable*. London: Kogan Page.
Strycharczyk, D., & Elvin, C. (2014). *Developing resilient organizations*. London: Kogan Page.
Sun, T. Z. U. (2011). *The art of war* (S. G. Griffith, Trans.). London: Watkins Publishing.
Tichy, N. M., & Cardwell, N. (2002). *The cycle of leadership. How great leaders teach their companies to win*. New York: Harper Business.
Tichy, N. M., & Devanna, M. A. (1986, July). The transformational leader. *Sloan Review.*
Tobin, C. (2005). *The original all blacks 1905-06*. Auckland: Hodder Moa Beckett.
Tuchman, B. W. (1985). *March of folly from troy to Vietnam*. New York: Random Publishing House.
van Creveld, M. (1982). *Fighting power*. Westport, CT: Greenwood Press.
Various. (2001). Break though leadership. *Harvard Business Review.*
Vennell, J. (2014). *The forgotten general*. St. Leonards, Australia: Allen & Unwin.
Vincent, E. (2003, June). Nelson and mission command. *History Today.*
von Clausewitz, C. (1982). *On war* (1832, J. J. Graham 1908, Trans.). London: Penguin Classics.
Watson, P. (2005). *Ideas: A history of thought and invention from fire to freud*. New York: Harper Collins.
Weber, M. (1922). *Economy and society*. Berkeley, CA: University of California Press. Republished 2013.
Weber, M. (1948). *From Max Weber: Essays in sociology* (Translated, edited and with an introduction by H. H. Gerth and C. W. Mills). London: Routledge and Kegan Paul.
Wheeler, S., Lucier, C., & Habbel, R. (2007, August 16). The era of the inclusive leader. *Strategy and Business.*
Wind, J. R., & Main, J. (1998). *Driving change: How the best companies are preparing for the 21st century*. London: Kogan Page.
Young, D. (1950). *Rommel*. London: Collins.
Zaleznik, A. (1992, March-April). Managers and leaders: Are they different? *Harvard Business Review.*

Index

B. Dive, *Mission Mastery*, Management for Professionals,
DOI 10.1007/978-3-319-25223-0

MIX
Papier aus verantwortungsvollen Quellen
Paper from responsible sources
FSC® C105338

If you have any concerns about our products,
you can contact us on
ProductSafety@springernature.com

In case Publisher is established outside the EU,
the EU authorized representative is:
Springer Nature Customer Service Center GmbH
Europaplatz 3, 69115 Heidelberg, Germany

Printed by Libri Plureos GmbH
in Hamburg, Germany